CONSTITUTIONAL LAW

CONSTITUTIONAL LAW

Third Edition

JEROME A. BARRON

Lyle T. Alverson Professor of Law, National Law Center
George Washington University

C. THOMAS DIENES

Professor of Law, National Law Center
George Washington University

BLACK LETTER SERIES

WEST PUBLISHING CO.
ST. PAUL, MINN.
1991

COPYRIGHT © 1991 By WEST PUBLISHING CO.
　　　　　　　　　　50 West Kellogg Boulevard
　　　　　　　　　　P.O. Box 64526
　　　　　　　　　　St. Paul, MN 55164–0526

Library of Congress Cataloging-in-Publication Data

Barron, Jerome A.
　　Constitutional law / Jerome A. Barron and C. Thomas Dienes. — 3rd ed.
　　　　p.　　　cm. — (Black letter series)
　　ISBN 0–314–80211–8
　　1. United States—Constitutional law.　I. Dienes, C. Thomas.
II. Title.　III. Series.
KF4550.B28　1991
342.73—dc20
[347.302]
　　　　　　　　　　　　　　　　　　　　　　90–49934
　　　　　　　　　　　　　　　　　　　　　　CIP

ISBN 0–314–80211–8

PUBLISHER'S PREFACE

This "Black Letter" is designed to help a law student recognize and understand the basic principles and issues of law covered in a law school course. It can be used both as a study aid when preparing for classes and as a review of the subject matter when studying for an examination.

Each "Black Letter" is written by experienced law school teachers who are recognized national authorities in the subject covered.

The law is succinctly stated by the author of this "Black Letter." In addition, the exceptions to the rules are stated in the text. The rules and exceptions have purposely been condensed to facilitate quick review and easy recollection. For an in-depth study of a point of law, citations to major student texts are given. In addition, a **Text Correlation Chart** provides a convenient means of relating material contained in the Black Letter to appropriate sections of the casebook the student is using in his or her law school course.

If the subject covered by this text is a code or code-related course, the code section or rule is set forth and discussed wherever applicable.

FORMAT

The format of this "Black Letter" is specially designed for review. (1) **Text.** First, it is recommended that the entire text be studied, and, if deemed necessary, supplemented by the student texts cited. (2) **Capsule Summary.** The Capsule Summary is an abbreviated review of the subject matter which can be used both before and after studying the main body of the text. The headings in the Capsule Summary follow the main text of the "Black Letter." (3) **Table of Contents.** The Table of Contents is in outline form to help you organize the details of the subject and the Summary of Contents gives you a final overview of the materials. (4) **Practice Examination.** The Practice Examination in Appendix B gives you the opportunity of testing yourself with the type of question asked on an exam, and comparing your answer with a model answer.

In addition, a number of other features are included to help you understand the subject matter and prepare for examinations:

Short Questions and Answers: This feature is designed to help you spot and recognize issues in the examination. We feel that issue recognition is a major ingredient in successfully writing an examination.

Perspective: In this feature, the authors discuss their approach to the topic, the approach used in preparing the materials, and any tips on studying for and writing examinations.

Analysis: This feature, at the beginning of each section, is designed to give a quick summary of a particular section to help you recall the subject matter and to help you determine which areas need the most extensive review.

Examples: This feature is designed to illustrate, through fact situations, the law just stated. This, we believe, should help you analytically approach a question on the examination.

Glossary: This feature is designed to refamiliarize you with the meaning of a particular legal term. We believe that the recognition of words of art used in an examination helps you to better analyze the question. In addition, when writing an examination you should know the precise definition of a word of art you intend to use.

We believe that the materials in this "Black Letter" will facilitate your study of a law school course and assure success in writing examinations not only for the course but for the bar examination. We wish you success.

The Publisher

SUMMARY OF CONTENTS

APPENDICES

*

TABLE OF CONTENTS

APPENDICES

*

CAPSULE SUMMARY OF CONSTITUTIONAL LAW

PART ONE: THE ALLOCATION OF GOVERNMENTAL POWER: NATIONAL AND STATE

I. JUDICIAL REVIEW

Jurisdiction is the power to hear a case. In addition to jurisdictional rules there are prudential principles limiting the occasions when a federal court will decide a case on the merits. If jurisdiction is present and these prudential limits are overcome, courts can exercise the power of judicial review.

A. Establishing Judicial Review

1. Judicial Review Defined

Judicial Review is the doctrine that the courts have the power to invalidate governmental action which is repugnant to the Constitution.

2. Review of Federal Action

While there is no explicit textual authority for federal court review of the acts of the President and the Congress, this power has been inferred from a number of sources, including the Art. III grant of judicial power to the Supreme Court and inferior federal courts and the principle that it is the judicial power to say what the law (i.e., the Constitution) is.

3. **Review of State Action**
   a. The Supremacy Clause of Art. VI establishes federal judicial power over the acts of state officials.

   b. Art. VI requires state courts to make decisions in conformity with the U.S. Constitution. These "cases arising under the Constitution" are reviewable by the Supreme Court under Art. III.

B. Source of Judicial Power: Article III Jurisdiction
The "judicial power" is vested by Art. III in the Supreme Court and inferior federal courts created by Congress.

1. **Federal "Judicial Power" Defined**

   a. Unless a case falls within one of the "cases or controversies" identified in Art. III, § 2, an Art. III federal court (as distinguished from an Art. I court) must dismiss the case for want of subject matter jurisdiction.

   b. Congress exercises broad powers over the existence and jurisdiction of lower national courts.

2. **Supreme Court Jurisdiction**
   a. Original Jurisdiction
      Supreme Court original jurisdiction is defined by Art. III. It cannot be enlarged or diminished by Congress.

   b. Appellate Jurisdiction—Congressional Power
      The Supreme Court's appellate jurisdiction is vested by Art. III subject to congressional exceptions. This congressional power may be subject to limitations arising from separation of powers principles and constitutional rights and liberties.

   c. Form of Review
      Supreme Court review of lower court decisions is almost entirely a matter of discretion.

C. Constitutional and Policy Limitations on Judicial Review
Even where an issue concerns the subject matter set forth in Art. III, it may not *necessarily* be heard on the merits. For example, Art. III requires that a "case or controversy" must be present for an Art. III court to have jurisdiction. Further, there are prudential limitations borne of judicial self-restraint limiting the use of judicial review. The jurisdictional requirements and policy restraints are frequently referred to as justiciability.

1. **Constitutional Limitations**
   a. Eleventh Amendment
   The Eleventh Amendment as interpreted, provides that the judicial power does not extend to suits against a state or its agencies by citizens of another state or of a foreign country or by its own citizens. However, there are exceptions:

   (1) local governmental units not covered;

   (2) states may clearly waive sovereign immunity;

   (3) unconstitutional acts of state officials are not state acts. But, if suit involves a retroactive charge against the state or violation of state law, the Eleventh Amendment is a bar. Prospective relief and ancillary relief are permitted;

   (4) acting under the Fourteenth Amendment, § 5, or the Commerce Clause, Congress can grant remedies against the state action if it makes its intent to abrogate state immunity unmistakably clear.

   b. Case or Controversy
   A case must be in an adversary form and a context that is capable of judicial resolution and its resolution must not violate separation of powers principles, or an Art. III federal court lacks jurisdiction.

   Advisory Opinions—Art. III federal courts cannot furnish advisory opinions.

2. **Policy Limitations (Judicial Self-Restraint)**
   a. Rules for Constitutional Review

   b. Presumption of Constitutionality

   c. Judicial Restraint to Avoid Unnecessary Use of Judicial Review. The Court follows a policy of "strict necessity" before deciding constitutional questions.

D. Specific Doctrines Limiting Judicial Review
There are specific doctrines, based on the case and controversy requirement and judicial self-restraint, through which Art. III federal courts determine *who* may litigate a constitutional question, *when* the constitutional question may be litigated, and *what* constitutional questions may be litigated.

1. **The Standing Limitation**—*Who* Can Litigate?
   a. Constitutional Standards
      (1) Art. III requires that a plaintiff seeking to litigate a federal constitutional question demonstrate a personal stake in the outcome by establishing (1) injury in fact (2) caused by the government act being challenged. This assures the requisite adversity.

         (a) *"Injury in Fact."* Any significant factual injury, economic, aesthetic, etc., will suffice.

         (b) *Causation.* Plaintiffs must show that the injury is "fairly traceable" to the government action being challenged. They must also demonstrate a "substantial likelihood" that the injury is "redressable" if the court grants the requested relief.

      (2) Taxpayer and Citizen Standing

         (a) *Federal Taxpayers.* A federal taxpayer must allege (1) that the enactment being challenged is an exercise of the taxing and spending power, and (2) that the challenged enactment offends a specific limitation on the taxing and spending power.

         (b) *Citizen Standing.* At least in the absence of congressional legislation authorizing the suit, a citizen lacks a sufficient personal interest to raise the constitutional claim.

         (c) *State Taxpayers.* A state taxpayer has standing if she demonstrates a direct and substantial expenditure of public funds, i.e., a good faith pocketbook injury.

   b. Prudential Standing
      (1) *Third Party Standing.* A litigant usually lacks standing to raise the rights of others, but there are exceptions.

         (a) The jus tertii rule is a rule of judicial self-restraint which can be overcome when the balance of interests warrants hearing the claim.

      (2) An association can raise the rights of its members if the members have Art. III standing to sue in their own right, the suit is germane to the organization's interests and there is no need for individual participation.

2. The Timing Limitation—*When* Can Constitutional Litigation Be Brought

a. Mootness

Art. III requires dismissal of a case when, because of changes, the court's determination of the legal issue cannot have any practical effect in achieving the desired result. But there are exceptions to the doctrine:

(1) voluntary cessation of the allegedly illegal conduct;

(2) unsettled collateral consequences remain unsettled;

(3) there is a reasonable likelihood that the constitutional issue is "capable of repetition, yet evading review".

b. Ripeness and Justiciability

(1) The Art. III requirement of ripeness requires that there be *present* injury or an *imminent threat* of injury.

(2) Even if jurisdiction is technically present, judicial self-restraint may dictate dismissal of issues as premature and abstract.

c. Discretionary Abstention

(1) *Vagueness*

If a state statute is capable of a narrow saving construction, federal courts should exercise restraint and abstain from decisions on constitutional issues.

(2) Pending State Proceedings

Absent a showing of bad faith harassment, a federal court should abstain in a suit seeking declaratory or injunctive relief if state criminal and analogous civil proceedings are pending.

3. The Subject Matter Limitation—*What* Can Be Litigated

a. The Political Question Doctrine

Political questions, which are non-justiciable, have their origin in classic, functional, and prudential considerations.

(1) Constitutional commitment to another branch;

(2) lack of judicial resources and capabilities;

(3) prudential or policy considerations relating to the proper use of judicial power.

     b.   Adequate and Independent State Grounds
Where adequate and independent substantive or procedural state grounds for a lower court decision exist, the Supreme Court will decline to exercise jurisdiction.

II. NATIONAL LEGISLATIVE POWERS

Congress has only such powers as are granted by the Constitution. Under the Tenth Amendment, powers not granted to the national government are retained by the states and the people. The crucial inquiry is whether there is a constitutional source of power for congressional legislation.

A. The Scope of the National Legislative Power

1. Express Powers
Art. I, § 8, expressly grants specific powers to Congress.

2. Implied Powers
Under the Necessary and Proper Clause of Art. I, § 8, Congress can enact laws which are reasonably designed to achieve its delegated powers.

3. Inherent Powers
Congress has no inherent domestic legislative powers. This does not preclude the existence of inherent foreign affairs powers.

4. Delegation of Powers
Congress can delegate legislative authority so long as it prescribes some standards to guide use of the granted powers.

5. The Origination Clause
A bill which only incidentally raises revenue is not a "Bil[l] for raising revenue" which must originate in the House of Representatives.

B. Commerce Power

1. Definition
Congress has power to regulate "commerce among the states" which has come to mean interstate commerce. However, the commerce power provides the basis for congressional regulation even of local intrastate activities.

2. Achieving Social Welfare Objectives—A National Police Power
Congress' power to regulate commerce is plenary, permitting it to prescribe rules for the protection of commerce. Courts will not probe Congress's purpose in regulating interstate commerce.

     a.   Congress can achieve social welfare objectives through regulating interstate commerce.

b. *Tenth Amendment.* When Congress regulates *private* action, the Tenth Amendment is no limitation on Congress' regulatory power.

3. **Stream of Commerce**
Local activities can be regulated if they are part of the "stream" of interstate commerce.

4. **The Affectation Doctrine**
a. Substantial Effects
Under the necessary and proper clause, Congress can regulate local activities if it can rationally conclude that such activity has a substantial effect on interstate commerce. The courts defer to the congressional judgment.

b. Cumulative Effects Doctrine
In assessing the effect, Congress may consider the cumulative or aggregate impact of all regulated activities.

C. **The Taxing Power**
Congress has the fiscal power of raising monies through taxes. However, this is not a regulatory power and "penalties" may not be imposed in the guise of taxes.

1. Courts today tend to accept any tax as a fiscal measure if, on its face, it is a revenue producing measure.

2. Disclosure requirements will not make a tax into a penalty but such provisions raise problems of self-incrimination.

D. **The Spending Power**
Congress can spend, but not regulate, for the general welfare.

1. **General Welfare**
The spending clause of Art. I, § 8, cl. 1, is in an independent fiscal power to spend for general welfare objectives. It is not limited to the regulatory powers of Art. I, § 8. Congress determines the scope of the general welfare.

2. **Reasonable Conditions**
Congress may impose any reasonable conditions for participation in federal spending programs even if this induces states to conform to federal standards. The courts defer to Congress' judgment of reasonableness. Such conditions must be explicitly stated so that states can make informed choices.

E. Intergovernmental Immunities
The national government has greater immunity from state regulation and taxation and greater power to tax and regulate state functions (Art. VI Supremacy Clause).

1. State Taxation and Regulation
States cannot directly tax or regulate the federal government or federal instrumentalities. They cannot discriminate against the federal government or those who deal with the federal government.

2. Federal Taxation and Regulation
a. Federal Taxation of States
Non-discriminatory federal taxes, which reasonably reflect the benefits provided the state, are constitutional.

b. Federal Regulation of States
(1) *State Sovereignty Limitation.* Principles of state sovereignty, embodied in the Tenth Amendment, previously were interpreted to limit Congress' Commerce Clause power to regulate state activities. Three conditions were used in determining if state sovereignty was violated:

(a) "States as states" (Direct regulation of state or its agencies)

(b) "Traditional state functions"

(c) Impairment of state ability "to structure integral operations in areas of traditional functions"

(2) The national interest in including the states under the regulation was balanced against the intrusion on state sovereignty.

(3) *Minimal State Sovereignty Limitation.* Today principles of state sovereignty, embodied in our constitutional structure, impose only minimal limits on congressional power, assuring that the national political process is functioning.

(a) Federal courts should not determine what are "traditional" or "integral" functions of state government.

(b) It is the structure of the federal government itself that protects federalism.

III. STATE POWER IN AMERICAN FEDERALISM

States have inherent police power to legislate for the public health, morals, and well-being of its citizens. But this power is limited by the constitutional division of powers.

A. State Power to Regulate Commerce

1. Establishing the Foundations

Where a subject requires national regulation or where the particular state regulation would excessively burden interstate commerce, the state may not regulate absent congressional authorization.

a. The Nature of the Power

The commerce power is, at least partially, a concurrent power.

b. The Nature of the Subject—*Cooley* Doctrine

When subjects of commerce regulation are national in nature, i.e., require a uniform system or plan of regulation, they are not amenable to state regulation.

2. The Modern Focus: The Dormant Commerce Clause

The Dormant Commerce Clause, as interpreted by the courts, limits state power to enact regulations affecting interstate commerce. States may not discriminate against interstate commerce absent substantial justification or place excessive burdens on it.

a. Rationale

(1) Common Market Philosophy. No trade barriers.

(2) Lack of political protection for out-of-state interests.

b. Discrimination

If a state regulation is labeled "discriminatory" against interstate commerce, it is likely to be held unconstitutional. Economic protectionism violates the Dormant Commerce Clause.

(1) Purposeful Discrimination

A state law which intentionally discriminates against interstate commerce is virtually per se invalid

(2) Discriminatory Means and Effects

Even if a state law serves a legitimate police power objective, the law must regulate evenhandedly. A law having using discriminatory means or having a discriminatory impact must serve a legitimate local purpose that cannot be served as well by nondiscriminatory means.

(a) Extraterritorial operation of state laws

(b) Facial imposition of unequal burdens

(c) Discriminatory impact or effects of market structure

c. Undue Burdens—Ad Hoc Balancing
In determining if a nondiscriminatory state regulation of interstate commerce is valid, the courts balance the local interests in maintaining the law against the burden on interstate commerce. Some members of the Court reject undue burdens balancing, limiting the Dormant Commerce Clause to a ban on discrimination.

(1) Important state interests in trade, conservation, and environment weigh heavily in the balance but cannot be achieved by means which excessively impede the free flow of interstate commerce.

(2) State highway laws enjoy a heavy presumption of validity but, even here, states cannot unreasonably burden our national Common Market system.

d. State as Market Participant
When the state acts, not as a regulator, but as a participant in the marketplace, the Dormant Commerce Clause doctrine doesn't apply. Even state discrimination in favor of its own citizens is permissible. The more state actions effect parties not in privity with the state, the more likely the state will be held to be a regulator.

e. Protecting Personal Mobility
(1) Commerce Clause
The Commerce Clause protects the free movement of persons from state to state.

(2) Interstate Privileges and Immunities
Art. IV, § 2, prohibits unreasonable discrimination against out-of-state citizens in regard to fundamental interests basic to the livelihood of the Nation. There must be a substantial reason for the discrimination and the discrimination must bear a close relation to that reason. There must not be any less burdensome alternatives. The clause provides an alternative means for attacking state discrimination against out-of-state citizens.

3. **When Congress Speaks**
a. Preemption
(1) If a state law conflicts with a valid federal law so that it is impossible to comply with both or if it impedes achievement of

the federal legislative objective, the state law is invalid under the Art. VI Supremacy Clause.

(2) Congress may expressly preempt state law.

(3) If there is no conflict or express preemption, the courts must still determine if Congress intended to occupy the field and exclude the state regulation. Courts consider:

   (a) need for uniformity;

   (b) legislative history;

   (c) the pervasiveness of the federal regulation;

   (d) historic roles of national and local interest in regulating in the area (Presumption of no preemption in areas of traditional state authority);

   (e) potential for future conflict;

   (f) availability of a federal agency to maintain continued control.

   b. Legitimizing State Burdens on Commerce
      In exercising its plenary powers, Congress may authorize the state to regulate even where the state law would otherwise violate the negative implications of the Dormant Commerce Clause.

4. **The Compact Clause**
   Art. I, § 10, cl. 3, requires congressional consent to any agreement between states if it increases the political power of the states so as to potentially interfere with federal supremacy.

B. State Power to Tax Commerce
1. General Principles
   a. Interstate commerce can be forced to pay taxes which reasonably reflect the benefits derived from the taxing state.

   b. States *may not discriminate* against interstate commerce.

   c. *Due process* requires that the taxpayer have some minimal contacts with the taxing state.

   d. The *Commerce Clause* requires that a state tax be apportioned to reflect the extent of the taxable status the taxpayer has in the taxing state to avoid *multiple burdens*.

2. **Modern Applications**
Identify the local incidents being taxed and inquire into the actual
economic effect of the tax. The tax is valid if:

(1) the activity taxed is sufficiently connected to the taxing state;

(2) the tax fairly reflects the benefits received;

(3) the tax does not discriminate against interstate commerce;

(4) the tax is fairly apportioned.

IV. CONGRESS AND EXECUTIVE POWER

When Executive and Congressional powers conflict, consider whether one
Branch is invading the constitutional prerogatives of another Branch or is
usurping powers properly shared. Formalist and functional approaches are
used.

A. The Domestic Arena
1. **Executive Law-Making**
   a. Domestic Law-Making Powers
   Absent an emergency, the President has no inherent domestic law-
   making power. His powers as Chief Executive and his power to take
   care that the laws are faithfully executed may create some emergency
   powers subject to congressional review.

   b. Veto Power
   A presidential refusal to sign an act into law can be overridden by a
   two-thirds vote of both houses.

2. **Executive Impoundment**
It has not yet been decided whether a President's withholding or delay in
expending appropriations is a constitutional exercise of his power to
faithfully execute the laws or an unconstitutional interference in
Congress's law-making power.

3. **Delegation and Control of Legislative Power**
   a. Congress can delegate power to the executive if it formulates
   reasonable standards to guide discretion. The courts defer to Congress
   in determining reasonableness.

   b. *The Legislative Veto*. Retention of power by Congress to review and
   veto executive exercise of delegated power is legislative action which
   violates the Presentment and Bicameralism provisions of Art. I, § 7.

4. The Appointment and Removal Power

a. Art. II, § 2, cl. 2, vests the power to appoint federal officials, subject to the Senate's advice and consent, in the President. Congress may vest appointment of inferior officers in the President, courts of law, or heads of departments.

(1) Congress may not vest the appointment power in persons other than those specified in Art. II, § 2, cl. 2.

(2) Whether an official is a principal or an inferior officer depends on a functional analysis of her independence, power, jurisdiction, and tenure.

b. The President has the power to remove quasi-judicial or quasi-legislative officials subject to the standards established by Congress. The President has greater freedom to remove purely executive officials. But consider whether Congress' removal restrictions impede the President's ability to perform his constitutional duty.

c. Congress may not vest executive functions in officials subject to congressional removal by means other than impeachment.

5. Separation of Powers Generally

Consider generally whether the challenged actions excessively intrude on the constitutional functions of another Branch or consolidate powers that should properly be dispersed.

B. The Foreign Arena

1. Foreign Affairs

Foreign affairs powers are shared powers between the President and Congress. States and courts play a limited role.

2. Treaties and Executive Agreements

a. *Treaties* are made by the President with the advice and consent of two-thirds of the Senators present. They prevail over state law but are subject to constitutional limitations.

b. *Executive Agreements,* not requiring Senate concurrence, are legal even though they are not mentioned in the Constitution and prevail over contrary state law.

c. Congressional legislation, which would not otherwise survive constitutional review, may be a legitimate means of implementing a treaty.

3. **The War Power**
While Art. I gives the Congress alone power to declare war, the President's Art. II power as Commander-in-Chief affords him power in making war.

C. **Privileges and Immunities**
1. **Executive Privilege**
The Court has recognized the existence of an executive privilege for internal confidential communications based on the separation of powers principle and Art. II. A claim of privilege is presumptively valid and the judiciary determines whether a sufficient need has been shown by the party seeking disclosure.

2. **Impeachment**
A President may be impeached by the House and tried by the Senate for "high crimes and misdemeanors."

3. **Presidential Immunity**
The President is absolutely immune from civil liability for actions within the "outside perimeters" of his official responsibility. Presidential aides have a qualified immunity.

4. **Congressional Immunity**
Members of Congress and their aides enjoy absolute immunity under Art. I, § 6, for "legislative acts."

PART TWO: INDIVIDUAL RIGHTS AND LIBERTIES: CONSTITUTIONAL LIMITATIONS ON GOVERNMENT POWER

V. **PRIVILEGES AND IMMUNITIES OF NATIONAL CITIZENSHIP**
The Fourteenth Amendment Privileges and Immunities Clause has been narrowly interpreted to protect only those rights relating to a citizen's relationship to the national government, *e.g.,* to vote in federal elections, the right to travel interstate.

VI. **DUE PROCESS OF LAW**
A. **Traditional Substantive Due Process**
1. **Impairment of Obligation of Contract**
Art. I, § 10 limits state legislative ability to impair substantive contract obligations and the Fifth Amendment Due Process Clause prevents congressional impairment of substantive contract rights.

a. Private Contracts
A state law substantially impairing pre-existing contractual relationships violates this guarantee unless the state establishes that

the law is a reasonable means for achieving a significant and legitimate public purpose.

b.   Public Contracts
A state may contract away its fiscal powers and may impair its contracts only if it is reasonable and necessary to serve important state interests.

2.   Bills of Attainder
Neither Congress (Art. I, § 9) nor a state legislature (Art. I, § 10) may punish an individual without the benefit of judicial trial.

3.   Limitations on the Eminent Domain Power—"Taking" of Property
a.   The power of the federal and state governments to "take" private property for public use is subject to the Fifth and Fourteenth Amendment requirement that just compensation be given.

b.   The fact that property values and investment expectations are impaired by government regulation, while relevant, does not necessarily make it a *"taking"*. If the regulation is a reasonable use of a governmental power, it is probably not a "taking". Factors to be considered include: economic impact, investment expectations, occupation of the property.

4.   Modern Substantive Due Process: Non-fundamental Rights
In reviewing federal (Fifth Amendment) and state (Fourteenth Amendment) laws, the courts usually defer to the legislative judgment. If there is any *rational* basis that the legislature might have had for concluding that a law would further permissible legislative objectives, it does not violate due process. This deferential standard is used in reviewing most social and economic legislation.

a.   Burden of Proof
The law is presumed constitutional and the burden of proof (which is essentially insurmountable) is on the challenging party.

b.   Legitimate Objective
Any permissible government objective will suffice.

c.   Rational Means
In assessing the rationality of the law in achieving the government's objective, the courts will not second-guess legislative fact finding or question the wisdom of the law.

d. Fundamental Rights Exception
    Due Process challenges based on fundamental personal rights invoke a
    more searching judicial scrutiny.

B. The Process of Incorporation
1. Selective Incorporation
Only those provisions of the Bill of Rights which are "essential to the
concept of ordered liberty" or "fundamental in the American scheme of
justice" are made applicable to the states through the Due Process Clause.
Rights thus far not incorporated include the Seventh Amendment right to
jury trial on some civil cases, grand jury indictment, excessive bail, 12-
person juries and a unanimous verdict for conviction.

2. Full Incorporation
The incorporated right applies against the states in the same manner as
the Bill of Rights provision applies against the federal government.

C. Substantive Due Process Revisited: The Right of Privacy and Other Unenumerated Rights

1. Fundamental Rights
When laws burden the exercise of "fundamental rights" protected by the
Due Process guarantee, the courts apply stricter scrutiny. The
government bears the burden of showing that the law is narrowly tailored
to further an overriding government interest.

2. Express, Implied, and Unenumerated Rights
A more stringent standard of review is used for all express rights, those
rights implied from the express rights or the constitutional structure, and
other unenumerated fundamental rights recognized by the courts.
Occasionally, the Court holds that there is a significant burden on due
process liberty and balances the competing interests.

3. The Right of Privacy: Contraception and Abortion
While a variety of constitutional sources have been cited for the right of
privacy, it has been held to protect the use of contraceptives and the
abortion decision.

a. State Interest
    States have an interest in maternal health sufficient to allow
    reasonable regulation of abortion procedures. The state interest in
    the potentiality of life is compelling after viability permitting
    prohibition of abortion unless necessary to the life or health of the
    mother.

b.   Rights of Minors
The minor woman's right of privacy also protects her contraception
and abortion decisions. However, the greater state interest in minors
and their usual lesser capacity, permits a greater amount of state
regulation. Parents cannot be given an absolute veto over the
minor's decisions but requiring parental consent or notification, if a
judicial by-pass is provided, has been upheld.

c.   Abortion Funding
There is no right to abortion funding. Neither the right of privacy
nor equal protection requires the state to make the abortion right
effective even if maternal funding is provided.

4.   Sodomy Laws
There is no fundamental right of homosexuals to engage in private
consensual sodomy.

5.   Rights to Marriage and Family Life
The institutions of marriage and family, which are deeply rooted in our
nation's history and traditions, are fundamental rights subject to the
stricter form of judicial review.

6.   Right of Travel
a.   Interstate Movement
While the source of the right of interstate travel is unclear, it is a
fundamental personal right subject to more stringent judicial
protection.

b.   Foreign Travel
The right to travel abroad guaranteed by Fifth Amendment due
process is subject to reasonable regulation by the national government.

7.   The Right to Care and Protection
Government has no affirmative constitutional duty, absent special
circumstances, to provide care and protection for individuals. A limited
duty may arise if Government assumes custody of an individual.

8.   The Right to Refuse Treatment
A person has a liberty interest in avoiding unwanted medical treatment.
The government's interest may justify the regulatory burden on liberty.

9.   Rights in Restricted Environments
Stricter standards of due process review do not apply. Balancing of the
competing interests tend to reflect greater judicial deference.

D. Procedural Fairness
1. Ex Post Facto Laws
Neither the federal (Art. I, § 9) nor the state (Art. I, § 10) government may enact retroactive criminal laws significantly disadvantaging an offender.

2. Procedural Due Process: Civil Cases
Whenever the government deprives a person of a significant life, liberty, or property interest, it must afford due process.

   a. Life, Liberty, and Property Interests
      (1) *Right-Privilege Rejected.* Whether the interest is a right or a privilege, if it is a significant due process interest and is presently enjoyed, it is protected.

      (2) *Property* is limited to interests created by government, i.e., entitlements.

      (3) Liberty is not limited to freedom from confinement. It includes marriage, raising a family, etc. But, reputation, without more does not constitute a sufficient liberty interest.

   b. Procedures Required
The question of what process is due is a matter of federal constitutional law for the courts. It is not determined by state law. In determining what procedures are required to assure due process, courts balance the competing interests, considering three factors:

      (1) the severity of the harm to the litigant if the procedures are not provided;

      (2) the risk of error if the procedures are not afforded; and,

      (3) the administrative difficulty and other costs of providing the requested procedures.

   c. "Deprivation"
Negligent injury by government officials to life, liberty or property interest does not constitute a deprivation.

   d. Due Process Contexts
      (1) Welfare Benefits
Welfare benefits, once received, constitute a property entitlement. Courts balance the state interest in conserving resources against the recipient's interest in uninterrupted benefits.

(2) Use and Possession of Property
Wages or a purchaser's interest in goods received under a contingent sales contract constitute property. Normally, notice and hearing are required prior to depriving the property interest.

(3) Public Employment Rights
The mere subjective expectancy of continued employment or employment terminable at will are not property interests. There must be a state created entitlement. A state-created cause of action is a property entitlement.

(4) Institutional Due Process
While officials in public institutions do exercise broad discretion, liberty interests resulting from compulsory attendance at a school or involuntary confinement in a hospital require due process to be satisfied. The appropriate procedures are determined by balancing the liberty interest against institutional considerations.

(5) Parental Rights
The important liberty interests of natural parents in the care, custody, and management of their children require significant procedural protection.

(6) Student Rights
Due process does protect the liberty and property interests of a student. But the courts are reluctant to intrude on academic decisionmaking and the discretion afforded school authorities.

(7) Access to Courts
Due process does not require that indigents be given free access to the courts in civil cases absent state monopoly of processes affecting fundamental due process interests. Procedures available in civil proceedings are determined by the balancing test, although there is a presumption against a right to appointed counsel.

(8) Due Process Rights in the Military Sector
(a) *Status.* Military court jurisdiction is generally limited to military personnel.

(b) *Types of Crimes.* Military courts have jurisdiction over military personnel solely on the accused's status as a member of the Armed Forces, and not on the "service connection" of the offense charged.

e.   Conclusive Presumptions
When critical due process interests are lost through government action, due process generally requires that the individual be afforded an opportunity to prove that the facts presumed are not true in the particular case. But if the case involves a non-contractual claim to public benefits, it is possible that no liberty or property interest is involved.

VII. EQUAL PROTECTION
A. General Standards
The Fourteenth Amendment Equal Protection Clause and the Fifth Amendment Due Process Clause (which is read to guarantee equal protection) prohibit the state and federal government respectively from using unreasonable classifications. Reasonableness is dependent on: (1) the basis of the classification; (2) the character of the interests burdened by the classification; and (3) the government objectives supporting the classification.

B. Traditional Equal Protection
1. The Rational Basis Test
In most cases, a classification will be upheld if it is rationally related to any permissible government objective. The fact that a classification is under- or over-inclusive will not result in its unconstitutionality.

a.   Burden of Proof
The law is presumed valid and the burden of proof of its invalidity is on the challenger. The burden is usually insurmountable.

b.   Permissible Government Objective
If the classification is rationally related to a permissible government objective, even if it is not the actual objective, it will be upheld.

c.   Rational Means
If any facts can be ascertained that will sustain the classification, the existence of such fact finding by the legislature will be assumed. Only arbitrary classification is proscribed.

d.   Recent Trends
In a few recent cases, the Court has engaged in a more demanding balancing of the competing interests in determining the reasonableness of the challenged classification.

C. The New Equal Protection
1. Suspect Classifications
When a law purposely employs a suspect classification, the classification is subject to strict scrutiny. The ordinary presumption of validity no longer

applies and the burden is on the government to demonstate that the classification is necessary to a compelling government interest.

a. Purpose, Not Effect
Only intentional discrimination will trigger strict scrutiny.

(1) Discriminatory impact, while evidence of discriminatory purpose, is not enough to trigger strict scrutiny review.

(2) Even if discriminatory purpose is shown, government can avoid strict scrutiny if it can prove it would have taken the same action even apart from the discriminatory purpose.

b. Legislation and Administration
Legislation or administrative action which is purposely discriminatory, is subject to strict scrutiny. A law or policy may be overtly or covertly discriminatory in purpose.

2. **The Limits of Suspectness**
a. Race and National Origin
Racial and National origin classifications are suspect.

(1) Segregation in Education
(a) *De Jure Segregation.* Intentional racial segregation in public schools is inherently unequal and violates equal protection.

(b) *De Facto Segregation.* Government has no affirmative constitutional duty to remedy school segregation which it has not intentionally created.

(c) *Duty to Desegregate.* A *de jure* segregated school system is under an affirmative constitutional duty to desegregate. Action having a discriminatory *effect* impeding desegregation is prohibited.

(e) *Desegregation Remedies.* In remedying *de jure* segregation, equal protection does not require racial balancing, although racial composition may be used in measuring desegregation. District courts have broad equity powers, including the use of busing.

(e) *Interdistrict Segregation.* Segregation between school districts in a state does not violate equal protection unless it is caused by the government.

(2) Affirmative Action
Equal Protection does not prohibit the voluntary use of racial classification where a proper factual showing is made by the government.

   (a) State and localities must prove that the race conscious program is necessary to a compelling government interest.

   (b) Since deference is accorded congressional judgments, congressionally sanctioned programs need only be substantially related to important government interests.

c. Alienage—The "Sometimes Suspect" Classification
(1) Strict Scrutiny
When a state classifies on the basis of alienage, strict scrutiny normally applies.

(2) Political Function Exception
Only rationality is required when the state sets voter qualifications or defines the qualifications for appointment to important government positions involving governance of the political community, *e.g.,* state police, teachers, probation officers.

(3) Preemption
State classifications involving aliens are preempted if they interfere with national policies regarding immigration and naturalization.

(4) Federal Discrimination
Action by the national government does not violate the Fifth Amendment if it is a reasonable means of implementing its immigration and naturalization powers.

3. **"Almost Suspect" Classifications—Gender and Illegitimacy**
When reviewing gender and illegitimacy classifications, courts generally use an intermediate standard of review. The classification must be substantially related to an important government interest.

a. Gender Classification
(1) Sex Discrimination
Use of classifications that intentionally discriminate against women based on stereotypes seldom survive intermediate review. If the classification reflects real differences between the sexes, it is more likely to be upheld.

(2) Discriminatory Purpose
While a discriminatory impact on women is evidence of impermissible intent, it is only a discriminatory government purpose that will trigger use of the intermediate standard of review.

(3) Non-sex Classifications
Not all classifications that operate to the disadvantage only of women will be treated as discriminatory sex classifications.

(4) Affirmative Action
Classifications providing benefits only to women which are designed to remedy past discrimination are likely to be upheld if they are narrowly tailored to achieve this important benign objective.

(5) Mothers and Fathers
A law which discriminates against fathers, in favor of mothers, where the parents are similarly situated, is subject to intermediate review and generally violates equal protection.

b. Illegitimacy Classifications
An intermediate standard of review is also used for classifications burdening illegitimates—the classification must be substantially related to an important government interest. The more that it appears that a law is based on prejudice against illegitimates, the more likely it is that the law will be held unconstitutional.

4. Other Classifying Traits
Other classifying traits, *e.g.,* those which operate to disadvantage the poor or the aged, without more, are reviewed under the traditional rational basis test.

5. Fundamental Rights
When a classification significantly burdens the exercise of fundamental personal rights, the government usually must prove that the classification is necessary to a compelling governmental interest.

a. In cases where the law does not deter, penalize, or otherwise *significantly* burden the constitutional right, the Court applies the traditional rational basis test.

b. Increasingly, the Court has moved to a variable standard of review. The more significant the burden on fundamental rights, the greater the degree of scrutiny used.

    c.   Examples of fundamental rights include:

        (1) First Amendment Rights

        (2) the Right of Interstate Travel

        (3) the Right of Privacy

        (4) the Right to Marry

6. Fundamental Interests

The Court also has used a stricter standard of review to prevent discrimination in access to certain fundamental interests that are not technically constitutional rights but are protected by the Equal Protection Clause when discrimination is involved. This use of stricter review has been applied to the following interests:

a.   Voting

    (1) When the government discrimination significantly burdens the *exercise of the franchise,* in general or special purpose elections, strict scrutiny is applied.

        (a) *Special Purpose Districts.* A unit may be so special purpose and its effects on citizens so disproportionate that strict scrutiny will not be applied.

        (b) *Durational Residency Requirements.* While reasonable residency requirements are constitutional, durational residency requirements burden the vote and the right of interstate travel.

    (2) *Diluting the Franchise.* Dilution of the effectiveness of a vote of a particular class will often be reviewed under a more stringent standard of review than rationality.

        (a) *Access to the Ballot.* The requirements must be fair and not virtually exclusionary of independents and minority parties.

        (b) *Reapportionment.* The one person-one vote principle is applied to congressional districting as a command of Art. I, § 2, and to both houses of a bicameral state legislature as a mandate of equal protection.

        (c) *Multi-member Districts.* Multi-member districting violates equal protection and the Fifteenth Amendment if it is a purposeful device to exclude racial minorities from effective political participation.

    (d) *Political Gerrymanders.* Political gerrymanders that are proven to be intentionally discriminatory and which have actual discriminatory effects on an identifiable political group violate equal protection.

b. Access to Criminal Justice

Differences in wealth should not determine the ability of a person to secure criminal justice.

c. Education

While education is an important social and individual interest, the rational basis test is generally used for reviewing classifications burdening the interest on education. But when education is totally denied to a discrete underclass of children, the Court has required government to prove substantial justification.

7. Other Interests

Classifications burdening other social and economic interests, such as welfare, housing, medical care, are reviewed under the traditional rational basis test.

VIII. FREEDOM OF EXPRESSION

A. The Basic Doctrine

While the First Amendment is addressed only to Congress, its guarantees, express and implied, have been applied to the states as incorporated in due process liberty. When these rights are burdened, the courts employ heightened judicial scrutiny.

1. First Amendment Rationale

a. Marketplace of Ideas

Government must not prevent the free exchange of ideas in the marketplace. Free competition is the best test of an idea's worth.

b. Citizen Participant

Free expression is necessary so that citizens can perform their democratic obligations of criticizing the government and public policy.

c. Individual Liberty

Freedom of expression promotes individual autonomy and self-determination.

2. **Content Control v. Indirect Burdens**

   a. Some speech is categorically excluded from First Amendment protection, *e.g.,* obscenity, fighting words, or given lesser First Amendment protection, *e.g.,* commercial speech, defamation of private persons.

   b. When government directly burdens speech within the freedom of expression because of the content of the speech, the courts demand substantial justification, *e.g.,* clear and present danger, strict scrutiny.

   c. But when government only indirectly burdens speech by regulating, in a content-neutral way, the conditions under which expression takes place, *e.g.,* time, place, manner controls, the courts employ a lesser degree of judicial scrutiny (*e.g.,* interest balancing).

3. **The Clear and Present Danger Test: Content Control**
   Advocacy of the abstract idea of illegal conduct, without more, is constitutionally protected. Only where the advocacy is directed to inciting imminent lawless action and is likely to produce such action may the speech be suppressed because of its content. Both incitement and danger are required.

4. **The Balancing Test: Indirect Burdens**
   Reasonable content-neutral laws are constitutional even though freedom of expression is incidentally burdened.

   a. Balancing
   Reasonableness is determined by balancing the governmental interests in regulating against the extent of the burden on the protected constitutional right. This may take the form of simple ad hoc interest balancing or may involve a more intensive judicial scrutiny of the competing interests.

   b. Speech-Conduct
   When speech is joined with conduct, it is often not afforded as much protection as "pure speech".

5. **The Doctrine of Prior Restraint**
   Government restraints which operate prior to the time speech enters the marketplace of ideas are highly suspect, both substantively and procedurally. The government bears a heavy burden of justification when it uses such restraints, *e.g.,* clear and present danger test.

6. First Amendment Due Process and Equal Protection: Facial Validity and Validity as Applied
Laws may be facially invalid or invalid as applied in a particular case. The former generally results in invalidation of the law itself.

a. Vagueness
A law is facially invalid under freedom of expression and due process if it is not drawn with sufficient clarity and definiteness to inform persons of ordinary intelligence what actions are proscribed.

b. Overbreadth
A law may be void on its face if it is overbroad, in that the law indiscriminately reaches both constitutionally protected and unprotected activity. Substantial overbreadth is required.

c. Less Burdensome Alternatives
In some cases, when a permissible governmental objective can be achieved by means which are less burdensome on First Amendment expression than the means selected, the government must use the less burdensome means.

d. Equal Protection
When classifications significantly burden First Amendment rights by discriminating among speech activities, the classification will be closely scrutinized, *e.g.*, it must be narrowly tailored to serve substantial government interests.

7. Corporate Speech
Expression which is protected under the First Amendment does not lose that protection simply because the source of the speech is a corporation.

B. Freedom of Association and Belief
The First Amendment guarantees a right of expressive association for First Amendment objectives, not a general right of social association. The validity of government burdens on the implied rights of association and belief is usually determined by a balancing test. A law is reasonable if the government interest outweighs the individual's right to associate and hold particular political, economic, or social beliefs. Increasingly the Court has employed more stringent forms of interest balancing including strict scrutiny.

1. Restraints on Membership and Associational Action
a. Membership in an organization cannot be penalized or punished unless the law is limited to active membership, which requires:

(1) membership knowing of the group's illegal objectives (scienter);

(2) specific intent to further those illegal objectives.

b. The right includes the right to engage in legitimate group activity to further associational objectives but does not impose any constitutional duty on government to promote the group.

2. Group Registration and Disclosure Requirements
In judging the validity of laws requiring groups to register and disclose their membership lists, the courts balance the burden on the right of association and belief against the interests of government in securing the information.

3. Government Employment and Benefits
Civil penalties for group membership and activities must satisfy First Amendment standards; the right-privilege distinction has been rejected. Government may not condition the receipt of government benefits on the surrender of First Amendment rights (*i.e.*, Unconstitutional Conditions). When reviewing restraints on expression by government employees, the courts employ a balancing test, weighing the interest of the government as employer against the burden on First Amendment rights.

a. Loyalty Programs
Programs designed to review the loyalty of government employees must be narrowly drawn to serve the government interest in security.

b. Loyalty Oaths
While narrowly drawn oaths are constitutional, broader oaths probing associational activities must be clear (vagueness) and narrowly drawn to include scienter and specific intent (overbreadth).

c. Individual Membership Disclosure: Bar Admission Requirements
(1) Failure to cooperate with a bar commission's inquiry, when the questions are narrowly drawn and have a substantial relevance to determining an applicant's fitness and competence to practice law, is a grounds for denying bar admission.

(2) Broad-ranging inquiries into associational memberships which are not limited by scienter and specific intent requirements violate freedom of expression.

4. Legislative Investigations and Forced Disclosure
a. First Amendment Limitations
While the Court has used ad hoc balancing in reviewing the validity of legislative investigations burdening First Amendment rights, more

recently it has required that government demonstrate a substantial relation between the information sought and an overriding governmental interest.

b. Self-Incrimination
(1) An employer cannot be required to surrender her privilege against self-incrimination as a condition of continued employment.

(2) Under a grant of immunity, an employee can be required to cooperate with an inquiry which is narrowly focused on her performance of official duties.

5. Group Litigation
Group litigation, a form of expressive and associational conduct, can be regulated only for substantial reasons and only by specific regulations.

C. Freedom From Compelled Expression
The First Amendment protects the freedom to speak freely and the right to refrain from speaking. The constitutional right to associate and believe implies a correlative right to be free of compelled association and beliefs. If freedom from compelled expression is significantly burdened, strict scrutiny applies.

D. The Electoral Process
Speech and association for electoral ends are "core" First Amendment rights. Strict scrutiny usually applies.

1. Campaign Speech
When government seeks to control what a candidate may say during an election campaign, it must show that the restraint is necessary to a compelling government interest or is a form of unprotected expression.

2. Regulating Political Parties
A heavy burden of justification is imposed when states seek to legislate extraterritorially by regulating national political parties.

3. Limitations on Contributions and Expenditures
a. Campaign Spending
(1) Noncorporate Spending
Restrictions on *expenditures* by individuals and groups violate freedom of speech. Reasonable limitations on *contributions* by individuals and groups are permissible since such laws further the interest in avoiding the actuality or appearance of corruption.

(2) Corporate Spending
Restrictions on expenditures by corporations are constitutional if
they are narrowly drawn to serve the state's compelling interest
in preventing the distortion and corrosive effect of corporate
wealth on the political process.

b.   Ballot Referenda
State interests in restricting contributions for ballot referenda are
inadequate to justify the burden on freedom of speech and association.

4. **Forced Disclosure Requirements**
Forced disclosure of campaign contributions can be upheld only if the law
is narrowly drawn to further overriding government objectives, *e.g.*,
informing the electorate.

5. **Political Patronage**
Dismissal, hiring, promotion, transfer or recall of public employees because
of their political affiliation is constitutional only if the government shows
that party affiliation is, in fact, an appropriate measure of performance
for the public office involved.

E. **Speech in the Local Forum: The Right to Assemble and Petition**
Basic doctrines of First Amendment law outlined above (vagueness and
overbreadth, prior restraint, equal protection), especially the distinction between
laws directly regulating speech content and laws indirectly burdening freedom
of expression, apply to the right to assemble and petition government.

1. **Controlling Speech Content**
a.   The Danger of Disorder
(1) The Clear and Present Danger Doctrine
Government must establish incitement to likely, imminent lawless
conduct.

(2) The Fighting Words Doctrine
Words which have a direct tendency to cause acts of violence by
the person to whom, individually, the remarks are addressed may
be punished by government under carefully drawn statutes not
susceptible of application to protected expression.

(a) Such verbal assaults are categorized as unprotected speech.

(b) *Overbreadth and Vagueness.* Laws which are not specifically
limited to fighting words are typically held overbroad and
vague.

(c) *Hostile Audiences.* If the source of a threatened disruption is a crowd of listeners hostile to the speaker's message, and the speaker is not seeking to incite a hostile reaction, the police must usually proceed against the crowd and protect the speaker.

b. Offensive and Abusive Language
Government has no power to punish the use of words that are merely offensive, abusive, profane, or vulgar.

c. Equal Protection
Discrimination in the use of the public forum generally involves content-based distinctions subject to strict scrutiny.

2. **Regulating the Public Forum**
If government regulates speech in the public forum, the law must be content-neutral, narrowly serve a significant governmental interest, and must leave open alternative channels of communication.

If government regulates public property determined to be a nonpublic forum, the law must be viewpoint-neutral and rational.

a. The Nature of the Forum
(1) *Traditional Public Forum.* Government cannot bar public access to places historically open to expression, *e.g.*, streets, sidewalks and parks.

(2) *Limited or Designated Public Forum.* Government may designate other public property as open to First Amendment activity.

(3) *Nonpublic Forum.* Public property not traditionally open or open by designation is a nonpublic forum. Government can regulate based on speech content or speaker identity.

(4) Only when privately-owned property has taken on all of the attributes of publicly-owned property is it labeled part of the public forum.

b. The Demand for Reasonable Regulation
Regulation of the time, place and manner of expression in the public forum must be clear and precise, content-neutral, narrowly drawn to reflect a significant government interest and leave open alternative forums for expression. Narrowly tailored does not mean that government must use the least burdensome means. It is sufficient if the government interest would be achieved less effectively absent the regulation.

(1) Speech Plus
When expression takes the form of speech plus conduct, it is not as entitled to protection as pure speech.

(2) Sound Amplification and Interest Balancing
While sound broadcasting is constitutionally protected, it may be subject to content-neutral, reasonable regulation.

(3) Protecting the Homeowner
Canvassing, handbilling and solicitation of homeowners are constitutionally protected but may be subjected to clear, narrowly-drawn, non-discriminatory regulation protecting the privacy of homeowners, *e.g.*, targeted picketing.

(4) Licensing, Prior Restraint and the Duty to Obey
Prior restraints on access to the public forum, *e.g.*, licensing, injunctions, are constitutional if they are clear, narrowly-drawn, time, place and manner regulations.

    (a) *Balancing.* The public interest in preserving the normal usage of public places is balanced against the free expression interests.

    (b) *Facial Validity—Vagueness and Overbreadth.* Laws vesting discretion in administrators must be drawn with precision, specificity, and clarity.

    (c) The Duty to Obey
        (1) *Laws.* If a licensing law is valid on its face, it must be obeyed, and its application must be judicially determined. However, if a licensing law is facially invalid, it may be ignored and its invalidity established at the time of prosecution.

        (2) *Injunctions.* Only if a court order is frivolous or the issuing court lacks jurisdiction may it be disobeyed prior to appellate review.

F. Symbolic Speech

When conduct is alleged to embody the idea itself, the Court employs a two-part inquiry: (1) Is the conduct communicative? (2) If so, is the speech protected under First Amendment law?

1. **Is the Conduct Communicative?**
    The nature, factual context, and environment are examined to determine if the actor has an intent to communicate and whether the viewing audience would understand the communication.

2. **Is the Speech Protected?**
    a. Government regulation of symbolic speech is permissible if:

        (1) it furthers an important or substantial government interest;

        (2) the governmental interest is unrelated to the suppression of the idea; and,

        (3) the incidental restriction on alleged First Amendment freedom is no greater than is essential to furtherance of that interest.

    b. If the regulation is based on the content of the symbolic speech, *e.g.,* flag burning, the most exacting scrutiny applies.

G. Commercial Speech
Regulation of commercial speech, *e.g.,* lawyer advertising, is constitutional if it satisfies a four-part test:

(1) the speech is actually or inherently misleading or related to unlawful activity since such speech is not protected by the First Amendment;

(2) the asserted government interest must be substantial;

(3) the government regulation must directly advance the governmental interest asserted;

(4) the regulation must not be more extensive than is necessary to serve that interest. This does not mean that government must use the least burdensome alternatives, only that the law directly and effectively furthers the interest.

H. Freedom of the Press
The press clause is read with the speech clause as a single guarantee. The press enjoys no privileges or immunities beyond those afforded the ordinary citizen.

1. **Newsgathering**
    While newsgathering is protected by the First Amendment, the protection is less than that accorded when government restrains publication.

a. Journalist's Privilege
The First Amendment affords journalists no privilege, qualified or absolute, to refuse to give evidence to a grand jury at least so long as it is conducted as a good faith law enforcement effort. The Supreme Court has not decided whether a qualified First Amendment-based journalist's privilege is available in the context of civil litigation.

b. Access to Public Information and Institutions
    (1) Prisons
        (a) Censorship of prisoners' outgoing mail is permitted only when the censorship is no greater than necessary to further a substantial public interest. Incoming and internal mail may be regulated if the law reasonably furthers legitimate penological objectives.

        (b) A non-discriminatory, reasonable regulation limiting press interviews with prisoners is constitutional.

    (2) Judicial Proceedings
        (a) *Criminal Trials.* Closure of criminal trials, voir dire and preliminary hearings violates the First Amendment guarantee of access unless record findings establish that closure is necessitated to preserve higher values and is narrowly drawn.

        (b) *Newsroom Searches and Seizures.* The press, like the public, may be subjected to reasonable searches but warrant requirements are to be applied with searching exactitude.

        (c) *Cameras in the Courtroom.* Due process is not violated by broadcast media coverage of trials, absent a showing of prejudice to the defendant depriving him of a fair trial.

        (d) *Copyright.* The First Amendment does not protect the publishing of as yet unpublished copyrighted expression of a public figure from copyright liability.

2. **Public Access to the Media**
The First Amendment protects the public's right to receive suitable access to ideas and experiences.

a. Public Access to the Electronic Media
Government can require broadcasters to discuss public issues and provide balanced coverage or provide for a limited reasonable statutory right of access to broadcast time. But the First Amendment does not afford a constitutional right of public access to broadcasting.

   b. Public Access to the Print Media
Since the First Amendment protects journalistic integrity and the editorial process, the print media cannot be compelled to publish that which they do not choose to publish.

   c. Access to Cable
First Amendment considerations are implicated when cable franchises are denied but the standards are yet to be determined.

3. Defamation and Privacy
   a. Defamation
     (1) Public Officials and Public Figures
Public Officials and Public Figures may be awarded damages for publication of a defamatory falsehood only if they prove by clear and convincing evidence that the publication was made with actual malice, *i.e.*, subjective knowledge of its falsity or reckless disregard of its truth or falsity.

        (a) In all matters of public interest, the plaintiff also bears the burden of proving falsity.

        (b) A public figure may be an all-purpose public figure (*i.e.*, general fame or notoriety) or a limited purpose public figure (*i.e.*, voluntary involvement in a public controversy).

     (2) Private Figures
        (a) So long as a state does not impose strict liability, it may define for itself the appropriate standard of liability for a publisher or broadcaster in defamation actions by a private figure.

        (b) Presumed and punitive damages cannot be recovered, absent a showing of actual malice, unless the subject of the defamation is a matter purely of private concern.

        (c) The private figure plaintiff also bears the burden of proving falsity, at least where the statements involve matters of public concern.

     (3) There is no constitutional privilege for opinion, although there cannot be liability if the publication cannot reasonably be interpreted as stating a defamatory fact.

b. Privacy
    (1) False Light Privacy
        At least at present, a privacy action against the media cannot be maintained solely on the basis that the report was false—actual malice must be shown.

    (2) Public Records
        Truthful reports, but not inaccurate reports, of facts disclosed in the public record are constitutionally protected. Truthful publication of materials legally obtained cannot be punished absent a need to further a state interest of the highest order.

    (3) Right of Publicity
        Government protection of a person's "right of publicity" is subject to constitutional limitation.

c. Intentional Infliction of Mental Distress
    Public officials and public figures must show that the defendant published with actual malice.

I. Obscenity
1. No First Amendment Protection
Lewdness, indecency, offensiveness, and profanity are not excluded from First Amendment protection, but obscenity, which lacks social importance, is entitled to *no* protection under the First Amendment.

2. Defining Obscenity
Each element of a three-part test must be satisfied in order to define material as obscene:

    (1) whether the average person, applying contemporary community standards, would find that the work taken as a whole appeals to the prurient interest;

    (2) whether the work depicts or describes, in a patently offensive way, sexual conduct specifically defined by the applicable state law; and,

    (3) whether the work, taken as a whole, lacks serious literary, artistic, political, or scientific value. *Miller v. California.*

3. Applying the Standards
a. No National Community Standard
    (1) In determining pruriency and patent offensiveness, the jury may apply "contemporary community standards."

    (2) Sensitive persons, but not children, are part of the community.

(3) No expert testimony is constitutionally required.

(4) Jury determinations are subject to appellate review to assure constitutional requirements are met.

b. Defining the Relevant Audience
(1) The Average Person
Obscenity is to be judged by the effect of the material on a person of average susceptibility.

(2) Variable Obscenity: Minors and Deviants
But if the material is directed at a particular audience, obscenity may be judged by its probable effects on that audience.

c. The Demand for Specificity
(1) Vagueness

(a) If the three-part test is satisfied, a vagueness challenge to a law will fail.

(b) The conduct to be proscribed must be specifically defined by applicable state law, but this specificity may be satisfied by judicial construction of state law in conformity to the *Miller* obscenity standards. Only the overbroad provisions of the statute are to be invalidated.

(c) *Pandering.* In determining whether the material is obscene, the circumstances of the presentation and dissemination of the material may be considered.

(d) *Serious Value.* "Serious" value (which is not judged by local community standards) can save material from being labeled obscene.

4. Privacy and Obscenity
The mere possession of obscene material cannot constitutionally be made a crime but possession of child pornography can be criminalized.

5. Civil Control of Obscenity and Indecency
a. Zoning laws, usually treated as time, place and manner regulations, must be designed to achieve a substantial government interest and leave open reasonable alternative channels of communication.

b. Civil controls of obscene material, e.g., nuisance laws, must satisfy the three-part *Miller* test; indecent expression is protected. But if a regulation is directed to unlawful activity and does not significantly burden protected expression, only rationality is required.

6. **Broadcasting and Indecency**
FCC regulation of indecent, although not obscene, material in broadcasting is constitutional.

7. **Child Pornography**
Sexually indecent live productions or reproductions of sexually indecent live productions involving minors is not protected speech. Knowing distribution of such material may be criminally punished.

8. **Administrative Censorship**
   a. Procedural Fairness
   Prior restraints on publication, alleged to be obscene, are burdened procedurally. Censorship must satisfy the following requirements:

   (1) burden on censor;

   (2) prompt judicial proceeding;

   (3) censor must secure judicial approval.

   b. Search and Seizure
   While seizure of a single copy of an allegedly obscene work, pursuant to a warrant for use as evidence is permissible even without a prior adversary determination of obscenity, large scale seizure for purposes of suppression must be preceded by a determination of obscenity.

J. SPECIAL CONTEXTS
In certain "restricted environments" like prisons, government employment, schools and prisons, First Amendment protections of expression is diminished.

1. **Government Employees**
   a. In determining if a restraint on political activity and public speech by government employees is constitutional, the courts normally balance the interests of the employee as citizen against the government's interest as employer.

   b. When government employee speech involves matters of private interest rather than public concern, the courts exercise deference and apply a rationality test.

   c. The employee must prove that the protected activity was a cause of the adverse government action.

2. **The Academic Forum**
    a. Library Censorship
        The First Amendment does impose limits on library book removal in an effort to limit student access to offensive ideas.

    b. Student Speech
        (1) Schools can bar speech or expressive action which intrudes on the work of the schools and their educational mission or which violates the rights of other students.

        (2) Schools are public forums only if school officials have by policy or practice opened those facilities for general public use or for use by some segment of the public.

        (3) Schools can regulate "school sponsored" student speech that occurs in "curricular" activities if there is some pedagogical reason for the regulation.

    c. Academic Freedom
        The First Amendment embraces a concept of academic freedom but it does not protect against all incidental burdens.

IX. FREEDOM OF RELIGION

The First Amendment guarantees of free exercise of religion and freedom from religious establishment are applicable to the states as part of Fourteenth Amendment due process liberty. The basic command is government neutrality.

A. The Meaning of the Establishment Clause

The Establishment Clause is not limited to a command of equal treatment of religions. While the Court has increasingly asked whether the challenged law *endorses* religion, a three-part test is usually used to determine if the Establishment Clause is violated:

(1) the government action must have a secular legislative purpose;

(2) the primary effect of the government action must neither advance nor inhibit religion;

(3) the government must not foster an excessive entanglement with religion.

1. Religion in School

a. Released Time
    While released time for religious education is a constitutional accommodation of religion, on-premises religious instruction has the primary effect of advancing religion.

b. Prayers, Bible Reading, and Devotional Exercises
    Required prayers, including moments of silent prayer, even when non-denominational and where objectors are excused, have the purpose and primary effect of aiding religion.

c. Teaching Religious Values
    While a state has broad discretion over its curriculum and may foster the teaching of basic values and tradition, a program violates the Establishment Clause if it is primarily religious in character or has the purpose of advancing religion.

d. Equal Protection
    Discrimination among groups in the use of the public forum based on the fact that they are engaged in religious expression can be justified only by a compelling government interest. Laws promoting equal access to schools by religious groups do not violate the Establishment Clause.

2. **Financial Aid to Religious Schools**
    a. Public Benefits: Busing and Books
        If the state provides transportation or books to private school children only for the secular purpose of serving the public welfare, the incidental benefit to religion does not condemn the program.

    b. Financial Aid for Schools
        While financial aid usually is considered to be for a secular purpose, it often is found to have a primary effect that is sectarian or to involve excessive government entanglement with religion.

        (1) Elementary-Secondary v. Higher Education
             Since pupils in lower levels of education are likely to be more impressionable and political divisiveness is more common, aid to such schools is more likely to be held unconstitutional.

        (2) Financial Aid
             Aid directly to the religious institution rather than to citizens is more likely to be held unconstitutional. Financial support directed only to parents having children in private schools has the primary effect of aiding religion. Tax breaks for educational expenses available to citizens generally is constitutional.

        (3) Testing, Recordkeeping, and Other Services
             The dangers of religious indoctrination from a particular form of aid and the location where it occurs influence the constitutional validity of the program.

3.   Other Establishment Contexts
   a.   Blue Laws

      Thus far, Sunday closing laws have been upheld against Establishment Clause challenge on grounds that they serve the secular purpose of promoting a common day of rest.

   b.   Tax Exemptions

      Tax exemptions for religious and other charitable institutions are constitutional given the historical experience with such benefits. But an exemption from sales and use taxes solely for religious activities has been held violative of the Establishment Clause.

   c.   Legislative Prayer

      History and tradition support the conclusion that opening prayer at the state legislature, led by government paid clergyman, does not violate the Establishment Clause.

   d.   Public Displays

      Public recognition of traditional holidays is permissible when the religious effect is only indirect, remote, and incidental. However, if the display endorses religious beliefs, the antiestablishment principle is violated.

   e.   Denominational Preference

      When government provides benefits to only selected religions, it must demonstrate that the law is narrowly tailored to further a compelling public interest. The *Lemon* tripartite test must be satisfied.

   f.   Internal Church Disputes

      While courts may not decide purely internal church disputes, they can decide legal questions when they involve only application of neutral principles of law.

B.   The Meaning of the Free Exercise Clause

If a law significantly burdens the free exercise of religion by compulsion or coercion, government must demonstrate a compelling or overriding government interest. The availability of less burdensome alternatives will be considered. General First Amendment law will be applied.

There are increasing indications that a law that is generally applicable and religion-neutral, which imposes only incidental burdens on a particular religion, will not be judged by strict scrutiny. Incidental discriminatory impact on a religious practice or belief, even if it is significant, may not be sufficient to trigger strict scrutiny review.

1. **Belief-Conduct**
   While religious belief is absolutely protected, religious conduct must be accommodated to valid government interests.

2. **Centrality and Sincerity**
   While the courts cannot probe the truth or falsity of a religious belief, they can probe whether the belief is sincerely held. While courts have also probed the centrality of a belief or practice to a religion, there are indications that this approach may be eliminated from free exercise review.

3. **General Indirect Burdens**
   Absent some significant burden on a claimant's free exercise of religion, strict scrutiny is not appropriate.

4. **Blue Laws**
   Thus far, the Court has upheld Sunday closing laws against free exercise challenges by characterizing the burden as only an indirect economic hardship, outweighed by the public interest in a uniform day of rest.

5. **Conditioning Public Welfare Benefits**
   The government cannot condition the receipt of public benefits on the surrender of constitutional rights, such as free exercise of religion. Even if the burden is indirect, loss of such benefits constitutes a significant burden on religion, requiring government to demonstrate a compelling interest which cannot be satisfied by less burdensome means. Benefits can be denied if this is only an incidental effect of applying a generally applicable and otherwise valid religion-neutral criminal law.

6. **Compelled Action**
   Outside of the military context, when government requires an individual to engage in practices contrary to central tenets of his or her religion, only the showing of a compelling interest will justify such a direct (significant) burden on religion.

7. **Noncoercive Laws**
   If the government regulation has the incidental effect of making it significantly more difficult to practice a religion, but does not compel or coerce action contrary to a religious belief, strict scrutiny does not apply. Government is not required to accommodate its internal practices to religious needs and desires.

8. **Proscribed Religious Practices**
   Strict scrutiny is not applicable to a generally applicable, religion-neutral criminal law which has the incidental effect of prohibiting a religious

practice. Application of the law is constitutional, even if the practice is central to a religion.

C. The Meaning of Religion
1. Defining Religion
While "religion" is not limited to theistic beliefs and practices, the Court has not yet defined the outer limits of religion.

2. Conscientious Objection—Parallel Beliefs
In conscientious objector cases, the Court has asked whether a given belief which is sincere and meaningful occupies a place in the life of its possessor parallel to that filled by the orthodox belief in God.

X. STATE ACTION
Most of the rights and liberties protected by the Constitution require a showing of "state action." It is government wrongdoing, not private misconduct, that is the focus of constitutional judicial review.

A. The State Action Requirement
1. The Civil War Amendments
While the Thirteenth Amendment prohibits the imposition of slavery or involuntary servitude regardless of its source, the Fourteenth and Fifteenth Amendments, at least in the absence of congressional legislation, require that governmental action be present in order to establish a violation.

2. The Present Standard—State Responsibility
It is only when government is so significantly involved in the challenged action that it can be said that government is actually responsible for it, that the state action threshold is satisfied. There must be a close nexus between government and the particular action being challenged. These requirements have become harder to satisfy.

B. Official Misconduct and Joint Action
1. Action Contrary to State Law
Laws and official action pursuant to law involve state action. Even if a state official acts contrary to state law, the state action requirement is satisfied since government has put the official in a position of power.

2. Public Administration
Official supervision, control, or management of a facility, even where the government is only indirectly entwined in the management, constitutes state action.

3. Joint Action
If a private individual engages in joint activity with government officials, state action is established.

C. Public Functions
If performance of a function is traditionally and exclusively a function of government, it will constitute state action, *e.g.,* white primaries, company towns.

D. Significant State Involvement
1. Symbiotic Relationships
In weighing the facts and circumstances to determine the significance of a public-private relationship, the existence of mutual benefits and supports (i.e., symbiotic relationship) is critical. Only if the acts of the private actor may fairly be treated as the acts of the government itself, is there state action.

2. Government Regulation and Licensing
Even licensing and extensive government regulation of a private activity will not, without more, constitute state action.

3. Government Financial Support
Financial support of a private activity, unless it makes the government responsible for the challenged private action by encouraging, authorizing, or approving it, does not constitute state action.

E. Encouragement, Authorization, and Approval
1. Neutral Law Enforcement
Neutral state enforcement of state laws, without a showing of encouragement, authorization, or approval of the particular action being challenged, does not constitute state action.

2. Involuntary Discrimination
However, even a neutral enforcement of state laws cannot be used to force racial discrimination on unwilling parties.

3. Significant Encouragement
When the challenged private actions are overtly or covertly encouraged by government, state action is present.

4. Authorization and Approval
a.   While acquiescence in conduct is not enough to establish state action, government compulsion or authorization of the particular act being challenged, whereby the state becomes responsible for it, is state action.

b.	The Court has indicated that the challenger must show that the action being challenged is borne of a state policy, rule, right or privilege, and that the party charged with the action may be said to be a state actor.

XI. CONGRESSIONAL LEGISLATION IN AID OF CIVIL RIGHTS AND LIBERTIES
### A.	In General: Federal Legislative Jurisdiction
1.	Pursuant to the commerce and spending powers, Congress has power to legislate for social welfare purposes, including the protection of civil rights and liberties.

2.	Congress can also legislate to protect "federal rights" against state or private interference.

3.	The Civil War Amendments and a number of other amendments grant Congress power to enact legislation, which is reasonably appropriate, to enforce the rights secured by the amendments.

### B.	Enforcing the Thirteenth Amendment
1.	Under the Thirteenth Amendment, § 2, Congress has power to enact legislation which is rationally related to eliminating all badges and incidents of slavery in the United States.

2.	Pursuant to the power, Congress can legislate against even private conduct.

### C.	Enforcing the Fourteenth Amendment
The Fourteenth Amendment, § 5, authorizes Congress to enact legislation which is rationally related to protecting the privilege and immunities, due process and equal protection guarantees.

#### 1.	Defining Remedies
It is clear that Congress can enact remedies for Fourteenth Amendment rights as defined by the courts, even if the action proscribed would not violate the Fourteenth Amendment in the absence of congressional legislation.

#### 2.	Defining Rights?
There are indications that Congress can define the substantive scope of the Amendment's guarantees, at least where it acts to increase the constitutional protection afforded, and legislate pursuant to the right so defined. Alternatively, Congress' remedial power extends to determining the adequacy of state justification for discriminatory practices.

a.	The Rachet Theory
Congress cannot dilute Fourteenth Amendment guarantees.

b.   **Constitutional Limitations**
Congress cannot violate other constitutional provisions through the exercise of its Fourteenth Amendment, § 5, powers.

3.   Private Action
There is some judicial authority for the principle that Congress can legislate against even private action under the Fourteenth Amendment, § 5, powers, at least in regard to some Fourteenth Amendment rights.

D.   Enforcing the Fifteenth Amendment
The Fifteenth Amendment, § 2, gives Congress power to enact legislation which rationally implements the Fifteenth Amendment's prohibition against racial discrimination in voting.

PERSPECTIVE

THE STUDY OF CONSTITUTIONAL LAW

(1) THE DOCUMENT AND JUDICIAL REVIEW

Constitutional law is concerned primarily with the exercise of judicial review. The focus is on the manner in which the courts generally, but the Supreme Court in particular, have interpreted the sometimes cryptic provisions of the United States Constitution. In your study, you should emphasize not only the principles and doctrines developed in the cases but also the policies and values reflected in these rules. Further, you should consider the principles and policies rejected by the Court. The collegial character of the Supreme Court demands attention not only to the opinion of the Court but also to concurring and dissenting opinions which indicate alternatives and often suggest future currents and trends in constitutional decision-making. Remember, stare decisis, the rule of precedent, has less force in constitutional law than in other areas of your law studies. Constitutional law is an unsettled and rapidly evolving field. Its touchstone may be variously constitutional text, constitutional history, or even recently-fashioned doctrine and practice.

(2) APPROACHES TO CONSTITUTIONAL INTERPRETATION

Two general approaches to constitutional interpretation and analysis should be noted. While these approaches are especially vital in the context of defining rights and liberties, they also inform the exercise of judicial review in the area of the allocation of powers.

(a) Interpretivism emphasizes reliance on the Constitution itself as the basic norm for decision in constitutional cases. The approach assumes various forms. Interpretivists may look to the "plain meaning" of the textual language, the original understanding of the framers, the historical exegesis of the constitutional provision or the structure and relationships reflected in the document. A broad or narrow reading of the provisions may be adopted. But the focus of judicial review, the source of the principles and policies for decision, are all, according to the Interpretivists, to be derived from the Constitution.

(b) Non-interpretivism acknowledges the existence of an "unwritten constitution." Principles and policies used in judicial review are derived not only from the document but from external sources, such as historical experience, political realities, traditional social values, societal consensus or evolving concepts of justice and morality. The constitutional text and the historical origins of the provisions in question are, at best, only starting points for judicial review.

PRINCIPLES OF CONSTITUTIONAL LAW: COURSE OVERVIEW

The course in constitutional law is traditionally divided into two major parts. The first part is devoted to the allocation of powers at the national level (separation of powers) and between the national government and state governments (division of powers). The second part of the course focuses on the limitation of government power resulting from the guarantee of rights and liberties. The allocation of government powers is designed not only to assure that government can govern effectively but also to limit the exercise of government powers. In Madisonian democracy, which is reflected in the original Constitution, abuse of power is avoided primarily through the distribution and blending of power. The Bill of Rights (the first ten amendments) was added *after* the Constitution was ratified.

The subject matter of constitutional law reflects the following basic principles of American constitutionalism that find expression throughout the course.

(1) LIMITED GOVERNMENT AND POPULAR SOVEREIGNTY
The premise of American constitutionalism is that the national governmental power is derived from the people—government acts with the consent of the governed. The national government properly exercises such powers as "we the people" have delegated to it through the Constitution and subject to the limitations we have imposed. Thus, the political sector has a limited, essentially fiduciary, role to play in fulfilling the purposes for which government was created. This is a government of limited powers.

(2) SEPARATION OF POWERS

Limited government is achieved in part through the separation of powers at the national level. Under the Articles of Confederation, the only national government unit was the Congress. But the Constitution created a separate national executive and judiciary as well as a Congress. The U.S. Constitution, Art. I, vests the legislative power in a bicameral Congress. Art. II vests the executive power in a President, and Art. III vests the judicial power in a Supreme Court and such inferior federal courts as Congress may create (i.e., Art. III federal courts).

(3) DIVISION OF POWERS

Governmental power is divided not only horizontally, but vertically—we are a nation of states. This is the division of powers. Federalism reflects a belief in the value of diversity and the need to prevent accumulation of power even while seeking the benefits of union. Under the Tenth Amendment, powers not delegated to the national government "are reserved to the states respectively, or to the people." The national government is limited to the exercise of powers delegated to it by the Constitution, either expressly or by reasonable implication. But if the national government constitutionally uses its delegated power, the U.S. Constitution, Art. VI (the Supremacy Clause), provides that the federal law, as the "Supreme Law of the Land," shall supersede inconsistent state law (preemption). The student should consider the extent to which the protection of the values of federalism is achieved through the constitutional division of powers or through the system of political representation in the Congress and the workings of our political system.

(4) CHECKS AND BALANCES

The separation of powers and division of powers principles in the American Constitution reflect the principle of checks and balances. Power is divided among institutions but the functions of government are blended. Congress legislates but the President can veto. The President makes treaties, but only with the advice and consent of the Senate. The federal courts can hold congressional or executive acts unconstitutional but the jurisdiction of the federal courts is largely subject to congressional control.

(5) RIGHTS AND LIBERTIES

The principle of limited government is achieved not only by the distribution of governmental powers but also by the protection of rights and liberties. Some rights were recognized in the original Constitution, *e.g.*, Art. I, § 9, limits suspension of the writ of habeas corpus, Art. I, §§ 9 and 10 proscribe bills of attainder or ex post facto laws, neither Congress nor the states may impair the obligation of contract (Art. I, § 10 and Fifth Amendment due process). A Bill of Rights was the price for ratification. Most of the guarantees of the Bill of Rights have been applied to the states through the Due Process Clause of the Fourteenth Amendment. Using the amending process of Art. V, another sixteen amendments have been added. Other rights have been implied from those that are granted and still others have been read into the Constitution. The First and Fourteenth Amendments will be especially important in your study of Constitutional Law.

GUIDE TO ANALYSIS: COMMON ISSUES

While the uncertainties of constitutional law adjudication and decision-making make any "all-purpose" guidelines questionable, there are certain basic issues that a student should consider in analyzing cases in this area.

(1) COURT JURISDICTION AND REVIEWABILITY

Before a constitutional case can be considered on the merits, the Court must decide whether it will review the constitutional issue. If the federal court lacks jurisdiction, it lacks power to determine the issue and the case will be dismissed, regardless of the merits of the constitutional claim. Even if jurisdiction is technically present, the court may, for a variety of functional and prudential reasons, exercise discretion and decline to decide a constitutional claim. These jurisdictional and prudential concerns are sometimes referred to as justiciability. Therefore, the student should first consider whether the court has jurisdiction and whether it might decline to review the constitutional claim. *NOTE:* Even if you decide that the court cannot or will not reach the merits of the case, do *not* end the analysis. You should always consider what would happen if the court does reach the merits. Your judgment on the questions of jurisdiction and reviewability could be wrong—protect yourself.

(2) SOURCES OF POWER
(a) National Law

If the court reaches the merits of the constitutional claim and the question involves the constitutionality of national law, ask yourself—does the government have the *power* to act? Since our government is one of enumerated powers, it must be ascertained whether there is a power, express or implied, delegated to the national government.

(b) State Law

If the court reaches the constitutional merits and the question involves the constitutionality of state or local action, it is *not* necessary (at least in the constitutional law course) to determine whether there is power to act. States and localities have inherent fiscal and police powers to legislate for the health, morals, and well-being of their citizens.

(3) LIMITATIONS ON POWER—NATIONAL AND STATE LAW

Even if the national or state government has the power to act, this does not mean that its actions are constitutional. The student must consider whether the exercise of the power violates some constitutional limitation. Remember, there are two sources of limitation on governmental power: *First,* the separation and division of powers; *second,* rights and liberties guaranteed by the Constitution.

Always consider whether the manner in which the government actor has exercised its power excessively intrudes on the constitutional powers of another government actor, *e.g.,* the President takes action that constitutionally is the province of Congress, a state regulates in such a way as to unduly burden the free movement of interstate commerce.

Consider also whether the way in which the government has acted may unconstitutionally burden some right or liberty, *e.g.,* freedom of speech or religion, rights of association and belief, the right of privacy. Remember constitutional rights and liberties are not limited only to express guaranteed rights. Nor does the fact that a right is burdened mean that the government action is unconstitutional—burdens on rights can be justified.

APPROACH TO CONSTITUTIONAL LAW

Alexis deTocqueville wrote, more than a century ago, that in America every question ultimately becomes a constitutional question. With the expanded role of the Supreme Court, this is particularly true. More and more legal questions have a constitutional dimension. The course in constitutional law, like all courses in law school, is, to some extent, a course in a new vocabulary. Phrases that pepper the case law in the fields of free expression and equal protection will become second nature to you. You will find yourself talking easily about standards of review, about the differences among the rational basis standard of review, the intermediate standard of review, and the strict scrutiny standard of review. These are standards of review that have distinct meanings in constitutional law. In the free expression area, terms like the two level theory of speech, categories of speech, the public forum, the public law of libel, the distinction between political speech and commercial speech and obscenity and indecency, will become terms of art to you. That constitutional law will open up a new vocabulary to you is to be expected. What, perhaps, requires emphasis is that the course in constitutional law is for the law student also a course in humanities and a course in the social sciences. The basic values to which a society is dedicated and about which a society may be in conflict is the bedrock of a course in constitutional law.

DAY–TO–DAY STUDY

Because the course in constitutional law is so fundamental, the student's approach to study in constitutional law must be somewhat different than in other courses. In a course in torts or in contracts, the names of particular cases may not be especially important. Abiding principles may emerge in those fields of law. But the particular names of the plaintiffs and defendants who gave play to those principles usually are not particularly significant. This is not so in constitutional law.

After all, one of the greatest cases in constitutional law, *Marbury v. Madison,* does not involve just an ordinary person. Madison was Secretary of State of the United States and he later became President. To a very large extent, cases in constitutional law involve the way our society should be governed and the way our polity should be structured. Students sometimes ask their instructors in law school, are we responsible for the names of the cases? The classic response to this question by most law instructors is that what they are interested in is that students learn the basic legal method to approach particular problems and that the names of particular cases are irrelevant. But in constitutional law, case names like *Marbury v. Madison* (1803) or *United States v. Nixon* (1974) involve controversies and principles which are part of the liberal learning of any literate and educated lawyer. These cases are documents in American history and government to a degree not encountered in other courses. With respect to these most famous cases, the student should at least have an idea when he hears the name of cases like *Marbury v. Madison* or *United States v. Nixon* of the context in which those cases arose and of the principles for which they stand. In short, case names are more important in constitutional law than in other areas.

THE ROLE OF CASE LAW

If the case law is important in constitutional law, how should one approach those cases? The short answer to this question is—slowly. A case like *Marbury v. Madison* cannot be read quickly. Embedded in the magisterial prose of Chief Justice Marshall, one will find condensed the substance of controversies about the role of the Judiciary vis-a-vis the Executive and the Congress, which still absorb us as a people. A student in constitutional law will often say that it took her an hour or two to read ten pages. In the early period of a course in constitutional law, this should be considered standard rather than remarkable. It should take you an hour or an hour and a half to read the edited version of *Marbury v. Madison* that is found in most contemporary constitutional law casebooks. In the formative constitutional law cases, you are reading about fundamental and enduring controversies. These controversies raise deeper and more profound issues than obtain in the resolution of cases which involve automobile accidents or commercial disputes.

THE SIGNIFICANCE OF THE CONSTITUTIONAL TEXT

We have spoken about the role of case law and of how carefully it should be approached and studied in constitutional law courses. What about the constitutional text itself? There was a great constitutional law teacher at Harvard several generations ago named T. R. Powell. The story goes that Professor Powell used to tell his classes that they need not bother to read the Constitution because they would only find it distracting. This was Professor Powell's mischievous way of telling his students that the overlay of case law in the constitutional law text was what was truly significant and that the constitutional document is continually interpreted by each new generation of Americans through the doctrine of judicial review.

All this is true, but in our opinion, Professor Powell's witticism overstates the matter. You *should* read the constitutional text, particularly in those parts of the course which deal with the relationships between the three branches of government. Reading the text of the Constitution will bring directly to your attention the difficulty and the magnitude of the task people like Chief Justice Marshall faced. Questions such as whether or not the Supreme Court could invalidate acts of Congress or whether the Supreme Court of the United States could review constitutional decisions of state courts are questions upon which there was very little prior law. In a sense, the prior law that had existed had been repudiated. The people who wrote the American Constitution had, to a considerable extent, rejected much of the body of English law when they declared their independence from the Crown. People like John Marshall wrote on a largely blank slate. There were few cases for them to construe. Their opinions were going to become the case law for tomorrow and they knew it. If you tackle the question of whether or not there is a basis for judicial review in the text of the American Constitution as an original proposition, you will be giving yourself the same task that John Marshall and his colleagues faced.

For this reason, many teachers of constitutional law—and we are among them—do not believe that it is wise for students new to the subject of constitutional law to attempt to bury themselves too quickly or too deeply in treatises or hornbooks. We think it is more profitable for the student to do what Marshall did—analyze the facts of a great case like *Marbury v. Madison,* read the constitutional text, try to identify the large principles which the framers had in mind, and then to reach a decision which seems to flow from the interstices of the document. If you take this approach, you will find that your task, at least initially, will take more time. But the conclusions you reach are likely to stay with you longer than if you merely parrot the summary of these great cases which you can easily find in some hornbook or treatise.

OUTSIDE READING

This is not to say that outside reading should be discouraged in a course in constitutional law. It is only to say that the timing of the appropriate moment for outside reading is crucial. One should not go too quickly to what others have thought about problems that you have been asked as students to confront for the first time. After you have spent a significant part of the course struggling with these ideas themselves, it may then be appropriate for you to seek some help on a particularly troubling point with the vast constitutional law literature. For many years there was a dearth of constitutional law treatises particularly for students. This was partially because the Warren Court so rapidly changed our understanding of constitutional law. The law in this area, therefore, was thought to be too much in flux to warrant any easy summary. To a considerable extent, in the past few years this situation has altered. One recent book which can provide you a crisp and accurate summary of basic principles is the treatise, *Constitutional Law* (3d ed., 1986), by Nowak, Rotunda, and Young. Professor Tribe has written a one volume treatise, *American Constitutional Law* (2d ed., 1988), which deals in a very sophisticated and thorough way with some of the more subtle and complex issues in contemporary constitutional law. This is a good book to turn to if you want the variety of possibilities which a particular constitutional problem presents. Particular fields in constitutional law have benefited from considerable scholarship that has been expended on it. The study of judicial review in cases involving constitutional rights, for example, has profited from John Hart Ely's *Democracy and Distrust* (1980) and Michael J. Perry's, *The Constitution, the Courts and Human Rights* (1982). J. Choper, *Judicial Review and the National Political Process* (1980), provides valuable insights on judicial review of the allocation of governmental powers. Capsule summaries, such as some of the Constitutional Law Nutshells, can prove helpful. Illustrative is *Constitutional Law* (2d ed., 1990), by the authors of this outline.

An outline such as this is helpful. But if it is going to be helpful, it should be approached with a clear understanding of what it can do and what it cannot do. What it can do is to put an organizational structure on a body of learning that you are already significantly familiar with. It can identify the highlights in that body of learning, and it can serve as a refresher for what you have, through your own study, both earned and learned. What this outline cannot do—and what no outline can do—is to serve as a substitute for the course itself. If you have not read the great cases in constitutional law, if you have not struggled with the text as Marshall did, for example, the principles and examples summarized here cannot mean as much to you as they will mean for those who have, to put it plainly, done their homework.

APPROACH TO THE EXAMINATION

(1) STUDYING FOR THE EXAMINATION

How does one review for an examination in constitutional law? There are so many cases to read. Your class notes usually are quite extensive. Furthermore, your instructor may have mentioned or discussed a number of books and law review articles which bear on various aspects of the course. One good technique is to look at the table of contents of your casebook. The table of contents of the book will usually give you a detailed skeletal outline of the course. Since it lists the leading cases under the various topics, *e.g.*,

Marbury v. Madison under Judicial Review, *Roe v. Wade* under Substantive Due Process and the Right of Privacy, and *Warth v. Seldin* under Standing, the table of contents will itself serve to refresh your recollection. After you have looked at the Table of Contents, you probably will want to read your notes once through. Then you will want to read this outline because it provides a crisp review of the whole subject and it will put flesh and structure on the course. After having read your notes and the outline, certain aspects of the course may be less clear to you than others. For example, in the equal protection area, the constitutional significance of the distinction between discriminatory purpose and discriminatory effect may be unclear to you. In that case, you may want to reread a leading case in the field, such as *Washington v. Davis* (1976).

In studying for the examination, does it make a difference whether the examination is an open-book exam or a closed-book exam? It probably does not make a great deal of difference in terms of how you study for the examination. It is possible, however, that if you know you are going to take an open-book examination you should spend more time on analyzing concepts than devoting yourself to the brute memorization of facts. Does it make any difference whether the examination is entirely essay or semi-objective? On this point, it probably does make a difference. If the examination is semi-objective, you probably want to focus your study to a higher degree on detail; but principles and their application remain vital even in objective exams.

A problem that is particularly troubling to students in constitutional law vis-a-vis the examination is how can they be sure, in a course so studded with doctrinal principles, that they have captured the critical issues that a particular question may present. A helpful technique is to prepare lists of key words. For example, if you want to remember some of the key ideas in terms of congressional power in the constitutional system, you might want to prepare a list which will have terms or central ideas on them, such as:

(1) achieving social welfare through the federal commerce clause;

(2) the affectation doctrine;

(3) federalizing crime through the affectation doctrine;

(4) when is a tax not a tax?

- penalty doctrine

- doctrine of judicial obtuseness

If you are preparing for First Amendment law, you may want a list which will just identify some issues in that area of the law:

(1) clear and present danger doctrine;

(2) prior restraint;

(3) fighting words;

(4) time, place, and manner controls;

(5) symbolic speech;

(6) corporate speech;

(7) commercial speech;

(8) public law of libel;

(9) indecent speech;

(10) obscene speech.

Such a checklist, or even one oriented toward more particular issues, *e.g.*, restraints on speech content, can be helpful to you. Just seeing a phrase may immediately help your mind connect with some set of facts or some question in the examination. The summary outline and word glossary in this Outline should assist you in preparing such a checklist.

(2) GETTING STARTED

All right, you are now at the examination. You have studied hard and you are ready to take the examination. What do you do first? The first thing you do—we are going to say that again—THE FIRST THING YOU DO is READ THE EXAMINATION. This may seem like an easy thing to do—it isn't. Some of your classmates will be writing away as soon as they get their bluebooks passed to them. You may be tempted, because they are writing, to start writing too. Resist this temptation. Read the question first, read it carefully, and read the question in terms of the answer you are specifically requested to provide. For example, the first question might be a question that seems to involve interstate commerce. Some students will attempt immediately to convey to the instructor everything they know about the commerce clause. They will, therefore, recite the case law from *Gibbons v. Ogden* to *Wickard v. Filburn.* Now such a chronological history of the commerce clause could make an impressive answer if anybody had asked you for it. But usually the constitutional law instructor will be asking you to apply specific principles to specific facts. The question will usually be directed to some such specific matter. If the question is, should the court order an injunction, you should begin with "yes" or "no" and then give your supporting reasons. Obviously, "yes" or "no" is not enough of an answer but at least you are, by answering the question, doing two things: you are flagging your view of the situation to the instructor and you are organizing your answer around a particular conclusion. On the other hand, some instructors will not even ask you to reach a conclusion. They are interested only in your analysis of the issues. In either case, keep your answer relevant to the particular issues raised by the facts.

(3) ANALYSIS

How do you analyze the question itself? You should try to keep five things in mind when you are answering the examination questions. This is your Analysis Check List. (We are assuming as the norm for this check list the typical law school essay examination. The technique will be the same whether the format is short answer or long answer essay although if it is short answer essay, your answers must be particularly concise and terse.):

(1) The first thing you should try to do is to try to identify the issues.

(2) You should identify the principle or principles which apply to the resolution of those issues.

(3) You should try to provide a supporting rationale as to why the particular principle or principles might be applicable to this set of facts.

(4) You should be sure that you apply the principle to the facts in question.

(5) You should include the principle or principles which may compete for application to the resolution of the particular facts presented. This demonstrates that, although you have chosen a particular principle to resolve the facts, you are aware that strong arguments exist for the applicability of a competing principle.

The technique of including in your answer competing principles even though you do not think they are the most appropriate principles is an excellent one. First, you may be wrong in your assessment of what is the best principle available to govern the facts. If you have included the competing principle, the instructor will be aware that you saw this clash of principles. Usually, the instructor will not mind that the principle you selected is not the one he thought the best available if you at least present the one he thought the best available as an alternative. After all, we all have read enough five to four decisions of the Supreme Court to know, as Justice Frankfurter said, that constitutional issues are non-Euclidean problems.

From the checklist that we have set forth above, you can see why it is the sheerest folly to waste precious time setting forth all the case law in a particular area just because the examination question happens to involve that area. There is an easy guide to the successful taking of constitutional law examinations. It is, like all good counsel, magnificent in its simplicity. First, READ THE QUESTION; SECOND, ANSWER THE QUESTION. In other words, answer the question you have been asked, not the question you would like to have been asked. The authors of this outline have been reading answers to constitutional law questions in bluebooks for many years. A phenomenon we have frequently encountered is that students answer the question they expected to be asked or that they would like to have been asked. That this is so is only human nature. We prefer to write about what we know more than what we do not know. The instructor, however, will be more impressed if you take a stab at what he asked than if you provide a great deal of information for which he did not ask.

Here is another technique for successful examination taking. What do you do if a particular question or sub-question draws a complete blank from you? Do you leave it blank? Here is our advice. Unless the instructor tells you that he will deduct for wrong answers, it usually is worth your while to attempt some kind of answer. Even the most liberal instructor cannot give a sympathetic construction to nothing. So try to write something.

(4) TIME CONSTRAINTS

You have to be mindful of the time problem in taking an examination. Many instructors will assign a specific number of minutes to a particular question. This allocation of time by the instructor has to be taken with the greatest seriousness by the student. If the instructor says that a particular question is worth thirty minutes, then it is worth no more than that. Some students decide to put an hour into a thirty minute question. Their idea is that by fully exploiting a question where they happen to be comfortable, they will do so well it will out-balance the question which, by definition, they will not be able to answer as well since they have exceeded the time allocation. This is a fallacious way to proceed. Following the time allocations in an examination is a form of showing your mastery of the course. If the instructor gives you a series of questions and says that you should answer each sub-question in one or two sentences: DO THAT. The instructor is well aware that many times you would be able to answer the same sub-question in a hundred sentences. He knows that. What he is trying to do, however, is to give a comprehensive examination raising a large number of questions to test your overall knowledge of constitutional law. He cannot do that if you insist on saying more than he has asked for. The end result of doing that will be that toward the last third or half of the examination you will be way out of time. The solution for this problem is not to write TIME at the end of the bluebook because this is only a way of telling the instructor you did not follow instructions.

We have taken a great deal of space to emphasize the importance of respecting the time allocation of the instructor. We would like to make a couple of other observations with respect to time allocation. First, if you draw a blank on a question, although you certainly should plan to say something on the question, do not tarry over such a question. Go on to the next one and come back to it. The blank you drew may be only a temporary one. Furthermore, leave a couple of minutes in your time allocation for reading what you have written at the end of the examination. Did you by mistake leave out the answer to part of a question? Did you by mistake forget to turn the examination over and miss two questions on the other side? One way to find this out is to turn the examination paper over. These errors may seem obvious but experienced instructors will tell you that they happen with surprising frequency.

A question students often have is this: If I am going to be taking an open-book examination in constitutional law, is there any particular technique I should bear in mind while taking an examination? Some students develop elaborate colored tab indexes so they can reach a relevant point in their materials instantly. Is this kind of thing worth it? In our opinion, this kind of thing usually is not worth the time. The examination is not usually intended to be a research experience. Most instructors designate their examinations as open-book examinations in order to help their students relax so that they will not freeze if they forget a particular point or case. Usually, time is such a pressing problem during a constitutional law examination that the best thing one can do is to have such a mastery of the subject that you don't need to refer to your books and notes at all. If you do refer to them, you should do so rarely. If you are referring to the materials all the time, this could be a signal to you that you are going to run into a time problem. If you are allowed to use study-aids, such as this Outline, you may find time to at least refer to the Summary Outline. If you can bring only your own material into the exam, prepare an outline, or at least a checklist, to jog your memory.

There is a technique for taking examinations which somehow law students resist which is the most effective guarantee for success that we can think of. This is to look at the past examinations of your instructor from previous years, if possible, and then to take those examinations for practice. You would not think of learning to drive a car by just reading the rules in the operator's manual. You would want to drive a car at some point before you are given your road test. Similarly, if you are going to take a test in constitutional law, does it not make sense that you actually practice by taking constitutional law examinations? We think it does. However, for this technique to work, you have to be honest. If the practice examination that you are taking is a closed-book examination, then you should not look at anything else when you are taking that particular examination. Also, you should follow the specific time allocations. In other words, you should make the simulated practice examination as close to the real thing as possible. At this point you may say, how do I know that what I am saying is right? You don't. But if you don't overdo it, some instructors will be willing to read at least one of your answers to any old question. Similarly, you probably have an idea of who seems to have a gift for constitutional law among your classmates and who does not and you might run your practice answer past such a person. Or, at least, you can check your answer against the course material.

The last thing you should do as part of the examination taking process is to forget the examination after you have written it. Do not engage in post-mortems with your classmates. They will invariably have put something on the examination that you did not. What they put in may have been right, but it also may have been wrong. The best thing to do after you complete the constitutional law examination is to go to a movie—unless you have another exam!

PART ONE

THE ALLOCATION OF GOVERNMENTAL POWER: NATIONAL AND STATE

Analysis

I

JUDICIAL REVIEW

Analysis

A course on American constitutional law deals primarily with the exercise of the power of judicial review. But before a court can review government action on its constitutional merits, the court must have jurisdiction, i.e., power to hear the case. Even when a court has technical jurisdiction to decide a case, there are various policies and principles whereby final decision can be avoided, at least temporarily. This chapter deals with the jurisdiction of the federal courts, including the power of judicial review, and the constitutional, congressional and self-imposed limitations on the exercise of that judicial power.

A. ESTABLISHING JUDICIAL REVIEW

1. "JUDICIAL REVIEW" DEFINED
Judicial review is the doctrine that the courts have the power to invalidate governmental action which is repugnant to the Constitution. "It is emphatically the province and duty of the judicial department to say what the law is." Marbury v. Madison (1803).

2. REVIEW OF FEDERAL ACTION
State and federal courts have the power to review and invalidate the acts of Congress and of the Executive which are contrary to the Constitution. Although the power of judicial review over the Congress has been long established and rarely used, this power has now been explicitly extended to executive action as well.

a. Reviewing Acts of Congress—*Marbury v. Madison*
1) In *Marbury v. Madison* (1803), the Supreme Court held § 13 of the Judiciary Act of 1789 unconstitutional. The Act was read by Justice Marshall, perhaps erroneously, to enlarge the Supreme Court's original jurisdiction beyond the limits defined in Art. III of the Constitution. Since the Constitution prescribes the powers delegated by the people to the national government, a congressional act contrary to the Constitution is invalid. The Constitution is supreme over ordinary federal or state law under the Supremacy Clause of Art. VI.

2) There is no explicit textual authority for judicial review in the Constitution. But Art. III does extend the judicial power to cases arising under the Constitution. Marshall reasons that it is the judicial duty to say what the law is. When the constitutionality of a congressional act is drawn into question, the Court must give effect either to the Act or to the Constitution. Only federal laws "made in pursuance" of the Constitution are the Supreme Law of the Land under Art. VI.

3) The critical issue is whether Marshall is correct that the judicial judgment on constitutionality is controlling. The Court could have held that the judgment of Congress, the popularly elected branch of government, binds the courts on the meaning of the Constitution. Many countries, even some with written Constitutions, do not accept judicial review. The student should consider whether constitutional interpretation is analogous to judicial functions such as statutory interpretation or common law decision-making or is qualitatively different. The student should also consider the capabilities of the branches of government for interpreting the Constitution.

4) While the holding in *Marbury v. Madison* might have been limited to Acts of Congress dealing with federal court jurisdiction or to cases where judicial action is necessary to give effect to congressional legislation, it has come to stand for the proposition "that the federal judiciary is supreme in the exposition of the law of the Constitution, and that principle has ever since been ∗ ∗ ∗ a permanent and indispensable feature of our constitutional system." *Cooper v. Aaron* (1958).

b. Reviewing Executive Action
The doctrine of judicial review also applies to executive action. Courts may call executive officers to answer for their actions and review those actions as to their constitutionality.

1) In *Marbury,* the Court reasoned that where the executive possesses legal or constitutional discretion, judicial review would be precluded. But it is the nature of executive action and not the office of the person that determines the appropriateness of judicial review. A mandamus order, therefore, could issue to an executive officer requiring the performance of ministerial (non-discretionary) duties.

2) While the President takes an oath to uphold the Constitution, his decisions regarding constitutionality are not decisive. The federal judiciary is supreme in the interpretation of the Constitution.

Example: The federal courts have the power to review claims of the Executive to withhold tape recordings and documents relating to conversations among staff subpoenaed by the Special Prosecutor for use in a pending criminal prosecution. "Notwithstanding the deference each branch must accord the others, the 'judicial power of the United States' vested in the federal courts by Art. III, § 1 of the Constitution can no more be shared with the Executive Branch than the Chief Executive, for example, can share with the Judiciary the veto power." *United States v. Nixon* (1974).

3. REVIEW OF STATE ACTION
The Supremacy Clause of Art. VI establishes that the Constitution of the United States binds state officials, "anything in the Constitution or laws of any state to the contrary notwithstanding." Thus, the federal courts can review the constitutionality of state statutes and the actions of state officials.

When the state courts decide federal constitutional questions, the Supreme Court has appellate jurisdiction under Art. III, § 2, over such decisions. A principal policy justification for extending Supreme Court appellate jurisdiction to the federal constitutional decisions of state courts is the need for uniformity in federal constitutional interpretation.

Examples: (1) Section 25 of the Judiciary Act of 1789 conferring appellate jurisdiction on the Supreme Court over the decisions of a state court is constitutional for the reasons stated above. *Martin v. Hunter's Lessee* (1816).

(2) The governor and legislature of a state act unconstitutionally in attempting to interpose state sovereignty as a justification for refusing to obey the Supreme Court's decision declaring state mandated school segregation unconstitutional. *Cooper v. Aaron* (1958).

B. SOURCE OF JUDICIAL POWER: ARTICLE III JURISDICTION

The "judicial power," consisting of defined "cases and controversies," including cases involving constitutional questions, is vested by the U.S. Constitution, Art. III, in the Supreme Court and such inferior courts as Congress may establish. The U.S. Supreme Court, the U.S. Courts of Appeal, and the U.S. District Courts are created pursuant to this authority. The judicial power has been interpreted to include the power to review and invalidate as unconstitutional both federal and state action.

1. FEDERAL "JUDICIAL POWER" DEFINED
Art. III, § 2, defines the subject matter jurisdiction of the Art. III federal courts. Unless a case falls within one of the "cases and controversies" identified in Art. III, § 2, an Art. III federal court must dismiss the case for want of jurisdiction. While Art. III is the source of federal judicial power, its implementation is largely dependent on congressional legislation.

a.   Art. III and Art. I Courts
1) The Supreme Court of the United States is the only federal court specifically required by the Constitution. Whether other federal

courts were needed was left to Congress to determine. In the Judiciary Act of 1789, Congress created federal trial courts (district courts) and intermediate courts of appeal. Independence of Art. III judges is assured by protecting "their offices during good behavior" and prohibiting their salaries from being "diminished."

2) Art. III federal courts must be distinguished from "legislative" or Art. I courts created by Congress pursuant to its various powers under Art. I, *e.g.,* the military justice system, courts of the District of Columbia. Art. I legislative courts are not limited to the jurisdiction specified in Art. III and the judges do not enjoy the tenure and salary protections provided by Art. III.

b. Subject Matter Jurisdiction

Art. III federal courts are courts of limited jurisdiction. They may hear and decide only those "cases and controversies" identified in Art. III, § 2. The more important categories of Art. III jurisdiction for you to remember are cases arising under the Constitution, laws and treaties of the United States, *i.e.,* federal question jurisdiction and cases involving citizens of different states (diversity jurisdiction). If litigation does not fall under the designated categories, an Art. III federal court lacks subject matter jurisdiction and must dismiss the case.

c. Congressional Control

While the source of the federal judicial power is Art. III, the extent to which it is exercised is generally determined by Congress. This is especially true for the inferior federal courts whose very existence was left to the pleasure of Congress. But Congress cannot authorize the Art. III federal courts to take jurisdiction or perform functions beyond the limits of Art. III. *Marbury v. Madison* (1803).

2. SUPREME COURT JURISDICTION

The "judicial power" vested by Art. III in the Supreme Court may be exercised in two ways: original or appellate jurisdiction.

a. Original Jurisdiction

Congress has passed legislation implementing the grant in Art. III to the Supreme Court of original jurisdiction in all cases affecting ambassadors, other public ministers and consuls, and those in which a state shall be a party. By assigning original jurisdiction, it is meant that such cases may commence in the Supreme Court. Congress cannot grant original jurisdiction to the Court beyond those cases specified in Art. III.

b. Appellate Jurisdiction—Congressional Power to Confer and Withdraw

Art. III, § 2, provides that in all other cases to which the federal judicial power extends, the Supreme Court shall have appellate jurisdiction. But this power is given "with such Exceptions, and under such Regulations as the Congress shall make." Congress must authorize the Court's appellate jurisdiction, and Congress may withdraw subjects from the Court's appellate jurisdiction. Congressional failure to authorize jurisdiction is considered an implied exception. How extensive such withdrawal can be is a matter of dispute.

1) Essential Functions: Internal Restraints

While Art. III, § 2, may be a grant of power to Congress to withdraw subjects from the Supreme Court's appellate jurisdiction, congressional powers are subject to constitutional limitations. It has been argued by commentators that a statute preventing the Court from performing its essential role of preserving the uniformity and supremacy of federal law would violate the principle of separation of powers.

2) Rights and Liberties: External Restraints

Congressional statutes withdrawing Supreme Court review might also invade rights and liberties guaranteed in the Constitution, *e.g.*, Fifth Amendment due process. Even withdrawal of a particular remedy might, in some cases, prevent judicial protection of a constitutional right, *e.g.*, busing to implement a school desegregation order, and thus could be argued to violate that right.

> ***Example:*** A congressional statute withdrawing Supreme Court appellate jurisdiction to issue writs of habeas corpus was held constitutional, even though the case was already pending. But note that other methods for Supreme Court review still were available. The congressional statute did not foreclose all Supreme Court review of the constitutional issue but only precluded one particular remedy. Nevertheless, the Court did use sweeping language in describing congressional power over Art. III appellate jurisdiction. *Ex parte McCardle* (1869).

c. **Discretionary Review**

1) Certiorari

With a few minor exceptions, Supreme Court review of lower court decisions is discretionary. The losing party below petitions the Court for a writ of certiorari. Certiorari is usually granted when four Justices vote to review the decision (the Rule of Four). A denial of certiorari is not a decision on the merits.

2) Basis for Review

a) Supreme Court Rules indicate that certiorari will be granted only for special and important reasons and suggest the character of the considerations that govern the decision whether or not to grant certiorari. But these rules are not meant to be exhaustive.

b) Court Conflict—Certiorari is often granted when federal courts of appeal are in conflict or there is a conflict between the highest courts of different states or between a state high court and a federal court of appeals.

c) Novel Federal Questions—The exercise of certiorari often reflects the novelty of the federal question presented or the fact that an important federal question may have been incorrectly decided.

C. CONSTITUTIONAL AND POLICY LIMITATIONS ON JUDICIAL REVIEW

Even if a case appears to be within the technical jurisdiction of a federal court under Art. III, there is no assurance that the Art. III court will reach a decision on the merits. There are a number of doctrines, based either on the Constitution or on the policy of judicial self-restraint, whereby the federal courts may avoid a decision on the merits. Together these textually-required doctrines and judicially fashioned policies reflect a concern with justiciability—*the proper use of the judicial review power.* For example, the Court asks whether constitutional rights and duties can be judicially defined and appropriate relief fashioned. The student should try to develop an appreciation of the difference between doctrines which are constitutionally mandated and those which are not.

1. CONSTITUTIONAL LIMITATIONS
a. Eleventh Amendment
The Eleventh Amendment provides that the judicial power granted in Art. III does not extend to suits against a state by citizens of another state or of a foreign country. Through judicial interpretation, the Eleventh Amendment has been extended to provide a bar to suits against the state by its own citizens. Hans v. Louisiana (1890). The Eleventh Amendment does not prevent the Supreme Court from reviewing cases arising in state courts which involve questions of federal law, even though the suit could not have been heard originally in federal court. The preservation of uniformity of federal law requires Supreme Court review of such decisions under the Constitution. *McKesson Corp. v. Division of Alcoholic Bev. and Tobacco, Fla. (1990).*

1) State Immunity
The Eleventh Amendment grant of sovereign immunity is limited to the states and their agencies. It does not bar suits against cities, counties, local school boards or other local agencies. *Lake County Estates, Inc. v. Tahoe Regional Planning Agency* (1979).

2) Waiver

A state may intentionally waive its Eleventh Amendment immunity if it does so expressly by statute or waiver is otherwise clearly implied. But state waiver cannot be inferred simply from participation in a program funded by the federal government. *Atascadero State Hospital v. Scanlon* (1985). "The Court will give effect to a State's waiver of Eleventh Amendment immunity 'only where stated by the most express language or by such overwhelming implication from the text as [will] leave no room for any other reasonable construction.'" *Port Authority Trans-Hudson Corp. v. Feeny* (1990).

3) Congressional Limitations

The Eleventh Amendment bar to suits against the state is limited by the power of Congress to authorize such remedies. *Fitzpatrick v. Bitzer* (1976) (Fourteenth Amendment, § 5); *Pennsylvania v. Union Gas Co.* (1989) (Commerce Clause). But such an intent must be made "unmistakably clear in the language of the statute." *Atascadero.*

4) Unconstitutional Official Acts

A suit against a state officer acting unconstitutionally is not a suit against the state and the Eleventh Amendment is therefore not a bar. Ex parte Young (1908). For example: The Eleventh Amendment did not bar a suit against named state officials for allegedly unconstitutional acts which resulted in the death of students at Kent State. *Scheuer v. Rhodes* (1974). The fact that the state is required to expend monies in order to comply with a court decree does not infringe the Eleventh Amendment prohibition. *Milliken v. Bradley* (1977). But the Eleventh Amendment does bar a suit against state officials where the official action violates only state law—federal court review is not then necessary to assure supremacy of federal law. *Pennhurst State School & Hospital v. Halderman* (1984).

> *Exception:* Where a suit directed against a public official results in a *retroactive* charge on the general revenues of the state and cannot be distinguished from an award of damages against the state, the Eleventh Amendment bars the award. *Edelman v. Jordan* (1974) [award of retroactive welfare benefits held to violate Eleventh Amendment]. But the award of attorney's fees or other forms of ancillary relief requiring expenditure of state money does not violate the Eleventh Amendment even if paid by the state. *Hutto v. Finney* (1978).

b. **Case and Controversy**

The federal judicial power granted in Art. III is limited to certain defined "cases and controversies." This requires that a case be in an adversary form and context that is capable of judicial resolution and that its resolution would not violate separation of powers principles. If this requirement is not met, the federal courts lack jurisdiction, and therefore, power to act.

1) No Advisory Opinions
   The federal courts may not furnish opinions on constitutional matters in a "friendly" nonadversary proceeding even at the request of a coordinate branch of government.

   Example: The Supreme Court held that Congress could not authorize a certain class of Indians to bring suit against the United States to test the constitutionality of federal legislation limiting the property rights granted by earlier federal legislation to the same Indians. The Supreme Court held that what Congress sought was an impermissible advisory opinion because the interest of the defendant United States was not adverse to the Indians. Therefore, there was no case and controversy. *Muskrat v. United States* (1911).

2. POLICY LIMITATIONS (JUDICIAL SELF–RESTRAINT)

a. Rules for Constitutional Review

Constitutional issues affecting legislation will not be determined: (1) in advance of the necessity of deciding them; or (2) if there are alternative grounds of disposition; or (3) if a construction of a statute is fairly possible by which the constitutional question may be avoided; or (4) in broader terms than are required by the precise facts to which the ruling is to be applied. *Ashwander v. TVA* (1936).

b. Presumption of Constitutionality

Some of the policies recited above are exemplified in the long-standing canon of constitutional construction, sometimes honored more in the breach than in the observance, that legislation challenged on constitutional grounds should be accorded a presumption of constitutionality by the reviewing court.

c. Judicial Restraint

The federal courts, where possible, have conventionally avoided judicial review, given: (1) the delicacy of the function; (2) the potential consequences; (3) the finality of the court's judgment; (4) the principle of separation of powers; and (5) the inherent limitations of the judicial process. The Courts follow a policy of "strict necessity" in using the judicial review power.

d. Congressional Role
While Congress cannot directly remove an Art. III jurisdictional obstacle to judicial review, the above prudential limitations can be overcome by congressional legislation.

D. SPECIFIC DOCTRINES LIMITING JUDICIAL REVIEW

There are a number of specific doctrines, based on the case and controversy requirement and policy considerations, through which the federal courts avoid a decision on the merits. They relate to WHO may litigate a constitutional question, WHEN a constitutional issue may be litigated, and WHAT constitutional questions may be litigated.

1. THE STANDING LIMITATION—WHO CAN LITIGATE?
    a. Constitutional Standing
        1) General Standards
        Art. III case and controversy requires that the party seeking to litigate a constitutional question, originally or on appeal, demonstrate "such a personal stake in the outcome of a controversy as to assure that concrete adverseness which sharpens the presentation of issues upon which the Court so largely depends for illumination of difficult constitutional questions." Baker v. Carr (1962). A litigant has such a "personal stake" if he alleges (1) an injury in fact (2) caused by the government action being challenged. The focus is on the party who is litigating, not on the issue being litigated.

        a) "Injury in Fact"
        Standing does not usually turn on the legal claim but on the existence of factual injury. *The focus is on injury in fact, not legal injury.* It may be economic, aesthetic, environmental injury, or even an intangible injury such as the ability to live in an integrated community. Congress can, by statute, create an interest, the denial of which satisfies the injury in fact requirement. *Warth v. Seldin* (1975).

        Examples: (1) A physician has standing to maintain a civil action challenging the constitutionality of a state criminal abortion statute since he suffers economic injury. He is prevented from performing abortions by the statute. *Singleton v. Wulff* (1976).

                (2) A village has standing to sue real estate brokers alleged to have engaged in "steering" prospective home buyers to different areas according to their race in violation of federal civil rights laws. The

consequences of changing the village from an integrated to a segregated neighborhood are sufficiently concrete to give the village standing. Residents of the 12–13 block neighborhood to which blacks were alleged to have been steered also have standing, because the transformation of their neighborhood from integrated to segregated, denied them the social and professional benefits of living in an integrated community. *Gladstone Realtors v. Village of Bellwood* (1979).

(3) An individual school board member lacks standing to appeal from a judgment against the school district and school board members in their official capacities where the school board has chosen not to appeal. *Bender v. Williamsport Area School District* (1986).

(4) A physician who intervened in the lower court on behalf of the state does not have standing to appeal from a judgment that the state abortion statute is unconstitutional where the state had chosen not to appeal. The physician has no personal judicially cognizable interest in a criminal statute's defense or in the enforcement of the law. *Diamond v. Charles* (1986).

(5) An exhibitor of certain foreign films (a state senator), who is required to label the films as "political propaganda" has standing to challenge the federal law requiring the labeling. The exhibitor suffers more than a "subjective chill" since he could not exhibit the labeled films without incurring a risk of injury to his reputation and an impairment of his political career. A judgment declaring the Act unconstitutional would redress this reputational injury. *Meese v. Keene* (1987).

(6) Members of an association of landlords have Art. III standing to challenge a city's rent control ordinance, which allowed consideration of "hardship to a tenant" in determining whether to approve a proposed rent increase. The requirement of actual injury was satisfied by the probability that enforcement would result in the reduction of rent below that which would be obtained by a landlord in

the absence of the ordinance. *Pennell v. City of San Jose* (1988).

(7) Bookseller associations and general-purpose bookstores have standing to challenge a state law prohibiting the display of certain sexually explicit material in areas where they may be examined by juveniles. Plaintiffs would suffer a clear injury from the law because of the costly compliance measures required to avoid criminal prosecution. *Virginia v. American Booksellers Ass'n* (1988).

(8) A white defendant has standing to raise a Sixth Amendment challenge to the exclusion of blacks from his jury. Every defendant can object to a venire that does not represent a fair cross section of a community whether or not the systematically excluded group is a group to which he himself belongs. *Holland v. Illinois* (1990).

b) Causation
Plaintiffs must demonstrate that the injury is "fairly traceable" to the government action being challenged. Plaintiffs must demonstrate further that the injury is "redressible" if the court grants the requested judicial relief. This establishes that the injury was, in fact, caused by the wrong complained of. Recent judicial application of the causation requirement has stressed separation of powers concerns, *i.e.,* the danger of judicial interference with administrative policy choices. *Allen v. Wright* (1984).

Examples: (1) Black and low income litigants lack standing to challenge racially exclusionary zoning in the absence of any showing that a developer who would build housing suitable to their needs is prevented from doing so because of the zoning ordinance. Nor was there a developer who could identify a specific project then being impeded by the restrictive zoning. *Warth v. Seldin* (1975).

But a black litigant who seeks housing near his employment and shows that the zoning ordinance is barring a developer from building low income housing suitable to his needs, has standing. The developer, who had expended funds and had a desire to build the low income housing, also has Art. III standing. *Village of Arlington Heights v. Metropolitan Housing Development* (1977).

(2) Indigents and organizations composed of indigents lack standing to challenge a federal revenue ruling allowing favorable tax treatment to non-profit hospitals even though those hospitals provide only limited services to indigents. While the plaintiff may suffer from denial of services by the hospital, this is insufficient injury to maintain the present action since the hospital is not the defendant. It is pure speculation that the hospital's denial of services to indigents is in any way encouraged by the government's grant of tax exempt status. *Simon v. Eastern Kentucky Welfare Rights Organization* (1976).

(3) A resident of a community in which a nuclear power plant is to be built has standing to challenge the Price-Anderson Act, limiting potential tort liability from nuclear accidents. He is threatened with environmental injury if the plants are built. The lower court's determination that there is a "substantial likelihood" that the plants would not be built "but for" the federal law is not clearly erroneous. *Duke Power Co. v. Carolina Environmental Study Group* (1978).

(4) An allegation that the IRS failed in its legal duty to deny tax-exempt status to racially discriminatory private schools is a sufficient claim of injury to minority public school children in a suit by parents where such failure diminishes the ability of their children to be educated in a racially integrated school. (A claim of stigmatic injury to racial minorities was held to be too general to confer standing.) However, the plaintiffs failed to prove that the alleged injury is fairly traceable to the IRS action. It is uncertain how many racially discriminatory schools received tax exemptions. And, it is speculative whether withdrawal of tax exemption from any particular school would lead that school to change its policies. Separation of powers principles bar suits simply designed to challenge the policies government agencies adopt to carry out their legal obligations. *Allen v. Wright* (1984).

2) Taxpayer and Citizen Standing
    a) Federal Taxpayers
        (1) In general, the interest of a federal taxpayer in the expenditures of federal monies is too fluctuating, remote, and imprecise to provide a basis for invoking federal jurisdiction to challenge such an expenditure. A showing that a federal enactment violates the federal taxing and spending powers delegated to Congress by Art. I, § 8 is insufficient in itself to furnish a basis for taxpayer standing in a federal court. *Frothingham v. Mellon* (1923) (federal taxpayer lacks standing to challenge federal law providing grants to states as violative of Tenth Amendment).

        (2) *Exception*—Federal taxpayer status may be a basis for Art. III standing if the taxpayer can satisfy a two part test: (1) the taxpayer must be challenging an exercise of Congress' Art. I, § 8 taxing and spending power; and, (2) the enactment must be alleged to offend a specific constitutional limitation on the taxing and spending power. *Flast v. Cohen* (1968). In *Flast,* the taxpayer challenged a federal spending law as violative of the Establishment Clause of the First Amendment which limits government spending in support of religion. While *Flast* has not been overruled, it has been confined to its facts. It is unlikely today, in light of the citizen standing cases cited below, that some other constitutional claim will satisfy the *Flast* test.

    b) Citizen Standing
        At least in the absence of congressional legislation authorizing the suit, a citizen lacks a sufficient personal interest to challenge government acts as unconstitutional. Her interest is viewed as a "generalized grievance" held in common with citizens generally. While individual justices have argued that the bar to citizen standing is a prudential rule of judicial self restraint, the Court has generally treated it as an Art. III impediment.

        Examples: (1) A citizen lacks standing to challenge the constitutionality of a federal statute authorizing the director of the CIA to certify expenditures as a violation of the constitutional requirement of a regular accounting of the use of public funds. *United States v. Richardson* (1974).

        (2) A citizen has only a generalized interest, insufficient to maintain standing, in challenging the holding of reservist status by a congressman in

violation of the Incompatibility Clause which prohibits members of Congress from holding other office. *Schlesinger v. Reservists Comm. to Stop the War* (1974).

(3) A citizen and taxpayer lacks standing to challenge an HEW grant of surplus land under a federal statute to a religious institution as a violation of the Establishment Clause. Since the challenge was to an HEW action rather than a federal statute and since the government grant was based on the property power rather than the Taxing and Spending Clause, the challengers did not have standing under *Flast* as taxpayers. Nor does a citizen qua citizen have standing to challenge government action merely to correct constitutional wrongs. An Establishment Clause claim does not eliminate the Art. III requirement of personal injury. *Valley Forge Christian College v. Americans United For Separation of Church and State* (1982).

c)   State Taxpayers
A state taxpayer does have standing if she demonstrates a direct and substantial expenditure of state funds, i.e., a good faith pocketbook injury. *Doremus v. Board of Educ.* (1952). A party who will suffer "direct, specific and concrete injury" as a result of an adverse state court judgment involving federal law has standing to seek review in a federal court. *Asarco Inc. v. Kadish* (1989).

b.   **Prudential Standing**
1)   Third Party Standing—Raising the Rights of Others. *A litigant usually lacks standing to raise the rights of third parties not before the court.*

Example: Litigants lack standing as city taxpayers to raise the rights of low income persons excluded by suburban restrictive zoning practices even though their city taxes are increased by the need to provide increased low income housing. There was no showing that either the rights of third persons would be adversely affected by denying standing or that there existed a special relationship between the litigants and those they sought to represent. *Warth v. Seldin* (1975).

2)   *The third party standing doctrine is a rule of judicial self-restraint, not an Art. III requirement. Therefore, it can be outweighed by competing*

considerations in a particular case. Further, Congress can grant a cause of action to persons who would otherwise be barred by prudential standing rules so long as Art. III requirements are satisfied.

Examples: (1) Physicians may raise the rights of their patients to an abortion given: (a) the intimacy of the relationship of the physician to the patient; and (b) the relative inability of the patient to assert her own rights since she may be chilled from litigating by the desire to avoid publicity and by the imminent technical mootness. *Singleton v. Wulff* (1976).

(2) If a litigant has a substantial interest which depends on establishing the rights of the third person, the Third Party rule will not be applied. Thus, a beer vendor has standing to challenge a state law barring sales to males under 18 but not minor females as a violation of equal protection, [*Craig v. Boren* (1976)] and a physician defending against a criminal charge for providing contraceptives has standing to raise the privacy rights of his patients. *Griswold v. Connecticut* (1965).

(3) Provisions of the Federal Black Lung Benefits Act limit, and require prior judicial approval of, attorneys fees paid by claimants. An attorney, disciplined for violating the provisions, sought to argue that these provisions limited a claimant's access to legal representation in violation of the due process guarantee. The attorney has third party standing to litigate the claim. When enforcement of a restriction against a litigant prevents a third party from entering into a relationship, to which relationship the third party has a legal entitlement, third party standing exists. On the merits, the attorney failed to prove that the Act caused any lack of legal representation to claimants. *United States Dep't of Labor v. Triplett* (1990).

3) An association has standing to assert the claims of its members even if it has suffered no personal injury from the challenged activity. It must satisfy the following three requirements: (1) the members would otherwise have standing to sue in their own right; (2) the interest the association seeks to protect is germane to its organizational purpose; (3) neither the claim asserted nor the requested remedy would require participation by the individual members in the lawsuit. *Hunt v. Washington State Apple Adv. Comm'n.* (1977).

Example: A Union has standing to challenge the Secretary of Labor's interpretation of a law providing benefits to workers laid off because of competition from imports. Some Union members would suffer personal injury since the interpretation would limit their ability to qualify for benefits. Since Unions represent their members' economic interests, the subject is germane. Individual participation in the lawsuit is not required since eligibility of individual claimants will be subsequently determined by appropriate agencies. *Int'l Union v. Brock* (1986).

2. THE TIMING LIMITATION—*WHEN* CAN CONSTITUTIONAL LITIGATION BE BROUGHT?

a. Mootness

When a federal court's determination of a legal issue submitted by the parties is no longer necessary to compel the result originally sought because of changes after the suit was brought, the case is said to be moot and federal courts are without power to decide such an issue. The constitutional underpinning of the doctrine derives from the Art. III requirement that there be a case or controversy.

Examples: (1) An action brought by a rejected nonminority applicant to a state university law school who asserts that the equal protection clause of the Fourteenth Amendment is violated because minority applicants with lesser credentials are admitted is rendered moot when he is registered for his last year of study at the school and will complete his studies regardless of the Court's decision. *DeFunis v. Odegaard* (1974).

(2) An action brought by members of Congress, challenging the President's "pocket veto" of a bill limiting further grants of military aid to El Salvador, was rendered moot since the bill expired by its own terms before the matter was reviewed by the Court. *Burke v. Barnes* (1987).

Exceptions: (1) Voluntary Cessation. The voluntary cessation of allegedly illegal conduct will not render a case moot where there is a reasonable expectation that the wrong will be repeated.

(2) Collateral Consequences. A case will not be rendered moot if there remain unsettled important collateral consequences which may still have an adverse impact on the litigant, *e.g.,* a challenge to a criminal conviction following completion of the prison sentence.

(3) Repetitious Issues. *A constitutional issue will not be rendered moot when it is "capable of repetition, yet evading review."* If the suit is maintained as a class action, mootness is avoided if it is "capable of repetition, yet evading review" for any members of the class. There must be a "reasonable likelihood that the wrong complained of will reoccur.

Examples: (1) The fact that a woman who was pregnant when the case was instituted is no longer pregnant will not prevent her and members of her class from challenging the constitutionality of state abortion laws before the Supreme Court. Pregnancy will almost always end prior to appeal but is capable of repetition. *Roe v. Wade* (1973).

(2) A suit by an emotionally disturbed student under the Education of the Handicapped Act seeking injunctive relief against school officials who suspended him for violent and disruptive behavior related to his handicap was not moot although he was no longer enrolled in school. Absent evidence that the student has overcome his disabilities, there is a "reasonable expectation" that he would again be deprived of his rights because of classroom misconduct. A similar suit by a student who was no longer entitled to the benefits of the statute because of his age was held to be moot. *Honig v. Doe* (1988).

(3) The federal Bank Holding Company Act authorizes states to prevent out-of-state holding companies from owning in-state "banks," a term specifically defined in the federal Act. A Commerce Clause challenge to a Florida statute prohibiting out-of-state holding companies from operating certain kinds of banks in Florida was rendered moot when Congress amended the federal Act expanding the definition of "banks" in a way which authorized and approved the Florida statute, thereby assuring the constitutionality of the state law under the Commerce Clause. The alleged injury to the claimant was not "capable of repetition, yet evading review" because the state statute was constitutional with regard to the type of bank involved in the controversy, and also because the state's future refusal to issue a bank charter would be effectively reviewable at that time. *Lewis v. Continental Bank Corp.* (1990).

b. Ripeness Prematurity and Abstractness

A prerequisite to the adjudication of constitutional issues is the presentation for decision of concrete legal issues, presented in actual cases, not abstractions. For a case to be ripe, there must be present injury, or an imminent threat of injury. Further, a federal court will not decide a case where the controversy is at too premature a stage to permit proper judicial resolution.

1) Ripeness is generally considered to be a mandate of the Art. III case and controversy requirement. However, it blends almost imperceptibly into a prudential rule of judicial self-restraint based on the timing of the constitutional litigation.

2) Even when jurisdiction is technically present, a federal court will sometimes dismiss the issue as premature and abstract. This reflects the concern that a case be "justiciable"—the proper use of the power of judicial review.

3) In determining whether a constitutional case has sufficiently matured to permit judicial resolution, consider whether there are any significant events yet to occur which will sharpen the dispute, whether the issues are sharply defined or remain speculative and uncertain and whether there is a realistic expectation that a threatened government action (*e.g.*, enforcement of a statute) will occur.

> *Examples:* (1) Government employees who plan to engage in activities that might infringe the Hatch Act prohibition against political activities fail to present an Art. III case and controversy. It is uncertain what political actions they would engage in and how the Civil Service Commission would react. *United Public Workers v. Mitchell* (1947).
>
> (2) A ban on the use of contraceptives which is not being enforced is not justiciable. *Poe v. Ullman* (1961).

c. Discretionary Abstention

1) Vagueness

If a state statute is capable of a narrow saving construction, federal courts should abstain from decision even though important constitutional questions may be involved. This policy is based on the desire to avoid needless friction with state courts (comity) and unnecessary resolution of constitutional decisions. If the statute is unambiguous and not capable of a savings construction, abstention is inappropriate.

Example: Abstention is inappropriate in a case involving a First Amendment challenge to an ordinance making it unlawful to intentionally interrupt a police officer in the performance of his duties. The case involved a facial challenge to a law that was not ambiguous and was not fairly subject to a construction that would overcome the overbreadth claim. There was no core of constitutionally unprotected expression to which the law might be limited. *Houston v. Hill* (1987).

2) Pending State Proceedings
    Absent a showing of bad faith harassment, a federal court should abstain in a suit seeking declaratory and/or injunctive relief if a state criminal prosecution is pending even though the statute is alleged to be a vague and overbroad invasion of First Amendment rights. Younger v. Harris *(1971).*

    (a) The principle of *Younger v. Harris* has been extended to civil proceedings analogous to state criminal proceedings, *e.g.,* enjoining operation of a state public nuisance statute used to close a porno movie house. *Huffman v. Pursue, Ltd.* (1975).

    (b) No Pending Proceeding. Where there is no pending state court proceeding, a federal court need not abstain from granting either declaratory or injunctive relief where a statute is alleged to be a vague and overbroad invasion of First Amendment rights even though there is no showing of bad faith harassment. *Steffel v. Thompson* (1974) (declaratory relief); *Wooley v. Maynard* (1977) (injunctive relief).

3.   THE SUBJECT MATTER LIMITATION—WHAT CAN BE LITIGATED?
a.   The Political Question Doctrine
Political questions, which does not mean cases dealing with political subjects, are non-justiciable. In defining what questions are political, the Court in Baker v. Carr *(1962) provided criteria, reflecting classic, functional, and prudential considerations. The Court has generally limited the doctrine to cases involving the federal court's role vis-a-vis co-equal branches rather than cases involving state power but it has been suggested as applicable to constitutional cases generally.*

1) Classic Doctrine
    If the issue has been committed by the Constitution to the discretion of another government decisionmaker, federal courts will treat it as a political question. But whether the issue is constitutionally committed to a particular branch is itself a judicial question. Only the manner in which discretion is exercised is inappropriate for federal review.

2) Functional Considerations

A question may be labeled "political" because the Court determines that the judicial branch lacks the resources and capabilities for resolving it. For example, "a lack of judicially discoverable and manageable standards for resolving [the question]" or "the impossibility of deciding without an initial policy determination of a kind clearly for nonjudicial discretion", *e.g.,* foreign affairs issues, may render the question political.

3) Prudential Considerations

Constitutional issues may also be labeled political because of prudential or policy considerations relating to the proper use of the judicial power. For example, *Baker v. Carr* (1962), noted as relevant: "the impossibility of a court's undertaking independent resolution without expressing lack of the respect due coordinate branches of government" or "an unusual need for unquestioning adherence to a political decision already made" or "the potentiality of embarrassment from multifarious pronouncements by various departments on one question."

Examples: (1) The question whether state legislative apportionment satisfies equal protection is not a political question since it does not involve separation of powers concerns and equal protection standards for decisions are available. *Baker v. Carr* (1962). Similarly, the issue of partisan or political gerrymandering is justiciable. Judicially discernible and manageable standards for decision could be formulated as they were in the reapportionment context. *Davis v. Bandemer* (1986).

(2) The question of whether the House of Representatives' refusal to seat Adam Clayton Powell was constitutional was held justiciable. The Supreme Court determined that Art. I, § 5, making each House "the Judge of the * * * Qualifications of its own members," is limited to the qualifications specified in the Constitution, i.e., age, citizenship, and state residence. *Powell v. McCormack* (1969).

(3) Questions concerning the duration for state ratification of a constitutional amendment and whether a state can withdraw a prior ratification appear to be left to Congress by Art. V. These questions are non-justiciable. *Coleman v. Miller* (1939).

(4) The ability of a grand jury to subpoena documents in the possession of the President against a claim of

executive privilege for confidential communications does not present a political question at least apart from a claim based on national security and/or foreign affairs. *United States v. Nixon* (1974).

(5) A plurality of the Court would treat the question of a President's power to unilaterally terminate a treaty as a political question since no constitutional provision directly controls the issues, the political branches have adequate resources to decide the issue, and the issue involves foreign affairs. *Goldwater v. Carter* (1979).

(6) The question of whether a bill which originated in the Senate is valid under the Origination Clause is not a non-justiciable political question. If the Court refused to hear such cases out of respect for Congress, which had considered the constitutional issue, every challenge to a federal statute would be non-justiciable. The Court has a duty independently to review the constitutional question. *United States v. Munoz–Flores* (1990).

b.   Adequate and Independent State Grounds

Where a decision of a state court includes a "plain statement" that it rests on adequate and independent state grounds, the Supreme Court will not take jurisdiction even though the state court may also have erroneously decided a federal constitutional question. A litigant's failure to adhere to fair and reasonable state procedural rules can also result in Supreme Court dismissal of an appeal from a state court. Such failure would provide an adequate and independent state ground for the decision. But the state procedural rule must advance substantial state interests and must not unnecessarily impair decision of the federal constitutional question.

Example: The Court invoked the principle of "comity," or proper respect for state functions, to bar a suit in federal court which raised a constitutional challenge against a state civil judgment. Since the movant had not sought the requested relief in the state court, the Court assumed that state procedures could have afforded an adequate remedy. The moving party did not sustain its burden of forwarding unambiguous authority to the contrary. Although the question presented in federal court had never been addressed by the relevant state courts, there was no evidence that the state courts lacked the authority or inclination to address it. *Pennzoil Co. v. Texaco, Inc.* (1987).

E. REVIEW QUESTIONS

1. T or F   There is explicit textual authority for the doctrine of judicial review.

2. T or F   The doctrine of judicial review only applies to legislation as the facts of *Marbury v. Madison* (1803) illustrate.

3. T or F   State courts have the power to invalidate acts of Congress or Presidential acts on the grounds of their inconsistency with the federal Constitution.

4. T or F   The Supreme Court of the United States does not have appellate jurisdiction over cases coming from the state courts because the only reference in Art. III to Supreme Court appellate jurisdiction is directed to such inferior federal courts as Congress may create.

5. T or F   When a federal constitutional issue is presented along with nonconstitutional issues, the federal constitutional issue should be decided in order to remove uncertainty.

6. T or F   As a textual matter, the Congress can abolish federal courts, other than the Supreme Court.

7. T or F   The Eleventh Amendment does not bar federal courts from enforcing federal constitutional obligations against state officials.

8. T or F   In order to have standing to litigate a federal constitutional question in an Art. III federal court, the litigant must demonstrate both (1) injury in fact and (2) causal relation.

9. T or F   A federal citizen has standing to challenge violations by federal officials of constitutionally imposed duties.

10. T or F   Art. III prevents the plaintiff from litigating the legal rights of a party not before the court.

11. T or F   If a state criminal prosecution is pending, a federal court generally should abstain from granting declaratory or injunctive relief with regard to the controversy even though a First Amendment claim is involved.

12. T or F   A question is "political" and, therefore, non-justiciable not because in some way it affects the political process but because the problems the question presents are not appropriate for judicial resolution.

13. Which of the following is an Art. III requirement?

   a. The presumption of constitutionality.

   b. Third party standing rule.

   c. Ban on advisory opinions.

   d. Avoidance of prematurity and abstract questions.

14. Which of the following is *not* an exception to the Eleventh Amendment limitation on federal court jurisdiction?

   a. State waiver of immunity.

   b. Retroactive charges on state revenues.

   c. Suits against state officials acting unconstitutionally.

   d. Ancillary monetary relief.

   e. Prospective relief which involves expenditures of state funds.

15. Suburbia, which adjoins the city of Metro, maintains a racially exclusionary zoning ordinance. Which of the following parties would be most likely to have the requisite standing to challenge Suburbia's law?

   a. Metro taxpayers.

   b. A builder who has been denied a permit to build a racially integrated housing project in Suburbia.

   c. Black persons living in Metro.

   d. An association of homebuilders.

16. A federal court, pursuant to the 1972 amendments to Title VII of the Civil Rights Act of 1964, has awarded back pay and attorneys' fees against the state to present and retired male state employees where the latter had suffered from state discrimination against them because of their sex. Congress had enacted this legislation pursuant to legislative authority granted it under Section 5 of the Fourteenth Amendment. The state has argued that the award is unconstitutional on the ground that it offends the Eleventh Amendment. Is it?

17. The state of Purity maintains a law prohibiting any person from sterilizing females. Doctor Kildare, a licensed physician in Purity, brings suit in federal district court seeking to enjoin the Purity Sterilization Law, alleging that the Sterilization Law violates the right of privacy of his female patients who wish to be sterilized. The state of Purity has moved to dismiss Doctor Kildare's suit for want of jurisdiction and, in the alternative, that Doctor Kildare cannot raise the rights of his patients. Discuss the validity of the state's claims.

*

II

NATIONAL LEGISLATIVE POWERS

Analysis

A. *The Scope of the National Legislative Power*
B. *Commerce Power*
C. *The Taxing Power*
D. *The Spending Power*
E. *Intergovernmental Immunities*
F. *Review Questions*

American Government is limited government. The national government has only such powers as are granted to it by the people through the constitutional text, either expressly or impliedly. Powers not delegated are retained by the states and the people (Tenth Amendment). A broad view of the constitutional basis for federal legislative power originated with Marshall in the early nineteenth century, then a more or less contracted view of federal congressional power emerged, to be followed in turn by Supreme Court decisions which since the New Deal have once again taken a very expansive view of congressional power based on a generous interpretation of the implied powers granted to Congress in the Constitution.

In analyzing the constitutionality of federal statutes, always ask two questions: (1) Is there a constitutional source of power and, if so, (2) is there a constitutional limitation on the exercise of the power? Remember, limitations on the exercise of government power include both constitutional rights and liberties and the constitutional distribution of powers (i.e., separation and division of powers).

A. THE SCOPE OF THE NATIONAL LEGISLATIVE POWER

1. EXPRESS POWERS

Art. I, § 8, expressly grants a variety of powers to Congress including the powers to regulate commerce with foreign nations and among the several states and to lay and collect taxes to pay the debts and provide for the defense and general welfare of the United States.

2. IMPLIED POWERS

a. "Necessary and Proper" Clause

Art. I, § 8 also provides that Congress shall have power "To make all Laws which shall be necessary and proper for carrying into Execution the foregoing Powers, and all other Powers vested by this Constitution in the Government of the United States, or in any Department or Officer thereof."

b. Interpretation of "Necessary and Proper"

The terms "necessary and proper" have been interpreted to mean that if the end for which Congress legislates is legitimate, within the scope of the Constitution, then "all means which are appropriate, which are plainly adapted to that end, which are not prohibited, but consist with the letter and spirit of the Constitution are constitutional." McCulloch v. Maryland *(1819).* Congress may use "reasonable" means for achieving its delegated powers.

Example: In an action to collect state taxes against a federal corporation, the Bank of the United States, the question was raised as to whether Congress had the power to incorporate the bank. The Court noted that among the enumerated powers of government the word "bank" or "incorporation" is not found. Nevertheless, the Constitution did not enumerate all the means by which the powers it confers may be executed. Congress has implied power to create such a corporation if it is appropriate to the beneficial exercise of an enumerated power, *e.g.*, incorporation of a national bank by Congress is a useful instrument for pursuing the fiscal powers of Congress. *McCulloch v. Maryland* (1819).

3. INHERENT POWERS
Consistent with the principle that this is a limited government, i.e., a government of enumerated powers, Congress has no inherent domestic legislative powers. Kansas v. Colorado *(1907).* This does not necessarily preclude inherent foreign affairs powers. The Court has indicated that the national government has inherent powers of external sovereignty which do not depend on the Constitution. *United States v. Curtiss-Wright Export Corp.* (1936).

4. DELEGATION OF POWERS
Congress is free to delegate legislative authority provided it has exercised the essentials of the legislative function by determining the basic legislative policy and by formulating standards to guide subsequent conduct. The courts today are very liberal regarding what will suffice as adequate standards, *e.g.*, "just and reasonable", "fair and equitable".

5. THE ORIGINATION CLAUSE
Art. I, § 7 provides that "[a]ll Bills for raising Revenue shall originate in the House of Representatives; but the Senate may propose or concur with Amendments as on other Bills." While this section requires that revenue raising bills originate in the House of Representatives, a bill which merely produces revenue as an incidental effect of furthering its primary goal may originate in the Senate. It is not a "Bil[l] for raising revenue." *United States v. Munoz–Flores* (1990) [monetary assessment paid to Crime Victims Fund imposed on any person convicted of a federal misdemeanor held constitutional].

B. COMMERCE POWER

1. DEFINITION
In *Gibbons v. Ogden* (1824), Marshall broadly defined "commerce among the States" as "commerce which concerns more states than one," including those activities "which affect the states generally."

a. Territorial Movement
In subsequent years, the courts have required a showing of movement of goods across state lines, i.e., "interstate commerce". Production, mining, etc., were held antecedent to, and not part of, interstate commerce as such.

b. A Broader Commerce Power

However, as indicated below, the territorial limitation on the Clause is not indicative of the scope of Congress' commerce power which today has been interpreted to encompass a wide range of activity.

2. ACHIEVING SOCIAL WELFARE THROUGH THE COMMERCE POWER—A NATIONAL POLICE POWER?

Congress is not given express authorization to legislate for police power purposes, i.e., to legislate on a national basis concerning the morals, health, well-being of the people. However, Congress' power to "regulate" interstate commerce is plenary, is complete in itself, and is subject only to constitutional limitations. Congress can legislate to protect interstate commerce and prevent it from being misused. The courts will not probe the motive or purpose of Congress' regulation of interstate commerce. Congress, therefore, can achieve social welfare objectives by using its broad commerce powers.

a. Pretext Principle

In *McCulloch,* Justice Marshall indicated that if Congress uses its delegated powers as a pretext for regulating activities properly in the domain of the states, the Court would hold the law unconstitutional. In *Hammer v. Dagenhart* (1918), the Court held that federal regulation of the interstate transit of goods produced by child labor was an unconstitutional intrusion on state police powers and violative of the Tenth Amendment.

b. Protective Principle—The Modern View

Today, it is accepted that Congress can legislate for social welfare objectives using its commerce power. It can close the channels of interstate commerce activities and regulate locally to protect interstate commerce from pollution and misuse. *The Tenth Amendment, insofar as federal regulation of private activity is concerned, is a truism—anything not delegated is reserved to the states.* But if Congress exercises its delegated powers, express or implied, the Tenth Amendment is no limitation on Congress' power to regulate private activity.

Examples: (1) Congressional wage and hour legislation prohibiting the interstate transit of goods produced under substandard conditions and regulating the wages and hours of employees is constitutional. *Hammer v. Dagenhart* is overruled. Since Congress can close the channels of interstate commerce, it also can regulate locally to effectuate the prohibition. Congress can also legislate to prevent unfair competition which would adversely affect interstate competition. *United States v. Darby* (1941).

                 (2) Congress may prohibit racial discrimination in places of public accommodation serving interstate travellers since

Congress could rationally conclude that such discrimination in service impedes interstate travel by Negroes. The fact that national police power purposes, i.e., terminating racial discrimination, are accomplished by such legislation does not make the legislation an improper use of the commerce power. *Heart of Atlanta Motel, Inc. v. United States* (1964).

3. STREAM OF COMMERCE

Local activities can be regulated by Congress if they are part of the "stream" or "current" of interstate commerce. In defining interstate commerce, the Court has rejected a technical inquiry into the non-interstate character of some of the incidents of the activity, focusing instead on the overall movement of which they are a part.

Example: Congress has the power to regulate the activities of local dealers in the Chicago Stockyards since the stockyards are but a throat through which the current of commerce flows from West to East. *Stafford v. Wallace* (1922).

4. THE AFFECTATION DOCTRINE

Congress has power to regulate local activities to the extent such regulation is necessary and proper to fostering and protecting interstate commerce. The fact that the federal law has the purpose or effect of displacing state police power will not affect the validity of the federal law.

a. Direct-Indirect Test

Prior to the New Deal, Congress was limited to regulating only those local activities having a "direct" effect on interstate commerce. This excluded consideration of the magnitude of the effect of local activities on interstate commerce, limiting the inquiry to the manner in which the effect was brought about.

b. The Modern Affectation Doctrine

Congress may reach even local activity if it can rationally conclude that such activity has a substantial adverse effect on interstate commerce, regardless of whether the effect is "direct" or "indirect". The Courts defer to the congressional judgment. Again, the fact that the law has the effect of displacing state police power regulation does not affect the validity of the federal law.

c. Cumulative Effects Doctrine

In determining the adequacy of the effect, Congress may consider the cumulative effect of all the activities regulated even though the contribution of a particular activity may be trivial.

Examples: (1) A farmer's own contribution to the demand for wheat through home consumption may be trivial by itself but that is not enough to remove him from the scope of federal regulation where his contribution, taken together with that of many others similarly situated, is far from trivial. *Wickard v. Filburn* (1942).

(2) Congress may prohibit racial discrimination in restaurants serving food which has traveled through interstate commerce since Congress could rationally conclude that such discrimination causes less interstate goods to be sold, that it impedes interstate travel by Negroes and causes business to suffer generally. Even a small restaurant whose purchases of interstate goods is insignificant in itself may be regulated since the cumulative effect with others similarly situated is substantial. *Katzenbach v. McClung* (1964).

(3) A congressional statute prohibiting the use of extortionate credit transactions is within the power of Congress to regulate interstate commerce. A class of activities may be properly regulated by Congress in spite of its police power purpose without proof that the particular intrastate activity against which a sanction is laid has an effect on interstate commerce. Congress could reasonably conclude that local loansharking supports interstate crime; the courts will not consider the separate effect of the individual case. *Perez v. United States* (1971).

(4) The Surface Mining Act of 1977 establishing an extensive federal-state program for curbing the negative effects of coal strip-mining is a constitutional exercise of the Commerce power. The congressional finding that surface coal mining affects interstate commerce is rational because: (1) coal is a commodity that moves in interstate commerce, (2) surface mining standards serve to prevent destructive interstate competition, and (3) environmental hazards have effects in more than one state. *Hodel v. Virginia Surface Mining and Reclamation Ass'n.* (1981).

(5) A federal law, designed to encourage energy conservation by electric utilities, was held to be a valid exercise of the federal commerce power. The legislative history established that Congress could reasonably conclude that regulation of local power transmission was a reasonable means of energy conservation given the interstate nature of the generation and

supply of electric power. *Federal Energy Regulatory Commission v. Mississippi* (1982).

(6) A federal statute which allows parties to preserve railroad rights of way which are to be abandoned for future railroad use by providing for interim use of the routes as recreational trails is a constitutional exercise of the commerce power. Preventing reversion of the route to local reversion holders by providing for interim use is a rational means of furthering the valid Commerce Clause objective of preserving the right of way for future railroad use. *Preseault v. ICC* (1990).

C. THE TAXING POWER

*Art. I, § 8 provides that "Congress shall have power to lay and collect taxes, duties, imposts, and excises, to pay the debts and provide for the common defense and general welfare of the United States * * *." While this textual authority gives Congress the power to raise revenue, it is a fiscal power and not an independent source of regulatory power. Congress can, of course, impose a tax as a necessary and proper means of achieving a granted regulatory power. And, taxes do not lose their character as taxes because of an incidental regulatory motive or effect. However, a taxing measure which betrays on its face penalizing features loses its character as a tax and becomes a regulatory penalty not authorized under the fiscal taxing power.*

1. OBJECTIVE CONSTITUTIONALITY
This doctrine, sometimes called the doctrine of judicial obtuseness, permits the Court to uphold taxing measures by focusing only on the portions of the legislation which disclose a taxing purpose while ignoring other manifest regulatory features.

Example: The Court upheld a $0.10 per lb. tax on colored oleo but taxing white oleo at a rate of only $0.0025 per lb. The motive of the statute was clearly to give the dairy industry's butter a competitive advantage over colored oleo. However, by just looking at the four corners of the statute, the Court, using the doctrine of objective constitutionality, upheld the statute. *McCray v. United States* (1904).

2. THE PENALTY DOCTRINE
A taxing measure with the characteristics of regulation and punishment must be judged as a penalty, and not a tax. Note that the law may still be constitutional as a means of achieving one or more of the regulatory powers, *e.g.*, under the Commerce Clause. The constitutional problem arises only where Congress does not have power to regulate the activity that is taxed.

While the Court today is less willing to probe the congressional purpose, it will look for facial features extraneous to any tax need. It will consider: (1) the amount of the tax; (2) the consequences of a failure to pay; (3) scienter requirements; (4) the identity of the administering authority; and (5) the detail of the scheme or administration.

Example: The Federal Child Labor Tax imposing a heavy tax on employers using child labor was held an invalid penalty rather than a tax. Among other regulatory features was the provision that the employer would be liable only if he knew that a child was under the proscribed age limits. The Court held that scienters are associated with penalties and not with taxes. *Bailey v. Drexel Furniture Co.* (1922).

3. MODERN TREND

The modern judicial trend is to accept any tax as a valid taxing measure if it purports to be and is, on its face, a revenue-producing measure.

Example: A tax on persons engaged in the business of gambling, having a regulatory effect but producing revenue, even though negligible in amount, was held to be a valid tax. Filing and disclosure provisions were held to be reasonable regulatory features incidental to effectuation of the tax. *United States v. Kahriger* (1953).

4. SELF–INCRIMINATION

a. While disclosure requirements may not make a tax into a penalty, such provisions may violate the privilege against self-incrimination.

b. Where the information required would be a significant link in the chain of evidence tending to establish guilt, presenting a "real and appreciable" and not merely an "imaginary and unsubstantial" danger of self-incrimination, the Fifth Amendment is violated and the taxpayer need not provide the information. *Marchetti v. United States* (1968).

D. THE SPENDING POWER

Congress is expressly empowered to spend for the general welfare. While this does not permit Congress to regulate for the general welfare, it does authorize expenditures for any general welfare purpose. The Spending Power is a fiscal, not a regulatory power. Nevertheless, Congress can attach reasonable conditions to its grant of money.

1. **GENERAL WELFARE**
   a. Under the Necessary and Proper Clause, Congress can spend for the purpose of achieving any of its delegated regulatory powers.

   b. But the Spending Clause is an independent source of fiscal power authorizing Congress to spend for general welfare objectives. General Welfare is not limited to the specific objectives specified in the Art. I, § 8 regulatory powers but includes all matters of national concern. Today, the Court defers substantially to Congress in determining the scope of the general welfare.

2. **REASONABLE CONDITIONS**
   In implementing this spending power, Congress may impose any reasonable conditions upon the states as a prerequisite for participation in federal spending programs. While a condition that is totally unrelated to any federal interest in the program might be illegitimate, this limitation has little practical significance today given the judicial deference accorded congressional spending measures.

   The Tenth Amendment, historically considered to be the barrier to a plenary exercise of the congressional spending power, has generally been viewed as only a truism. Furthermore, the Twenty-First Amendment is not in itself an independent constitutional limitation on the spending power. The states remain free to reject the federal grant and its attached conditions. While there is an inducement to participate, this is not the equivalent of coercion.

   Examples: (1) The Court upheld a tax on employers under the Social Security Act to be used for payment of unemployment compensation to employees against a claim that the legislation violated the Tenth Amendment on the ground that Congress may spend money to avoid the severe national consequences of unemployment. *Steward Machine Co. v. Davis* (1937).

   (2) An act of Congress which authorized the withholding of a percentage of federal highway construction funds from states where the drinking age was under 21 is a valid exercise of the spending power; the Twenty-first Amendment granting the states control over importation and sale of liquor and the structure of the liquor distribution system is not, as South Dakota contended, an independent constitutional bar to the conditional grant of federal funds. Although in some situations financial inducements offered by Congress might be so coercive as to pass the point at which "pressure turns into compulsion," all South Dakota would lose if it did not comply was 5 percent of the funds otherwise obtainable under the highway grant program. The coercive argument was "more rhetoric than fact." Even if Congress lacked the power to impose a national minimum drinking age directly,

the federal statute's relatively mild encouragement to the states to enact a higher minimum drinking age than they would otherwise choose was a valid use of the spending power. *South Dakota v. Dole* (1987).

3. SPENDING AS A CONTRACT: EXPLICIT CONDITIONS

Conditions imposed in federal grants are akin to contractual provisions and must be clear and unambiguous to be enforced. The conditions must be clearly delineated so that the states can make informed choices as to whether or not they will accept the grant subject to the condition. Language not sufficiently clear is to be considered only as a policy statement and not as a binding commitment on the part of the state.

Example: The words in the federal Developmentally Disabled Bill of Rights Act calling for "appropriate treatment" in "the setting that is least restrictive of personal liberty" was held to be only part of congressional findings of fact and policy statements and not to create a statutory right to treatment conditioning grants to the state made under the Act. *Pennhurst State School and Hosp. v. Halderman* (1981).

E. INTERGOVERNMENTAL IMMUNITIES

Intergovernmental immunities deals with two problems: (1) the power of the state or local government to tax or regulate federal activities and (2) the power of the federal government to tax or regulate the states. When dealing with questions in this area, remember that the Supremacy Clause (Art. VI) runs in one direction. It makes the Constitution "and the Laws of the United States" made pursuant to it the Supreme Law of the Land. This suggests that the national government has greater immunity from state taxation and regulation and greater power to tax and regulate state functions.

1. STATE TAXATION AND REGULATION

a. *The state cannot directly tax or regulate the federal government or a federal instrumentality.* A state tax, for example, is unconstitutional if the legal burden of the tax falls on the federal government. The power to tax is the power to destroy. *McCulloch v. Maryland* (1819) [state tax on notes issued by the Bank of the United States held unconstitutional].

b. Nor can a state discriminate against the federal government or those who deal with the federal government absent proof that there are significant differences between the classes that justify the inconsistent treatment.

Examples: (1) Imposition of state gross receipts and use taxes on contractors conducting business with the federal government in the state did not violate the Supremacy Clause. Only when the levy falls on the United States itself, or its agencies or instrumentalities so closely tied to the government that the two cannot realistically be viewed as separate entities is the state tax barred—the taxed entity must be "incorporated into the government structure" to be immune. Since the legal incidence of the present tax is on the contractors rather than the government and since the contractors are entities independent of the federal government, the state taxes are constitutional. *United States v. New Mexico* (1982).

(2) A state statute imposed a sales tax on federal contractors for materials purchased for federal projects. The tax for nonfederal projects was imposed on the project landowner, rather than the contractor. The tax on federal contractors does not violate the Supremacy Clause. The tax is not directly laid on the federal government but on the private contractor. Nor does the tax impose a discriminatory economic burden on the federal government and those with whom it deals since, in fact, they pay less tax than other projects in the state. No one is treated better than the federal government, and therefore, the Constitution is not violated. *Washington v. United States* (1983).

(3) A state law discriminating in favor of its own state securities and against obligations of the federal government in computing the net earnings of banks for state bank tax purposes is unconstitutional. While only the economic incidence, and not the legal incidence of the tax falls on the federal government, the Constitution prohibits discrimination against the federal government and those with whom it deals. *Memphis Bank & Trust Co. v. Garner* (1983).

(4) A state law exempting from taxation all retirement benefits paid by the state to its former employees, but taxing benefits to federal government retirees, violates the doctrine of intergovernmental immunities. The imposition of a heavier tax burden was not "justified by significant differences between the two classes." Although the state had a "rational reason" for the discrimination given its objective of hiring and retaining state employees, this does not prove that there were significant differences between the two classes to justify the discrimination. Nor does the allegedly higher benefits received by some federal retirees justify the discrimination since there are undoubtedly individual instances in which

state employees receive larger pensions than federal employees. *Davis v. Michigan Dept. of Treasury* (1989).

(5) A state statute which requires out-of-state liquor distributors to report the volume of liquor shipped into the state and to label all bottles bound for a federal enclave for consumption within the enclave only, does not violate the intergovernmental immunity doctrine. Although the state regulations impose extra expenses upon the federal government in purchasing liquor for its military bases in the state, the law is not a regulation of the government itself, but only operates against out-of-state distributors. The law also does not impose a discriminatory regulatory burden on the federal government but actually favors the government. Unlike in-state liquor retail purchasers, the federal government has the option to purchase liquor from unlicensed, out-of-state distributors. *North Dakota v. United States* (1990).

2. FEDERAL TAXATION AND REGULATION
a. Federal Taxation of States
If a federal tax imposed on state activities is non-discriminatory (i.e., applicable only to the state), is based on a fair return for federal benefits and the cost is not excessive in light of the benefits provided the state, the federal tax will be upheld. *Massachusetts v. United States* (1978) [federal tax on all civil aircraft using federal facilities, applied to state police aircraft, held constitutional].

b. Federal Regulation of States
The principle that state sovereignty embodied in the Tenth Amendment constitutes a significant substantive limitation on Congress' commerce power has been rejected. *Garcia v. San Antonio Metropolitan Transit Auth.* (1985). It is the political process, not judicial determination of what state activities must be immune from federal regulation, that protects federalist values. The judicial role is limited to compensating for possible failings in the national political process.

1) In *National League of Cities v. Usery* (1976), the Court held that Congress' power to regulate the states under the commerce power was limited by principles of state sovereignty. Subsequent cases, held that, under the Tenth Amendment, a federal law must satisfy each of three requirements.

"First, there must be a showing that the challenged statute regulates 'States as States'. Second, the federal regulation must address matters that are indisputably 'attributes of state sovereignty.' And third, it must be apparent that the States' compliance with the federal law would directly impair their ability 'to structure integral operations in areas of traditional functions' ". *Hodel v. Virginia Surface Mining & Reclamation Ass'n* (1981).

2) In *Garcia, National League of Cities* was overruled 5–4. Judicial determination of which state government functions are "traditional" or "integral" was said to be unworkable and inconsistent with principles of federalism.

   a) In cases following *National League* the courts were unable to fashion objective criteria for identifying the essential functions of the states in our federal system.

   b) *Garcia* emphasizes that it is not the function of an unelected federal judiciary to define the nature and content of the limitations that our federal structure imposes on the commerce power. It is the structure of the federal government, *e.g.,* the role of the states in the selection of the Executive and the Congress that defines these limits. "State sovereign interests are more properly protected by procedural safeguards inherent in the structure of the federal system than by judicially created limitations on federal power."

   c) The *Garcia* Court did indicate that state sovereignty does impose some "procedural" affirmative limitations on congressional regulation of the states. But such restraints which the *Garcia* Court does not define, appear to be minimal, designed only to provide a safeguard if the political process fails, *e.g.,* a congressional effort to dictate where a state locates its capitol. *Coyle v. Oklahoma* (1911).

3) The *Garcia* dissent argues that it is the judicial role under *Marbury* to enforce the Tenth Amendment, that federal usurpation of the traditional functions of the states undermines their role as a counterpoise to federal power and that the political process is an inadequate safeguard for federalism. The dissent contends that the courts should balance the respective interests of the states and the federal government.

F. REVIEW QUESTIONS

1. T or F Congress has inherent power to legislate in matters where the states separately are incapable of acting.

2. T or F   Congress can use its granted powers, *e.g.* the commerce power, in order to achieve social welfare objectives.

3. T or F   Congress can regulate local activities which have a substantial adverse effect on interstate commerce even if the law displaces state police powers.

4. T or F   If a law purports, on its face, to be a revenue producing measure, it is a valid taxing measure.

5. T or F   Congress can regulate to further the general welfare.

6. T or F   Congress can impose reasonable conditions as a precondition to receiving federal grants.

7. T or F   A federal law, even if otherwise valid under the commerce power, is unconstitutional if it regulates the state itself in an area of its traditional governmental functions.

8. T or F   Congress can use reasonable means for implementing its granted powers, even if this involves regulation of matters traditionally subject to state regulation.

9. Congress imposes a $.10 tax on every gallon of gas sold, the revenues to be used to make federal grants to states for energy conservation programs. States' programs which are funded must meet federally-imposed standards. Which of the following is most accurate?

    a. The tax is an unconstitutional penalty since it is intended to discourage use of gasoline.

    b. The law is a valid regulation for the general welfare.

    c. These exercises of the tax and spending powers are both constitutional.

    d. The federal law violates the Tenth Amendment since it coerces the states to conform to federal standards.

10. Assume that the life guards who work at the municipal beach of Magnolia Beach, State of West Jefferson, were paid the federal minimum wage, but were not paid the federal overtime rate of time and a half by Magnolia Beach. In the summer, the life guards there worked eight hours a day, seven days a week. The federal government contends that the Fair Labor Standards Act requires that the federal overtime rate should be paid to the life guards. The largest part of the municipal payroll for the tiny resort town of Magnolia Beach consists of its life guard salaries. If overtime has to be paid, the city

contends that it might have to dissolve itself and ask for annexation by its neighbor Jackson City.   If the government seeks to enforce the FLSA against the town of Magnolia Beach, does the town have a constitutional defense or must the town bankrupt itself?

*

III

STATE POWER IN AMERICAN FEDERALISM

Analysis

While the national government can exercise only such powers as are expressly or impliedly delegated in the Constitution, states have inherent police power to act for the health, morals, and well-being of their citizens. When dealing with the constitutionality of state laws, therefore, the student should focus on constitutional limitations on state power. Such limitations may take the form of constitutional rights and liberties or limitations arising from the constitutional allocation of powers. The focus of this Chapter is on federalist values reflected in the Division of Powers principle.

A. STATE POWER TO REGULATE COMMERCE

1. ESTABLISHING THE FOUNDATIONS
Some constitutional powers are exclusively national, *e.g.*, the power to declare war or to legislate for the District of Columbia. Other powers are shared by both the states and the federal government. If the power is concurrent, in some instances, where Congress has not acted to exclude the states, the states may regulate even though Congress, if it chose, could also legislate in the same area. In other instances, however, where Congress could act, the particular state regulation is proscribed by the constitutional grant of power to Congress. *The rationalizing principle is that where a subject of the state regulation is by its nature national or where the state regulation would place an excessive burden on national concerns, the states may not regulate in the absence of congressional authorization.*

a. The Nature of the Power—Exclusive or Concurrent
  1) The Commerce Power Is, at Least Partially, a Shared Power
     The existence of a plenary power over interstate commerce in Congress is not necessarily inconsistent with the existence of state regulatory power over that commerce. *Cooley v. Board of Wardens* (1851).

  2) Primacy of Federal Regulation
     When a state regulation conflicts with a federal law in a shared area or impedes the achievement of the federal objectives, the federal regulation must prevail by force of the Supremacy Clause (Art. VI) which states: "This Constitution, and the Laws of the United States which shall be made in Pursuance thereof * * * shall be the supreme Law of the Land * * *."

b. The Nature of the Subject—The Cooley Doctrine
     In the determination of whether a state regulation of interstate commerce is permissible, the Cooley *doctrine focuses on the subject of the regulation. When subjects of commerce regulation are national in nature, i.e., require a uniform system or plan of regulation, they are not amenable to state regulation.* Cooley v. Board of Wardens *(1851)* [held

that, in the absence of applicable federal legislation, a state may regulate local pilotage for navigation].

The *Cooley* doctrine is criticized for focusing excessively on the subject of the state regulation rather than the nature of the regulation, i.e., its effect on interstate commerce. Nevertheless, it continues to be occasionally used as a test of the state power to regulate interstate commerce.

2. THE MODERN FOCUS: THE DORMANT COMMERCE CLAUSE

Even when Congress is silent, the Commerce Clause itself, as interpreted by the courts, imposes some limitation on the ability of states to regulate when the state regulation affects interstate commerce. In determining whether a state regulation is barred by the negative implications of the Dormant Commerce Clause, the course of decisional law has moved away from nominalistic tests of direct and indirect interference with commerce to a new inquiry. Today, the student should ask two questions derived from *Pike v. Bruce Church* (1970): *(1) does the state regulation impermissibly discriminate against interstate commerce, or, (2) are the incidental burdens imposed on interstate commerce "clearly excessive in relation to the putative local benefits."* If the answer to either question is "yes", the state law is unconstitutional. It should be noted that there are a number of Justices on the Court who would limit the negative implications of the Dormant Commerce Clause to state regulations that are discriminatory.

a. Rationale
1) Common Market Philosophy
   The central purpose of the Commerce Clause was the avoidance of state custom barriers and other economic barriers which spawn trade rivalries and retaliation. The Constitution "was framed upon the theory that the peoples of the several states must sink or swim together, and that in the long run prosperity and salvation are in union and not division." *Baldwin v. G.A.F. Seelig, Inc.* (1935).

2) A Political Rationale
   When a law is framed so that its negative impact is directed solely at out-of-state interests, "legislative action is not likely to be subjected to those political restraints which are normally exerted on legislation where it affects adversely some interests within the state." *South Carolina Highway Dept. v. Barnwell Bros.* (1938).

b. Direct and Indirect Effects
An early effort to reconcile national and local interests in regulating commerce focused on whether the state regulation imposed a "direct" or an "indirect" burden on interstate commerce. The test provided little

indication of how burdens were to be classified as direct or indirect and the distinction has been abandoned.

c. The Modern Standards
1) Discrimination
   a) Intentional Discrimination
   A state law which purposefully discriminates against interstate commerce in favor of local interests is invalid regardless of the importance of the local interests involved. Simple economic protectionism is "virtually per se" invalid.

   > ***Example:*** A state law prohibiting the sale of milk bought out-of-state at a price lower than the price set by law for the sale of milk in the state is unconstitutional. "[W]hen the avowed purpose of the [state law], as well as its necessary tendency, is to suppress or mitigate the consequences of competition between the states," it violates the Commerce Clause. *Baldwin v. G.A.F. Seelig, Inc.* (1935).

   b) Discriminatory Means and Effects
   Even if a state regulation is intended to serve a legitimate police power interest rather than economic protectionism, the law must regulate evenhandedly. "The statute must serve a legitimate local purpose and the purpose must be one that cannot be served as well by available nondiscriminatory means." Maine v. Taylor *(1986).*

   (1) If a state law operates extraterritorially to regulate activities occurring outside the state's borders, it is likely to be labeled discriminatory and be subjected to more stringent judicial review.

   > ***Examples:*** (1) A New York law requiring liquor distillers selling to wholesalers in New York to sell at a price that is no higher than the lowest prices that it charges wholesalers in other states violates the Commerce Clause. While a state may seek lower prices for its consumers, it may not insist that producers or consumers in other states surrender competitive advantages. The New York law impermissibly regulates extraterritorially. *Brown–Forman Distillers Corp. v. New York State Liquor Auth.* (1986).
   >
   > (2) A state law requiring out-of-state shippers of beer to affirm that their monthly posted prices for beer

sold in the state are no higher than prices for their product in bordering states, including any price inducements, violates the Commerce Clause. The statute has the practical effect of "controlling commercial activities" occurring wholly outside the state. The law also serves as a disincentive for companies doing business in the state from engaging in interstate commerce. *Healy v. The Beer Institute, Inc.* (1989).

(2) If a state law facially imposes burdens on out-of-state interests that are not imposed on in-state interests, it is likely to be labeled as discriminatory in means and be subjected to more searching judicial review.

Examples: (1) A state law which prohibits the importation of wastes from out of state for dumping in local landfills while allowing local traffic and dumping of wastes is unconstitutional. "[T]he evil of protectionism can reside in legislative means as well as legislative ends." While the law serves legitimate interests of the state, there is no reason to discriminate against interstate commerce. *City of Philadelphia v. New Jersey* (1978).

(2) A state statute forbidding the transportation out of state for sale of free-swimming minnows taken from waters within the state, but not restricting local sales, was held to violate the Commerce Clause. While conservation of natural resources is a legitimate state purpose, states may not seek to achieve this goal by choosing discriminatory means where non-discriminatory means are available. *Hughes v. Oklahoma* (1979).

(3) An order of the New Hampshire Public Utilities Commission, pursuant to a state statute, requiring New England Power to sell locally produced hydroelectric energy solely within New Hampshire in order to satisfy local needs is unconstitutional under the Commerce Clause. The Commerce Clause precludes a state from requiring that its residents be given a preferred right of access over out-of-state consumers to privately-owned national resources or the products derived therefrom. Such an exportation ban is the type of simple protectionist regulation

that the Commerce Clause prohibits and places a direct and substantial burden on interstate commerce. Nothing in the Federal Power Act was found to authorize such discrimination. *New England Power Co. v. New Hampshire* (1982).

(4) Nebraska's permit system limiting out-of-state export of ground waters to states granting reciprocity for sale of its waters in Nebraska is unconstitutional. The law did not satisfy the "strictest scrutiny" applicable to facially discriminatory laws. While Nebraska has an "unquestionably legitimate and highly important" conservation and health interest in ground waters, the state failed to show that the reciprocity requirement was narrowly tailored to this end. Even if the water could be used most beneficially in another state, the reciprocity requirement could bar the sale. *Sporhase v. Nebraska* (1982).

(5) A Maine criminal statute banning the importation of live baitfish from out-of-state is constitutional. The district court finding that the law served the state's important interest in protecting the integrity of its natural resources and that alternative means would not adequately serve that interest was not "clearly erroneous." The law was not deemed economic protectionism. *Maine v. Taylor* (1986).

(6) An Ohio law awarding a tax credit against the Ohio fuel sales tax for each gallon of ethanol sold as a component of gasohol, but only if the ethanol is produced in Ohio or in a state that grants similar tax advantages to Ohio ethanol, violates the Commerce Clause. The law imposes a facial disadvantage on out-of-state sellers. Reciprocity provisions would not justify such disparity of treatment but would enhance the discrimination by seeking more favorable treatment for Ohio-produced ethanol. The state's health and commerce justifications were merely speculative and would not justify "this plain discrimination against products of out-of-state manufacture." *New Energy Co. of Indiana v. Limbach* (1988).

(3) Even if a state law is evenhanded in purpose and is facially neutral between out-of-state and in-state interests (i.e., it is not discriminatory in means), it may impact more severely on interstate commerce than on local commerce and be labeled discriminatory. However, if the different effect is due to the way in which the market is structured rather than the operation of the state law, the Court might not label it discriminatory. *Exxon v. Governor of Maryland* (1978) [state law prohibiting oil producers or refiners from operating retail service stations held nondiscriminatory even though almost all oil producers and refiners were out-of-state concerns].

Example: A North Carolina state law requiring all closed containers of apples sold in the state to bear no grade other than the U.S. grade operates to discriminate against the Washington state apple industry. The law raises the costs of doing business in North Carolina thereby depriving Washington apple dealers of an economic competitive advantage over local sellers. Washington's apple industry is deprived also of its competitive marketing advantage resulting from displaying the superior Washington state grades. Even when considered as a law to prevent consumer deception, the law fails since marketing is permitted with no grades at all, sales in closed containers would apply only to wholesalers and brokers who are knowledgeable, and Washington state grades are in fact superior to U.S. grades. Finally, there are non-discriminatory alternatives to an outright ban such as requiring U.S. grades when other grades are used or banning state grades which are not equal to U.S. grades. *Hunt v. Washington State Apple Advertising Comm'n* (1977).

2) Undue Burdens—Ad Hoc Balancing
Even if a state law is held to be nondiscriminatory, it may still violate the Dormant Commerce Clause if it imposes an undue burden on interstate commerce. In determining if a non-discriminatory state regulation of interstate commerce imposes an undue burden on interstate commerce, the Court balances the local interests in maintaining the regulation against the burden on the free movement of interstate commerce. This approach inquires into: (1) the nature and function of the regulation; (2) the character of the business involved; and (3) the actual effect on the flow of commerce. As a result of this inquiry, a court may conclude that a state law that burdens interstate commerce may be sustained because the regulation pertains to matters peculiarly

local and does not unduly infringe the national interest in maintaining freedom of commerce across state lines.

A number of Justices argue that such judicial balancing of interests is improper. They argue that if the law is nondiscriminatory the rationale of the Dormant Commerce Clause no longer applies, that courts lack the capacity for such interest balancing, that such balancing makes the courts a superlegislature, that federalism counsels judicial restraint and that Congress can legislate to relieve any excessive burdens on interstate commerce. This approach would limit the Dormant Commerce Clause to cases of discrimination.

a)   Important State Interests
     Certain state interests receive greater weight in the balancing test, *e.g.,* health, safety, prevention of fraud, conservation of resources, regulation of highways.

b)   Trade, Conservation, Environment
     A state may regulate incoming and outgoing commerce in goods pursuant to its interests in protecting the health, safety, and well-being of its citizens, including the economic well-being of citizens. But the states cannot hoard their resources or adopt laws that are essentially protectionist. It cannot use means which, while rationally designed to achieve permissible police power objectives, excessively burden the free flow of interstate commerce.

     Examples: (1) An Arizona statute requiring a grower of cantaloupes to package its produce in the state at an added cost of $200,000 was held unconstitutional. The state interest in having the produce identified with the producing state was viewed as minimal and less substantial than the cost burdens on the grower. *Pike v. Bruce Church, Inc.* (1970).

     (2) A state ban on plastic nonreturnable milk containers was held not to violate the Commerce Clause. The statute did not discriminate between interstate and intrastate commerce, but rather prohibited all milk retailers from selling their products in plastic containers. The incidental burden imposed on interstate commerce, i.e., the statute was more burdensome on the out-of-state plastics industry than the Minnesota pulp wood industry, was not excessive in light of the local benefits achieved. The state demonstrated substantial interests in promoting

conservation of energy and other natural resources and easing solid waste disposal problems. Most out-of-state dairies package their products in more than one type of container and it was only minimally inconvenient to conform to the particular packaging requirements of Minnesota. *Minnesota v. Clover Leaf Creamery Co.* (1981).

(3) The Illinois Business Takeover Act imposing restrictions on corporate takeovers (not limited to Illinois corporations), beyond those imposed by federal law, is unconstitutional. Applying a balancing test, the Court held the state law excessively burdened interstate commerce. The ability to block nationwide tender offers substantially burdened interstate commerce and "directly" regulated commerce outside the state. The state interests were deemed speculative. *Edgar v. MITE Corp.* (1982).

(4) An Indiana statute providing that, when an entity or person acquires controlling stock of an Indiana corporation having a substantial number of Indiana shareholders, the acquiring party obtains no voting rights unless the shareholders agree to give voting rights, does not violate the Commerce Clause. The law is not discriminatory since it applies to all tender offers whether or not the offeror is an Indiana resident. Since the law applies only to Indiana corporations, there is no danger of businesses being subjected to inconsistent state regulation. The law does not impose an undue burden on interstate commerce since the statute is limited to Indiana corporations and is designed to protect the shareholders of such corporations, including Indiana residents, from takeovers and to prevent the corporate form from being used as a shield for unfair business dealing. *CTS Corp. v. Dynamics Corp. of America* (1987).

c) Transportation
A state may regulate traffic passing through the state in order to achieve permissible police power objectives. *State highway laws enjoy a heavier presumption of validity given the historic and local interest in highway management. But the states may not regulate where the national interest requires uniformity of regulation, nor*

otherwise excessively burden the movement of interstate commerce. State laws granting exceptions in favor of local interests are more closely scrutinized. State adoption of a regulation more burdensome than that used by surrounding states also increases the likelihood of its being held unconstitutional.

> ***Example:*** An Iowa statute generally prohibiting the use of 65 foot double-trailer trucks within its borders was held to impose an unconstitutional burden on interstate commerce. While the Court accords special deference to state legislative judgments regarding highway safety regulations, in the present case the state did not prove that its safety interests justified the significant burden on efficient and safe interstate transportation. Studies indicated that the 65-doubles are safe and that the Iowa law would severely impair trucking firms using interstate highways. The use of smaller trucks being driven through the state or larger trucks being driven longer distances to bypass Iowa increased the danger of traffic accidents. Various exemptions in the state statutory scheme benefited only state residents while shifting to neighboring states many of the costs associated with the statutory requirement. *Kassel v. Consolidated Freightways Corp.* (1981).

d. State as Market Participant

> *1) When the state acts, not as a regulator but as a participant in the marketplace, it is not subject to the ordinary constraints of the Commerce Clause. The Dormant Commerce Clause does not prohibit the state from discriminating in favor of its own citizens in subsidies or incident to engaging in market transactions.* It has been suggested that this principle may not extend to state discrimination in regards to natural resources which the state has not expended effort to develop, but the Court has not, thus far, adopted such an exception.

> ***Examples:*** (1) A state law discriminating in the sale of cement marketed by the state (i.e., preference for in-state residents) does not violate the Commerce Clause. The negative implications of the Dormant Commerce Clause do not apply when the state acts as a market participant rather than as a market regulator. The historical purposes of the Commerce Clause and respect for state sovereignty indicate that any restraint should come from Congress rather than from the courts. *Reeves v. Stake* (1980).

(2) An executive order of a mayor requiring all construction projects funded wholly with city funds or with city and federal funds be performed by a work force at least half of which are bona fide residents of the city does not violate the Dormant Commerce Clause. Since the city acted as a market participant rather than as a regulator, the negative implications of the Commerce Clause do not apply. The impact of the law on out of state firms and residents is relevant only if the state is regulating the market. Everyone affected by the law can be said to be working for the city. Insofar as federal funds were used, federal statutes and regulations permitted the parochial favoritism in the order—Congress can exempt states from the negative implications of the Dormant Commerce Clause. *White v. Massachusetts Council of Const. Employers* (1983).

2) The more that state action impacts on persons who are not parties to the state contract, the more likely it is that the state action will be treated as a regulation.

Example: A four-justice plurality determined that a state statute requiring buyers of timber sold by the state to process that timber in the state violated the Commerce Clause. While the state participated in the marketplace in selling its timber, its conditions on downstream processing constituted a regulation of the processing market. That regulation is subject to the Dormant Commerce Clause and is clearly unconstitutional. *South-Central Timber Dev., Inc. v. Wunnicke* (1984).

3) Note that even if a law survives Commerce Clause scrutiny, it may violate the Privileges and Immunities Clause of Art. IV, § 2, or the Equal Protection guarantee.

Example: A Camden municipal ordinance requiring contractors and subcontractors working on public work projects to use their best efforts to employ no less than 40% Camden residents is subject to Art. IV, § 2, even if the Commerce Clause is satisfied. Art. IV, § 2's concern with interstate comity in matters of fundamental concern applies whether the state is acting as a regulator or a participant. The opportunity to seek employment with a private employer is of fundamental national concern to come within Art. IV, § 2. The case was remanded to determine if Art. IV,

§ 2, was violated. *United Bldg. & Constr. Trades Council v. Camden* (1984).

c. Protecting Personal Mobility

1) The Commerce Clause

The Commerce Clause has been used to invalidate state restrictions on the free movement of persons into the state.

> ***Example:*** A state statute making it a misdemeanor to bring an indigent person into the state was held an unconstitutional burden on interstate commerce. While the influx of indigent migrants might burden the state, the problem of indigency is a national burden which must be shared and no state can isolate itself. *Edwards v. California* (1941).

2) Interstate Privileges and Immunities

Art. IV, § 2, providing that "the Citizens of each State shall be entitled to all Privileges and Immunities of Citizens in the several States," has been interpreted as a prohibition against unreasonable discrimination against out-of-state citizens in regard to fundamental national interests. The Court employs the following test. First, is the activity in question "fundamental" in that it is sufficiently basic to the livelihood of the Nation as to be within the privileges and immunities protected by Art. IV, § 2. Second, is there a substantial reason for the discrimination. Third, does the discrimination bear a close relation to that reason, including consideration of the availability of less restrictive means.

a) The term "citizens" does not include aliens or corporations.

b) State A must treat the citizens of state B in the same way it treats its own citizens with the exception that some reasonable distinctions such as a slightly higher fishing license fee for out-of-state fishermen to pay state administration and conservation costs may be justifiable.

c) But Art. IV, § 2, does not apply to all forms of interstate discrimination. It applies only if fundamental national interests are burdened, *i.e.*, those which bear on the vitality of the Nation as a single entity.

> ***Examples:*** (1) A state statute requiring preferential employment treatment of residents in oil- or gas-related jobs was held to violate the Art. IV Privileges and Immunities Clause. Non-residents were not the peculiar source of the evil attacked, i.e., high unemployment among

residents. Even if non-residents were the peculiar source of the evil, the broad employment preference given *all* residents was too loosely related to the goal of aiding unemployed residents. The state's interest in the oil and gas was inadequate justification for the discrimination. *Hicklin v. Orbeck* (1978).

(2) A state's imposition of substantially higher elk-hunting license fees on non-residents than on residents was held not to violate the Art. IV Privileges and Immunities Clause. Elk Hunting is not a fundamental interest, so it does not fall within the scope of the Art. IV Privileges and Immunities Clause. The distinction between residents and nonresidents is a rational means of preserving a finite natural resource. *Baldwin v. Fish & Game Comm'n of Montana* (1978).

(3) A state Supreme Court rule limiting bar admission to state residents violates Art. IV, § 2. The opportunity to practice law is a national "fundamental right" under the Clause given the role of lawyers in national commercial intercourse and the importance of out-of-state counsel in protecting federal rights. There was no evidence indicating nonresidents would be deficient in practice. State interests in assuring the ready availability of counsel could be satisfied by less restrictive means. *Supreme Court of New Hampshire v. Piper* (1985).

(4) A state Supreme Court rule requiring out-of-state lawyers to become permanent residents of the state in order to be admitted to the state bar violates the Art. IV, § 2, Privileges and Immunities Clause. In applying *Piper*, the Court held that it was not necessarily true that lawyers admitted in other states are less likely to respect the bar and further its interests solely because they are nonresidents. *Supreme Court of Virginia v. Friedman* (1988).

(5) Virgin Islands' court rules requiring applicants for admission to the bar to live in the Virgin Islands for one year and to declare an intention to reside and practice law there following admission violate the Art. IV, § 2, Privileges and Immunities Clause. Applying *Piper,* the discrimination against

nonresidents was not justified by any substantial state objective. Less restrictive means existed to address the problems relating to the unique nature of the legal practice in the Virgin Islands. For example, assuring the presence of counsel could be met by requiring nonresident lawyers to retain a local counsel. *Barnard v. Thorstenn* (1989).

3. WHEN CONGRESS SPEAKS
a. Preemption

CONFLICT. Under the Supremacy Clause (Art. VI), if a state regulation of interstate commerce conflicts with a federal regulation, the state law is invalid. Conflict arises if it is impossible to comply with both federal and state law or if the state law impedes the achievement of the federal objectives.

EXPRESS PREEMPTION. In the exercise of its plenary commerce power, Congress may expressly prohibit a specific form of state regulation or may entirely preclude state regulation of the subject. Where the area is one that has traditionally been occupied by the states, the congressional intent to supersede state law must be clear and manifest.

OCCUPYING THE FIELD. In the absence of conflict or express exclusion of state regulation, the courts must determine if Congress intended to occupy exclusively a field of regulation. The courts consider: (a) the need for uniformity; (b) legislative history; (c) the pervasiveness of the federal regulatory scheme; (d) the historical dominancy of national or local interest in the area; (e) the potential for conflict from dual administration; and (f) the use of a federal regulatory agency to maintain continued regulatory control of an area in determining whether Congress has preempted the field. Preemption, therefore, turns on the particular facts of each case.

Examples: (1) A state sedition law was preempted by federal sedition legislation based on the following considerations: (1) numerous federal statutes in the field were so pervasive as to compel the conclusion that Congress intended to leave no room to the states to supplement the federal legislative program; (2) the state law touched a field in which the federal interest was so dominant that enforcement of state legislation on the same subject was assumed to be precluded; and (3) the enforcement of the state sedition law presented a serious threat of conflict with the administration of the federal program. *Pennsylvania v. Nelson* (1956).

(2) A California moratorium on certifying nuclear power plants until the state determined that there exists a means

for disposal of nuclear waste is not preempted. The Court interpreted atomic energy legislation as limited to radiological safety. Congress did not intend to usurp the state's traditional authority over economic regulation. California's moratorium was found to be supported by a non-safety economic objective. *Pacific Gas & Elec. Co. v. State Energy Resources Conservation & Dev. Comm.* (1983).

(3) A state statute requiring employers to provide leave and reinstatement to employees disabled by pregnancy was not pre-empted by Title VII of the Civil Rights Act of 1964, which prohibits employment discrimination based on sex, or its amendment extending Title VII to cover pregnancy. The Court interpreted Congress' intent under Title VII to preempt state laws only if they conflict with federal law. The state antidiscrimination law furthered the Title VII purpose of "equal employment opportunity" and is not preempted. The state statute providing that women will not lose their jobs on account of pregnancy is narrowly tailored to cover only the "actual physical disability" period and therefore promotes Title VII's objectives. *California Fed. Sav. & Loan Ass'n. v. Guerra* (1987).

(4) A state regulation providing for the permanent cancellation of producers' entitlements to natural gas for excessive delay in extraction does not violate the Supremacy Clause. In the National Gas Act, Congress divided the field of natural gas regulation, allocating to states the regulation of the production and gathering of natural gas. This was precisely the field of state regulation at issue. The regulation does not conflict with federal law regulating interstate purchasers' cost structures since there was no showing that the state regulation impaired the federal objective of promoting production of low cost natural gas. *Northwest Central Pipeline Corp. v. State Corp. Comm'n of Kansas* (1989).

(5) A state tort claim for intentional infliction of mental distress is not preempted by provisions of the Federal Energy Reorganization Act which prohibit employers from discharging nuclear plant employees who report safety violations and provide a federal remedy for unlawful discharge of whistleblowers. Congress has not explicitly precluded state tort recovery in the Act nor does the provision of a federal remedy establish Congress' intent to occupy the field. While the threat of state tort actions might influence some nuclear safety policy decisions, this effect is neither sufficiently direct

or substantial enough to place the tort claim in the preempted field of nuclear safety. There was no instance of "actual conflict" with provisions of the federal Act sufficient for preemption. *English v. General Electric Co.* (1990).

(6) The Rock Creek hydroelectric project is licensed by both the Federal Energy Regulatory Commission (FERC) and the California State Water Resources Control Board (WRCB). An order issued by WRCB setting minimum water flow rates for the river on which the licensee operated higher than those set by FERC is preempted by the Federal Power Act (FPA). The FPA had previously been interpreted by the Court as limiting state regulation of hydroelectric power to regulating proprietary rights and Congress had not altered that statutory interpretation. Instead Congress had affirmed the Court's reading of the FPA to establish a broad and paramount federal regulatory role and the field had been governed by that understanding for 44 years. *California v. FERC* (1990).

b. **Legitimizing State Burdens on Commerce**
In the exercise of its plenary powers, Congress may decide to permit state regulation of an area even though the state would be barred from such regulation by the Commerce Clause in the absence of such congressional authorization.

Examples: (1) A discriminatory state tax imposed on out-of-state but not domestic insurance companies is valid where Congress expressly authorized states regulation and taxation of interstate insurance. *Prudential Insurance Co. v. Benjamin* (1946).

(2) State statutes permitting regional out-of-state bankholding companies to acquire in-state banks provided the other New England state accords reciprocity is sanctioned by federal statute. The language of the federal act allowing states to lift the ban entirely gives the states flexibility in choosing the mode of regulation, including a partial removal of the ban against local bank acquisition by out-of-state holding companies. *Northeast Bancorp, Inc. v. Board of Governors* (1985).

4. **THE COMPACT CLAUSE**
Art. I, § 10, cl. 3, requires that Congress consent to any agreement or compact by a state with another state or with a foreign country. This consent requirement is limited to agreements which increase the political power of the states in such a way as to potentially interfere with federal supremacy.

Examples: (1) The Multistate Tax Compact does not give any member state powers beyond those a member state possesses when acting individually. Further, each state retains complete freedom to accept or reject rules of the governing commission and may withdraw from the compact at any time. There is no actual or potential interference with federal supremacy. *United States Steel Corp. v. Multistate Tax Commission* (1978).

(2) State statutes authorizing regional bank holding companies to acquire in-state banks if the other state accords reciprocity does not create a compact. No mutual obligations are created and no regional authorities are established. Further, the laws do not enhance the political power of the states in the region or impact on our federal structure. *Northeast Bancorp, Inc. v. Board of Governors* (1985).

B. STATE POWER TO TAX COMMERCE

State and local taxation of interstate commerce has increasingly become a subject for specialized courses. Therefore, no effort is made to survey this extensive and technical body of case law. Rather, the general principles governing the area and some of the modern applications of these principles will be provided.

The fact that a state tax burdens the free flow of interstate commerce does not necessarily mean it's unconstitutional. Interstate commerce can be made to pay its own way. In determining whether a state tax on interstate commerce is constitutional, the student should generally consider the following: (1) Is the tax discriminatory?; (2) Is the activity being taxed sufficiently related to the taxing state?; (3) Is the tax fairly related to the benefits provided the taxpayer?; and (4) Is the tax fairly apportioned in light of the local contracts and benefits received by the taxpayer? Complete Auto Transit, Inc. v. Brady (1977). Remember, Congress has plenary commerce power to determine the permissible extent of state taxation.

1. GENERAL PRINCIPLES
a. Concurrent Power
Not all state taxation of interstate commerce is impermissible. Interstate commerce can be forced to pay its own way as long as the burden imposed by the taxing state is commensurate with the benefit the taxpayer receives from the taxing state.

b. Discrimination
A state may not discriminate against interstate commerce in imposing taxes. It cannot, for example, use one tax rate for local commerce and a higher rate for interstate commerce if there is no essential difference between the two classes. *Nippert v. City of Richmond* (1946).

Example: A Florida statute prohibiting out-of-state banks, bank holding companies and trust companies from owning or controlling businesses selling advisory services violates the Commerce Clause. Since only out-of-state banking interests were subject to the regulation, it was discriminatory. There was no showing that this disparate treatment was only an incidental product resulting from furthering legitimate local concerns. *Lewis v. BT Investment Managers, Inc.* (1980).

c. Due Process

In order for a state to levy a tax on an interstate concern, the taxpayer must have a taxable situs in the state. *Minimum Connection*—If a state seeks contribution from a person, the Fourteenth Amendment Due Process Clause requires some benefit to justify the burden, i.e., some definable link, some minimum connection (jurisdictional contacts) between the taxpayer and the taxing state. The taxing formula used must be reasonable "in relation to the opportunities which [the state] has given, to protection which it has afforded, to benefits which it has conferred." *Wisconsin v. J. C. Penney Co.* (1940).

d. Interstate Commerce

1) "Multiple Burdens"

Since a taxpayer frequently acquires more than one taxable situs, there is a danger of an excessive burden on interstate commerce if each state is allowed to impose an unapportioned tax. Interstate commerce would be placed at a competitive disadvantage to local competition.

2) Apportionment

The taxing state must apportion its tax to reflect the extent of the taxable situs the taxpayer has acquired with the taxing state.

2. MODERN APPLICATIONS

Even a state tax nominally imposed on the "privilege of doing business" which is applied to the taxpayer doing interstate business may be constitutional if it satisfies the *Complete Auto Transit, Inc. v. Brady* test. The Court's modern focus is increasingly on the actual economic effects of the state tax.

a. The court will determine if there are local activities severable from the interstate transaction of which they are a part. The tax must be nondiscriminatory and reflect the benefits provided the taxpayer by the taxing state.

Examples: (1) A state severance tax on each ton of coal mined in the state was held constitutional, using the four-part *Complete Auto Transit* test. Since the act of severance occurs in

Montana and no other state could tax that local activity, the first two parts are satisfied. Since the tax is computed at the same rate regardless of the final destination of the coal, it was not discriminatory. Finally, because the tax is measured as a percentage of the coal mined, it reflects the taxpayer's activities within the state and thus is fairly related to the services provided by the state. *Commonwealth Edison Co. v. Montana* (1981).

(2) A state levied a tax upon photography galleries and persons engaged in photography. If the photography business was conducted "at a fixed location," the tax in large cities was $25 a year for each county, town or city. For each "transient or traveling photographer," the tax is $5 per week for each county, town or city in which he works. The tax was deemed to be valid because the local activity of photography which was made the nominal subject of the tax was not such an integral part of the flow of interstate commerce that it could not be realistically separated from it. The essentially local character of the activity is emphasized by the intimate connection between appellant's photographers and the local stores in which they set up their temporary studios. Engaging in such local business may constitutionally be made subject to local taxation. *Dunbar-Stanley Studios, Inc. v. Alabama* (1969).

(3) A fairly apportioned and nondiscriminatory corporate franchise tax upon the "incident" of qualifying to carry on or carrying on business in the taxing state does not violate the Commerce Clause as applied to an interstate carrier who does no business in the state but who does employ persons in the state to inspect and maintain its local facilities. The taxpayer had voluntarily qualified to do business in the state, and gained benefits from the state for its local activities which were of value to the business, and thus could be required to pay its fair share. *Colonial Pipeline Co. v. Traigle* (1975).

(4) A New Jersey "add-back" tax provision preventing oil companies from deducting federal windfall profit taxes on oil production outside the state in computing their New Jersey business income tax does not violate the *Complete Auto Transit* test. The state has a "substantial nexus" with oil production occurring outside the state since all of the taxpayer's New Jersey operations were part of an integrated unitary business which included oil production. The tax was

fairly apportioned, based on in-state property, receipts and payroll, having already received Supreme Court approval. The tax does not discriminate against companies operating in interstate commerce; any difference in the effect of the tax was due to the nature of the business, not the location of the activities. There was no pressure on companies to locate more activities in New Jersey. Finally, there was "no doubt" that the tax was fairly related to the benefits New Jersey provides to the company. *Amerada Hess Corp. v. Director* (1989).

b.   States may not assess taxes on out-of-state businesses by methods which discriminate against interstate commerce.

The Commerce Clause prohibits a state from imposing taxes placing a much heavier burden on out-of-state businesses that compete in an interstate market than it imposes on its own residents who also engage in interstate commerce.

Examples: (1) A state, through a business and occupation tax, taxed the gross receipts of all manufacturing with the state but only those manufacturers selling their product outside the state were required to pay the tax. Those selling products within the state were exempt if they paid the state gross receipts tax on wholesale and retail selling. As a result, through payment of either the wholesaling or retailing tax, the manufacturer selling goods within the state gained an exemption from the state manufacturing tax. However, companies doing interstate business received no such manufacturing tax exemption from the state when paying business taxes in other states. In such circumstances, a state's manufacturing tax imposed on products manufactured in the state that are sold out of state but not on products manufactured and sold within the state discriminates against interstate commerce in violation of the Commerce Clause. *Tyler Pipe Industries, Inc. v. Washington State Department of Revenue* (1987).

(2) Two successive state statutes imposed lump sum annual taxes on the operation of trucks on the state's highways. One state statute imposed an annual per axle fee on trucks weighing over 26,000 pounds. However, the law fell almost exclusively on truckers not based within the state because in-state truckers were given a corresponding reduction in registration costs. An earlier state law had imposed an annual fee on trucks that were registered outside the state

which weighed more than 17,000 pounds and used the state's highways. No fees were imposed on trucks registered within the state. Both statutes were held to unduly discriminate against interstate commerce. The Court pointed out that the administrative machinery for revenue collection for highways should take into account "at least the gross variations in cost per unit of highway usage" between state-based and out-of-state-based carriers. *American Trucking Associations, Inc. v. Scheiner* (1987).

C. REVIEW QUESTIONS

1. T or F   The plenary power of Congress over interstate commerce precludes state regulation of such commerce.

2. T or F   In the absence of congressional legislation, states are free to regulate interstate commerce.

3. T or F   State regulation which purposefully favors local economic interests against out-of-state concerns is permissible under the Commerce Clause if it is reasonably related to a valid state interest.

4. T or F   When a state law is discriminatory in means or effect, a state must use any less burdensome alternatives available.

5. T or F   A state law which does not discriminate against interstate commerce will not be held invalid under the Commerce Clause.

6. T or F   State highway laws are presumed to be valid in spite of the negative implications doctrine but factual balancing may result in their invalidity.

7. T or F   Under contemporary Commerce Clause decisions a state may discriminate in favor of its own citizens when it acts as a participant in the marketplace.

8. T or F   State discrimination against out-of-state citizens does not violate the Art. IV, § 2, Privileges and Immunities Clause, unless fundamental national interests are involved.

9. T or F   If a state cuts and sells timber from its own lands, it may choose to sell only to its own citizens without violating the Commerce Clause.

10. T or F   State taxation of business concerns is prohibited by the Commerce Clause.

11. T or F A state tax on the "privilege of doing business" in the state imposed on an out-of-state business is unconstitutional.

12. The state of Montana imposes a substantial severance tax on each ton of coal mined in the state regardless of the coal's destination. Which of the following is most accurate?

    a. The tax is unconstitutional because of the economic costs to out-of-state users.

    b. The tax discriminates against interstate commerce and is, therefore, unconstitutional.

    c. The tax is constitutional even though it imposes an excessive burden on out-of-state businesses.

    d. The tax is constitutional since the tax is on the local act of severance, is nondiscriminatory, and reflects the services provided by the state.

13. T or F When Congress regulates in a field, state regulation in the same field is preempted.

14. T or F Congress cannot authorize the states to regulate in a manner that would violate the Dormant Commerce Clause.

15. Which of the following factors are considered in determining if a federal law is intended to preempt state law?

    a. The pervasiveness of the federal law.

    b. The need for uniformity.

    c. The potential for administrative conflict.

    d. The existence of a federal regulatory agency.

    e. All of the above.

16. During the 1973 oil embargo, the state of West Lincoln conducted a study which showed that gasoline stations operated by producers or refiners received preferential treatment in terms of oil supplies during this scarcity. As a result, the West Lincoln legislature enacted a law which prohibits producers or refiners from operating retail service stations within West Lincoln. Furthermore, producers or refiners now are required in West Lincoln to extend all "voluntary allowances" uniformly to all stations that are supplied. Colossal Oil Company, one of the nation's largest producers and refiners, has brought

suit in the federal district court in West Lincoln on the ground that the state law is unreasonable and will frustrate rather than enhance competition. Colossal Oil also argued that the West Lincoln scheme discriminated against out-of-state competitors in favor of in-state independent dealers, since the burden of the legislation fell on interstate companies which will have to divest themselves of their West Lincoln service stations. Is the West Lincoln legislation constitutional? Why or why not?

*

IV

CONGRESS AND EXECUTIVE POWER

Analysis

A. The Domestic Arena
B. The Foreign Arena
C. Privileges and Immunities
D. Review Questions

Art. II, § 1, vests the Executive Power in the President of the United States. It has never been determined whether this Vestiture Clause is itself a separate source of power, only a reference to all Art. II powers, or a reference to the Framer's choice of a single rather than a plural Executive. In any case, the modern presidency has broad domestic and foreign affairs powers. He is Head of State, Chief Executive, Chief Legislator, and Commander-in-Chief. But in examining the constitutional place of the Executive in our separation of powers system, keep in mind the wide gap between the President's paper powers and his real powers. A reading of the Constitution provides only a shadow of the modern presidency.

Most of the express executive powers are vague and lie in areas where power is shared with Congress. What happens when the executive and congressional exercises come into conflict? In the past, the tide of power has tended to flow to the Executive. But Congress has been trying to stem the tide by enacting laws which at least ostensibly seek to promote Executive responsibility and accountability. This may be due, in part, to the fact that the Branches are controlled by different parties. The question is whether such laws unconstitutionally invade the constitutional prerogative of the Executive or usurp powers properly shared by the other Branches.

In answering the question, the Court at times adopts a formalist approach. This approach stresses a stricter emphasis on constitutional text and on a strict separation of powers between the Branches. At other times, the Court adopts a more functional approach stressing the interrelation of the Branches and the need for checks and balances. Constitutional text tends to be downplayed and the focus is on the balancing of competing interests.

A. THE DOMESTIC ARENA

1. EXECUTIVE LAW–MAKING

a. Limited Domestic Law-Making Powers
The President has no inherent domestic law-making powers, at least in the absence of extreme emergency. In emergencies, his power as Chief Executive under Art. II, § 1, and his power to "take care that the laws be faithfully executed," (Art. II, § 3), do appear to create some power to act subject to congressional authority.

Example: The seizure of the steel mills by President Truman to avert a crippling strike during the Korean War was held unconstitutional since Congress had previously legislated regarding the scope of executive power to curtail strikes. Art. I gives Congress the power to make law. A majority of the Justices indicated that, in the absence of such a specific congressional negative, the President would have independent power to act in an emergency. *Youngstown Sheet & Tube Co. v. Sawyer* (1952).

b. Veto Power

1) A bill passed by Congress and signed by the President is law. If the President refuses to sign, he returns it to Congress with a statement of objections. Congress may make the bill law by a two-thirds vote of both houses. Art. I, § 7.

2) Pocket Veto. The President has ten days to determine if he will veto a bill or it automatically becomes law unless Congress by its adjournment prevents its return. The President is thus able to "pocket veto" a bill by not acting on it prior to adjournment. While a brief recess is not an adjournment [*Wright v. United States* (1938)], the nature of an adjournment permitting use of the pocket veto has not been judicially determined.

2. EXECUTIVE IMPOUNDMENT

The President impounds when he withholds or delays the expenditure of congressionally appropriated funds. This may defeat a congressional program or policy.

a. Justification

It is argued that such impoundment is justified by statutorily-imposed budgetary constraints in the light of the constitutional mandate that the President should faithfully execute the laws.

b. Critique

Conversely, it is claimed that such frustration of a congressional program or policy violates Congress' power to make the law and hence the separation of powers principle. Further, it arguably constitutes an executive veto in a manner not prescribed by the Constitution. The Supreme Court has not yet ruled on the constitutionality of impoundment. Congress has enacted legislation limiting the executive power to impound. The constitutionality of such a restraint on executive power has not been judicially tested. The decision of the Court in *Chadha,* discussed below, raises serious doubt as to the validity of the provisions in the impoundment legislation embodying a legislative veto of executive deferral of expenditures.

3. DELEGATION AND CONTROL OF LEGISLATIVE POWER

a. Legislative Delegation

Much executive law-making results from conscious congressional delegation of legislative power. Such delegation is constitutional provided Congress exercises the essentials of the legislative function by determining policy and formulating reasonable standards to guide the exercise of executive discretion. The courts have generally exercised restraint and deferred to Congress in reviewing the adequacy of such standards.

Example: (1) Congressional legislation creating the United States Sentencing Commission in the Judicial Branch and delegating to it power to formulate Sentencing Guidelines binding on the courts does not violate the Separation of Powers Principle. The Act set forth the policies and principles governing Commission operations and provides specific directives to govern formulation of the Guidelines. There was, therefore, no violation of the nondelegation doctrine.

Delegation of some rulemaking authority to a Commission located in the Judicial Branch does not violate separation of powers if it does not intrude on the prerogatives of another Branch and is appropriate to the central mission of the Judiciary. Setting sentencing policy is a shared responsibility of the Branches and the Judiciary has always played a role.

The fact that Art. III judges serve on a Commission with nonadjudicatory functions does not violate separation of powers. Art. III judges may perform extrajudicial duties if such service does not "undermine the integrity of the Judicial Branch." Nor does the fact that the President appoints and removes members of the Commission for good cause pose a sufficient threat to judicial independence to violate separation of powers. *Mistretta v. United States* (1989).

b. The Legislative Veto

One method by which Congress has sought to achieve executive accountability in exercise of broad delegated power is the legislative veto. Congress delegates power to the Executive but reserves authority to review and veto executive action taken pursuant to the grant. The Supreme Court has held that such a veto is legislative action violative of the Art. I, § 7, separation of powers requirements of Bicameralism and Presentment.

Example: In the Immigration and Naturalization Act, Congress delegated authority to the Attorney General to suspend deportation of aliens. However, Congress reserved control over executive action by allowing either House to review and veto the suspension order. This legislative veto violates the Presentment Clause which requires legislation be presented to the President for approval or veto. The one House veto also violates Bicameralism (Art. I, §§ 1, 7), requiring that both houses exact a measure in order for it to become a law. The veto in this case was "legislative" in both purpose and effect in that it altered "legal rights, duties and relations of persons." Thus, the structural requirements of Art. I, designed to preserve checks and maintain the separation of powers must be followed. The veto provision is severable from the remainder of the Act and is unconstitutional. *Immigration and Naturalization Service v. Chadha* (1983).

4. THE APPOINTMENT AND REMOVAL POWER

a. The Appointment Power

Art. II, § 2, cl. 2, provides that the President "shall nominate, and by and with the advice and consent of the Senate, shall appoint Ambassadors, other public Ministers and Consuls, Judges of the Supreme Court, and all other Officers of the United States, whose appointments are not herein otherwise provided for, and which shall be established by law, but the Congress may by law vest the Appointment of such inferior Officers, as they think proper, in the President alone, in the Courts of Law, or in the Heads of Departments."

1) *Congress may not vest the Appointment Power in persons other than those specified in Art. II, § 2, cl. 2.*

> ***Example:*** A majority of the voting members of the Federal Election Commission were appointed by the President pro tem of the Senate and the Speaker of the House. Neither the Speaker of the House, nor the President pro tem of the Senate comes within the terms "Courts of Law" or "Heads of Departments" as required by Art. II, § 2, cl. 2. The power given to Congress under the Twelfth Amendment to regulate parties in connection with presidential elections does not permit Congress to create a federal commission to regulate such elections in a manner violative of the appointments clause. Accordingly, except in the case of its investigatory and informative power, Congress in permitting the Commission to exercise administrative and law enforcement powers violated Art. II, § 2, cl. 2. *Buckley v. Valeo* (1976).

2) *Whether an officer is a principal or inferior officer depends on a functional analysis of the extent to which there is subordination or independence, the scope of the officer's jurisdiction and the extent of the functions performed.* If the officer is an inferior officer, interbranch appointments are permissible unless it impairs the ability of a Branch to perform its functions or is incongruous.

> *Example:* Congressional legislation vesting the appointment of independent counsel to investigate and prosecute executive officials in a Special Division of the U.S. Court of Appeals does not violate the Appointments Clause. The independent counsel is an "inferior officer." She is subject to removal for good cause by the Attorney General and has a limited jurisdiction. She performs only limited duties of investigation and prosecution, and does not make general policy. The office is limited in tenure to the completion of the appointed task. *Morrison v. Olson* (1988).

b. The Removal Power
1) Executive Removal

The scope of the President's power to remove executive officials has turned on whether the official was deemed a "purely executive" official or an official who exercised "quasi-legislative" or "quasi-judicial" powers. In the former case, the President had exercised unfettered removal power. In the latter case, the removal power was subject to congressional restrictions. The Court recently has cast doubt on excessive use of these "rigid categories" to define the removal power. *While accepting the relevance of the categories, the Court emphasized a functional approach focusing on "whether the removal restrictions are of such a nature that they impede the President's ability to perform his constitutional duty."* Morrison v. Olson (1988).

> *Example:* The provision of the Ethics in Government Act that the Attorney General can remove an independent counsel only for good cause is not of such a nature as to interfere impermissibly with the President's constitutional obligation to ensure the faithful execution of the laws. Law enforcement functions are executive functions. But, the President's need to control the exercise of discretion of the independent counsel, an "inferior official" with limited jurisdiction, tenure and power, is not so central to the functioning of the Executive Branch as to require as a matter of constitutional law that counsel be terminable at will by the President. Counsel can still be removed for misconduct. Independence could be achieved only by limiting the removal power. Congress has not sought to usurp any added role in the removal of executive officials. *Morrison v. Olson* (1988).

2) Congressional Removal
Congress may not constitutionally vest executive functions in officials who are subject to removal by Congress by means other than impeachment.

Example: Provisions of the Gramm-Rudman Act vesting in the Comptroller General authority to specify spending reductions binding on the President violate the separation of powers. The Act vests executive functions in the Comptroller since he has the ultimate authority to determine the budget cuts to be made; he interprets and implements the legislative mandate and this constitutes execution of the laws. The Comptroller is an agent of Congress since by earlier legislation he is removable for designated, but broadly-phrased, causes (*e.g.*, inefficiency, neglect of duty). This allows removal for transgressing of the legislative will. By retaining in its own agent control over the execution of the Gramm-Rudman Act, Congress intruded into executive functions in violation of separation of powers. *Bowsher v. Synar* (1986).

5. SEPARATION OF POWERS GENERALLY
Apart from the specific contexts discussed above, the Court will often examine the separation of powers question generally. *The Court examines the degree of intrusion on the constitutional functions of the other Branch and the extent to which the challenged actions consolidate powers that should properly be shared.* Balancing of the competing interests is the dominant methodology.

Example: The Ethics in Government Act, providing for the appointment of independent counsel to investigate and prosecute high executive officials, taken as a whole, does not unduly interfere with the role of the Executive Branch. Nor is there any congressional usurpation of any Executive Branch functions. The Attorney General has sole and unreviewable power to request the appointment of the independent counsel. He retains several means for supervising and controlling the independent counsel's prosecutorial powers. He may remove the independent counsel for good cause. While the counsel is to some degree independent and freer from Executive supervision than most federal prosecutors, the Act provides the Executive Branch "sufficient control * * * to ensure that the President is able to perform his constitutionally assigned duties." *Morrison v. Olson* (1988).

B. THE FOREIGN ARENA

The respective roles of Congress and the Executive in the exercise of foreign affairs and the war powers remain unclear. The Court in *United States v. Curtiss-Wright Export Corp.* (1936) spoke of inherent foreign affairs powers vested in the national government and suggested an executive primacy in their exercise. The Constitution, however, provides a wide range of express and implied foreign affairs powers to each branch. Whatever the source of the national foreign powers, their distribution has yet to receive a consistent and clear judicial definition. A few items should be noted. Congress has broad discretion to vest foreign affairs powers in the Executive. Since foreign affairs and the war powers are exclusive, states have a very limited role to play. Finally, remember that the political question doctrine plays an especially important role in the foreign affairs arena, inviting judicial avoidance of constitutional questions.

1. FOREIGN AFFAIRS
a. Presidential Powers
The President has power to receive Ambassadors and other public ministers (Art. II, § 3), to recognize or withdraw recognition of foreign governments, and to act on behalf of the United States in day to day dealings with foreign governments. This is augmented by his role as Commander-in-Chief.

b. Congressional Powers
Congress has express authority to regulate foreign commerce, to fashion a uniform rule of naturalization, to raise and maintain armies and to declare war as well as the vital power to tax and spend.

c. Shared Powers
The power to determine foreign policy then is arguably a shared power, although the executive has become dominant. The executive control of information and its ability for quick response gives it an advantage in this area. When the Executive acts with congressional authorization, its constitutional powers are maximized. When it acts contrary to congressional action, its powers are at their lowest. *Youngstown Sheet & Tube Co. v. Sawyer* (1952) (Jackson, J., concurring).

> ***Example:*** In his Executive Order nullifying attachments on Iranian assets and transferring Iranian assets the President acted within his statutory authority. Prior legislation reflects a congressional purpose to put control of foreign assets in the hands of the President for use in negotiating the resolution of a declared national emergency. With respect to his order suspending claims against Iran in U.S. courts, congressional acquiescence in past presidential action supports such authority. Past practice does not by itself create power but

"long continued practice known to and acquiesced in by Congress raises a presumption that the action has been taken in pursuance to its consent." When the President acts on a vital issue of foreign affairs with congressional approval and authorization, his constitutional power is maximized. *Dames and Moore v. Regan* (1981).

2. TREATIES AND EXECUTIVE AGREEMENTS

a. Treaties

The President has the power to make treaties with the advice and consent of the Senate provided that two-thirds of the senators present concur.

b. Executive Agreements

Executive Agreements do not require Senate concurrence. While Congress is often consulted concerning such agreements, this is not required. While there is no express constitutional authority for such agreements, their legality is now established. *United States v. Belmont* (1937).

c. Supremacy

Art. VI provides that all treaties which are made "under the authority of the United States" are the supreme law of the land. They prevail, as do Executive Agreements, over inconsistent state law. Treaties and Executive Agreements are subject to constitutional limitations. *Reid v. Covert* (1957). Treaties and Acts of Congress are on a par, i.e., the last in time controls. *Chinese Exclusion Cases* (1889).

d. Self-Executing Treaties

Some treaties are self-executing and do not require congressional implementing legislation. Congressional legislation, which would not be constitutional otherwise, is constitutional when it reasonably implements a treaty.

> *Example:* Legislation implementing a treaty with Canada regulating the movement of migratory birds was held constitutional even though the Court had previously indicated that the Commerce Clause was not a source of power for the legislation. *Missouri v. Holland* (1920).

3. THE WAR POWER

a. Shared Power

1) Congress has the power to declare war, to create and regulate the armed forces, and to provide for the general defense. From these express powers are implied broad powers to prepare for war (*e.g.,* to assure electricity, to register and draft), to regulate during wartime (*e.g.,* economic controls, Japanese-American internment in World War

II), and to remedy wartime disruptions (*e.g.,* veteran's benefits, rent controls).

2) The President is Commander-in-Chief but the scope of this power is not clear. An executive claim of national security does not justify an injunction against newspaper publication of classified material, at least in the absence of congressional authorization or a direct, immediate, and irreparable damage to the Nation. *New York Times Co. v. United States* (1971).

b. Declaring and Making War
Since Congress has the constitutional power to declare war (Art. I, § 8), the President cannot formally initiate a "war." But, as Commander-in-Chief (Art. II, § 2), the President has power to repel sudden attack, to make war, and to control the disposition of our armed forces. These powers may often be used in such a way that the country may be committed to hostilities.

1) War Powers Resolution
   Congress has enacted a War Powers Resolution which seeks to limit executive power to engage the armed forces in hostilities. Sixty days after the President is required to report the use of the armed forces, such use shall terminate unless Congress affirmatively acts. Whether the War Powers Resolution is an unconstitutional delegation of Congress' power to declare war or excessively intrudes on the President's power as Commander-in-Chief, his duty to execute the laws and his status as Chief Executive, has not been judicially determined. The constitutionality of the legislative veto provision of the War Powers Resolution is in doubt as a result of *Chadha.*

C. The Militia Clauses
The Militia Clauses of Art. I, § 8, cls. 15 & 16, do not limit the war powers of Congress. Instead they are additional grants of power to Congress. The Clauses recognize the supremacy of federal power in the areas of military affairs.

Example: The "Montgomery Amendment" which provides that the consent of the Governor of a state is not required for assignment to duty outside the United States of the State National Guard called to active service, is constitutionally valid. *Perpich v. Department of Defense* (1990).

C. PRIVILEGES AND IMMUNITIES

1. EXECUTIVE PRIVILEGE
While nowhere expressly mentioned, the need for candor and objectivity in confidential communications has been held to give rise to a privilege against

disclosure which is constitutionally based. It is based on the separation of powers principle and flows from the need to implement the powers enumerated in Art. II.

a.   Limitations

However, this privilege, at least in the domestic sphere, is not absolute and may yield when the proven need for disclosure is sufficiently great. While a claim of privilege for confidential communication by the President is presumptively privileged, it is the duty of the judiciary to determine if sufficient need has been demonstrated by the party seeking disclosure.

b.   Unsettled Areas

The treatment of claims of executive privilege for military, diplomatic or sensitive national security matters, or the claim of privilege against congressional demands for information, have not yet been determined by the Supreme Court.

Example: President Nixon's claim of privilege for tapes and other materials relating to Watergate from disclosure to a grand jury for use in a criminal proceeding was held subject to judicial review. The generalized interest in confidentiality did not prevail over the fundamental demands of the fair administration of criminal justice to prevent *in camera* judicial determination of what materials were relevant to the criminal proceedings and what should remain confidential. *United States v. Nixon* (1974).

2.   IMPEACHMENT

a.   Grounds

Art. II, § 4, provides that "[t]he President, Vice-President and all civil Officers of the United States, shall be removed from Office on Impeachment for, and Conviction of Treason, Bribery, or other high Crimes and Misdemeanors."

b.   Procedure

The House of Representatives has the sole power to impeach (Art. I, § 2) and the Senate the sole power to try impeachments (Art. I, § 3). Conviction requires the concurrence of two-thirds of the members present. The Chief Justice presides when the President is tried.

c.   Unsettled Questions

Whether "High Crimes and Misdemeanors" is limited to criminal offenses or includes some acts of political maladministration or failure to discharge the constitutional duties of the office has not been judicially determined since Richard Nixon resigned from office while impeachment charges were pending. Moreover, while Andrew Johnson was impeached, he was not convicted by the Senate. As a result, the full meaning of the clause "High Crimes and Misdemeanors" has yet to be resolved.

3. PRESIDENTIAL IMMUNITY

a. A civil damages suit cannot be maintained against the President for action taken while in office that is within the "outside perimeter" of his official responsibility. The President's unique role in the constitutional scheme demands that he be free to vigorously execute the duties of his office without the distraction of civil suits. Consequently, he is accorded absolute immunity from damages for all action taken under any of his broad areas of constitutional authority. Other measures, including congressional oversight, impeachment, and scrutiny by the press still exist to deter presidential misconduct. *Nixon v. Fitzgerald* (1982).

b. Presidential aides generally have only a qualified immunity—they are subject to liability only for violation of clearly established constitutional or statutory rights which would have been known by a reasonable person. *Harlow v. Fitzgerald* (1982). The Attorney General enjoys only a qualified immunity even when performing national security functions. *Mitchell v. Forsyth* (1985).

4. CONGRESSIONAL IMMUNITY

a. Art. I, § 6, provides immunity for members of Congress "for any Speech or Debate in either House." Legislative aides enjoy immunity when performing acts for which a member would be immune.

b. Only "legislative acts," *i.e.*, matters which are "an integral part of the deliberative and communicating processes" by which Congress acts are protected. *Gravel v. United States* (1972).

> *Example:* Neither Senator Gravel nor his aide could be questioned or prosecuted for reading portions of the Pentagon Papers into the public record at a subcommittee meeting. Immunity also extended to preprations for the meeting. However, arrangements between Senator Gravel and a private publisher to publish the Papers was not an immune legislative act. *Gravel v. United States* (1972).

D. REVIEW QUESTIONS

1. T or F The President has inherent domestic law making power.

2. T or F There is a constitutionally based executive privilege against disclosure.

3. T or F The President is free to remove any public official he selects.

4. T or F   Foreign affairs powers are shared powers.

5. T or F   Executive agreements, even when made without congressional consultation, prevail over state law.

6. T or F   Under the Constitution, Congress has the exclusive power to declare war.

7. T or F   The President can be made to answer in civil damages for his wrongful acts even if committed in an area of his constitutional authority.

8. Which of the following is the most accurate?

    a.   The President has absolute executive privilege.

    b.   The Court engages in ad hoc balancing in assessing a claim of executive privilege.

    c.   A claim of executive privilege is presumptively valid.

    d.   It is for Congress to finally resolve whether a claim of executive privilege should prevail.

9. Which of the following is most accurate?

    a.   Members of Congress enjoy absolute immunity from criminal prosecution.

    b.   Legislative aides do not share in legislative immunity.

    c.   Only acts pursuant to the legislative process are immune.

    d.   Art. I, § 6, does not provide any protection to members of Congress from criminal prosecution for bribery and fraud.

10. In the original legislation creating the Federal Election Commission, Congress provided that a majority of the voting members of the Commission should be appointed by the President pro tem of the Senate and the Speaker of the House. The selection procedure mandated by this legislation was challenged on the ground that it was unconstitutional. Was it?

*

PART TWO

INDIVIDUAL RIGHTS AND LIBERTIES: CONSTITUTIONAL LIMITATIONS ON GOVERNMENTAL POWER

Analysis

V

PRIVILEGES AND IMMUNITIES OF NATIONAL CITIZENSHIP

Analysis

A. Background
B. Definition and Scope
C. Review Questions

INDIVIDUAL RIGHTS IN THE ORIGINAL CONSTITUTION:
The allocation of governmental power discussed above is only one method of limiting government power. Specific enumeration of individual rights and liberties is another. The original Constitution contained a few such specific provisions such as the prohibition against Ex Post Facto laws and Bills of Attainder [Arts. I, §§ 9 and 10], suspension of Writs of Habeas Corpus except in cases of rebellion or invasion [Art. I, § 9], the use of religious tests as a qualification for public office [Art. IV, § 2].

BILL OF RIGHTS:
One of the acts of the first Congress was to initiate the enactment of ten amendments to the Constitution, popularly called the Bill of Rights. These amendments were designed to protect the individual from various infringements on freedom which might emanate from the newly created federal government.

SUBSEQUENT AMENDMENTS:
The Constitution has subsequently been enlarged to a total of twenty-six amendments protecting the individual against abuses from state, national, and in some instances, private action. The focus of this part of the outline is on the guarantees in the First, Thirteenth, Fourteenth, and Fifteenth Amendments.

A. BACKGROUND

1. UNENUMERATED RIGHTS

Despite some contrary judicial opinion, the Court has rejected the idea that there are extra-constitutional "natural rights" limiting governmental power. If Congress exercises one of its delegated powers or the states exercise their reserved powers, some express or implied constitutional provision must be found if the government act is to be held unconstitutional.

2. BILL OF RIGHTS

The Court has held that the Bill of Rights operates only on the federal government, not on the states. *Barron v. Baltimore* (1833). There was, therefore, a felt need for finding some constitutional provision which could be used against abuses of state governmental power.

B. DEFINITION AND SCOPE

1. THE SLAUGHTERHOUSE CASES

In the *Slaughterhouse Cases* (1873), the Supreme Court definitively held that the Privileges and Immunities Clause of the Fourteenth Amendment did not make the Bill of Rights applicable to the states.

a. Function of the Clause

It was held in the Slaughterhouse Cases that the sole function of the Privileges and Immunities Clause of the Fourteenth Amendment was to protect the rights secured to individuals in their relationship to the federal government, i.e., in their capacity as federal citizens. The fairly narrow list of rights of federal citizenship secured by the Privileges and Immunities Clause of the Fourteenth Amendment was declared to include the following rights: (a) to petition Congress; (b) to peaceably assemble; (c) to use the Writ of Habeas Corpus; (d) to use the navigable waters of the United States; (e) to claim the benefits secured by treaties with foreign nations; (f) the right to interstate travel; (g) to claim the rights secured by the Thirteenth and Fifteenth Amendments; and (h) the right to vote in federal elections.

b. Rationale

The Court in the *Slaughterhouse Cases* reflected federalism values in rejecting the view that the Privileges and Immunities Clause was intended to make all the fundamental rights traditionally protected by state law into federal constitutional rights which could be protected in federal court.

2. ENDURANCE OF THE NARROW VIEW

This limited interpretation of the Privileges and Immunities Clause of the Fourteenth Amendment dashed the hopes of those who sought to use the clause to protect fundamental rights whenever endangered as a result of state action or inaction. Yet this narrow view has endured and the Privileges and Immunities Clause of the Fourteenth Amendment has failed to this day to be a wellspring of constitutional litigation except for the rights listed above, particularly the right to vote in federal elections and the right of interstate travel. Even the right of interstate movement has not been made to rest solely on the Privileges and Immunities Clause.

C. REVIEW QUESTIONS

1. **T or F** The Fourteenth Amendment Privileges and Immunities Clause protects essentially the same rights as the Due Process Clause.

2. Recently, a legislature of the state of West Lincoln enacted a statute stating that before a new entrant into the dry cleaning industry can be licensed, the State Board of Dry Cleaners must ascertain the "necessity" for the new entrant and find that the existing dry cleaning establishments in the state "are not adequate to meet the public needs." Kris Kleen wants to go into the dry cleaning business in the state of West Lincoln. He has consulted a lawyer. His lawyer thinks that the statute is constitutionally invalid on a number of grounds. He thinks that the statute is particularly vulnerable because he believes it violates the Privileges and Immunities Clause of the

Fourteenth Amendment. Kris Kleen's lawyer has filed suit in the appropriate state court. He alleges that the right to choose one's calling is one of the privileges and immunities of United States citizenship protected by the Fourteenth Amendment. Is he right?

VI

DUE PROCESS OF LAW

Analysis

A. TRADITIONAL SUBSTANTIVE DUE PROCESS

The failure of the Fourteenth Amendment Privileges and Immunities Clause as a substantive limit on state police power left few significant constitutional impediments on state power, *e.g.*, provisions against impairment of contract obligations, and against Bills of Attainder. During the last part of the nineteenth century, the Court began to strike down state social and economic legislation as unreasonably interfering with the liberty and property rights guaranteed by the Fourteenth Amendment Due Process Clause. Federal socio-economic legislation was similarly invalidated under the Fifth Amendment Due Process Clause.

The exercise of judicial review in this area intruded substantive economic concepts such as freedom of contract and the principles of free market economics into the process of due process interpretation, hence the description, substantive due process. Reaction against large-scale Court invalidation of social and economic legislation gradually produced judicial restraint and a new deference to the legislative judgment in economic matters and finally today to almost total judicial abdication with respect to due process challenges to economic legislation.

1. IMPAIRMENT OF OBLIGATION OF CONTRACT
a. Constitutional Text
Art. I, § 10, provides that "no state shall * * * pass any * * * law impairing the obligation of contract." While there is no comparable clause applicable to the federal government, the Fifth Amendment Due Process Clause guarantees procedural fairness which would bar unreasonable impairment of substantive vested legal rights. Fifth Amendment review has been characterized by the Court as "less searching" then review under the Contract Clause.

b. Present Scope
By giving a broad construction to the concept of "contract," courts could invalidate state police power measures. During most of the twentieth century, the clause has been accorded only limited importance, but recently, the Court has revived it.

c. Judicial Construction
The guarantee applies only against legislative (not judicial) action impairing substantive legal rights (not procedures for enforcement of contracts). While both private and public contracts are protected, the state may reserve the power to subsequently revise its licenses and other contracts.

1) Private Contracts
In the case of private contracts, a challenger must initially establish that the law substantially impairs pre-existing contractual relationships. If this threshold is met, the government must demonstrate that the law imposes

reasonable conditions appropriate to achieving a significant and legitimate public purpose.

A severe impairment will be particularly vulnerable (1) if it is not designed to deal with a broad generalized economic or social problem, (2) if it is a permanent rather than a temporary impairment, (3) if the area regulated has never before been subject to regulation by the state, and (4) if the impairment in question has an extremely narrow focus. *Allied Structural Steel Company v. Spannaus* (1978) (state statute providing for vesting of employee pension rights if an employer closes a facility in the state or terminates a pension program held unconstitutional).

> **Example:** A state law imposing price controls on interstate natural gas sales, and retroactively prohibiting application of private contract clauses allowing (1) price escalation if the government fixes prices at higher than the contract price and (2) redetermination of prices, does not violate the Contract Clause.
>
>> First, the state act does not meet the threshold test since it does not operate as a substantial impairment of the contractual relationship. The heavily-regulated character of the natural gas industry and the inclusion of the contract clauses indicate that the parties knew that their contractual rights were subject to price regulation. Even assuming the Act substantially impaired the contractual relation, the Act was a reasonable means of achieving the significant and legitimate public purposes of protecting consumers from the escalation of prices caused by deregulation and preventing imbalances in intrastate and interstate markets. The Act's prohibitions are limited to the context posing the greatest dangers from price escalation. *Energy Reserves Group, Inc. v. Kansas Power & Light Co.* (1983).

2) Public Contracts
In the case of public contracts, (1) the state may reserve the power to subsequently revise its licenses and other contracts; (2) a state may not abandon its sovereign power to legislate for the public health, safety, and well-being by a contract and if it does so then any such contract is invalid; and (3) while the state may contract away its financial powers, it may impair such contracts if this is reasonable and necessary to serve important state interests.

>   ***Example:*** State statutes repealing a statutory covenant made by the
>   two states limiting the ability of the Port Authority of
>   New York and New Jersey to subsidize rail passenger
>   transportation from revenues and reserves violates the
>   Contract Clause. The repeal on the limitation eliminated
>   an important security provision of bondholders and thus
>   impaired the obligation of the state's contract. In this
>   instance the repeal was not necessary to encourage users
>   of private automobiles to shift to public transportation,
>   and it was not reasonable in light of any changed
>   circumstances since the contract was entered into. *United
>   States Trust Co. of New York v. New Jersey* (1977).

2. BILLS OF ATTAINDER
a. Constitutional Text
Art. I, § 9 prohibits Congress from enacting Bills of Attainder and Art. I, § 10 contains a similar prohibition directed to the states. In a sense, a Bill of Attainder is a specific illustration in the Constitution of the separation of powers principle, *i.e.*, punishment is a judicial and not a legislative function.

b. Punishment Without Trial
Functionally, the Bill of Attainder clauses prohibit the legislature from punishing individuals without the benefit of judicial trial. The meaning of punishment in this context is not limited to imprisonment.

3. THE TAKINGS CLAUSE
a. Definition
The federal and state governments have power to take private property for public use (eminent domain). The federal government must show that such a taking is authorized under its Art. I powers, *e.g.*, condemnation of land to build a post office under the postal power.

b. Constitutional Text
The Fifth Amendment provides that private property is not to be taken for public use without just compensation. A similar limitation is applicable to the states as part of Fourteenth Amendment due process.

c. Public Use
The courts will not generally review government policy decisions on what is a public use. If the taking is for a public purpose, this is sufficient.

d. "Taking"
A "taking" is not limited to condemnation of land but the mere fact that property values are diminished by government action does not create a "taking" of property. If a regulation is a reasonable exercise of governmental

power, even though it diminishes property values, it is probably not a compensable "taking," e.g., rezoning of permissible land uses. Factors considered include: (1) the economic impact of the regulation to the claimant; (2) the extent to which the regulation has interfered with distinct investment expectations; and, (3) the character of the governmental action, e.g., is there a physical occupation of the property. Where a regulation is subsequently overturned, even a temporary denial of all economic use of the property will constitute a "taking." Compensation for the period during which the use is denied is required. First English Evangelical Lutheran Church v. County of Los Angeles (1987).

Examples: (1) A municipal zoning ordinance, enacted after plaintiff's purchase of land, which limits the uses of the land is not a "taking" without just compensation in violation of the Fifth and Fourteenth Amendments. The ordinance, as interpreted, did not bar all residential uses. The ordinance substantially advanced the public's interest in avoiding the ill effects of urbanization by controlling land development. Plaintiffs share in the benefits and burdens of the controls. The ordinance neither prevents economically viable uses of the land nor extinguishes fundamental attributes of ownership. There has been no denial of "justice and fairness." *Agins v. City of Tiburon* (1980).

(2) A New York statute which requires owners of rental housing units to permit the installation of cable T.V. equipment on their property constitutes a state "taking" for which the owner is entitled to just compensation under the Fifth Amendment. Since the cable equipment is affixed to the building, there is a physical occupation which deprives the owner of his rights to possession, use, and disposition of his property. No balancing of interests is required. Requiring the property owner to install equipment such as smoke alarms, *which would be owned by the property owner* is distinguished. *Loretto v. Teleprompter Manhattan CATV Corp.* (1982).

(3) A Pennsylvania statute prohibiting mining of 50% of the coal beneath certain pre-existing public buildings, dwellings, and cemeteries in order to prevent damage to these structures does not constitute a state "taking" for which the owner is entitled to compensation. The owners of the mining rights are not denied economically viable use of their property. The Court deferred to the legislature's finding that mining damage posed a significant threat to the common welfare. The prohibition was a legitimate exercise of state police power,

narrowly tailored to its significant and legitimate purposes. *Keystone Bituminous Coal Association v. DeBenedictis* (1987).

(4) A state requirement that an ocean-front property owner grant a public easement across his property for beach users as a condition of securing a permit to rebuild a residence on the property is a compensable taking. Assuming that the state might have denied the permit if it reasonably determined that the proposed development would impair legitimate state interests, conditioning of the permit would be allowed only if it served the same governmental purpose as the ban. If it did serve that objective, it would be a reasonable regulation of land use rather than a compensable taking. *Nollan v. California Coastal Comm'n* (1987).

(5) A federal statute providing for a 1½% deduction from awards received by claimants from the Iran–United States Claims Tribunal does not violate the Fifth Amendment Takings Clause. The change was imposed in order to compensate the United States government for costs arising from the arbitration of claims and the maintenance of a Security Account for payment of awards. Since the fee was reasonable as reimbursement of the costs incurred and the claimant benefited from the Tribunal's existence and functions, the charge was a reasonable "user fee" rather than a "taking" of property requiring just compensation. *United States v. Sperry Corp.* (1989).

e. Just Compensation
Just compensation is measured by the loss to the owners of fair market value, and not gain to the government.

4. THE RISE AND FALL OF ECONOMIC SUBSTANTIVE DUE PROCESS
a. Rise of Economic Substantive Due Process
Prior to the New Deal, the courts used the Due Process Clauses of the Fifth and Fourteenth Amendments to invalidate a variety of federal and state social and economic laws as arbitrary and unreasonable interferences with the freedom to contract protected by the Due Process guarantees of liberty and property.

Example: In the heyday of economic substantive due process, the Supreme Court invalidated a state law setting maximum hours of employment for bakery employees on the ground that the statute unreasonably interfered with the right of contract between the employer and the employee. Freedom of contract was declared to be part of the liberty of the individual protected by the Fourteenth Amendment.

The Court probed the purpose of the law, questioning whether it was a police power measure designed to serve the general public interest or secure private public interests. Further, the Court closely scrutinized the reasonableness of the hours requirement as a means of promoting employees' health, holding the law to be an excessive burden on liberty. In a famous prophetic dissent, Mr. Justice Holmes insisted that constitutional interpretation should be governed, not by the economic theories of the justices, but by whether the legislative judgement was reasonable. *Lochner v. New York* (1905).

b. Decline of Economic Substantive Due Process

In the 1930s, in the face of rising adverse public reaction to judicial invalidation of the New Deal, the doctrine of economic substantive due process began to ebb in importance and the doctrine followed a process of steady decline and erosion.

Example: The Court upheld state legislation setting milk prices against a due process challenge. While the Court spoke of the milk industry as a business "affected with a public interest," this meant only that the law was a reasonable exercise of the police power. Questions concerning the wisdom of the law are for the legislature, not the courts. The Court's evaluation of the reasonableness of the regulation reflected deference to the legislative judgment. *Nebbia v. New York* (1934).

5. MODERN SUBSTANTIVE DUE PROCESS: NON–FUNDAMENTAL RIGHTS

RATIONAL BASIS. *Today, social and economic regulatory and tax legislation which does not interfere with specific fundamental rights will not be closely scrutinized by the federal courts. If there is any rational basis that the legislature might have had for concluding that the legislation would further permissible legislative objectives, it will be sustained. The law must not be arbitrary or irrational. But the law is presumed to be constitutional and the burden of proof is on the challenging party. This burden is essentially insurmountable and no economic legislation has been held unconstitutional by the Court, using this rationality test, since the New Deal.*

GENERAL APPROACH. *When examining a statute under the Due Process Clause, if there is no basis for invoking a stricter standard of review, the rationality test should be adopted. Use the following approach: (1) ascertain the objective of the law (a court will not probe for the true purpose of the law); (2) identify the means used by the state to achieve the objective; and (3) examine the rationality of the means for achieving the objective by reviewing the relevant facts. In your analysis, remember that the courts adopt a position of extreme deference to the legislative policy judgment when this standard is used.*

a.   In using the rationality test, the courts will not question the legislative objective. In the case of state laws, any permissible police power objective (public health, morals, and well-being) will suffice. If the law serves a valid purpose, the fact that the law incidentally serves other purposes will not make it unconstitutional.

b.   While the law must be rationally related to the achievement of the objective, the courts will not second-guess the legislative fact finding. If there are facts that would sustain the law, the courts will generally assume the legislation was based on those facts.

> ***Examples:***   (1) The federal Price Anderson Act setting maximum limits on tort liability for nuclear power plant accidents is constitutional. The law is rationally designed to promote nuclear power development while providing a fair and adequate basis for recovery. Any dollar ceiling is necessarily an arbitrary determination. *Duke Power Co. v. Carolina Environmental Study Group* (1978).
>
> (2) A state law requiring pharmacies to be operated or controlled by pharmacists does not violate due process despite the fact that the state supreme court had relied on an earlier substantive due process Supreme Court precedent to the contrary. *North Dakota State Board of Pharmacy v. Snyder's Drug Stores, Inc.* (1973).
>
> (3) A heavy municipal gross receipts tax on private parking garages which put them at a disadvantage with public parking is not violative of due process. Due process is not violated because legislation renders a business unprofitable. Although substantive due process could be violated by a taxing law, the legislation is invalid only if it is so arbitrary as to compel a conclusion that it is not a tax or amounts to a confiscation of property. *Pittsburgh v. Alco Parking Corp.* (1974).
>
> (4) Retroactive application of a federal statute imposing a user fee on claimants who win an award from the Iran–United States Claims Tribunal does not violate the Fifth Amendment Due Process Clause. The law's retroactive application is rationally designed to insure that all successful claimants are treated alike in that all have to contribute to the costs of the Tribunal. If the fee had been prospective

only, claimants whose award was delayed would be disadvantaged and be required to bear a disproportionate share of the costs. *United States v. Sperry Corp.* (1989).

c. *Fundamental Rights Exception.* Due process challenges to legislation involving fundamental personal rights which invoke a more searching standard of judicial review, will be discussed below. (See, Pt. Two, VI, C).

B. THE PROCESS OF INCORPORATION

As economic substantive due process died, the courts began to use the Due Process Clause as a vehicle for making various specific personal rights applicable to the states. The present section deals with whether the Due Process Clause makes all of the Bill of Rights applicable to the states, whether the clause has an independent meaning, and whether Bill of Rights guarantees made applicable to the states apply to the same extent and in the same manner as it operates against the federal government.

1. TOTAL INCORPORATION
The Court has rejected the argument that the Due Process Clause incorporates all of the Bill of Rights and makes them applicable against the states.

2. FLEXIBLE DUE PROCESS
In the 1940s and 1950s, a Court majority employed a flexible approach which viewed the Due Process Clause as having a meaning independent of the Bill of Rights. The Court determined whether a proceeding was so unfair as to offend fundamental standards of decency.

3. SELECTIVE INCORPORATION
The Court has held that some, but not all, of the provisions of the Bill of Rights are incorporated by the Due Process Clause and thus made applicable to the states.

a. Standard of Incorporation
The standard of incorporation has been variously stated as whether the Bill of Rights guarantee is essential to "the concept of ordered liberty" or whether it is "fundamental to the American scheme of justice."

b. Provisions Not Incorporated
Most of the provisions of the Bill of Rights have been incorporated. Those which today do not apply to state governments are the Seventh Amendment right to trial by jury in civil cases, the right to grand jury indictment, freedom from excessive bail, the requirements of a 12-person jury and of a unanimous verdict for conviction.

4. FULL AND PARTIAL INCORPORATION

The Court has held that the incorporated right applies against the states to the same extent and in the same manner as the Bill of Rights provision applies against the federal government. Caveat: Later cases appear to have narrowed the scope of certain Bill of Rights guarantees to accommodate state procedures.

Example: The Sixth Amendment right to trial by jury is "fundamental to the American scheme of justice" and thus is incorporated in Fourteenth Amendment due process, *Duncan v. Louisiana* (1968). But the right to a 12-person jury is not a Sixth Amendment right and thus is not constitutionally required in federal or state criminal trials. *Williams v. Florida* (1970). A jury of five persons is not constitutionally permissible (*Ballew v. Georgia* (1978)) and a state conviction by a non-unanimous six-person jury for a non-petty offense violates due process (*Burch v. Louisiana* (1979)). While the requirement of unanimity is not incorporated in Fourteenth Amendment due process, a split among the Justices indicates it may still be a Sixth Amendment requirement. *Apodaca v. Oregon* (1972).

C. SUBSTANTIVE DUE PROCESS REVISITED: THE RIGHT OF PRIVACY AND OTHER UNENUMERATED RIGHTS

1. FUNDAMENTAL RIGHTS

Just as procedural rights were incorporated into due process and made applicable to the states, various substantive limitations on government power became part of Fourteenth Amendment due process. State legislation was declared unconstitutional not because it was an arbitrary and unreasonable deprivation of liberty but because it violated the guarantee of free speech, or religious freedom, or privacy which are fundamental rights guaranteed by due process.

"FUNDAMENTAL RIGHTS": STANDARD OF REVIEW. *When legislation intrudes on "fundamental rights" applicable to the states through the due process guarantee, courts do not apply the rational basis test. A more demanding standard of review is adopted. Often this takes the form of "strict scrutiny," i.e., the government must demonstrate that the legislation is narrowly tailored or necessary to further a compelling state interest.*

RATIONALITY TEST DISTINGUISHED. *This standard departs from the rationality test of due process in the sense that it requires a much more specific showing that the means are reasonable, a much more urgent showing of state interest must be made in order to validate the challenged legislation, and the burden of justification is on the government (i.e., the usual presumption of the law's validity does not apply). If such a law is not precisely drawn it can be held to be unconstitutionally overbroad.*

2. EXPRESS, IMPLIED AND UNENUMERATED RIGHTS

While a more stringent standard of review than the rationality standard is used for all express rights, *e.g.,* speech, religion, the Court has also applied the more demanding standard to rights that are not expressly enumerated in the Constitution. In some cases the rights are implied from the express rights, *e.g.,* rights of association and belief implied from the First Amendment. In other instances, the judicial recognition of a fundamental right reflects considerations such as traditional societal values, contemporary morals, logic and reason, or the consequences of the law for the individual. On occasion, the Court declines to fashion a separate right but determines that the government regulation does substantially burden a significant liberty interest guaranteed by the Due Process Clause. The Court then balances the government interest in regulating the conduct against the burden on protected liberty. While such substantive due process review does not reach the rigors of strict scrutiny, it does not necessarily reflect the deference of rationality review used for social and economic laws.

3. THE RIGHT OF PRIVACY: CONTRACEPTION AND ABORTION
a. The Source of the Right of Privacy
1) The Penumbral Right of Privacy

The Court, on one occasion, has said that there is a right of privacy which lies within the penumbras of the First, Third, Fourth, Fifth, and Ninth Amendments i.e., the right was implied from rights which are expressly enumerated.

> ***Example:*** A state criminal statute proscribing the use of contraceptives even by married persons or aiding and abetting the use of contraceptives is a violation of the right of privacy. It is an impermissible intrusion on the right of association protecting the marital relationship. Enforcement of the law threatens police intrusion into the marital bedroom. *Griswold v. Connecticut* (1965).

2) Alternative Sources of the Right of Privacy

In the abortion decisions, the Court declared that the right of privacy has its source in the Fourteenth Amendment's guarantee of personal liberty against restrictive state action without due process, but the Court also acknowledged that other courts have ascribed the source of the right of privacy to the Ninth Amendment's reservation of rights to the people. *Roe v. Wade* (1973).

b. The Scope of the Right of Privacy
1) In *Griswold v. Connecticut* (1965), the Court protected a right of privacy extending to the use of contraceptives within the *marital relationship*. Marital privacy reflects traditional values associated with marriage and family life. In *Eisenstadt v. Baird* (1972) [statute

prohibiting distribution of contraceptives to unmarried persons violates Equal Protection], the Court indicated that the right of privacy includes the right of an *individual* to be free from excessive governmental intrusion into decisions relating to procreation.

2) The right of privacy has now been extended to protect the use of contraceptives and a women's decision to terminate a pregnancy. In determining whether the state regulation is narrowly drawn to promote a compelling government interest in the abortion cases, the Court in *Roe v. Wade* (1973), employed a trimester test. *Webster v. Reproductive Health Services* (1989) indicated that the trimester test and *Roe v. Wade* itself might be reconsidered in an appropriate case.

Examples: (1) Citing the detrimental consequences to the woman of having an unwanted child, the Court held that the right of privacy is broad enough to encompass a woman's decision to terminate her pregnancy. The state's interest in protecting a mother's health becomes compelling after the end of the first trimester of pregnancy. Therefore, the state may regulate the abortion procedure at that point to the extent reasonably required to protect maternal health. Prior to the end of the first trimester, the attending physician and the patient are free to jointly determine without significant state regulation whether the pregnancy should be terminated. After viability, the state has a compelling interest in the potentiality of human life and the state regulation is permissible even if it goes so far as to prohibit abortion except when it is necessary to preserve the life or health of the mother. *Roe v. Wade* (1973).

(2) A state may not require consent of a spouse to an abortion since the balance of interests favors the woman who physically bears the child and is most affected by the pregnancy. *Planned Parenthood v. Danforth* (1976).

(3) The Court held unconstitutional provisions of a local ordinance regulating abortions which required: (1) that all abortions performed after the first trimester of pregnancy be performed in a hospital; (2) that the attending physician make certain specific statements to the patient "to insure that the consent for an abortion is truly informed consent"; (3) a 24-hour waiting period between the time the woman signs a consent form and the time the abortion is performed; and, (4) that fetal remains be "disposed of in a humane and sanitary manner." *Akron Center for Reproductive Health, Inc. v. City of Akron* (1985).

(4) The Court upheld a law requiring: (1) the attendance of a second physician at the abortion of a viable fetus and requiring the second physician to "take all reasonable steps in keeping with good medical practice to preserve the life and health of the viable unborn child; provided that it does not pose an increased risk to the life or health of the woman"; and, (2) that tissue removed in abortions be submitted to a pathologist for filing of a report. *Planned Parenthood Ass'n v. Ashcroft* (1983).

(5) A law requiring that all abortions after the first trimester be performed in a hospital is unconstitutional because it excessively inhibits the vast majority of abortions. *City of Akron v. Akron Center for Reproductive Health* (1983). But a state law requiring second-trimester abortions to be performed in licensed outpatient clinics, which comport with reasonable medical standards governing out-patient second-trimester abortions, is a reasonable means of furthering the state's compelling interest in protecting a woman's health. *Simopoulos v. Virginia* (1983).

(6) The states are not free, under the guise of protecting maternal health or potential life, to intimidate women into continuing pregnancies. Requirements that women be given certain printed materials which explain the abortion process, list risks, suggest alternatives, and explain psychological effects were held to constitute an attempt to discourage abortions. Extensive reporting requirements imposed on the physician concerning the abortion and public access to such reports were held to pose an unacceptable danger of harassing and deterring the exercise of the woman's right. A requirement which would require that physicians performing post-viability abortions exercise the degree of care required to preserve the life and health of any unborn child and that they use abortion techniques most likely to save the fetus unless it would present a "significantly greater medical risk" to the woman is unconstitutional since it requires the woman to bear increased medical risk. Requiring that a second physician be present when the fetus is viable was also held improper since it made no exception for emergencies. *Thornburgh v. American College of Obstetricians and Gynecologists* (1986).

(7) A state law, interpreted as requiring that after 20 weeks doctors perform tests of gestational age, fetal weight and lung maturity, if such tests are useful to making subsidiary

findings as to viability, prior to performing an abortion, is constitutional. The presumption of viability at 20 weeks created by the law reflects the possibility of a 4–week error in estimating gestational age. Thus, the state law safeguards potential human life from the point at which viable life is possible. Requiring the performance of useful viability tests, even though they add to the expense of an abortion, is reasonably designed to promote the state's compelling interest in protecting potential human life.

A three-Justice plurality would have overruled the trimester framework and Justice Scalia would have overruled *Roe* entirely. Justice O'Connor, while acknowledging that the *Roe* trimester framework is "problematic," limited her concurrence to holding that the viability testing law did not violate any Court precedent, including *Roe*. *Webster v. Reproductive Health Services* (1989).

3) The right of privacy protects the reproductive rights of the woman even if she is a minor. However, the Court, recognizing the greater state interest in protecting immature minors, has applied a less stringent standard of review in case involving minors and allows a greater degree of state regulation. Generally, parental notification and even parental consent can be required if provision is made whereby a judge can grant permission for the abortion if the minor has sufficient maturity or where parental involvement would not be in her best interests.

Examples: (1) A state may not require parental consent without providing for a judicial by-pass since this gives third persons a veto over the decision of a physician and his/her patient. *Planned Parenthood of Central Missouri v. Danforth* (1976). Similarly, the decision of a minor to use contraceptives free of parental consent is protected by the right of privacy. *Carey v. Population Services Int'l* (1977).

(2) A law prohibiting physicians from performing abortions on a minor under the age of 15, unless she obtains written consent from a parent or a court order, absent any provision affording an opportunity for a case-by-case evaluation of the maturity of a minor is unconstitutional. *City of Akron v. Akron Center for Reproductive Health* (1983). But a requirement that minors secure parental consent or consent from a juvenile court for an abortion is constitutional so long as

consent cannot be denied without an initial determination as to the maturity of the minor. *Planned Parenthood Ass'n v. Ashcroft* (1983).

(3) A parental notification statute which requires that a doctor notify both parents of a minor female seeking an abortion, without provision for a judicial bypass is unconstitutional. The requirement that both parents be notified serves no legitimate state interest and could have harmful effects on the pregnant minor. A provision in the law which provides that a judicial bypass procedure would be implemented if the dual parent notification section was enjoined by a court is constitutional, however, and saves the statute. By allowing a minor to show that she possesses sufficient maturity to make an informed choice or that parental notification was not in her best interests, the bypass procedure addresses the very concerns which rendered the original statute unconstitutional. *Hodgson v. Minnesota* (1990).

(4) A state statute which makes it a crime for a physician to perform an abortion on an unmarried, unemancipated minor unless one of her parents is notified or a juvenile court issues an order permitting the abortion is constitutional. The bypass provisions of the statute, which allow a minor to obtain an abortion if she can demonstrate sufficient maturity or a pattern of abuse on the part of a parent, satisfy constitutional requirements. *Ohio v. Akron Center for Reproductive Health* (1990).

c. Abortion Funding
But the right of privacy is not significantly burdened if government fails to make the right effective by funding abortions even for those dependent on government for their medical assistance. There is no affirmative right to government aid.

Examples: A state does not act unconstitutionally if it refuses to provide funding for indigent women who might otherwise be unable to secure an abortion. There is no constitutional obligation that government must affirmatively act to implement the abortion decision of the women. *Maher v. Roe* (1977). Nor does a federal statute denying public funding for certain medically-necessary abortions violate Due Process, Equal Protection or the Establishment Clause. While government may not place obstacles in the path of a woman's exercise of her freedom of choice, it need not remove those obstacles it did not create. *Harris v. McRae* (1980). States may prohibit public employees and public facilities from being used for facilitating abortions not necessary to save the life of the mother. States need not commit any resources to facilitating abortions. *Webster v. Reproductive Health Services* (1989).

4. SODOMY LAWS

There is no fundamental right of homosexuals to engage in consensual sodomy even in the privacy of the home. *Such a right has not been recognized as a matter of tradition and is not implicit in the concept of ordered liberty.* A sodomy law is rationally designed to further the presumed belief of a majority that such conduct is immoral and unacceptable. *Bowers v. Hardwick* (1986). Note that the Court did not reach questions of whether criminal punishment under such a law would violate the Eighth Amendment Cruel and Unusual Punishment Clause, whether the law could be constitutionally applied to heterosexual relations or whether Equal Protection might be violated by particular sodomy laws.

5. RIGHTS TO MARRIAGE AND FAMILY LIFE

The institutions of marriage and family life are deeply rooted in our nation's history and traditions. Through them, basic moral and cultural values are passed down. They are, therefore, fundamental rights guaranteed by the Due Process Liberty Clause. A more stringent standard of review is appropriate when these rights are significantly burdened.

Examples: (1) A state statute prohibiting interracial marriage violates due process liberty and the Equal Protection Clause. Marriage is one of the "basic civil rights of man" and is fundamental "to our very existence and survival." The state failed to prove that the law is necessary to the achievement of an overriding government interest. *Loving v. Virginia* (1967).

(2) A legal ordinance limiting occupancy of dwelling units to a single family and defining family so narrowly as to prohibit a grandmother from living with her two grandsons violates due process. Familial rights are not limited merely to the nuclear family. Laws limiting personal choice in matters of marriage and family life are subject to careful judicial scrutiny. The ordinance has only a marginal relation to valid government interests in preventing overcrowding, minimizing traffic and parking congestion, and avoiding excessive financial burdens on the school system. *Moore v. City of East Cleveland* (1977).

(3) A local ordinance limiting dwellings to a single family, but defining family to mean not more than two unrelated persons, does not violate due process. The law excludes land uses such as boarding houses, fraternities, communes, etc. No fundamental right of privacy or association is involved. The law is rationally related to permissible police power objectives of controlling population density and preventing noise and congestion. *Belle Terre v. Boraas* (1974).

(4) A state statute establishing a conclusive presumption that a child born to a married woman cohabiting with her husband is a child of the marriage does not violate the substantive due process rights of the natural father or the child. In a plurality opinion, Justice Scalia argued that our society has not traditionally awarded parental rights to a natural father when the child is born into an extant marital union. It is the relationships that develop within the unitary family that have traditionally been protected as due process liberty interests. However, it appeared that a majority of the Justices did accept the possibility that a natural father might have a constitutionally protected liberty interest in his relationship with a child born into an extant marital union. *Michael H. & Victoria D. v. Gerald D.* (1989).

6. THE RIGHT OF TRAVEL

a. Right of Interstate Movement

The Court has never clearly identified the source of the right of interstate movement. It has been variously ascribed to the Commerce Clause, to the Privileges and Immunities Clause of the Fourteenth Amendment or Art. IV, § 2, or has been held to be an inherent national right. If the right is burdened, the more stringent standard of judicial review applies. Since most of the cases involving this right have been decided under the Equal Protection Clause, it will be discussed more fully below.

b. Right of Foreign Travel

The right of travel abroad is a guarantee flowing from the Liberty Clause of the Fifth Amendment. Because of the national interest in foreign affairs and the behavior of citizens abroad, reasonable regulations, e.g., area restrictions on passport use, will be upheld. Zemel v. Rusk (1965).

Example: The Secretary of State has the power to revoke a passport when the holder's activities are causing or likely to cause serious damage to national security or foreign policy. Such a revocation does not constitute a violation of procedural due process, the right to travel or the First Amendment right to criticize the government. The right to travel abroad is subordinate to national security and foreign policy considerations and subject to reasonable government regulation. *Haig v. Agee* (1981).

7. THE RIGHT TO CARE AND PROTECTION

As the abortion funding cases indicate, government generally has *no affirmative constitutional duty* to provide care and protection for individuals. However, in some limited cases, *where the State exercises custody of an individual, the Due Process Clause imposes a duty on government to assume some responsibility for that person's care and well-being.*

Examples: (1) Due process liberty protects the right of involuntarily committed mentally retarded persons to "minimally adequate or reasonable training to ensure safety and freedom from undue restraint." When this right is burdened, the courts must undertake a balancing of the liberty interests against the relevant state interests. The judgments of the medical profession are presumptively valid and violation can be based only on a showing of a "substantial departure from accepted professional judgment." *Youngberg v. Romeo* (1982).

(2) The state's failure to protect a child from physical abuse by his father does not deprive the child of any due process liberty right. There is no affirmative right to government aid, even though the welfare department has investigated reports of child abuse, and after reports of continuing abuses, has taken various steps, short of removing the child, to try to protect him. *DeShaney v. Winnebago County Dept. of Social Servs.* (1989).

8. THE RIGHT TO REFUSE TREATMENT

A person possesses a significant liberty interest in avoiding unwanted medical treatment. But the state's regulatory interest may justify the burden on the protected liberty interest. See *Washington v. Harper* (1990) [involuntary administration of antipsychotic drugs to prisoners upheld], discussed below.

Example: Nancy Cruzan is in a persistent vegative condition. Her parents want artificial feeding and hydration terminated but the hospital refuses. In such circumstances a state may constitutionally require clear and convincing evidence of the patient's desire that life-sustaining treatment be withdrawn. The patient has a significant liberty interest in refusing unwanted medical treatment. The state's interest in the preservation of human life and its interest in safeguarding the personal element of the choice of life and death is sufficient to justify the imposition of heightened evidentiary standards. Such a standard protects against abuse, promotes more accurate fact finding and reflects the importance of the decision.

The state is not constitutionally required to repose judgment in such matters with anyone but the patient herself; it need not accept the substituted judgment of close family members. *Cruzan v. Director, Missouri Dept. of Health* (1990).

9. RIGHTS IN RESTRICTED ENVIRONMENTS

In certain special contexts, such as the military, schools, government employment and the prisons, the stricter standards of judicial scrutiny do not apply. While persons in such contexts do not lose their constitutional rights, the courts tend to defer to decisionmakers in the other branches of government. See *Goldman v. Weinberger* (1986) (military); *Bethel School Dist. v. Fraser* (1986) (schools); *Connick v. Myers* (1983) (government employees). In prison cases, for example, restrictions on fundamental rights are valid if they are reasonably related to legitimate penological objectives.

Examples: (1) A state restriction upon correspondence between inmates survives constitutional review, but a regulation that severely limits the ability of inmates to marry does not. Recognizing a special need for judicial deference in cases involving prison regulation, the Court employed a diminished standard of review—"the regulation is valid if it is reasonably related to legitimate penological objectives." The restraint on correspondence was not content-based and "logically advanced" the legitimate government interest in promoting institutional security and safety. It was not an "exaggerated response" to concerns over prison security; there were no "obvious, easy alternatives" available. In contrast, the restriction on marriage was not logically connected to the state's proffered objective of preventing "love triangles" that threaten prison security or to rehabilitation. Additionally, the almost complete ban on marriages was excessive in that it covered marriage with civilians and male inmates, whose marriages generally posed no security threat. *Turner v. Safley* (1987).

(2) A state Policy authorizing involuntary treatment with drugs of an incarcerated felon who suffers from a "mental disorder" and who is "gravely disabled" or poses a "likelihood of serious harm to himself, others or their property," does not violate substantive due process. While the inmate has a significant liberty interest in avoiding the unwanted administration of drugs, the state Policy recognizes both the prisoner's medical interests and the state interests. The policy is "reasonably related to legitimate penological interests of the State." Where the root cause of the threat to prison security is mental illness, the state interest encompasses provision of medical treatment. The impact of the due process right on guards, other inmates and prison resources generally also suggests the reasonableness of the Policy. Finally,

there were no "ready alternatives" to involuntary treatment. *Washington v. Harper* (1990).

D. PROCEDURAL FAIRNESS

1. EX POST FACTO LAW
Both the federal and state governments are expressly prohibited from passing any Ex Post Facto law. Art. I, § 9, cl. 3 and Art. I, § 10, cl. 1. The Ex Post Facto Clauses have been interpreted by the Court to prohibit the enactment of retroactive criminal legislation that significantly disadvantages the offender. The effect, not the form of the law, determines whether it is Ex Post Facto.

The restriction against Ex Post Facto laws would preclude the enactment of laws defining as criminal conduct which was not criminal at the time of its occurrence. Similarly, retroactively increasing the penalty for criminal conduct or denying a defendant a defense available when the act was performed are also impermissible. The standard derives from a basic legal precept in western civilization: *Nulla poena sine lege.* No penalty without a law.

Examples: (1) A state statute repealing an earlier statute and reducing the amount of "gain" time for good conduct deducted from a convicted prisoner's sentence, is an unconstitutional ex post facto law as applied to the petitioner, whose crime was committed before the new statute's enactment. Since the petitioner lost gain time that had been available under the repealed statute, the effect of the repealer statute was to retroactively impose a punishment more severe than that assigned when the defendant was convicted and thereby retroactively disadvantaged him. *Weaver v. Graham* (1981).

(2) A state statute altering sentencing guidelines was an unconstitutional ex post facto law as applied to petitioner, whose crime was committed before the statute was enacted. Under the old statute, petitioner's range of sentencing would have been 3½ to 4½ years' imprisonment, and a stiffer penalty could not be applied absent clear and convincing reasons for the deviation. Under the new statute the range was 5½ to 7½ years' imprisonment. The law was retroactive in that it changed the legal consequences of acts committed by petitioner before its effective date. The Court found that petitioner was "substantially disadvantaged" by the new law since he could receive a penalty prohibited under the old law in the absence of clear and convincing evidence. Also, a stiffer penalty was reviewable by a higher court under the old law; the new law did not allow review

of a sentence imposed within the range of sentencing. *Miller v. Florida* (1987).

(3) A Texas Statute, passed after respondent's crime, which allows an appellate court to reform an improper jury verdict is not an unconstitutional ex post facto law. The appellate court had reformed a jury verdict imposing both a fine and imprisonment contrary to state law by deleting the fine. Since the statute did not alter the offense, increase the punishment or deprive the respondent of a defense, its application to respondent was not prohibited by the Ex Post Facto Clause. *Collins v. Youngblood* (1990).

2. PROCEDURAL DUE PROCESS: CIVIL CASES

The Fifth and Fourteenth Amendment Due Process Clauses guarantee procedural fairness. Whenever a state or federal practice is challenged as violative of due process, two questions must be asked.

INTEREST INVADED. *First, is there a deprivation of a significant life, liberty, or property interest so that the Due Process Clause applies? It does not matter whether the interest is characterized as a "right" or a "privilege." If it is a significant due process interest, procedural fairness is required. However, thus far the Court has only recognized due process as applying to benefits that are "presently enjoyed," i.e., due process is not applied to the application for benefits. A negligent injury to life, liberty or property is not a "deprivation".*

PROCEDURES REQUIRED. *Second, in the particular factual context, what procedures are required to assure fundamental fairness? The question of what procedures are required is a federal constitutional question to be decided by the courts; it is not determined by the state law. The Court has rejected the proposition that an individual takes "the bitter with the sweet."*

The minimum procedures demanded by due process are notice and a hearing. What is fair is determined by balancing the interests favoring summary determination against the harm to the person aggrieved. Courts in making this determination consider three factors: (1) the severity of the harm to the litigant if the requested procedures are not granted; (2) the risk of error if the procedures are not afforded; and (3) the administrative difficulty and cost of providing the added procedures.

a. What Is "Property"?

While property is not limited to interests in realty or personalty, the fact that an interest is important to an individual is inadequate to create "property" for due process purposes. Property has thus far been limited to interests recognized by government. For government benefits to constitute property, therefore, the person seeking due process must show some entitlement created by government.

b. **What Is "Liberty"?**
Liberty is a broad concept not limited to conditions of confinement such as imprisonment. It includes interests such as marriage, raising a family, working in the common occupations of the community. It includes reputation but the Court has held that the imposition of stigma by government officials, without more, does not violate liberty.

Example: Distribution of a flyer by the police identifying a person as a shoplifter, even though the person had only been arrested, not convicted of the offense, does not violate due process liberty. The action of the state officials did not alter any status of the individual recognized and protected by law nor was he deprived of a tangible interest such as employment. Where there is no state created interest involved such as employment or schooling, even a charge of criminal conduct does not create a basis for an actionable due process violation although it may give rise to a claim for defamation. *Paul v. Davis* (1976).

c. **What Is a "Deprivation"?**
When an individual is injured by a negligent rather than a deliberate act, there is no "deprivation" requiring due process protection.

Examples: (1) A prison inmate who is injured as a result of slipping on a pillow negligently left on a stairwell by a prison guard cannot sue for damages for violation of procedural due process rights. There has been no "deprivation" of life, liberty or property to be remedied. *Daniels v. Williams* (1986).

(2) The negligent failure of prison officials to guard an inmate who informs the officials of threats made against him by another prisoner does not implicate the Due Process Clause. The lack of due care by government officials does not constitute the kind of abusive treatment that the Due Process Clause was designed to protect against. Since there is no "deprivation" of due process, no remedy is required. *Davidson v. Cannon* (1986).

d. **Due Process Contexts**
1) Welfare Rights
    a) The Statutory Entitlement Concept
        A person who qualifies to receive welfare benefits has a statutory entitlement to receive benefits. Whether welfare is deemed a

right or a privilege, this is a significant property interest and due process must be afforded when benefits are terminated.

b)   Balancing to Determine Fairness
     In determining what process is due, the state interest in conserving fiscal and administrative resources is balanced against the importance to the welfare recipient of uninterrupted benefits.

Examples: (1) Welfare benefits to a qualified AFDC recipient cannot be terminated prior to a hearing. Given the dependence of the recipient on the benefits for subsistence, the importance to the state that persons receive such subsistence and the absence of any emergency justifying summary procedures, due process requires timely notice indicating the basis for termination, and a hearing before an impartial examiner in which the recipient may appear personally, with or without counsel (counsel need not be provided by the state) to present evidence and confront and cross-examine adverse witnesses. *Goldberg v. Kelly* (1970).

(2) Social security disability benefits may be terminated without a prior hearing. *Goldberg* is distinguished. The individual hardship is not as great since disability benefits are not based on need, there is less risk of error given the medical basis of the disability determination, and the administrative difficulty and costs the additional procedural safeguards would entail would severely burden the government. *Mathews v. Eldridge* (1976).

2)   The Right to Use and Possess Property: Constitutionalizing the Consumer Credit Relationship
     a)   Wages as a Property Interest
          Wages constitute a specialized type of property interest protected by due process. Given the effect of even a temporary loss of such wages by garnishment, notice and a hearing must be afforded prior to statutorily-recognized garnishment. *Sniadach v. Family Finance Corp.* (1969).

     b)   Contingent Interests in Property
          The purchaser of goods under a contingent sales contract has a significant property interest in the use and possession of such goods. The due process guarantee has thus been extended in some situations to relationships which have not yet matured into

property rights. Due process must be afforded but in some cases summary adjudication may provide sufficient fairness.

Examples: (1) Procedural due process requires that before a state may authorize the summary seizure of goods or chattels in a person's possession under a writ of replevin, upon the mere *ex parte* application by a creditor to a court clerk, the state must provide an opportunity for hearing to the person in possession of the goods. The function of the hearing is to prevent unfair and mistaken deprivation of the "property" interest. *Fuentes v. Shevin* (1972).

(2) State sequestration laws permitting state courts to authorize seizure of goods, without prior notice to debtor in possession or opportunity for hearing, upon *ex parte* application of creditor who made installment sales of goods and whose sworn affidavit to a judge asserts delinquency in payment and belief that debtor would "encumber, alienate or otherwise dispose of" goods do not violate Fourteenth Amendment due process. The requirement of affidavits and the presence of direct judicial supervision satisfy the requirements of due process. *Mitchell v. W. T. Grant Co.* (1974).

(3) A state statute permitted garnishment of commercial accounts upon mere conclusionary allegations in an affidavit issuable by a clerk (not a judge) and made no provision for early hearing. The garnishment could be dissolved only by filing a bond to protect the creditor. The procedure was declared to violate due process. Since there still existed the likelihood of irreparable injury to property interests, the fact that the case involved garnishment of a corporation's bank account rather than household goods was deemed immaterial. *North Georgia Finishing, Inc. v. Di-Chem, Inc.* (1975).

c) Waiver of Civil Due Process Rights
The waiver of notice and hearing provisions in a cognovit note (a document confessing judgment) does not violate due process at least where no great disparity in bargaining power exists since constitutional rights can be waived where the waiver is undertaken voluntarily, knowingly, and intelligently. *D.H. Overmyer Co. v. Frick Co.* (1972).

3) Employment Rights of the Public Sector
    a) Conditions of Employment
        Whether a public employee has a due process property interest in continued employment, requiring at least notice and hearing, depends on the conditions of the employment. A person must have more than a subjective expectancy of continued employment. The expectation must be created by the state.

    Examples: (1) A state university teacher on a one-year contract has not suffered a due process violation by the refusal of the university to renew his contract. To have a property interest in a benefit, a person must have a legitimate claim of entitlement. If non-renewal is based on factors involving good name, reputation, honor or integrity (a liberty interest) then a hearing would be necessary. *Board of Regents v. Roth* (1972).

    (2) A state college teacher who has held his position for a number of years may be able to show a legitimate claim of entitlement to job tenure even in the absence of a formal tenure system. The college rules, regulations, and practices can create a de facto system of tenure, i.e., an entitlement. Although a mere subjective "expectancy" is not protected by due process, the teacher is entitled to be given an opportunity to prove the legitimacy of a claim of entitlement. If such a property interest is proved, the teacher is entitled to hearing by the college where he could be informed of the grounds for his nonretention and challenge the sufficiency of the grounds. *Perry v. Sindermann* (1972).

    b) Employment at Will—Conditional Property Interests
        (1) The termination of a policeman's employment without a hearing pursuant to a city ordinance providing for discharge for negligence, unfitness, and unsuitable conduct, was held not to violate due process. A public employee whose position is terminable at the will of the employer is not deprived of "liberty" when there is no public disclosure of the reasons for the discharge. Similarly, there is no "property" interest infringed when the ordinance involved is construed as "granting no right to continued employment" but merely conditions removal on satisfactorily complying with certain specified procedures. *Bishop v. Wood* (1976).

(2) *But remember, the issues of whether a life, liberty or property interest is implicated and what procedures are required to satisfy due process are separate. While a state may so condition the employment interest that it does not constitute "property", the courts, not state law, define what processes are due once a property interest is found to exist. The public employee does not take "the bitter with the sweet."*

> *Example:* In order to satisfy due process a statute governing discharge of public employees must provide at least for pretermination notice and an opportunity to respond, coupled with adequate post-termination administrative procedures. A public employee has a property interest in continued employment; property cannot be defined by the procedures provided for its deprivation.
>
> Nor does the fact that the statute defines applicable procedures determine the federal constitutional question of what procedures are due. Given the severity of depriving a person of a livelihood, the danger of factual error, the issues likely to surround the appropriateness of discharge, and the absence of any significant administrative burden on the state, due process requires at least pretermination notice and "some kind of hearing" designed to assure that there are reasonable grounds for the discharge. A fuller administrative proceeding can follow termination. Since the employees involved alleged they had not been given an opportunity to respond prior to discharge, they stated a cause of action. *Cleveland Bd. of Educ. v. Loudermill* (1985).

c) State-Created Causes of Action
A state-created cause of action which cannot be dismissed except "for cause," creates a due process property interest.

> *Example:* State termination of a complainant's cause of action because a state official, for reasons beyond the complainant's control, fails to comply with statutorily mandated procedures violates procedural due process. The Illinois Fair Employment Practices Act (FEPA) creates a cause of action for employment

discrimination based on physical handicaps unrelated to job ability. The plaintiff's FEPA claim constitutes an entitlement which cannot be denied except "for cause"—this suffices as a due process property interest. The Court applied the three-part test for determining what process is due. The employee's interest in retaining employment, disproving alleged inability and redressing discrimination are all substantial interests. Since termination of the claim is the result of random chance resulting from the Commission's failure to act, there is a high risk that meritorious claims will be defeated. Finally, there is no undue burden on the state in considering the merits of the employee's claim. *Logan v. Zimmerman Brush Co.* (1982).

4)   Institutional Due Process

Procedural due process issues have frequently arisen in the context of the judicial review of the practices of public institutions such as prisons, schools, and mental hospitals. While officials in such institutions exercise broad discretion, the courts have increasingly demanded adherence to fair processes in admission and administration. For example, while confinement in a mental hospital may not constitute imprisonment, it does involve significant curtailment of a liberty interest requiring due process. *Addington v. Texas* (1979) [involuntary confinement requires at least "clear and convincing evidence"].

Examples: (1) Transfer of an incarcerated prisoner to a mental hospital implicates a liberty interest protected by due process. A liberty interest is created by a statute specifying certain conditions for transfer and by commitment to the mental hospital. The stigma and subjection to mandatory behavior modification treatment also implicate significant liberty interests. The Court weighed the interest of the prisoner in not being arbitrarily stigmatized and subjected to involuntary treatment and the substantial risk of error against the state's interest in segregating and treating mentally ill prisoners. Due process requires written notice, a hearing at which evidence is heard, including a right of presentation, confrontation and cross-examination, an independent decisionmaker, a written statement by the fact-finder, effective and timely notice of rights, and qualified and independent assistance of legal counsel. *Vitek v. Jones* (1980).

(2) A child voluntarily committed by its parents to a mental institution has a constitutionally protectible liberty interest at stake given the confinement and stigma involved. In determining what procedures are due, the interests of the parents and the child are presumed to be the same since parents generally act in the child's best interests. State interests in effective use of its resources and avoidance of excessive procedures are also to be considered. The risk of error is sufficiently great to require some inquiry (an informal medical hearing would suffice) by a neutral fact finder to assure admission requirements are satisfied, and thereafter to assure that there is a continuing need for confinement. *Parham v. J.R.* (1979).

(3) Rescission of a decision to grant purely discretionary parole to a prisoner prior to actual release, without any hearing, based on alleged false statements by the prisoner to the parole board, does not violate due process. While the prisoner suffers grievous loss, this does not mean that he has a "liberty" interest. Neither his subjective expectation, even though based on understandings with the parole board, nor the state laws governing parole created a liberty interest. *Jago v. Van Curen* (1981).

(4) While a prisoner does not have a constitutionally protected liberty interest in remaining with other prisoners and not being administratively segregated following his involvement in a prison riot, explicit mandatory language in state statutes and regulations can create such a liberty interest. In this instance, due process was satisfied since the state met its minimal obligation "to engage in an informal, nonadversary review of information supporting [the prisoners] administrative confinement, including whatever statement respondent wished to submit, within a reasonable time after confining him to administrative segregation."

The prisoner's interest was not of great consequence since he was merely transferred from one extremely restricted environment to an even more confined situation. The government's interest in the safety of guards and inmates involved "the most fundamental responsibility of the prison administration." Informal procedures provided by the prison provided a reasonably accurate statement of probable cause to believe that charged misconduct occurred and the value of additional procedures was slight. *Hewitt v. Helms* (1983).

(5) Although the Due Process clause of the Fourteenth Amendment imposes procedural and substantive limits on the revocation of the conditional liberty created by probation, it does not generally require a sentencing court to indicate that it has considered alternatives to incarceration before revoking probation or to state explicitly why it rejected alternatives to incarceration. A general requirement that a fact finder elaborate upon the reasons for a course not taken would unduly burden the revocation proceeding without significantly advancing the interests of the probationer since procedures already afforded protect the defendant against revocation of probation in a constitutionally unfair manner. *Black v. Romano* (1985).

(6) A statute providing that a prisoner eligible for parole "shall" be released when there is a reasonable probability that no detriment to the community will result creates a liberty interest entitled to protection under the Due Process Clause. Mandatory language such as "shall" creates a presumption that parole will be granted under such circumstances and gives rise to a protected interest. *Board of Pardons v. Allen* (1987).

(7) Suspension of visitation privileges for particular visitors was held not to violate any liberty interest. First, the prisoners were not subjected to consequences qualitatively different from that of prisoners generally, since denial of access to particular visitors is well within the terms of confinement associated with imprisonment. Further, the prison regulations did not create any entitlement. Although the regulations did contain guidelines (*i.e.,* "substantive predicates") limiting official discretion on visitation, the regulations lacked the relevant mandatory language that would lead prisoners to reasonably expect that a visit would be allowed

absent one of the listed conditions. *Kentucky Dept. of Corrections v. Thompson* (1989).

(8) The failure of state employees to follow a state statutory procedure for the involuntary admission of mentally ill patients was sufficient to state a claim under the Due Process Clause. The fact that the very risk protected by the statute was predictable and that the employees were delegated the powers to implement the statute, rendered the availability of only postdeprivation remedies inadequate. Due process required a proper predeprivation hearing, and the fact that the employees did not follow the state procedures which were constitutional, did not render the patient's claim inappropriate. *Zinermon v. Burch* (1990).

(9) A state Policy establishing a nonjudicial procedure for involuntary treatment with antipsychotic drugs of mentally ill felons does not violate procedural due process. Although the inmate has a substantial liberty interest in avoiding unwanted administration of drugs, the state procedures satisfy due process. The treatment decision is made by a psychiatrist and is reviewed by a board of medical professionals not involved in the case. There is notice to the inmates and an opportunity to attend the hearing and cross-examine witnesses. A "clear, cogent, and convincing" standard is not required when medical personnel are making the treatment decision. *Washington v. Harper* (1990).

5) Parental Rights
The interest of natural parents in the care, custody, and management of their children involves a fundamental liberty interest. In determining what process is due, this liberty interest of the parents is commanding and weighs heavily. But the state interests may still outweigh the parental liberty interest.

Examples: (1) Due process requires use of the "clear and convincing" evidentiary standard before parental rights are terminated for unfitness. Use of the "fair preponderance" standard violates due process. There is a significant risk of error and the consequences of erroneous termination of parental rights generally outweigh the consequences of erroneous failure to terminate the parental relation. Accuracy in fact-finding also serves the state interest in the child's welfare by preserving the natural familial bonds while doubt remains. Since the clear and convincing standard is regularly used in other proceedings, there would be no excessive administrative burden on the state fact-finders. *Santosky v. Kramer* (1982).

(2) An indigent parent is not necessarily denied procedural due process guarantees where the state fails to appoint counsel in a parental-status termination proceeding. There is a general presumption that the due process safeguard of appointed counsel will only be required where there is a possible deprivation of personal liberty. To rebut this presumption, the private interests at stake, the risks of an erroneous decision, and the state's interest must be considered. While the balancing of these factors does favor the parent's interests in many cases, whether it is sufficient in a particular case to overcome the presumption against appointed counsel must be determined on a case-by-case basis. The record in the present case indicated that the absence of counsel had not denied fundamental fairness. *Lassiter v. Dept. of Social Services* (1981).

6) Student Rights
    Courts have been reluctant to intrude into the sensitive area of school-student relationships and have generally recognized broad power in school authorities to act in *loco parentis*. But the Court has now indicated that due process does protect the liberty and property interests of a student.

Examples: (1) A state statute allowing school principals to suspend students for misconduct for up to ten days without a hearing violates due process. Because the state confers a system of free public education on its children, there is an "entitlement," i.e., a property interest. Since the suspension could impose a stigma, the child's liberty interest is infringed. Balancing these interests against the state's interests in maintaining order and discipline, the Court held that due process requires that the student be furnished at least notice of the charges, an explanation of the evidence against him and an opportunity to reply. *Goss v. Lopez* (1975).

(2) Charlotte Horowitz failed to graduate from medical school because of poor performance in clinical courses and her lack of concern for personal hygiene. She was notified of the reasons for the school's actions and afforded a hearing and appeal at which she could respond. She was not, however, accorded an opportunity to appear personally. Assuming that such a dismissal denies a property or liberty interest, the Court was unanimous that due process was satisfied by the procedures afforded. A number of justices indicated that due process standards are more easily satisfied when the procedures involve academic rather than disciplinary considerations. *Board of Curators v. Horowitz* (1978).

7) Access to Courts
   a) Filing Fees
      While the Due Process Liberty Clause imposes significant demands to assure due process in criminal cases, with some exceptions, due process does not require that indigent plaintiffs be given free access to the courts in civil cases.

      Examples: (1) A filing fee imposed on indigents seeking a divorce violates due process. Marriage occupies a fundamental position in our society and the state monopolizes the means of dissolving it. *Boddie v. Connecticut* (1971).

      (2) A filing fee imposed on an indigent seeking a discharge in bankruptcy does not violate due process. The individual's interest in a bankruptcy is not as fundamental as marriage dissolution since the position of the individual who is denied is not materially altered. The government's role is qualitatively and quantitatively less than in *Boddie* since there are other methods for debt adjustment. *United States v. Kras* (1973).

      (3) A filing fee imposed on indigents seeking judicial review of an adverse welfare decision by an administrative board does not violate due process. The individual's interest is of inadequate constitutional significance and the State has provided an agency determination. *Ortwein v. Schwab* (1973).

b) Effective Access
The procedures that are available in civil proceedings are generally determined by the three-part balancing test. However, there is a presumption against a right to appointed counsel in civil proceedings that requires a case-by-case determination whether counsel is needed under the circumstances.

Example: A state statute which provides that in paternity actions the cost of blood grouping tests is to be borne by the party requesting them violates due process when applied to deny such tests to indigent defendants. Applying the three-part test for determining what process is due to the facts in the present case, the Court held that the denial of free blood tests denied the putative father a meaningful opportunity to be heard. First, the father has a strong pecuniary interest in avoiding support obligations and a liberty interest threatened by possible sanctions for non-payment as well as an interest in the creation of a parent-child relationship which is shared with the child. Second, blood tests are a highly effective method for negating paternity and thus avoiding the risk of error. Third, the state has an interest in securing support for a child on public assistance and securing a just determination of paternity. While the state seeks to determine paternity as economically as possible, federal reimbursement is available and costs can be offset. *Little v. Streater* (1981).

8) Due Process Rights in the Military Sector
a) Military Courts
Pursuant to its Art. I powers to provide regulations for the governance of the land and naval forces, Congress has created a system of military courts. Questions have arisen regarding the proper jurisdiction of these military courts.

b) Status
Military jurisdiction is generally limited to military personnel. It does not extend to military dependents or civilian employees (at least during peacetime) even when they are abroad.

c) Types of Crimes Not Basis of Jurisdiction
The jurisdiction of a military court does not depend on the "service connection" of the offense charged. Jurisdiction depends solely on the accused's status as a member of the Armed Forces

and not on the type of crime, *i.e.*, whether the offense charged is "service connected." The contrary doctrine of *O'Callaghan v. Parker* (1969) is reversed. This construction is supported by the natural meaning of Art. I, § 8, cl. 14, which confers plenary power on Congress "to make Rules for the Government and Regulations of the Land and Naval Forces." Civil courts are not equipped to develop policies on matters of military concern. *Solorio v. United States* (1986).

d) Primary Jurisdiction of Military Courts
When a serviceman charged with crimes by military authorities can show no harm other than that attendant to resolution of his case in the military justice system, the federal district courts must refrain from equitable intervention. If it subsequently is held that the military courts lacked jurisdiction, they would similarly lack power to impose any punishment. *Schlesinger v. Councilman* (1975).

9) Other Contexts
A taxpayer who challenged a state tax provision as unconstitutional under the Commerce Clause is entitled to retroactive relief from the State for unlawfully depriving the taxpayer of property. The Due Process Clause requires that a taxpayer have a fair opportunity to challenge the state tax, and that a "clear and certain remedy" exist to correct the effects of an unconstitutional tax. *McKesson Corp. v. Division of Alcoholic Bev. and Tobacco, Fla.* (1990).

e. **Conclusive Presumptions**
DEFINITION. *Conclusive presumptions are created when statutes conclusively presume that certain facts exist which categorize individuals into a class subjected to burdens not visited on others, even though the presumptions may be wrong in a certain case.*

The denial of an opportunity to challenge the presumption has generally been held to violate due process. When critical due process interests of the individual are lost by government action, he or she must normally be afforded an opportunity for a hearing to prove that the fact presumed is not true in his or her case.

1) A plurality of the Court argues that the conclusive presumptions doctrine does not rest upon procedural due process. Such cases, it is claimed, do not question the adequacy of the procedures, but the fit between the classification established by the law and the policy underlying the classification. *Michael H. & Victoria D. v. Gerald D.* (1989).

Example: School board rules requiring every pregnant school teacher to take a maternity leave without pay a specified number of months (five and four months in the two statutes challenged) before the expected birth of her child violate due process. To assume that all women teachers were physically unfit to continue employment beyond the designated date assumed a fact that was not true in individual cases. Since the critical interests in marriage and family life were at stake, the use of the conclusive presumption of unfitness violated due process. Individualized determinations were required to satisfy due process. The Court held also that the rules had no relationship to the school's interest in assuring continuity of instruction. *Cleveland Board of Education v. LaFleur* (1974).

2) *Exception.* When the irrebuttable presumption involves a non-contractual claim to receive public funds, and claimants are permitted to present evidence that they meet objectively defined statutory requirements for eligibility, the presumption is constitutional if rationally based. No significant liberty or property interest is impaired.

Example: A Social Security Act provision preventing wage earners, widows and step-children from recovering benefits if their relationships with the wage-earner began less than nine months before the wage earner's death is constitutional. Congress could rationally conclude that such a presumption would preclude the use of sham marriages to obtain Social Security benefits and that it would avoid the expense and difficulty of individualized determinations. It was therefore permissible to bar a widow from recovery even though the wage earner was in good health at the time of the marriage. *Weinberger v. Salfi* (1975).

E. REVIEW QUESTIONS

1. T or F   A reasonable law will generally be constitutional even if it retroactively impairs private contract relationships.

2. T or F   Once a state has contracted away its fiscal powers, it is thereafter barred from any changes in the contract.

3. T or F   If a state law has the effect of reducing property values, the law constitutes a "taking" requiring "just compensation."

4. T or F In most cases, due process is satisfied if the law is rationally related to a permissible government objective.

5. T or F The Court has now held all of the guarantees of the Bill of Rights applicable to the states as part of the Fourteenth Amendment Due Process "Liberty" Clause.

6. T or F An incorporated right applies against the states but the scope of the Bill of Rights guarantees which is being incorporated may be redefined by the Court.

7. T or F When a fundamental right is significantly burdened, the Court requires the government to justify the law under a stricter standard of review.

8. T or F Due process is not violated by a law which provides funding for maternity but denies funding for abortion.

9. T or F The Court has held that the right of interstate movement is a fundamental right derived from the Privileges and Immunities Clause of the Fourteenth Amendment.

10. T or F Whenever a state procedure is alleged to violate due process, the courts balance the interests of the person affected against the government interests in not affording the requested procedures.

11. T or F Reputation, when burdened by government, can qualify as a liberty interest.

12. T or F Conclusive presumptions always violate due process.

13. T or F Procedural due process applies only when life, liberty, or property rights are burdened.

14. Which of the following is *not* an element of the traditional rational basis test?

    a.   Probe to discover the true legislative objective.

    b.   Ascertain if the means are rationally related to the objective.

    c.   Assume any state of facts that would sustain the law.

    d.   All of the above (a, b, and c) are elements of the traditional due process rationality test.

15. Which of the following arguments would be least likely to succeed in constitutional challenges to sodomy convictions?

   a.   The law violates the Equal Protection Clause.

   b.   The law violates the fundamental right to engage in homosexual relations in private.

   c.   Criminal punishment violates the Cruel and Unusual Punishment Clause.

   d.   The law is an overbroad intrusion on the rights of heterosexuals.

16. Which of the following abortion laws would most likely survive constitutional challenge?

   a.   A substitute consent law for minors requiring approval of parents for the abortion.

   b.   A law requiring the presence of a second physician in post-viability abortions unless there is an emergency.

   c.   A law requiring abortions to be performed in a hospital.

   d.   A law requiring spousal consent.

17. Which of the following is *least* likely to qualify as a sufficient interest for invoking the due process guarantee?

   a.   The interest of a purchaser in a contingent sales contract.

   b.   The interest of a state employee under an "at will" contract.

   c.   The interest in a state cause of action.

   d.   A student's interest in not being suspended from school.

18. A state law requires that pharmacies be operated by pharmacists in good standing or by a corporation or association predominantly controlled by pharmacists. The West Lincoln State Board of Pharmacy denied a permit to a drugstore chain because it did not comply with the stock ownership requirements of the statute. The rejected drugstore chain has contended that the state statute violates the Due Process Clause of the Fourteenth Amendment. Is the West Lincoln statute constitutional?

*

VII

EQUAL PROTECTION

Analysis

A. GENERAL STANDARDS

1. CONSTITUTIONAL TEXT
The Fourteenth Amendment provides that no state shall deny to any person within its jurisdiction the equal protection of the laws. While there is no corresponding provision applicable to the federal government, unreasonable classifications by the federal government violate Fifth Amendment due process. *Bolling v. Sharpe* (1954).

2. UNREASONABLE CLASSIFICATION
Not all classification violates equal protection since law generally involves different treatment of persons. Only when a classification is unreasonable, arbitrary and invidious, does it violate equal protection.

3. STANDARDS OF REASONABLENESS
The reasonableness of a classification is dependent on: (1) the basis of the classification; (2) the nature of the interests impaired by the classification; (3) the government interests supporting the classification.

During the Warren Court era, the Court used a two-tier standard of judicial review. In reviewing socio-economic classification, the Court employs a traditional, deferential rational basis test. But when the law intentionally classifies on the basis of a suspect classification or significantly burdens fundamental rights, "strict scrutiny" is used, i.e., is the classification necessary to a compelling government interest. During the Burger Court era, a third intermediate approach emerged, primarily in gender and illegitimacy cases, asking whether the classification is substantially related to an important government interest. Various justices have suggested that there is only one standard of review, with the degree of judicial scrutiny varying with the nature of the discrimination and the significance of the burden on fundamental interests.

B. TRADITIONAL EQUAL PROTECTION

1. THE RATIONAL BASIS TEST
The Equal Protection Clause of the Fourteenth Amendment traditionally has been interpreted to grant the states a wide measure of discretion with respect to making classifications in enacting legislation. As long as the classification set forth in a statute has some rational basis, i.e, it is rationally related to a permissible government interest, the Equal Protection Clause is not violated because the particular measure results in some inequality.

This rational classification test operates as follows: (1) When a classification is challenged on the basis of the Equal Protection Clause, if any state of facts reasonably can be conceived that would sustain the law, the existence of that state of facts at the time the law was enacted will be presumed. (2) One who challenges a law on the basis of the Equal Protection Clause has the burden of showing that the classification has no rational relationship to a permissible governmental purpose and is essentially arbitrary. This burden of proof, until recently, has proven essentially insurmountable.

Examples: (1) A city ordinance prohibited ads on the side of trucks but made an exception for those who owned their trucks and used their vehicles to advertise their own business. It was contended that the prohibition drew an arbitrary line between advertisements of products sold by the owner of the truck and other truck and general outdoor advertising. The Court held that the local authorities may reasonably have concluded that those who advertise their own wares on their trucks do not present the same traffic safety problems in view of the nature or extent of the advertising which they use. *REA v. New York* (1949).

(2) A ban on plastic nonreturnable milk containers while permitting the sale of milk in other nonreturnable containers, such as paperboard milk cartons, does not violate the equal protection guarantee. The state legislature could rationally have decided that its ban on plastic milk jugs might foster greater use of environmentally desirable alternative containers. Where the evidence on whether the classification would help to conserve energy and landfill space was at least debatable, the courts are not to substitute their judgment for that of the legislature. *Minnesota v. Clover Leaf Creamery Co.* (1981).

(3) A state constitutional provision subjected corporations and other entities but not private individuals to *ad valorem* personalty taxes. The Court held that such a distinction did not violate the equal protection principle since states have wide latitude in defining what they deem to be reasonable tax classifications. *Lehnhausen v. Lake Shore Auto Parts Co.* (1973).

(4) A congressional statute providing that no household may become eligible for participation in the food stamp program while a member of the household is on strike or receive an increase in the allotment of food stamps because the striker's income has decreased does not violate equal protection. The discrimination against strikers and their households vis-a-vis "voluntary quitters" is rationally related to the legitimate government interest in maintaining neutrality in private labor disputes. It is for Congress to determine the wisdom of economic or social policy. *Lyng v. International Union, UAW* (1988).

(5) A federal statute imposing a user fee only on claimants winning awards from the Iran–United States Claims Tribunal does not violate equal protection. Congress could rationally conclude that only those who are successful before the Tribunal receive a benefit sufficient to justify assessment of the fee. Congress could also rationally conclude that imposition of the fee on all claimants would undesirably deter those whose claims were small or uncertain of success from filing. *United States v. Sperry Corp.* (1989).

2. RECENT TREND

In some cases, especially recently, the Court has indicated a willingness to utilize a somewhat more stringent approach in traditional review. In these cases, the Court's analysis more closely approximates true ad hoc balancing to determine the reasonableness of the law.

Examples: (1) A Food Stamp Act provision which generally excludes from participation any household containing an individual who is unrelated to any other member of the household violates equal protection. The provision does not rationally further any legitimate state objective. For example, it is clearly unrelated to safeguarding public health and raising the nutrition levels of members of low-income households. *Moreno v. United States Dept. of Agriculture* (1972).

(2) An Alaskan law whereby income derived from the state's natural resources is distributed to Alaskan citizens based on the length of residence violates equal protection. The Court found it unnecessary to determine whether a more stringent standard of review should apply since the law failed to satisfy even the minimal rationality test. While Alaska may have an interest in encouraging residents to remain in the state, and in promoting prudent use of the state's resources, these ends are not rationally furthered by distinguishing among past residents. Rewarding citizens for past contributions is not a legitimate state purpose. *Zobel v. Williams* (1982).

(3) A state domestic preference tax imposing a substantially lower tax rate on domestic insurance companies than on out-of-state insurance companies violates the Equal Protection Clause. A state may not constitutionally favor its own residents by taxing foreign corporations at a higher rate solely because of their residence. Promotion of domestic businesses within the state by discriminating against foreign corporations that wish to compete is not a legitimate purpose under the Equal Protection Clause, nor is the encouragement of investment in state assets and governmental

securities a legitimate purpose when furthered by discrimination. *Metropolitan Life v. Ward* (1985).

(4) Mental retardation is not a "quasi-suspect" classification calling for a more exacting standard of judicial review. But application of a zoning ordinance to exclude a group home for the mentally retarded but not other similar uses is not rationally related to any legitimate government interest. Denial of a special use permit in this case appears to rest "on an irrational prejudice against the mentally retarded." *City of Cleburne v. Cleburne Living Center* (1985).

(5) A county policy which assesses real property on the basis of recent purchase price, but which makes only minor modifications to assessments of properties not recently sold, violates equal protection. The valuation scheme results in a gross disparity in the assessed value of comparable properties over a long period of time. While the government may reasonably seek to promote tax appraisal based on the true market value of property, the law must provide for some seasonable attainment of a rough equality of similarly situated property owners. While the state purported to treat all property uniformly in determining tax assessments, the county had engaged in "intentional systematic underevaluation" for ten years. *Allegheny Pittsburgh Coal Co. v. County Com'n.* (1989).

C. THE NEW EQUAL PROTECTION
STRICT SCRUTINY

When a law employs a "suspect classification" or significantly burdens the exercise of a "fundamental right," the Court strictly scrutinizes the relation of the classification to the government purpose. When the Court uses strict scrutiny, the burden is on the government to demonstrate that the classification is necessary to achieve a compelling state interest. There must not be a less burdensome alternative available for achieving the government objective. The ordinary presumption of constitutionality no longer pertains. It is extremely difficult for the government to satisfy this burden.

1. SUSPECT CLASSIFICATIONS
Strict judicial scrutiny may be used when the basis of the classification, *i.e.,* the basis on which governmental benefits are awarded or penalties imposed, significantly burdens a protected group.

2. CRITERIA OF SUSPECTNESS
Some of the factors that have been considered in labeling a classification suspect include: (1) the historical purpose of the Equal Protection Clause; (2) a

history of pervasive discrimination against the class; (3) the stigmatizing effect of the classification (commentators sometimes refer to "caste" legislation); (4) classification based on an immutable status or condition which a person can't control; (5) discrimination against a "politically insular minority."

3. PURPOSE, NOT EFFECT

Before strict scrutiny is used, the challenger must prove that the discrimination was purposeful, either overtly or covertly. While discriminatory impact or effect may be evidence of discriminatory purpose, it is usually not sufficient in itself to prove discriminatory purpose. If a decision is motivated in part by discriminatory purpose, the state may avoid strict scrutiny if it proves that it would have reached the same decision regardless of the discriminatory purpose.

Examples: (1) The fact that Blacks are four times as likely as Whites to fail a police qualifying test does not establish an equal protection violation. Discriminatory impact, standing alone, does not trigger strict constitutional review. Such a rule would have far reaching effects, raising serious questions concerning the constitutional validity of a whole range of laws. Racially discriminatory purpose must be shown to justify strict scrutiny under the Equal Protection Clause. *Washington v. Davis* (1976).

(2) A zoning ordinance may not be challenged as racially exclusionary solely on the basis that it has a racially disproportionate impact. Racial discrimination need not be the sole basis for the law but it must be a "motivating factor." Racially discriminatory intent was not sufficiently evidenced by racially disproportionate impact, historical background, specific prior events, departures from usual procedures, or contemporaneous statements of the decision-makers involved. *Village of Arlington Heights v. Metropolitan Housing Development Corp.* (1977).

(3) Mobile's at-large election of city council members does not violate the rights of Black voters under the Fourteenth and Fifteenth Amendments unless it is purposely discriminatory. There is no right for a political group to have its candidate selected, only a right not to have a purposeful denial or abridgement of the franchise. There was inadequate showing that Mobile had "conceived or operated a purposeful device to further racial discrimination." *City of Mobile v. Bolden* (1980). Compare *Rogers v. Herman Lodge* (1982), where the Court upheld a lower court finding that the at-large voting scheme was maintained as a purposeful device to further racial discrimination. Looking at the totality of the evidence, the lower court had considered the historical discrimination in elections, the failure of any Blacks to

be elected to local government despite their majority status in the general population, the unresponsiveness of public bodies to the needs of Black constituents and other factors.

(4) A state statute affording veterans an absolute lifetime preference for civil service positions does not violate equal protection even though it impacts severely on public employment opportunities of women. Volition or awareness of consequences is not discriminatory purpose. Many male non-veterans are also disadvantaged. Absent a showing that the preference was established for the purpose of discriminating against women, the classification need not meet the more stringent standard of review. It was not shown that the statute was enacted "because of" a desire to discriminate. The law serves legitimate and worthy purposes of assisting veterans to readjust to civilian life, of encouraging military enlistments and rewarding those who have served the country. *Personnel Adm. of Massachusetts v. Feeney* (1979).

(5) A provision in a state constitution disenfranchising persons convicted of crimes involving moral turpitude violates the Equal Protection Clause. Even though the provision is racially neutral on its face, its original enactment was motivated by a desire to discriminate against Blacks on account of race and the provision continues to have a racially discriminatory impact today. Evidence of legislative intent consisting of the proceedings of the state constitutional convention, several historical studies and the testimony of two expert historians was sufficient to demonstrate conclusively that the provision was enacted with the intent of disenfranchising Blacks. The racial purpose is a "but for" cause of the racial impact. Where both impermissible racial motivation and racially discriminatory impact are demonstrated, evidence of another purpose to also discriminate against poor Whites does not negate the purpose of discriminating against all Blacks. *Hunter v. Underwood* (1985).

(6) A study showing that there is a statistically greater risk that race will be considered by state decisionmakers weighing whether or not to impose the death penalty upon racial minorities does not establish purposeful discrimination under the Equal Protection Clause. In the absence of evidence specific to the challenger's case, statistical evidence such as this study establish discriminatory purpose only where the statistics establish a "stark" pattern of discrimination. Most important, the Court stressed that the decision of a constitutionally-selected jury upon whether or not to impose the death penalty is entitled to great

deference. Finally, since discretion is essential to the criminal justice process, evidence of any type would have to be exceptionally clear in order to support the inference that this discretion has been abused. *McCleskey v. Kemp* (1987).

4. LEGISLATION AND ADMINISTRATION

Legislation may be challenged as overtly or covertly discriminatory, i.e., discriminatory on its face or by extrinsic evidence showing a racially discriminatory purpose. In such cases, the statutory classification is suspect. Even if the law is neutral, it may be administered or enforced in a discriminatory fashion. If it is shown that the purpose of the administrators is to classify on a suspect basis the government must show that the classification is necessary in order to achieve a compelling state interest.

Examples: (1) A state anti-interracial marriage statute, discriminatory on its face, violates equal protection. Racial classifications are suspect and cannot be upheld when there is patently no legitimate overriding purpose—invidious racial discrimination is not a legitimate objective—which justifies the classification. *Loving v. Virginia* (1967).

(2) Two hundred Chinese who applied for laundry licenses were denied, while all applications by persons who were not Chinese were granted. The Court held that even where legislation is racially neutral, if it is applied and administered by public authorities with an unequal hand so as to make unjust discriminations between persons in similar circumstances, a violation of equal protection has occurred. *Yick Wo v. Hopkins* (1886).

5. THE LIMITS OF SUSPECTNESS
a. Race and National Origin

The very purpose of the Fourteenth Amendment was to prevent legal discrimination against racial minorities. There is seldom any justification for a classification that discriminates against a racial minority. Race is a highly visible classifying trait, historically having a stigmatizing effect. It is an immutable condition. Black persons have been unable to protect their interests through ordinary political processes. Thus, race is a suspect classification. Purposeful racial discrimination imposes a heavy burden of justification on government, *i.e.*, strict scrutiny applies.

Examples: (1) An amendment to the city charter requiring voter referendum approval for any city council action involving racial discrimination in housing violated equal protection. The law imposed a heavier burden on legislation involving fair housing than on other legislation. Race classifications are "constitutionally suspect". The city could not meet its "far heavier burden of justification." *Hunter v. Erickson* (1969).

(2) A wartime conviction under a military order excluding Americans of Japanese ancestry from designated areas on the west coast was held constitutional. While racial classifications are subject to the "most rigid scrutiny", the law was justified by wartime necessity and the alleged inability to adequately separate the loyal from the disloyal. *Korematsu v. United States* (1944).

(3) A state court's overt consideration of the political harm to the child from community racial bias in determining whether a white natural mother cohabiting with a black male should retain custody violates equal protection. Private racial bias cannot be given legal effect. *Palmore v. Sidoti* (1984).

(4) A prosecutor cannot use his peremptory challenges to exclude certain jurors based solely on their race. The state denies a black defendant equal protection when it puts him on trial before a jury from which members of his race have been excluded. A defendant makes a prima facie case by showing purposeful discrimination in selection of a jury in his particular case. The burden then shifts to the state to come forward with a neutral explanation for challenging the black jurors. *Batson v. Kentucky* (1986).

(5) Without addressing the equal protection issue, the Court held that the use of peremptory challenges to exclude all black potential jurors from the petit jury of a white defendant did not violate his Sixth Amendment right to trial by an impartial jury. The peremptory challenge system preserves the impartiality of a jury, which is the basic command of the Sixth Amendment. *Holland v. Illinois* (1990).

1) Segregation in Education
   a) De Jure Segregation
   Intentional racial segregation in public schools is inherently unequal and violates equal protection. Brown v. Board of Education *(1954).* This principle was summarily extended to public facilities generally, *e.g.,* beaches, golf courses, parks, without any showing of particularized harm resulting from the racial classification.

b) De Facto Segregation
The Supreme Court has held that *de facto* segregation, i.e., segregation which is not intentionally created by government action, does not violate equal protection.

c) Duty to Desegregate
A de jure segregated school system has an affirmative duty to desegregate and achieve a unitary school system. Green v. County School Bd. of New Kent County (1968). A school district determined to be *de jure* segregated may not take any action that has the *effect* of impeding desegregation. *Wright v. Council of City of Emporia* (1972). Once a formerly *de jure* segregated school district has desegregated, a court may not require constant revision of attendance zones to reflect a changing racial composition. *Pasadena City Board of Educ. v. Spangler* (1976).

Examples: (1) Lower court findings that a school board's past actions were animated by a segregative purpose and had a current segregative impact throughout the school system provided adequate basis for finding a violation of equal protection. Actions having a foreseeable and anticipated disparate racial impact are relevant evidence of a forbidden racial purpose. Proof of purposeful segregation in a substantial part of a system is prima facie proof that a dual school system exists. There was no showing that the school board had satisfied its affirmative duty to disestablish its dual school system. *Columbus Board of Educ. v. Penick* (1979).

(2) Maintenance of a dual school system in 1954, coupled with a failure to disestablish that dual system, provides prima facie proof that present segregation was caused, at least in part, by prior intentionally segregative acts. The affirmative duty not to take any actions that have the *effect* of increasing or perpetuating segregation in the *de jure* segregated system had been violated. The school board was under a "heavy burden" of showing that pupil assignment policies and school construction and abandonment did not perpetuate its dual system and served legitimate and important objectives. *Dayton Board of Educ. v. Brinkman* (1979) (*Dayton II*).

d) Desegregation: Balancing, Quotas and Busing

    1) In *Brown v. Board of Education* (1955) (*Brown II*), the Court ordered the defendant school districts to desegregate "with all deliberate speed." Lower federal courts were to retain jurisdiction, apply equitable principles and assure that school districts sought, in good faith, to desegregate as soon as possible.

    Resistance to desegregation eventually produced Court holdings demanding prompt conversion to a unitary school district. *Alexander v. Holmes County Board of Education* (1969). Today, lower federal courts exercise broad supervisory powers over school districts that have engaged in de jure segregation.

    2) *In remedying de jure segregation, equal protection does not require racial balancing but racial quotas may be used as measures of desegregation.* A federal court, in the exercise of its broad equity powers, may order busing in order to achieve desegregation. *Swann v. Charlotte-Mecklenburg Bd. of Educ.* (1971).

        Examples: (1) A district court order increasing local taxes to satisfy a school desegregation decree violates the principles of federal/state comity. However, a district court may order local governments to levy taxes greater than the limit set by state statute and may enjoin the operation of state laws where they interfere with implementing federal constitutional guarantees. In providing desegregation remedies, the power of the federal courts to enforce the Fourteenth Amendment against the states is in no way diminished by the Tenth Amendment's reservation of nondelegated powers to the states. *Missouri v. Jenkins* (1990).

        (2) A district court order imposing monetary sanctions upon individual Yonkers city council members for failure to vote to implement a housing desegregation order was held invalid as an abuse of discretion. The imposition of sanctions upon individual legislators subverts the normal legislative process by forcing them to act for their own interests instead of the city's. The district court's imposition of a daily fine for the

duration of the contempt on the city had a reasonable probability of success. Imposition of contempt sanctions on individual legislators until they voted to implement the order would be permissible only if the sanction against the city failed. *Spallone v. United States* (1990).

3) *Anti-Busing Laws.* The Court has not yet formulated a clear position on the validity of laws designed to prohibit busing. If the anti-busing law restructures the government decision-making process for racial reasons or adopts different government processes for decisions involving race, it is likely to violate equal protection. *Washington v. Seattle School Dist.* (1982). Compare *Crawford v. Board of Educ.* (1982) [State amendment prohibiting state courts from ordering busing held constitutional. The law was racially neutral on its face and was not enacted for a racially discriminatory purpose.]

e)   Interdistrict Segregation
The mere showing of segregation between school districts does not establish an equal protection violation. "It must be shown that racially discriminatory acts of the state or local school districts, or of a single school district has been a substantial cause of interdistrict segregation." *Milliken v. Bradley* (1974).

2)   Affirmative Action
Equal protection does preclude the voluntary use of racial classifications where a proper factual showing is made. The standard of review depends on whether the affirmative action program is mandated by Congress or by state and local government.

a)   State and Local Programs—The government must establish that the race-conscious program is necessary to a compelling government interest. The state may seek to remedy its own wrong or its passive support of private discrimination. The plan must be narrowly drawn and race-neutral means must be considered.

Examples: (1) Where a state university medical school voluntarily set aside a set number of places for minority students, a non-minority, otherwise qualified, applicant who had no opportunity to be considered for any of these places cannot be denied admission solely because of his race. However, five justices held that race or ethnicity could be a factor in the decision to admit an applicant. *Regents of the University of California v. Bakke* (1978).

(2) Layoff provisions of a collective bargaining agreement between a school board and a union were held not to be narrowly tailored to achieving a compelling government interest. Remedying societal discrimination, not traceable to the board's actions, is not a compelling justification. Remedying past or present discrimination by the state actor would suffice as a compelling interest for a narrowly tailored affirmative action program. But the layoff plan in question was not narrowly tailored given the burden on white workers and the availability of less intrusive means such as hiring goals. A majority of the Justices agreed that there need not be contemporaneous findings of actual discrimination if there is clear evidence of such discrimination and that the plan need not be limited to remedying specific instances of identified discrimination. *Wygant v. Jackson Board of Education* (1986).

(3) A city ordinance requiring prime contractors awarded city construction contracts to subcontract at least 30% of the dollar amount of each contract to minority businesses violates equal protection. Elimination of government's passive support for private racial discrimination would be a compelling interest. But the city ordinance was not based on sufficiently specific statistical findings that the city was actually remedying the effects of identified past illegal racial discrimination in the city's construction industry. Further, the city's plan was not narrowly drawn. Racially neutral alternatives must be considered. Racial quotas may not be used where case-by-case consideration is available. The city must consider the effects of its program on third parties and must limit the program in duration and scope. *City of Richmond v. J.A. Croson Co.* (1989).

b) Congressional Programs—Given the deference accorded Congress, benign race-conscious programs need not satisfy strict scrutiny review. The law must serve important government interests within the power of Congress and must be substantially related to the achievement of those objectives. The program need not be remedial.

Examples: (1) A congressional statute requiring that 10% of federal funds granted for local public works projects must be used by the grantee to procure services or supplies from businesses owned and controlled by members of statutorily identified minority groups does not violate Fifth Amendment equal protection. The program is a limited and tailored program, operating prospectively, designed to remedy prior discrimination in the construction industry. There was no showing that Congress's choice of particular minority groups to benefit from the remedy worked an invidious discrimination against other identifiable minorities making it under-inclusive. The program is not facially over-inclusive since it provides reasonable assurances that it will be limited to the remedial objectives of Congress and that improper applications will be promptly remedied administratively. *Fullilove v. Klutznick* (1980).

(2) Two FCC minority preference policies designed to promote diversity in radio and television programming do not violate equal protection. After a number of efforts to promote greater minority participation in broadcast ownership and management, the FCC adopted the two challenged policies. First, the FCC awards an "enhancement" to a license applicant with minority participation in ownership and management which is then weighed with other factors in comparing applications for new broadcast stations. Second, the FCC maintains a "distress sale" policy which allows a licensee whose qualifications are questioned to transfer the license to a qualified minority enterprise without having to undergo an FCC hearing. The FCC policies were specifically approved and mandated by Congress.

The minority preference policies serve the important government interest of promoting program diversity. Such diversity is vital to the FCC mission of serving the public interest and serves First Amendment values. The programs are substantially related to this objective since the FCC and Congress found that a nexus exists between minority ownership and diversity. This conclusion does not rest on stereotyping but reflects studies indicating that, in the aggregate, such a nexus exists. The programs were adopted only after long study and the failure of alternative race-neutral means. Procedures are available for reassessment of the programs. The programs do not involve quotas and nonminorities are still free to compete for licenses. *Metro Broadcasting, Inc. v. F.C.C.* (1990).

b.   Alienage—The "Sometimes Suspect" Classification
1)   Compelling Justification
When a state classifies on the basis of alienage, strict scrutiny normally applies. Such a classification involves a discrete and insular minority requiring judicial solicitude.

> *Example:*   A state court rule restricting admission to the bar to United States citizens violates equal protection. The state failed to show that the classification was "necessary to the accomplishment of its purpose or the safeguarding of its interests." *In re Griffiths* (1973).

2)   Political Functions Exception
However, a state need only satisfy the rational relation test when it sets qualifications for voting or for appointment of officials to important government positions which involve the definition and self-government of a state.

> *Examples:*   (1) A state law limiting appointment to the state police to U.S. citizens was upheld under traditional equal protection standards. Generally alienage classifications are suspect. However, a state need only satisfy the rational relation test when defining eligibility for positions held by "officers who participate directly in the formation, execution, or review of broad public policy." Because of the high degree of discretion afforded police, police officers fall within this exception as officers who execute broad public policy. *Foley v. Connelie* (1978).
>
> (2) Elementary and secondary public school teachers play a vital role in preparing individuals to participate as citizens and in preserving basic societal value. A state law excluding from teaching all aliens who were unwilling to apply for United States citizenship satisfies traditional equal protection. The classification is rationally related to promoting civic virtues and understanding. *Ambach v. Norwick* (1979).
>
> (3) A provision of a state Constitution requiring that peace officers be citizens does not violate equal protection. Nor is the provision unconstitutional when applied to bar permanent resident aliens from serving as

probation officers. Probation officers have powers over those for whom they have supervisory authority, often exercise unsupervised discretion, and symbolize the political community's control over those who have violated its norms. *Cabell v. Chavez-Salido* (1982).

(4) A state requirement that notaries public be United States citizens was held unconstitutional under the Equal Protection Clause. Utilizing a two-part test, the Court first examined the specificity of the classification to determine if it was sufficiently tailored to serve legitimate ends. The Court did not resolve this issue, however, because the state requirement failed the second prong of the test—the classification did not apply to a position lying at the heart of representative government. Therefore, the notary position did not qualify for the political function exception. The state failed to show that the law furthers a compelling state interest by the least burdensome means available. *Bernal v. Fainter* (1984).

3) Preemption
Note that state classifications against aliens may interfere with the national power to legislate regarding matters of immigration and naturalization. Such laws would violate the Art. VI Supremacy Clause.

Example: A state university policy preventing "nonimmigrant" aliens from qualifying for tuition preference was held invalid under the Supremacy Clause. The policy imposed an ancillary burden on certain aliens not contemplated by the congressional laws admitting them. *Toll v. Moreno* (1982).

4) Federal Discrimination
The broad power given to Congress over immigration and naturalization (Art. I, § 8, cl. 4) results in a more limited standard of judicial review being applied to federal laws discriminating against aliens which are challenged under the Fifth Amendment.

Example: A federal statute conditioning an alien's eligibility for participation in a federal medical insurance program on continuous residence in the United States for five years and admission for permanent residence does not deprive ineligible aliens of due process of law guaranteed by the Fifth Amendment. Those qualifying under the test may reasonably be presumed to have a greater affinity to the

United States than those who do not and it is therefore rational. *Mathews v. Diaz* (1976).

INTERMEDIATE REVIEW: GENDER AND ILLEGITIMACY
In recent years the Court has reviewed equal protection classifications in selected areas using an intermediate standard of review. The Court examines the classification to assure that it is substantially related to achieving an important government objective. This intermediate form of equal protection review has been applied to sex discrimination and illegitimacy classifications.

c. Gender Classifications
1) Sex Discrimination
    No Supreme Court majority has held that sex classifications are suspect. As a result, the "strict scrutiny" standard is not used. However, discrimination against women does share common characteristics with race, *e.g.*, it has been historic and pervasive and gender is highly visible and immutable. Such discrimination often reflects archaic stereotypes rather than meaningful differences between the sexes.

    a) *The Court today applies an intermediate standard of review— purposeful gender classifications against women or men "must serve important governmental objectives and must be substantially related to achievement of those objectives."* Craig v. Boren *(1976). In most intermediate review cases, the Court will use the actual government purpose and demand close correspondence of the classification to that end. Classifications are most likely to fail because the classification is not substantially related to the government interest.*

    Examples: (1) A Louisiana statute granting the husband a right to unilaterally dispose of jointly held property without the consent of the wife is an unconstitutional gender-based discrimination. The Court held that such a statute is the type of gender-based discrimination that is unconstitutional absent a showing that the classification is narrowly tailored to further important government interests. The state failed to demonstrate any such important interest. *Kirchberg v. Feenstra* (1981).

    (2) A state law denying a widower death benefits under workmen's compensation laws unless he proves dependence or physical or mental disability while granting death benefits to widows without such proof violates equal protection. Such a law discriminates against women workers who receive less protection for

their spouses. And it discriminates against male widowers since they have a heavier burden than widows in order to recover. The classification was not substantially related to an important government interest. While providing for needy spouses is an important objective, the administrative convenience of presuming dependency will not support the discrimination. *Wengler v. Druggists Mutual Ins. Co.* (1980).

(3) A women-only admissions policy at a state nursing school violates equal protection. The classification, which the state claimed was compensatory, in fact served to reinforce a stereotype of nursing as a profession for women. Since women had not been discriminated against in nursing, there was no need for compensation. Compensation was not the *actual* purpose of the government. While promoting educational diversity might serve as an important interest, the law was not substantially related to that end since the choice was given only to women, not to men. *Mississippi University for Women v. Hogan* (1982).

b)   In some cases, the Court has determined that the sexes are not similarly situated. A gender classification based on real differences rather than sexual stereotypes is likely to be upheld. Perhaps reflecting a determination that the use of gender in classifying in such cases is not suspect, the Court tends to apply a lesser standard of review. Emphasis is on mixed legislative motives and less on a particular actual purpose. The fit of the classification to the state interest need not be as precise and close as in most intermediate review cases.

Examples: (1) A state "statutory rape" law which makes men alone criminally liable for the act of sexual intercourse with a female minor does not violate the equal protection guarantee. This gender-based classification realistically reflects the fact that the sexes are not similarly situated in certain circumstances. The different treatment of males and females bears a "fair and substantial relationship" to the "important" governmental interest of preventing illegitimate teenage pregnancies, which was at least one of the purposes of the law. Because virtually all the significant harmful and identifiable consequences of teenage pregnancies fall on the female, a legislature acts reasonably when it elects to punish only the male who suffers few of the consequences of his conduct. *Michael M. v. Superior Court* (1981).

(2) A federal statute authorizing male-only draft registration does not violate the Fifth Amendment equal protection guarantee since such a gender classification realistically reflects the fact that the sexes are not similarly situated in regard to the need to provide combat troops. In matters of national defense and military preparedness, great discretion must be given to Congress. Since women are not used for combat duty, the exemption of women from registration for the draft is "closely related" to Congress' "important governmental interest" in developing a pool of potential combat troops. *Rostker v. Goldberg* (1981).

2) Discriminatory Purpose
While discriminatory effect may be evidence of discriminatory purpose, it is not enough to trigger intermediate review. Only a governmental purpose to discriminate justifies departure from the traditional rationality standard.

   Example: While veteran preference laws have the effect of disadvantaging women, this is not their purpose. Therefore, only rational basis analysis applies. The laws rationally compensate veterans for the disruptions of military service. *Personnel Adm'r of Massachusetts v. Feeney* (1979).

3) Non-sex Classifications
Remember that not all classifications which operate to the disadvantage of women or classes of women are necessarily sex classifications.

   Example: A state public health program which exempts any work loss resulting from normal pregnancy from coverage is not a sex classification. The classification is not between men and women but between "pregnant women and non-pregnant persons." In the interests of economy, a state may reasonably exclude a particular physical condition. *Geduldig v. Aiello* (1974).

4) Affirmative Action
Classifications providing benefits to women (but not to men) to remedy disadvantages have been held constitutional if narrowly drawn to

compensate for past wrongs. But the Court will probe to determine if the alleged benign purpose is the real purpose.

Examples: (1) A state law granting a property tax exemption to female widows but not male widowers is constitutional given a lone woman's greater financial difficulty. *Kahn v. Shevin* (1974).

(2) A federal statute requiring discharge of male officers passed over twice for promotion after nine years of service and of female officers after 13 years is constitutional. Congress could reasonably conclude that women line officers had less opportunity for promotion. *Schlesinger v. Ballard* (1975).

(3) An amendment to the Social Security Act permitting women to exclude more lower earning years in computing benefits than males is constitutional. The classifications worked directly to achieve the important government interest in reducing the disparity in the economic condition between men and women caused by a long history of discrimination. *Califano v. Webster* (1977).

(4) A state statute authorizing courts to award alimony to wives but not to husbands violates equal protection. Sex was not a reliable proxy for need in this case since individualized hearings on financial need already occur— actual dependency could be determined on a gender-neutral basis. The law was not carefully tailored to achieving any compensatory objective. *Orr v. Orr* (1979).

(5) A state supported university's policy of denying admission to its nursing school to otherwise qualified males violates the Equal Protection Clause. This classification cannot be justified as compensating women for past discrimination, since women do not otherwise suffer a disadvantage in this area. The classification actually tends to perpetuate the traditional stereotype that nursing is a woman's job. *Mississippi University for Women v. Hogan* (1982).

5) Mothers and Fathers
A law which discriminates against fathers and in favor of mothers where the parents are similarly situated except for their gender violates equal protection under the intermediate standard of review.

Examples: (1) A state law permitting the mother, but not the father, of an illegitimate child to block the child's adoption by withholding consent, violates equal protection. The classification was based on the overbroad generalization that the maternal role is invariably more important for children, regardless of the child's stage of development. Nor did the law bear a substantial relation to the state's interest in securing homes for illegitimate children. *Caban v. Mohammed* (1979).

(2) A state law barring the father of an illegimate child who has not legitimated the child from suing for the child's wrongful death does not violate equal protection. A plurality in the 5-4 decision used only the rational basis test on grounds that the parents are not similarly situated where only the father is in a position to legitimate the child. The statute was rationally related to the state interest in proving paternity and the avoidance of spurious claims against intestate estates. The concurring opinion and the dissent would use intermediate review. *Parham v. Hughes* (1979).

d.   Illegitimacy Classifications

Illegitimacy classifications have many of the characteristics of suspectness, *e.g.*, they are based on a status beyond the control of the child, there is a history of pervasive discrimination, illegitimates are a politically insular minority. The Court has been ambivalent in its treatment of classifications based on the legitimacy of the child. *Today, the Court appears to use an intermediate standard of review, i.e., the classification must be substantially related to an important government interest. The more that it appears that a law is based on prejudice against illegitimates, the more likely it is that the law will be held unconstitutional.*

Examples: (1) Under a state workmen's compensation law, unacknowledged dependent illegitimate children would recover benefits only if there were not enough surviving legitimate dependents to exhaust the maximum statutory benefits. The Court declared that Louisiana's denial of equal recovery rights to the dependent unacknowledged illegitimate children violated equal protection. The Court said the inferior treatment of dependent unacknowledged illegitimates bore no significant relationship to those recognized purposes of recovery underlying workmen's compensation statutes. *Weber v. Aetna Casualty & Surety Co.* (1972).

(2) A state law providing that illegitimate children can inherit by intestate succession only if a court of competent jurisdiction has, during the lifetime of the father, made a finding of paternity is constitutional. The burden placed on illegitimates substantially furthers the important state interest in assuming the just and orderly disposition of property at death. The law aids in the difficult task of establishing paternity. *Lalli v. Lalli* (1978).

(3) A Texas statute providing that a paternity suit to identify the natural father for purposes of obtaining support must be brought before the child is one year old or the suit is barred violates equal protection. The state has a legitimate interest in preventing the prosecution of stale or fraudulent claims but the "unrealistically short time limitation" of one year is not "substantially related" to this interest. There is no real threat of loss or diminution of evidence or an increased vulnerability to fraudulent claims with the passing of one year. Nor does this period provide a time sufficiently long in duration to present a reasonable opportunity for those with an interest in such children to assert claims on their behalf. Five justices, concurring, noted that a longer period of limitations would probably also fail to justify the discrimination against illegitimates. *Mills v. Habluetzel* (1982). The Court later adopted this suggestion, holding a state's two-year limitation unconstitutional. *Pickett v. Brown* (1983).

(4) A six year statute of limitation does not necessarily provide a reasonable opportunity to assert a claim on behalf of an illegitimate child. Since the statute was not substantially related to the state's interest in avoiding litigation of stale or fraudulent claims, it violated equal protection. *Clark v. Jeter* (1988).

Other Classifying Traits. Thus far, stricter standards of equal protection review has been limited to classifications drawn on the basis of race and national origin, alienage, gender, and illegitimacy. All other classifying traits are inadequate, apart from the nature of the interest burdened by the classifications, to trigger a more exacting judicial surveillance.

Example: Mental retardation is not a "quasi-suspect" classification since it is a characteristic which government may legitimately consider in a wide range of its decisions. The question of how this class is to be treated under the law is more often a question for legislatures rather than courts. The class is not politically powerless and legislatures have been responsive to the needs of the mentally retarded. There are often real differences between the mentally retarded and others. It is difficult to find a principled means for distinguishing many other groups claiming prejudice based on an immutable trait if the mentally retarded were afforded special judicial protection. *City of Cleburne v. Cleburne Living Center* (1985). But note that the law in question was held unconstitutional.

e. Wealth and Age

In the absence of infringement on some fundamental right or interest, a classification which operates to disadvantage the poor or which classifies on the basis of age, is not suspect. The Court will use the traditional rationality standard of review.

Examples: (1) A state constitutional provision requiring referenda before any government-sponsored low income housing could be built in a community was held not to violate equal protection. The provision was not racially-discriminatory on its face or in its impact. *James v. Valtierra* (1971).

(2) A state law requiring retirement of police officers on attaining the age of 50 does not violate equal protection. Discrimination against the aged has not been as historically pervasive or been used as a stereotype to the degree of race, and there is no "discrete and insular minority" of elderly persons needing judicial protection. The law rationally serves the public interest in the physical preparedness of its police. *Massachusetts Bd. of Retirement v. Murgia* (1976).

6. FUNDAMENTAL RIGHTS AND INTERESTS

FUNDAMENTAL RIGHTS. Strict scrutiny is also used because of the nature of the interests which are burdened by the classification. When a classification significantly burdens the exercise of a fundamental personal right, the government usually must prove that the classification is necessary to a compelling governmental interest. But note that the Court has increasingly used varying terminology in defining the standard of review, suggesting a movement away from the strict scrutiny formulation. *Fundamental rights may be derived independently from provisions of the Constitution or may be dependent on the Equal Protection Clause itself, e.g., voting, access to justice.*

SIGNIFICANT BURDEN. The fact that a classification has some effect on the exercise of a fundamental right does not necessarily mean that a more stringent standard of review than rationality will be applied. *In some cases, where the law does not deter, penalize or otherwise significantly burden the exercise of the protected right, the Court has applied the traditional rational basis test.*

a.   First Amendment Rights
When the government classification significantly burdens the exercise of a fundamental First Amendment right such as freedom of speech, freedom of belief and association, or the free exercise of religion, the Court will apply a stricter standard of review.

> *Examples:* (1) A statute prohibiting the picketing of residences except where it involves a place of employment in a labor dispute was held to violate the First Amendment and the Equal Protection Clause. "When government regulation discriminates among speech-related activities in a public forum, the Equal Protection Clause mandates that the legislation be finely tailored to serve substantial state interests, and the justifications offered for any distinction it draws must be carefully scrutinized." Neither the state interests in maintaining the privacy of the home nor in controlling labor disputes justified this discrimination. *Carey v. Brown* (1980).
>
> (2) Application of state statute prohibiting corporations from making campaign expenditures out of general treasury funds to a nonprofit corporation does not violate equal protection. The law satisfies strict scrutiny. The regulation of corporation campaign spending is "precisely tailored to serve the compelling state interest of eliminating from the political process the corrosive effect of political 'war chests' amassed with the aid of the legal advantages given to corporations." The exemption of media corporations is justified by the state's compelling interest in recognizing the press' unique societal role in informing and educating the public. *Austin v. Michigan Chamber of Commerce* (1990).

b.   The Right to Travel
While the Court has never clarified its constitutional source, there is a fundamental constitutional right of interstate movement. When the government makes recent exercise of interstate travel a basis for denying benefits, the classification burdens the fundamental right to travel and the strict scrutiny standard of judicial review applies. But if the classification does not deter, penalize, or otherwise significantly burden the protected right, the Court will not apply strict scrutiny. In some cases, the Court has held that the law could not satisfy even rationality review and therefore has not considered whether a stricter standard should be used.

Examples: (1) A state law which denies welfare assistance to the residents of the state who have not resided within the jurisdiction for at least one year immediately preceding their application for assistance is invalid. Such a classification burdens the fundamental right of interstate movement, and, when judged by the stricter equal protection standard of whether it promotes a compelling state interest, clearly violates the Equal Protection Clause. *Shapiro v. Thompson* (1969).

(2) A one year state residency requirement for divorce was held valid against an equal protection attack because of the importance of the state interest in divorce and because of the different character of the alleged deprivation, *i.e.*, the petitioner was not foreclosed but merely delayed. *Sosna v. Iowa* (1975).

(3) In *Zobel v. Williams* (1982) the Court invalidated Alaska's scheme for distributing state income derived from its natural resources among its citizens on the basis of duration of residency on equal protection grounds using a rationality standard. A plurality, however, in a concurring opinion, urged that the law violated the right to travel, requiring "intensified equal protection scrutiny." Alaska's scheme was deemed "inconsistent with [our] Federal structure."

(4) A state statute granting a tax exemption only to the Vietnam veterans who resided in the state before May, 1976, violates the equal protection. The Court held that the law's distinction between resident veterans is "not rationally related to the State's asserted legislative goal" of expressing its appreciation to its own citizens for honorable military service. The Court did not consider whether heightened review would be appropriate. *Hooper v. Bernalillo County Assessor* (1985).

(5) A New York Civil Service law giving an employment preference solely to resident veterans who lived in the state at the time they entered military service violates the constitutionally protected right to travel *and* the Equal Protection Clause. A plurality reasoned that, since a penalty is put on the exercise of a fundamental right, the state must have a compelling justification. The benefits involved in this case are of substantial importance and the veteran is permanently deprived of them. Since New York could satisfy its interest by giving preference to *all* qualified veterans, there were "less drastic means" available. Two concurring

justices found the state law irrational and arbitrary. *Attorney General of New York v. Soto Lopez* (1986).

c. The Right of Privacy

The right of privacy is a fundamental right. Government classifications significantly burdening exercise of the right are subject to stricter scrutiny in determining if equal protection is violated. Eisenstadt v. Baird (1972). However, if the government does not penalize or otherwise significantly burden the right of privacy, the rationality test will be used.

Example: State denial of abortion funding for welfare recipients, even while funding childcare services, does not violate equal protection. The government does not interfere with or place any obstacle in the path of the woman seeking an abortion but only encourages an alternative activity. Since no fundamental right is significantly burdened, only rationality is required. The law rationally furthers the state's strong and legitimate interest in encouraging normal childbirth. *Maher v. Roe* (1977). This principle applies even when therapeutic abortions are involved. *Harris v. McRae* (1980) (federal law); *Williams v. Zbaraz* (1980) (state law).

d. Right to Marry

Marriage is one of the "basic civil rights of man." It is deemed fundamental "to our very existence and survival." Loving v. Virginia (1967). Government classifications which significantly interfere with this right are subject to a rigorous standard of review. But, if the classification does not significantly interfere with the exercise of the fundamental right, only the rational basis test is used.

Examples: (1) A statute requiring persons having minor children not in their custody to whom they owe support payments to get court approval before they marry was held invalid under "new equal protection" standards. The statute significantly interfered with the fundamental right to marry. If the person lacks financial means, the statute bars remarriage. The classification was not "closely tailored" to effectuate "legitimate and substantial" state interests in counseling parents regarding support obligations or protecting the welfare of the children. *Zablocki v. Redhail* (1978).

(2) A Social Security Act provision under which benefits received by a disabled dependent child of a wage earner terminate when the child marries an individual not entitled to benefits under the Act does not violate equal protection. The classification is rationally related to the need of a

recipient for continued benefits. Reasonable regulations that do not significantly interfere with the protected right to marry are constitutional. *Califano v. Jobst* (1977).

FUNDAMENTAL INTERESTS. *The Court has also used a stricter standard of equal protection review to prevent discrimination in regard to fundamental interests such as voting and access to criminal justice. Equality of access to these interests is protected by the Equal Protection Clause itself; the Court does not recognize an independent right. While the Court has not rejected this precedent, it has frequently rejected use of strict scrutiny based on the importance of other interests. Today, it is usually discrimination in the exercise of independent constitutional rights that triggers strict scrutiny under the Equal Protection Clause.*

e. Voting
There is no right to vote thus far recognized in the Constitution. However, the Court has indicated that voting is a fundamental interest, preservative of other rights and closely related to First Amendment rights. When government classifications discriminate in the ability to vote or otherwise significantly burden access to the franchise, the government must prove the classification is necessary to promote a compelling governmental interest. This principle applies whether a general or special purpose election is involved.

1) Exercising the Franchise
a) Voting Qualifications
When government significantly burdens the franchise by imposing qualifications on voting beyond age, citizenship and residence in the jurisdiction, a stricter judicial scrutiny generally applies.

Examples: (1) Imposition of a state poll tax as a precondition for voting is unconstitutional. A state violates the Equal Protection Clause whenever it makes the affluence of the voter or payment of any fee an electoral standard. Voter qualifications have no relation to wealth or to paying the tax. *Harper v. Virginia State Board of Elections* (1966).

(2) A state law providing that residents who are otherwise eligible to vote in state and federal elections may vote in the school district election only if they (1) own (or lease) taxable real property within the district, or (2) are parents (or have custody of) children enrolled in the local public schools is unconstitutional. The classifications permit inclusion of many persons who have, at best, a remote and indirect interest in school affairs and, on the other hand, exclude many who have a distinct and direct

interest in the school board decisions. The classifications are not necessary to assuring participation by an interested electorate. *Kramer v. Union Free School District* (1969).

b) Special Purpose Districts
However, if the unit has such a special limited purpose that it is not truly a governmental body and if the units affected have a disproportionate effect on certain segments of the populace, the franchise can reasonably be limited to the affected group. The Court will consider the nature of the district and the effect of the activities of the district on different classes in determining whether the franchise is significantly burdened. But even a limited purpose governmental body is subject to the equal protection requirement of reasonable classification.

Examples: (1) A law permitting only landowners to vote in water storage district general elections and apportioning votes in those elections according to the assessed valuation of land is constitutional. The Court reasoned that the water storage district by virtue of its special limited purpose and of the disproportionate effect of its activities on landowners was an exception to the requirements of *Kramer*. *Salyer Land Co. v. Tulare Lake Basin Water Storage District* (1973).

(2) A state constitutional provision requiring ownership of real property as a condition of membership on a board of freeholders is a form of invidious discrimination which violates equal protection. The requirement of land ownership is not rationally related to any legitimate state interest. Understanding the issues concerning one's community and attachment to the community do not depend on property ownership. The objectives of the state could be attained by means more finely tailored to achieve the desired goal. *Quinn v. Millsap* (1989).

c) Durational Residency Requirements
While residency requirements for voting do not violate equal protection, durational residency requirements significantly burden the exercise of the franchise and impair the fundamental personal right of travel.

> ***Examples:*** (1) A one year state residency requirement as a precondition for voting is an unconstitutional denial of equal protection. The restriction is not necessary to achieve the state interests in avoiding fraud and assuring an interested electorate. *Dunn v. Blumstein* (1972).
>
> (2) A 50-day duration residency requirement and a 50-day voter registration cut-off requirement for voting is a reasonable means of preventing fraud in the process of voter registration. *Marston v. Lewis* (1973).

2) **Diluting the Franchise**
    The right to equal protection in voting can be significantly burdened not only by a denial of the franchise to a particular class of citizens through numerous voter qualifications, but also by a dilution of the effectiveness of the vote of particular classes. But the Constitution does not guarantee that your candidate will win or that you will be in a voting district with like-minded voters.

    a) **Access to the Ballot**
        Attempts by the state to significantly limit access to the ballot by minority parties and independents will succeed only if the requirements imposed are fair and not virtually exclusionary. "The differences between requiring primary votes to qualify for a position on the general election ballot and requiring signatures on nominating petitions are not of constitutional dimension" Munro v. Socialist Workers Party *(1986)* [law requiring minor party candidate to receive 1% of primary vote to qualify for place on the general election ballot upheld].

        > ***Examples:*** (1) A state law provided that candidates of "major" parties could obtain ballot position by being nominated in a primary election. However, parties that polled less than 2% of the total gubernatorial vote in the preceding general election (or new parties) had to hold precinct, county and state nominating conventions and obtain signatures equalling at least 1% of persons voting in the last gubernatorial election. These and other distinctions for access to the ballot as between "majority" and "minority" parties were held not to violate equal protection since they were not unreasonably burdensome. *American Party of Texas v. White* (1974).

(2) A state law requiring a filing fee to obtain a place on primary election ballot or to be write-in candidate—in this case, 2% of the annual salary for the state office sought ($701.60)—violated equal protection when applied to indigents. In the absence of reasonable alternative means of ballot access, a state may not, consistent with constitutional standards, require from an indigent candidate filing fees he cannot pay. *Lubin v. Panish* (1974).

(3) A provision of the Texas state constitution that prevents state and local office holders from running for the state legislature before the term of their incumbency expires does not violate the Equal Protection Clause. In view of the minimal restriction on candidacy, and the fact that the candidacy is not itself a fundamental right, the law need only bear a rational relation to a legitimate state interest. The law was sufficiently related to the goal of insuring that office holders do not abuse their position or neglect their duties because of their aspiration for higher office. *Clements v. Fashing* (1982).

b) Reapportionment
"ONE MAN–ONE VOTE" PRINCIPLE. Geographical boundaries of a governmental unit for voting may not be defined in such a way as to deny numerical equality among voters. The basic command is one person-one vote—a voting district which has twice as many voters as another district is entitled to twice as many representatives.

(1) Congressional Apportionment. *Art. I, § 2, requires that representatives be chosen "by the People of the Several States". This is a command that, as nearly as is practicable, each person's vote be equivalent to that of another.* Wesberry v. Sanders *(1964).*

(a) *Limited Variance Permitted.* The Court has said that the constitutional provision permits only limited variances from numerical equality for which there is substantial justification. *Kirkpatrick v. Preisler* (1969). The Court in *Karcher v. Daggett* (1983) rejected a .7% maximum deviation between districts absent state showing "with some specificity that a particular objective required the specific deviation in the plan."

(2) State Legislative Apportionment. *The Equal Protection Clause of the Fourteenth Amendment requires the seats in both houses of a bicameral state legislature be apportioned on a population basis. A citizen has a right to equal representation and to have his vote weighted equally with those of other citizens.* Reynolds v. Sims *(1964).*

    (a) *Greater State Variance Permitted.* Greater flexibility is constitutionally permissible with respect to state legislative apportionment than in congressional districting. A state must make a good faith effort to construct districts as nearly of equal population as is practicable but it may rationally consider traditional political subdivisions and make the necessary minimum deviations from numerical equality. *Mahan v. Howell* (1973) [permitting deviations of 16.4% from the ideal].

(3) Local Apportionment. *Whenever a local government decides to select its officials by popular election to perform governmental functions, and selects these officials from separate districts, equal protection requires that each district be established on a one man-one vote basis.* Hadley v. Junior College Dist. *(1970).*

Exception: A district may be created for such a limited purpose that it is only marginally governmental, i.e., it doesn't provide the variety of services normally associated with government. One man-one vote does not apply. *Salyer Land Co. v. Tulare Lake Basin Water Storage Dist.* (1973).

Example: A system for electing the directors of a large water reclamation district which limits voting eligibility to landowners and which apportions voting power according to the amount of land the voter owns does not violate the equal protection guarantee even though it does not satisfy one man-one vote. The district was so specialized and narrow in purpose and its activities bore on the landowners so disproportionately as to distinguish the district from those public entities exercising more general governmental functions. While the district did regulate water supply and sell electricity to numerous consumers, this was not deemed a traditional element of governmental sovereignty. Since it was necessary to limit the franchise in order to get the district started, the voting scheme had a reasonable relation to the statutory objective of supplying water. *Ball v. James* (1981).

c) Multi-member Districts

(1) Representation by two or more legislators elected at large by voters of a district does not per se violate equal protection. Such representation does not inherently invidiously discriminate against racial or political minorities. *Whitcomb v. Chavis* (1971).

(2) *However, if a challenger proves that a particular multi-member district system purposely excludes racial minorities from effective political participation, it violates equal protection and the Fifteenth Amendment.* White v. Regester *(1973).*

Examples: (1) Mobile's at-large election of city council members does not violate the rights of Black voters under the Fourteenth and Fifteenth Amendments unless it is purposely discriminatory. There is no right for a political group to have its candidates selected, only a right not to have a purposeful denial or abridgement of the franchise or purposeful discrimination affecting voting. There was inadequate showing that Mobile had "conceived or operated a purposeful device to further racial discrimination." *City of Mobile v. Bolden* (1980).

(2) An at-large voting scheme that is maintained as a purposeful device to further racial discrimination violates equal protection. The Court declined to overturn the district court's findings of racially discriminatory intent. These findings were properly based on evidence of historical discrimination in elections, the failure of any Blacks to be elected to local government despite their majority status in the general population, the unresponsiveness of public bodies to the needs of Black constituents and other factors. *Rogers v. Herman Lodge* (1982).

d) Political Gerrymandering

Apportionment schemes whereby political districts are deliberately and arbitrarily distorted for partisan political purposes violate equal protection. The challenger must prove both intentional discrimination against an identifiable group and an actual discriminatory effect on this group. Although the Court remains divided on the appropriate standards, it is established that the mere lack of proportional representation does not prove unconstitutional discrimination.

Example: Indiana's 1981 state apportionment scheme did not violate equal protection even though Democrats receiving 52% of the vote received only 43% of the seats. A plurality held that "unconstitutional discrimination occurs only when the electoral system is arranged in a manner that will consistently degrade a voter's or a group of voters' influence on the political process as a whole." While the lower court's finding of discriminatory intent was not clearly erroneous, the plurality concluded that the challengers had failed to establish a prima facie case of discriminatory vote. In addition to discriminatory intent, there must be evidence of "continued frustration" of the majority will or of effective denial of a minority of voters of a fair chance to influence the political process. *Davis v. Bandemer* (1986).

f. Access to Criminal Justice
Access to the courts for a criminal defendant is of fundamental importance. Wealth differences should not determine the kind of criminal justice a person receives, at least when the initiative for the criminal proceeding comes from the government. Cases involving equal access to criminal justice are often decided on due process grounds.

Examples: (1) A state law which makes the only appeal which an accused criminal has of right under state law dependent on whether the accused can afford to hire counsel violates the Equal Protection Clause as such. *Douglas v. California* (1963). Moreover, the defendant is entitled to effective assistance of counsel. *Evitts v. Lucey* (1985).

(2) When an indigent criminal defendant, charged with a capital offense, makes a preliminary showing that his sanity at the time of the offense is likely to be a significant factor at trial, due process requires that he have access to the psychiatric assistance necessary to prepare an effective insanity defense. A criminal trial is fundamentally unfair if the state proceeds against an indigent without making certain that he has an adequate opportunity to present his claims fairly within the adversarial system. The prisoner's interest in life is compelling. The state's interest is in full and fair determination of guilt and the financial burden is not

excessive. There is a real risk of error if psychiatric assistance is not provided. *Ake v. Oklahoma* (1985).

OTHER IMPORTANT INTERESTS. *The fact that the classification significantly burdens critically important interests such as decent housing, medical care, welfare, or education will not itself trigger a stricter standard of review than rationality. Equal protection is satisfied so long as the classification is not arbitrary.*

g. Education

1) *While education is an important social and individual interest, it has not yet been held to be a constitutional right. The rational basis test is, therefore, usually the appropriate standard of review.*

Examples: (1) Use of local property taxes to finance local education does not violate equal protection even though there are wide differences in the value of property, and hence, educational resources, among school districts. There was no showing that the state was not providing at least the minimal skills necessary for the exercise of constitutional rights, such as speech and voting. The state financing scheme bears a rational relation to the state objective of promoting local control of education. *San Antonio Ind. School Dist. v. Rodriguez* (1973).

(2) A state law authorizing nonreorganized school districts to charge a fee for school bus service does not violate equal protection. The law applies equally to all families who pay a user fee for the service. The statute is rationally related to the state's legitimate interest in fulfilling the expectations of residents of reorganized districts that they would enjoying free busing arrangements as a result of the reorganization plans. *Kadrmas v. Dickinson Public Schools* (1988).

2) *However, when education is totally denied to a discrete underclass of children while it is freely provided for other classes, the Court has applied a more searching standard of review—only a law furthering a "substantial" state goal will satisfy equal protection.*

Examples: (1) A Texas statute that denies free public education to children of illegal aliens while providing it to children of citizens or legally-admitted aliens violates equal protection. While illegal alien children are not a suspect class, they do constitute an underclass ("a permanent caste") in our society. While education is not a constitutional right, it has "a fundamental role in maintaining the fabric of our society." The state failed to show that the discrimination was justified by a substantial state interest. *Plyler v. Doe* (1982). But note that the Court upheld a Texas law denying tuition-free education to a minor living apart from his or her parent or guardian whose presence in the school district is primarily for the purpose of attending a free public education. The law was held to be a bona fide residence requirement. *Martinez v. Bynum* (1983).

(2) In *Kadrmas, supra,* the Court distinguished *Plyler* since the child was not penalized because of any illegal conduct by her parents. She was denied bus service only because her parents would not pay the same user fee charged to all families using the service. *Plyler* involved "unique circumstances" that provoked a "unique confluence of theories and rationales."

h. Welfare
While welfare assistance involves basic human needs, welfare legislation is judged by the rational basis test unless a suspect classification or fundamental right is involved.

Example: A state law which imposes a dollar ceiling ($250 per month) on the amount of aid an AFDC family received was held constitutional. Each recipient child would receive benefits according to need until the ceiling was reached and after-born children would provide no additional benefits. Since this was deemed to be social and economic legislation, not involving any suspect classification or fundamental right, the rational basis test applied. The grant ceiling was rationally related to promoting employment among welfare recipients. *Dandridge v. Williams* (1970).

D. REVIEW QUESTIONS

1. T or F In most cases, a classification which is rationally related to a permissible government interest is constitutional.

2. T or F When a government enactment has the effect of discriminating on the basis of race, strict scrutiny applies.

3. T or F If a decision is motivated in part by racial discrimination, equal protection is violated.

4. T or F If a school district is adjudged to be *de jure* segregated, it may not take action that has a segregative effect.

5. T or F Voluntary use of racial classifications by government is constitutional if the plan is adopted to remedy racial segregation.

6. T or F Alienage classifications, imposed by a state, are subject to an intermediate form of review, i.e., the classification must be substantially related to an important government interest.

7. T or F State classifications which have the effect of burdening women more severely than men must be substantially related to an important government interest.

8. T or F Classifications which discriminate against men in order to remedy past discrimination against women are constitutional if they are narrowly drawn to achieve the benign purpose.

9. T or F Illegitimacy is a suspect classification subject to strict scrutiny.

10. T or F When a classification significantly burdens the exercise of a fundamental constitutional right, the Court generally requires that government prove that the classification is necessary to a compelling government interest.

11. T or F A classification which places an obstacle to free interstate movement will be judged by strict scrutiny standards.

12. T or F While voting has not been held to be a fundamental constitutional right, the Court has applied strict scrutiny to restrictions on the franchise.

13. T or F Residency requirements significantly burden the exercise of the franchise and the right of interstate travel and are generally held to violate equal protection.

14. T or F One person-one vote applies to all local apportionment schemes as a command of the Equal Protection Clause.

15. T or F Intentional political gerrymanders violate equal protection.

16. T or F Classifications which deny education to a discrete underclass of children are judged by a more demanding standard of review than rationality.

17. Which of the following are elements of strict scrutiny equal protection review?

    a. Burden of justification on the government.

    b. The government interest must be compelling.

    c. The classification must be necessary to achieve this objective.

    d. No less burdensome alternatives must be available.

    e. All of the above are elements of the strict scrutiny standard.

18. Which of the following classifying traits will *not* trigger a stricter standard of equal protection review?

    a. Race.

    b. National origin.

    c. Gender.

    d. Wealth.

    e. Illegitimacy.

19. Which of the following has *not* been held to be a fundamental right requiring a more stringent standard of equal protection review?

    a. Interstate travel.

    b. Privacy.

    c. Housing.

    d. Marriage.

    e. All of the above have been held to be fundamental rights.

20. Welfare recipients under the joint-federal state financed Aid to Families With Dependent Children program challenged a state of West Lincoln "maximum" grant regulation which set "an upper limit on the total amount of money any one family unit may receive" on the basis of a formula which did not take into account the fact that there was a disparity in family size among welfare recipients in the state. A three judge federal district court found the regulation violative of equal protection. The case was then appealed to the Supreme Court. Does the West Lincoln Welfare program described above

violate the Equal Protection Clause of the Fourteenth Amendment? Why or why not?

21. The state of Neuter enacts a law requiring the sterilization of all welfare recipients having a third illegitimate child. Statistics indicate that the state's welfare rolls have a disproportionate proportion of Blacks. A Black welfare recipient who has been ordered to be sterilized following the birth of her third illegitimate child has brought suit alleging the law violates the Equal Protection Clause. Discuss the issues that would be raised in determining if the sterilization law violates equal protection.

VIII

FREEDOM OF EXPRESSION

Analysis

A. THE BASIC DOCTRINE OF FREEDOM OF EXPRESSION

The First Amendment to the U.S. Constitution states: "Congress shall make no law respecting an establishment of religion, or prohibiting the free exercise thereof; or abridging the freedom of speech, or of the press; or the right of the people peaceably to assemble, and to petition for a redress of grievances."

The First Amendment has a specific addressee, Congress, by which is meant the federal government generally. It was only in 1925 that the Supreme Court held that the states were bound by the guarantees of the First Amendment through the Due Process Clause of the Fourteenth Amendment.

The First Amendment guarantees but does not define freedom of speech and press. Although it has often been contended that these guarantees provide absolute protection for speech and press, the course of constitutional interpretation does not support this contention. A variety of by no means consistent doctrines have emanated from the Supreme Court which seek to define the meaning and extent of the protection accorded to freedom of speech and press under the First Amendment. The Court has generally adhered to the principle that the vital functions served by the First Amendment require that it be given a "preferred position" in relation to other constitutional values. This requires close judicial scrutiny when First Amendment rights are burdened. The present chapter focuses on freedom of expression. Freedom of religion is discussed in Chapter IX.

1. FIRST AMENDMENT RATIONALE
a. Marketplace of Ideas
The marketplace of ideas theory is based on the principle that the First Amendment forbids government from taking sides in the natural struggle of ideas. If government does not limit or restrain the marketplace of ideas, full and free expression will push the best ideas toward triumph and lead to the defeat of less worthy ones. "[T]he best test of truth is the power of the thought to get itself accepted in the competition of the market." *Abrams v. United States* (1919).

b. The Citizen Participant Model
In the famous libel case, *New York Times v. Sullivan* (1964), the Court declared that the central meaning of the First Amendment was to encourage the vigorous robust discussion of public issues and public men. Such discussion is central to democratic government in order that the people may actively participate in governing.

c. The Individual Liberty Model
Freedom of expression serves individual values as well as societal goals. It promotes individual autonomy and furthers self-determination.

2.   CONTENT CONTROL v. INDIRECT BURDENS
When government undertakes to regulate expression because of the content of the speech, i.e., because of what is being said, the courts demand substantial justification. On the other hand, when government regulation only indirectly burdens freedom of expression, e.g., content-neutral time, place and manner regulations, a lesser degree of judicial scrutiny will be used.

In the former case, the government regulates because of some harm associated with the idea or subject matter of the speech itself. In the latter case, the government regulates because of some incidental harm arising from the speech, *e.g.,* littering caused by handbilling.

a.   Categories of Speech
At times, the Court has held that certain categories of speech are not entitled to full First Amendment protection (*e.g.,* commercial speech) or to any First Amendment protection (*e.g.,* fighting words, obscenity, child pornography). In the latter cases, laws based on the content of the expression are likely to be upheld. All that is required is rationality in law-making.

b.   Strict Scrutiny
On other occasions, the Court has employed tests which impose a heavy burden of justification on government when it seeks to regulate speech content (*e.g.,* clear and present danger test, compelling state interest test). In such cases, the ordinary presumption of constitutionality is not applicable.

Example: A New York Public Service Commission order prohibiting utilities from using bill inserts to discuss controversial political matters, used to prohibit activity bill inserts on the desirability of nuclear power development, violates freedom of expression. "The First Amendment hostility to content-based regulation extends not only to restrictions on particular viewpoints, but also to prohibition of public discussion of an entire topic." Such regulation can be sustained, "only if the government can show that the regulation is a precisely drawn means of serving a compelling state interest." There was no showing that substantial privacy interests were invaded in an essentially intolerable manner; there was no "captive audience" unable to avoid the speech. Nor was there a showing that ratepayers were subsidizing the costs of the bill inserts. *Consolidated Edison Co. v. Public Service Comm'n* (1980).

c.   Balancing
When a law only indirectly burdens freedom of speech, the Court is more likely to engage in some form of overt balancing of the competing

interests to determine if the law is *reasonable*. The interests of the government in regulating the activity are weighed against the burden on free speech interests. At times, the availability of less burdensome alternatives to achieve the government interests are considered. The degree of judicial scrutiny in interest balancing varies widely. In some cases the courts engage in simple ad hoc balancing of the competing interests. In other cases, a more weighted balancing is used, *e.g.*, the law must be narrowly tailored to achieve an important government interest. Some commentators view the clear and present danger doctrine and strict scrutiny as only forms of interest balancing.

3. THE CLEAR AND PRESENT DANGER TEST: CONTENT CONTROL

Advocacy of the idea of illegal conduct, without more, is constitutionally protected. Only "where such advocacy is directed to inciting or producing imminent lawless action and is likely to incite or produce such actions," may the speech be suppressed because of its content. Brandenburg v. Ohio *(1969).*

a. The Early Formulation

1) In its most influential formulation, the clear and present danger doctrine was defined as follows: A restraint on the rights to free speech and assembly can be held permissible only if there actually exists an imminent and probable danger and an apprehended evil so substantial as to justify the governmental restraint.

2) The clear and present danger test provides that where the threatened danger is serious and imminent, the state, in such extraordinary circumstances, will be permitted to do what in normal circumstances it is not permitted to do, *i.e.*, restrain expression because of its content. The reason such restraint is permitted is because it is concluded there is insufficient time to permit full and free discussion to achieve its normally curative function. As Mr. Justice Brandeis expressed it: "Only an emergency can justify repression."

3) A *legislative* judgment that the danger is too immediate and too serious to permit the normal reliance on free discussion is not conclusive even if it is reasonable. The *Court* must conclude that a particular restraint is justified because of the danger. *Whitney v. California* (1927) (concurring opinion of Mr. Justice Brandeis).

b. The Doctrine Distorted

In 1951, in the famous Smith Act case, the Supreme Court appeared to discount the importance of the criterion of time as an integral part of the clear and present danger doctrine and thereby removed an essential feature of the test designed to afford extensive protection to free expression. The clear and present danger doctrine, said the Court, does not mean that the governmental restraint on expression is prohibited "until the putsch is about to be executed". The contention was rejected that success or probability of success is the criterion. Instead, "[i]n each case, [courts] must ask whether the gravity of the 'evil', discounted by its improbability, justified such invasion of speech as is necessary to avoid the danger." *Dennis v. United States* (1951).

c. **Advocacy v. Incitement**
Later the Court retreated from the *Dennis* holding and declared that *Dennis* was only intended to uphold restriction on advocacy of unlawful action, i.e., incitement, and was not intended to restrict advocacy of abstract doctrine. *Yates v. United States* (1957). Although the *Yates* Court did not directly address the constitutional issue, *Yates* has been understood to impliedly repudiate the *Dennis* revision of clear and present danger.

d. **The Modern Test: Incitement and Danger**
1) *The modern formulation of the clear and present danger test focuses on both the nature of the speech and the danger it presents. First, only incitement of unlawful conduct, not advocacy of abstract doctrine, can be punished. Second, only incitement to "imminent lawless action" which is "likely to incite or produce such actions," may be reached.* Brandenburg v. Ohio *(1969).*

2) Some commentators argue that the clear and present danger test is simply interest balancing using the rubrics of a formula. Others perceive such incitement to be a form of speech categorically excluded from First Amendment protection.

4. **THE BALANCING TEST: INDIRECT BURDENS**
Laws which are neutral as to the content of the expression and are directed at conduct are constitutional if they are reasonable even though speech is indirectly burdened. The reasonableness of the burden is determined by a balancing test.

a. **Interests Balanced**
In balancing cases, the Court weighs the governmental interest (*e.g.,* in the national security area, the interest in self preservation) against the particular constitutional right alleged to be infringed, *e.g.,* to refuse to disclose political association. Some justices have urged that balancing as it is actually used works to the disadvantage of First Amendment rights because what should be balanced is the government interest against the *societal* interest in First Amendment values.

b. **Speech-Conduct**
The Court has, at times, indicated that when speech is joined with conduct (*i.e.,* "speech plus"), it is not as entitled to First Amendment protection as "pure speech". In any case, reasonable laws, directed at the

conduct element, are constitutional even though speech is incidentally burdened. The focus of the regulation must be on the associated conduct and not on the idea being expressed—government must remain neutral regarding the content of the expression.

Example: The Secretary of State has the power to revoke a passport when the holder's activities are causing or likely to cause serious damage to national security or foreign policy. To the extent that the revocation acted to inhibit movement, it was an inhibition of action rather than of speech. *Haig v. Agee* (1981).

c. Forms of Interest Balancing

There are a variety of formulations of interest balancing. Strict scrutiny, for example, is often treated as a balancing test. Ad hoc balancing, involves a case-by-case comparison of the competing interests with no apparent weighting in favor of First Amendment values. One of the most frequently used formulations is that of *O'Brien v. United States* (1968): "A government regulation is sufficiently justified * * * if it furthers an important or substantial government interest; if the governmental interest is unrelated to the suppression of free expression; and if the incidental restriction of alleged First Amendment freedoms is no greater than is essential to the furtherance of that interest." This does not require that government use the least burdensome means, if the means are direct and effective.

Example: The government's passive enforcement policy for draft registration, under which the government prosecutes only those who report themselves as having violated the law or who are reported by others, does not violate the First Amendment. The government retains broad discretion as to whom to prosecute and so long as the prosecutor has probable cause to believe that the accused committed the offense, the decision whether to prosecute generally rests entirely within his or her discretion. The policy satisfies the *O'Brien* test. It promotes the important government interest in promoting national security by furthering prosecutorial efficiency and general deterrence. It is narrowly tailored in that it imposes no special burdens on the nonregistrant and is an interim enforcement system. *Wayte v. United States* (1985).

5. THE DOCTRINE OF PRIOR RESTRAINT: FORMS OF CONTROL

Prior restraints involve government restraints on freedom of expression which operate prior to the time that the expression enters the marketplace of ideas, e.g., licensing, permit systems, censorship, injunctions. Such restraints on expression should be distinguished from restraints operating after speech, *e.g.*, breach of the peace, disorderly conduct, defamation laws.

Prior restraints are highly suspect, both substantively and procedurally, and there is a heavy presumption against their constitutionality. The government bears a heavy burden of showing justification for the imposition of such a restraint.

a. Historically, the original understanding of the First Amendment may have been limited to a prohibition on prior restraints. Attack on administrative censorship and licensing provided the spawning ground for the development of theories of freedom of expression. Also, prior restraints tend to be more sweeping and inhibiting than post hoc restraints. Such restraints impose immediate and irreversible sanctions. While not per se impermissible, they are subject to close judicial scrutiny. *Near v. Minnesota* (1931).

b. Generally, the Court has employed the clear and present danger test or a similar standard in reviewing such prior restraints.

>   ***Examples:*** (1) Absent a statute, a court could not constitutionally issue an injunction at the request of government restraining the publication by a newspaper of a classified study on the Vietnam War. The government failed to demonstrate that the publication would necessarily involve "direct, immediate, and irreparable damage to our Nation or its people." *New York Times Co. v. United States* (1971).
>
>   (2) Judicial orders restraining criminal pretrial news publications, while intended to preserve Sixth Amendment rights to a fair trial, involve prior restraints which are the most serious and least tolerable infringements on First Amendment rights. Only a showing by government that there is clear and present danger to the administration of justice could justify such a prior restraint. In imposing such an order, a trial judge must determine (1) the nature and extent of pretrial news coverage; (2) whether other measures would be likely to mitigate the effects of unrestrained pretrial publicity; (3) the effectiveness of a restraining order in avoiding the danger. The failure to consider alternatives to a restraining order and the probable ineffectiveness of the order in promoting fair trial made such a "gag order" impermissible in the present case. *Nebraska Press Assn. v. Stuart* (1976).
>
>   (3) A protective order prohibiting dissemination, prior to trial, of information gained through the pretrial discovery process

does not violate the First Amendment. The restraint was no greater than necessary to protect the integrity of the discovery process, *i.e.*, the danger to reputation and privacy resulting from disclosure of information obtained through discovery. Emphasizing the unique character of the discovery process, the Court concluded that the order was entered on a showing of good cause, was limited to the context of pretrial civil discovery and did not restrict dissemination of the information if gained from other sources. *Seattle Times Co. v. Rhinehart* (1984).

6. FIRST AMENDMENT DUE PROCESS AND EQUAL PROTECTION: FACIAL VALIDITY AND VALIDITY AS APPLIED

Throughout your review of First Amendment law, keep in mind that a law may be attacked as facially invalid or invalid as applied given the facts in the particular case. If the language of a law is unconstitutionally vague or overbroad, on its face, the fact that it is applied in a narrow, constitutional manner will not save the law. And even a precise, narrowly drawn law can be applied in a sweeping unconstitutional way in a particular case.

a. Vagueness

A law is facially invalid if it is not drawn with sufficient clarity and definiteness to inform persons of ordinary intelligence what actions are proscribed. A vague statute regulating the First Amendment activity is fundamentally unfair, violating both due process and freedom of expression. The First Amendment demands special clarity in both criminal and civil laws burdening freedom of expression so that protected expression will not be chilled or suppressed, *e.g.*, standards in administrative licensing laws must be drawn with precision and clarity.

b. Overbreadth

A law may also be void on its face if it is substantially overbroad in that the law indiscriminately reaches both constitutionally protected and unprotected activity. A statute regulating First Amendment activities must be precisely drawn so that protected behavior is not chilled or suppressed.

Examples: (1) A city ordinance making it a crime for "one or more persons to assemble * * * on any of the sidewalks * * * and there conduct themselves in a manner annoying to persons passing by * * *" is unconstitutional on its face. It is vague and an excessive intrusion on free assembly and association. *Coates v. Cincinnati* (1971).

(2) A resolution banning all "First Amendment activities" within the central terminal of a local airport is facially unconstitutional under the First Amendment overbreadth

doctrine regardless of whether or not the terminal is a public forum. The ban is so sweeping that virtually any individual within the terminal is subject to legal action for protected expression, even individuals not posing a threat to the proffered governmental interest in preventing congestion and disruption. Such an absolute prohibition is a substantially overbroad invasion of protected speech that could not be justified by any conceivable governmental interest. Thus, it was not necessary for the Court to rule whether the affected forum was public or nonpublic; under any degree of scrutiny the law would have been unreasonable. Further the resolution was not amenable to a saving construction—it was too broad to construe it differently from its plain meaning without a series of adjudications. *Bd. of Airport Comm'rs of Los Angeles v. Jews for Jesus, Inc.* (1987).

1) Third Party Standing
A litigant has standing to challenge the constitutionality of an overbroad statute even though his activities could be reached under a properly drawn statute. Persons whose conduct could not be reached under a properly drawn law may be chilled in the exercise of their First Amendment rights. Further, the overbroad law invites selective enforcement.

2) Substantial Overbreadth
Increasingly, the Court is requiring real and substantial overbreadth for facial invalidity. *Broadrick v. Oklahoma* (1973) [state law restricting political activities of state employees held constitutional]; *New York v. Ferber* (1982) [child pornography law held constitutional]; *Bd. of Airport Comm'rs of Los Angeles v. Jews for Jesus Inc.* (1987).

c. **Less Burdensome Alternatives**
The Court will often require (especially for content-based regulations) that when a permissible governmental objective can be achieved by means which are less burdensome on First Amendment expression than the means selected, government must use the less burdensome means.

Example: The Court struck down a local ordinance prohibiting the distribution of anonymous handbills. The state argued that the purposes of the statute were to prevent false advertising and libel but the Court pointed out that the statute was not limited to the accomplishment of such purposes but by its language barred all anonymous handbills under all circumstances. *Talley v. California* (1960).

d. Equal Protection
When a classification significantly burdens the exercise of First Amendment rights by discriminating among speakers or speech activities, the classification will generally be closely scrutinized. The classification must be finely tailored to serve substantial state interests.

> *Example:* A statute prohibiting the picketing of residences except where it involves a place of employment in a labor dispute was held to violate the First Amendment and the Equal Protection Clause of the Fourteenth Amendment. The Court held that the statute regulated conduct deserving of First Amendment protection and discriminated on the basis of the content of the picketer's communication, contrary to the Fourteenth Amendment. Neither the state interests in maintaining the privacy of the home or in protecting labor disputes justifies this discrimination. *Carey v. Brown* (1980).

7. CORPORATE SPEECH
The First Amendment does not indicate who may claim its protections and the Fourteenth Amendment Due Process Clause extends its protection of liberty to "persons." It has not yet been determined whether a business corporation, not chartered for expression purposes (i.e., newspapers, NAACP are chartered for expression), may claim First Amendment protection nor have appropriate standards of review been defined. However, expression which is protected under the First Amendment does not lose its protected status simply because the source of the speech is a corporation.

> *Example:* A state law prohibiting business corporations from expending funds for ballot questions unless they materially affect the business of the corporation is unconstitutional as applied to a referendum on a proposed graduated income tax. Such political speech is protected regardless of the source of the speech, unless the state demonstrates it substantially furthers a compelling interest. Since this burden was not met, the law violated freedom of expression. *First National Bank v. Bellotti* (1978).

B. FREEDOM OF ASSOCIATION AND BELIEF

While the freedom of association and belief is not expressly enumerated in the Constitution, it has been held that such a right is implicit in the First Amendment speech, press, assembly and the Fifth and Fourteenth Amendment due process "liberty" guarantees. *Increasingly, the Court has employed more stringent standards in reviewing government regulations significantly burdening the right to associate for politically expressive purposes. "Infringements * * * may be justified by regulations adopted to serve compelling state interests, unrelated to the suppression of ideas, that* *cannot be achieved through means significantly less restrictive of associational freedoms."* Roberts v. United States Jaycees *(1984).*

The First Amendment guarantee is limited to expressive association; it does not include a generalized right of social association. It is a right to associate for protected First Amendment purposes that is constitutionally protected. *City of Dallas v. Stanglin* (1989) [city ordinance limiting adult admission to teenage dance halls does not violate any First Amendment right of minors and adults to associate].

1. **RESTRAINTS ON MEMBERSHIP AND ASSOCIATIONAL ACTION**
   a. *Membership in an organization that engages in illegal advocacy cannot be punished or penalized unless the law is limited to active membership which requires (1) knowing membership in the organization (scienter); (2) with specific intent to further the illegal objectives of the organization.*

   Example: A membership clause in a federal statute which made it a felony for any person to be a member of an organization which advocated the forceful overthrow of the government knowing the purposes of the organization is valid. The Court validated the statute by declaring that the statute could only be enforced against a defendant if specific intent to engage in illegal advocacy could be shown. *Scales v. United States* (1961).

   b. The right of association includes the right to engage in joint political action to further the organization's legitimate objectives. But it does not impose on government any affirmative obligation to promote those objectives or to support the activity.

   Examples: (1) Neither the NAACP nor its members could be held liable for damages resulting from a civil rights boycott of white merchants absent a showing of participation in illegal activity causing the harm. There was no showing that any member had actual or apparent authority from the NAACP to foster illegal conduct. The fact that some participants in the boycott may have acted illegally does not justify liability for those engaged only in peaceful political associational activity. *NAACP v. Claiborne Hardware Co.* (1982).

   (2) A provision of the Internal Revenue Code granting certain tax breaks to groups which do not engage in lobbying while providing lesser tax benefits to lobbying organizations, does not violate the First Amendment. "Congress has simply chosen not to pay for [the organization's] lobbying." Congress is under no duty to subsidize the organization's political

activities. *Regan v. Taxation With Representation of Washington* (1983). *Compare F.C.C. v. League of Women Voters* (1984) [ban on editorials by public broadcasting stations receiving federal funds held violative of First Amendment].

(3) A federal statute providing that no household may become eligible for participation in a food stamp program while a member of the household is on strike or receive an increased allotment of food stamps because the income of a striking member has decreased does not violate the First Amendment. The law does not "directly or substantially" interfere with a striker's right to associate with his family or with the associational rights of strikers and their unions. Congress' decision not to subsidize the exercise of the First Amendment rights does not infringe the First Amendment. *Lyng v. International Union, UAW* (1988).

(4) A boycott, designed to force increased compensation, organized by lawyers representing indigents as court-appointed counsel, is a restraint of trade violative of the antitrust laws and is not protected by the First Amendment. The First Amendment does not protect illegal restraints of trade used as a means of securing favorable legislation. While the nonviolent activity of a political boycott is constitutionally protected under *NAACP v. Claiborne Hardware Co.* (1982) an illegal boycott designed to secure economic advantage for those who participate is not protected activity under the First Amendment. The expressive component of the attorneys' boycott activities is not sufficient to require special judicial sensitivity or prudence in applying the antitrust laws. *FTC v. Superior Court Trial Lawyers Ass'n* (1990).

2. GROUP REGISTRATION AND DISCLOSURE REQUIREMENTS

a. While a law prohibiting membership in an organization is a direct restraint on the right to associate, the restraint is generally more indirect, *e.g.*, requiring that an organization register and disclose its membership. In such cases, the Court balances the extent of the interference with the right to associate against the interests of government in the regulation.

b. In a series of cases involving subversive or extremist groups, the Court employed ad hoc balancing with deference to the legislative judgment. In other cases, involving more "legitimate" groups, the Court employed strict scrutiny. Comparing these two lines of cases, some commentators suggest that the right of association is essentially the right to engage in activities otherwise independently protected by the First Amendment. Alternatively, the enhanced review used in more recent cases may simply reflect the different times.

Examples: (1) A federal statute requiring registration of the Communist Party and disclosure of its membership as a condition for organizing was held constitutional. The Court deferred to the congressional findings concerning the magnitude of the public interests in disclosure, the pertinence of the requirement to protecting those interests, and the minimal burden on associational rights. *Communist Party of America v. Subversive Activities Control Board* (1961).

(2) A state law requiring that the Ku Klux Klan disclose the names of its officers and members, pursuant to the state's efforts to control the KKK's illegal activities is constitutional. The conviction of a member of the Klan for attending meetings knowing that the group had not satisfied the disclosure requirement was upheld. *New York ex rel. Bryant v. Zimmerman* (1928).

(3) A state attorney general may not require the NAACP to disclose to the state a list of its members in the state. Such compelled disclosure violates the First Amendment since the inviolability of privacy in group association and its indispensability to preservation of freedom of association, given the danger of reprisals, outweighs the governmental need for the information. *NAACP v. Alabama ex rel. Patterson* (1958).

(4) Application of a state law requiring political parties to report the names and addresses of campaign contributors and recipients of campaign disbursements to the Socialist Workers Party (SWP) (a minor political party which has historically been the object of governmental and private harassment), violates privacy of association and belief. The government interests in disclosure (i.e., enhancement of voters' knowledge, deterrence of corruption and enforcement of contribution limitations) are weaker in the case of minor parties while the threat to First Amendment values is greater when the disclosure involves contributors and recipients. Since the lower court concluded that the evidence established a reasonable probability that disclosure would subject contributors and recipients to threats, harassment and reprisals, the disclosure law cannot be applied to the SWP consistent with the First Amendment. *Brown v. Socialist Workers '74 Campaign Comm.* (1982).

3. RESTRAINTS ON GOVERNMENT EMPLOYMENT AND BENEFITS

a. General Principles

(1) Principles governing punishment of membership in an organization also apply to non-criminal penalties imposed on persons enjoying benefits and privileges provided by government, e.g., bar membership, government employment. No distinction can be made today regarding whether the person is exercising a right or a privilege. Civil penalties cannot be imposed for membership alone, absent scienter and specific intent.

(2) *Unconstitutional Conditions.* Government may not condition the receipt of government benefits on the surrender of First Amendment rights.

> *Example:* A refusal by a state board of bar examiners to admit an applicant to its bar solely because of past association, *i.e.*, the use of aliases, former connection with subversive organizations, and a record of arrests is invalid. In the light of the ancient vintage of the objectionable past associations and the forceful showing of good moral character in intervening years, the action of the state board violated the Constitution. *Schware v. Board of Bar Examiners of State of New Mexico* (1961).

(3) Government has a substantial interest in the fitness, qualifications, and loyalty of its employees. In implementing this interest, it has employed a variety of means, e.g., loyalty programs and loyalty oaths, disclosure requirements, legislative investigations. Reconciling these requirements with freedom of speech, association and belief has produced a mass of case law, varying over time, and often inconsistent in result. *Generally, however, the Court has employed a balancing approach, weighing the interest of government as employer in maintaining the particular regulation against the burden on First Amendment rights.*

b. Loyalty Programs and Loyalty Oaths

1) Loyalty Programs

Loyalty programs designed to remove risks from government employment cannot employ means which excessively intrude on First Amendment rights. Government must use means which have a less drastic impact on First Amendment rights. This frequently is determined by balancing the respective interests involved.

> *Examples:* (1) A federal statute which prohibited members of communist-action organizations under a final order to register from engaging "in any employment in any

defense facility" was held invalid. The statute was too broadly drawn (overbreadth) and Congress could have used less drastic means in terms of the effect on First Amendment prohibitions in order to accomplish its legislative purpose. *United States v. Robel* (1967).

(2) A complicated and intricate scheme for determining teachers' loyalty was held unconstitutional. Mere knowing membership, without any requirement of specific intent, was proscribed. The Court held that the law was insufficiently precise and not drawn with narrow specificity. Further, less drastic means were available. *Keyishian v. Board of Regents* (1967).

2) Loyalty Oaths
a) Positive Oaths
Employment may not be conditioned on an oath that one has not or will not engage in protected speech activities, such as criticism of government, discussing political doctrine, or supporting certain candidates for office. Positive oaths as a condition of government employment which promise support of the Constitution in the future are constitutional as long as the oath has reasonable relation to the individual's present and future competency for the position.

Example: Since there is no constitutionally protected right to overthrow a government by force, violence, or illegal or unconstitutional means, no constitutional right is impaired by a state requirement that a state employee must take an oath to live by the constitutional system in the future as a precondition to employment. *Cole v. Richardson* (1972).

b) Overbreadth
A broader oath probing the individual's association with organizations having illegal purposes must be limited to membership in the organization knowing its illegal goals with specific intent to promote those illegal objectives.

Example: A state loyalty oath which conditioned employment on taking an oath that the employer had not knowingly and wilfully become or remained a member of an organization seeking the forcible overthrow of government was held unconstitutional since there was no requirement of specific intent. *Elfbrandt v. Russell* (1966).

c) Vagueness
An oath cannot be framed in terms so broad that persons of ordinary intelligence could not know what is being attested. Such an oath would violate due process requirements of fairness and might chill individuals from engaging in constitutionally protected activities.

> *Example:* An oath requiring teachers to swear that they would "by precept and example promote respect for the flag and the institutions of the [United States] and that they were not members of a 'subversive organization'" was held unconstitutionally vague. *Baggett v. Bullitt* (1964).

c. **Individual Membership Disclosure: Bar Admission Requirements**
Government has an interest in limiting admission to the legal profession to those who establish their fitness and competency to practice law. Failure to cooperate with a bar committee's inquiry when the questions have a substantial relevance to such qualifications is a grounds for denying bar admission.

> *Example:* A bar applicant is not constitutionally authorized to refuse to say whether he was a member of the Communist Party. The Court declared that a state is not prohibited from denying admission to the bar to an applicant who refuses to provide unprivileged answers to questions having a substantial relevance to his qualifications. *Konigsberg v. State Bar of California* (1957).

1) But the questions must be relevant to the applicant's fitness and narrowly tailored to serve the government interest. Broad questions concerning associational memberships without reference to the character of the membership violate due process.

> *Example:* A state bar committee cannot deny admission to the bar to an applicant who refuses to answer questions concerning whether he had ever been a member of an organization advocating the forceful overthrow of the government. Since the questions did not probe knowledge or specific intent, the inquiry was an overbroad intrusion on First Amendment rights. *Baird v. State Bar* (1971).

2) But a more narrowly tailored inquiry into past associations, including inquiries into knowledge and specific intent, is permissible.

Example: A state bar committee may validly ask a bar applicant whether he or she belongs to an organization advocating the violent overthrow of the government and whether during the period of membership(s) he had the specific intent to further the organization's illegal goals. Bar examiners may inquire about Communist affiliations as a prelude to further inquiry about the nature of the applicant's association and an applicant may be excluded from admission to the bar for refusal to answer. *Law Students Civil Rights Research Council, Inc. v. Wadmond* (1971).

4. LEGISLATIVE INVESTIGATIONS AND FORCED DISCLOSURES
a. Investigatory Power
Pursuant to the necessary and proper clause, government can investigate in order to legislate. The grant of authority to an investigatory committee must be specific and explicit. Questions propounded to a witness must be "pertinent," *i.e.*, as precise and clear as due process requires in criminal cases.

b. First Amendment Limitations
In determining whether the investigation intrudes on First Amendment rights, the Court has at times balanced the government interests against the individual interests. Barenblatt v. United States *(1959). More recently, the Court has held that when an investigation intrudes on First Amendment rights of speech and association, government must show a substantial relation between that information sought and a subject of overriding and compelling government interest.* Gibson v. Florida Legislative Investigation Comm. *(1963);* DeGregory v. Attorney General *(1966).*

c. Disclosure Requirements and Self-Incrimination
1) Confessions given by government employees under threat of discharge cannot be used as a basis for a subsequent criminal prosecution since it violates the employee's privilege against self-incrimination. *Garrity v. New Jersey* (1967). The employee cannot be required to forego this privilege against self-incrimination as a condition of employment. *Gardner v. Broderick* (1968).

2) An employee who is granted immunity from criminal prosecution may not refuse to answer questions specifically, directly, and narrowly relating to the performance of his official duties. Failure to answer can be a grounds for dismissal. If the employee answers, he may be discharged because of his answers.

3) If the inquiry is broad-ranging into associations and beliefs, it is arguably barred by the First Amendment. However, it may be

possible for the employee to be removed for failure to cooperate with a relevant government inquiry.

5. GROUP LITIGATION

Litigation engaged in by groups to further organizational goals is viewed as expressive and associational conduct entitled to First Amendment protection. Government may regulate group litigation and legal services only for substantial reasons and with specificity.

> *Example:* A state may not punish a lawyer affiliated with a non-profitmaking organization who, seeking to further ideological and political goals, informs a lay person of her legal rights and tells her free representation is available from the organization. The lawyer's activity is a form of political expression and is near the core of the First Amendment. Regulations in this area must be narrowly drawn, and a showing of merely potential danger cannot justify punishment. *In re Primus* (1978).

C. FREEDOM FROM COMPELLED EXPRESSION

The First Amendment includes both the right to speak freely and the right to refrain from speaking at all. Since there is a constitutional right of freedom of association and belief, there is a correlative right to be free of compelled association and beliefs. "If there is any fixed star in our constitutional constellation, it is that no official, high or petty, can prescribe what shall be orthodox in politics, nationalism, religion, or other matters of opinion." *West Va. State Bd. of Educ. v. Barnette* (1943) [compulsory flag salute held unconstitutional].

1. In determining whether the right not to speak or associate is significantly burdened the Courts will consider factors such as whether there is a particular message prescribed by government, the probability that the public will mistakenly associate the idea with the claimant of the right, and the ability of the claimant to disavow the idea or message, the impact of the compelled expression on a group's structure or message.

2. If freedom from compelled expression is significantly burdened by government, the more stringent standards of review apply. The regulation must be narrowly tailored to serve a compelling or overriding government interest.

> *Examples:* (1) A state may not constitutionally enforce criminal sanctions against persons who cover the motto "live free or die" on passenger vehicle license plates because that motto is repugnant to their moral and religious beliefs. The right of freedom of thought protected by the First Amendment includes the right to

speak freely and the right to refrain from speaking at all. The latter limits the ability of the state to require an individual to participate in the dissemination of an ideological message by displaying it on his private property in a manner and for the express purpose that it be observed and read by the public. The state's interest in facilitating the identification of passenger vehicles and promoting the appreciation of history, individualism, and state pride are not sufficiently compelling to override the First Amendment interest at stake. *Wooley v. Maynard* (1977).

(2) Insofar as service charges imposed by a union on non-members as part of an agency shop arrangement permitted by state law are used to finance expenditures by the union for the purposes of collective bargaining, contract administration, and grievance adjustment, there is no First Amendment violation even for public employees. However, a state cannot constitutionally compel public employees to contribute to union political activities or ideological causes not germane to the union's duties as collective bargaining representative consistent with the First Amendment guarantee of freedom of belief and association. Such expenditures must be financed by charges on employees who do not object to advancing those ideas and who are not coerced into doing so against their will by the threat of loss of government employment. *Abood v. Detroit Board of Education* (1977).

(3) The use of mandatory membership dues by the California State Bar to promote political and ideological causes which some members disagree with violated those members' First Amendment rights. While California has an integrated bar, the State Bar is not designed to participate in the general government of the state and therefore is distinguishable from traditional government agencies and officials. *Abood* is controlling. In order to be permissible, the challenged expenditures must be "necessarily or reasonably incurred for the purpose of regulating the legal profession or 'improving the quality of legal service available to the people of the State.'" *Keller v. State Bar of California* (1990).

(4) An interpretation of a state human rights law barring gender discrimination by public business facilities to the males-only membership rules of the United States Jaycees does not violate the right to be free of compelled association. The state has a compelling interest in eliminating gender discrimination in publicly available goods and services. There was no showing that inclusion of females would impede the organization's ability to engage in protected activities or to disseminate its views. The

state had selected the "least restrictive means of achieving its ends." *Roberts v. United States Jaycees* (1984).

These principles were reaffirmed and applied in *Bd. of Dirs. of Rotary Int'l v. Rotary Club of Duarte* (1987).

(5) A city law prohibiting discrimination in institutions with over four hundred members, defined to include certain private clubs, is not unconstitutionally overbroad. On its face, the statute does not significantly affect the ability of individuals to form associations to advocate public or private viewpoints. Clubs are not required to abandon or alter any activities protected by the First Amendment. There is ample opportunity under the law to assure that any overbreadth in its coverage will be curable through case-by-case analysis of specific facts. *New York State Club Ass'n v. City of New York* (1988).

(6) The order of a state Public Utilities Commission requiring a public utility to place a newsletter of a rate-payers organization into its billing envelopes violates the utility's First Amendment rights. It penalizes the expression of particular points of view by the utility and forces it to alter its speech to conform to an agenda set by a third party. The utility is being compelled to use its property, *i.e.*, the billing envelope, to further views with which it may not agree. *Pacific Gas & Electric v. Public Utilities Comm. of California* (1986).

(7) However, a state law permitting the use of privately owned shopping centers for speech purposes does not violate the property owner's rights of belief and association. Since the shopping center is a public place, there is no likelihood that the property owners will be identified with the views being expressed and they can expressly disavow any such association. Finally, government is not prescribing the message being expressed. *PruneYard Shopping Center v. Robins* (1980).

D. THE ELECTORAL PROCESS

Speech involving the electoral process is at the "core" of the First Amendment. Similarly, First Amendment concerns are at their zenith when government seeks to regulate political association, including both the freedom the individual to associate and the freedom of political parties to pursue common action. *The Court will typically apply a strict scrutiny standard of review when government significantly burdens speech and association in the electoral process.*

1. CAMPAIGN SPEECH

Direct restrictions on what is said during an election campaign are tested under strict scrutiny. The restriction must be necessary to achieve a compelling government interest or be a form of unprotected expression.

Examples: (1) A state may not, consistent with the First Amendment, declare an election void because the victorious candidate violated a state law in announcing to voters during the campaign that he intended to serve at a salary less than that fixed by law. Such a statement differs from the corrupting agreements and solicitations recognized as unprotected speech. Nor can the proscription be justified as facilitating the candidacy of persons lacking independent wealth. The means are unacceptable since government cannot restrict the free exchange of ideas because voters may make a bad choice. Finally, the state interest in preventing factual misstatements is inadequate since the law excessively chills political debate—there was no showing of knowledge of falsity or reckless disregard of truth or falsity. *Brown v. Hartlage* (1982).

(2) A state law prohibiting the use of paid circulators to obtain sufficient voter signatures to place an initiative on a general election ballot violates the First Amendment right to engage in political speech. The law restricts core political expression by limiting the number of people who will convey a message and the size of the audience that can be reached. The statute also makes it less likely that the number of needed signatures will be obtained to place the initiative on the ballot for statewide discussion. The restriction was not so necessary to further the state interest in assuring grass roots support for initiatives and its interest in protecting the integrity of the process to meet the "exacting scrutiny" required to justify the burden. *Meyer v. Grant* (1988).

2. REGULATING POLITICAL PARTIES

State efforts to control national political parties are likely to be held unconstitutional. States cannot enforce their laws extraterritorially to regulate national parties. A heavy burden of justification is imposed.

Examples: (1) The First Amendment right of political association is violated when a state seeks to compel a national political party to seat a delegation at its convention chosen in a way that violates the party's rules. A state statute requiring that state delegates to the Democratic Party's national convention be seated even though those delegates were chosen through a process that included a binding state preference primary election in which voters do not declare their party affiliation was held unconstitutional. The

National Democratic Party requires that only Democrats select delegates to the convention. Even though a state has a substantial interest in the manner in which its elections are conducted, it has no compelling justification for this substantial interference with the national party's right of political association. *Democratic Party of U.S. v. Wisconsin ex rel. LaFollette* (1980).

(2) A state statute requiring voters in party primaries to be registered members of that party violates the First Amendment right to political association of the Republican Party which allows independent voters to participate in primaries. The state power to regulate the time, place, and manner of elections does not justify restricting political association. State interests in easing its financial burden in administrating the political process, preventing raiding, avoiding voter confusion and in maintaining political integrity are either not sufficiently substantial or not adequately furthered by the state law to justify the burden on constitutional association. A political party may determine its own sphere of association free from excessive state interference. *Tashjian v. Republican Party of Connecticut* (1986).

(3) A state law banning the governing bodies of political parties from endorsing candidates in the party primaries and regulating the governance of such bodies violates freedom of speech and association. The restriction directly affects speech at the core of the electoral process by hampering the ability of a party to spread its message and the ability of voters seeking information. It interferes with the freedom of association of political parties by limiting the ability to promote candidates through concerted action. The state lacks a compelling government interest in either promoting a stable political system or protecting primary voters from confusion or undue influence that would justify such burdens. Nor did the state establish that its regulation of internal party governance is necessary to the integrity of the electoral process. *Eu v. San Francisco Cty. Democratic Cent. Comm.* (1989).

3. **LIMITATIONS ON CONTRIBUTIONS AND EXPENDITURES**
    a. **Campaign Spending**
        1) *Noncorporate Spending—Attempts to limit contributions and expenditures for political campaigns constitute a burden on the rights of association and expression. However, reasonable limitations on contributions by individuals and groups, designed to serve substantial governmental interests, are permissible, since such laws permit display of support and do not impair the ability to discuss issues. Restrictions on expenditures*

by individuals and groups, however, excessively reduce the quality and quantity of communication, and are unconstitutional.

Examples: (1) The provisions of the Federal Election Campaign Act of 1971 limiting political *contributions* to candidates for federal elective office are constitutional but the provisions of the statute limiting *expenditures* by contributors or groups relative to a clearly identified candidate are not valid. The statute's primary purpose, *i.e.*, limiting the actuality and appearance of corruption resulting from large individual financial contributions, is a sufficient justification for the intrusion on freedom of political association which is a consequence of the limitation on political contributions. However, the expenditure limitations are invalid since they place substantial and direct restrictions on the ability of individuals, candidates, and associations to engage in political expression. *Buckley v. Valeo* (1976).

(2) Provisions of the Federal Election Campaign Act limiting the amount an unincorporated association may contribute to a multi-candidate political committee do not violate either the First Amendent or the equal protection guarantee of the Fifth Amendment Due Process Clause. The "speech by proxy" that the medical association was attempting to achieve by funding a multi-candidate political committee is not the sort of political advocacy entitled to full First Amendment protection. *California Medical Ass'n v. FEC* (1981).

(3) A section of the Presidential Election Campaign Fund Act making it a criminal offense for an independent political action committee (PAC) to expend more than $1000 to further the election of a presidential candidate who accepts public financing violates the First Amendment. Restrictions on the amount of money which a group can spend on political communication during a campaign would reduce the quantity of expression because virtually every means of expressing ideas in mass society requires the expenditure of money. While the government has a compelling interest in preventing corruption of the political process or the appearance of corruption, there is not sufficient evidence that PACs cause political corruption to enable the spending limitation provision to survive a rigorous First Amendment standard of review. Even if sufficient

evidence could be found, the section is fatally overbroad because it applies equally to multimillion dollar and small neighborhood PACs. *Federal Election Comm'n. v. National Conservative Political Action Committee* (1985).

2) *Corporate Spending*—Restrictions on expenditures by corporations are constitutional if they are narrowly drawn to serve the state's compelling interest in preventing the distorting and corrosive effect of corporate wealth on the political process. The unique state-conferred corporate structure that facilitates the amassing of large treasuries warrants such state spending limitations.

Examples: (1) A section of the Federal Election Campaign Act prohibiting direct expenditure of corporate funds applied to a nonprofit, voluntary political association in connection with elections to public office violates the First Amendment since it infringes upon protected political speech without a compelling government justification. The government interest in protecting the political marketplace from the corrupt influence of corporate wealth is absent when the Act is applied to a small, voluntary political association which does not engage in business activities, has no shareholders, and does not accept contributions from business corporations or labor unions. The government may only limit speech through narrowly tailored means and must not infringe speech simply because of a group's status. *Federal Election Comm'n. v. Massachusetts Citizens For Life* (1986).

(2) Application of a state statute prohibiting corporations from making campaign expenditures out of general treasury funds to a nonprofit corporation which does not have the distinctive features of the association in *FEC v. Massachusetts Citizens for Life,* supra, does not violate the First Amendment guarantee. Although the statute burdens corporate political speech, it is justified by the State's compelling interest in preventing political corruption or the appearance of undue political influence. The statute is narrowly tailored because it does not entirely prohibit corporate spending but allows expenditures from funds segregated for political contributions.

While the Chamber of Commerce is a nonprofit corporation, it lacks the three distinctive features that made Massachusetts Citizens for Life more akin to a voluntary political association than a business firm.

First, the Chamber is not formed solely for political expression but engages in a variety of nonpolitical activities. Second, members of the Chamber are like corporate shareholders who would be reluctant to leave the organization even if they disagree with its political agenda. Third, the Chamber is subject to influence from business corporations which might use the association as a conduit for political spending. *Austin v. Michigan Chamber of Commerce* (1990).

b. Ballot Referenda

Limitations on contributions in ballot referenda disputes are generally invalid. State interests supporting such laws are inadequate to satisfy the exacting scrutiny applicable to such significant restrictions on freedom of association and freedom of expression.

Example: A city ordinance placing a limitation of $250 on contributions by persons to committees formed to support or oppose a ballot referendum on rent control violates freedom of expression and association. A restriction on contributions to groups burdens freedom of association and is subject to "exacting scrutiny." The restriction also operates to significantly affect expenditures and thus restrains freedom of expression. The exception recognized in *Buckley* based on the public interest in preventing corruption of officials does not apply to ballot referenda campaigns. *Citizens Against Rent Control/Coalition for Fair Housing v. City of Berkeley* (1981).

4. FORCED DISCLOSURE REQUIREMENTS

Forced disclosure of campaign contributions by individuals and committees are subject to exacting scrutiny. However, they are upheld if narrowly drawn to serve government interests in informing the public, determining the reality and appearance of corruption and implementing valid contribution limitations. *Buckley v. Valeo* (1976). They are invalid if there is a showing of chill and harassment of associational rights. *NAACP v. Alabama ex rel. Patterson* (1958).

5. POLITICAL PATRONAGE

a. *Dismissal of public employees because of their political affiliation is permissible only if the government shows that party affiliation is, in fact, an appropriate requirement for the effective performance of the public office involved.*

Example: Attorneys in a county public defender's office cannot be dismissed on purely political grounds since this would violate their First and Fourteenth Amendment freedom of political belief and association. It would place an unconstitutional condition on receipt of a government benefit. *Branti v. Finkel* (1980).

b. The *Branti* principle also applies to decisions to hire, promote, transfer or recall public employees. Such patronage practices coerce belief and impose significant penalties on the exercise of First Amendment rights. The restrictions are not narrowly tailored to serve the government interests asserted since less intrusive means are available. *Rutan v. Republican Party of Illinois* (1990).

E. SPEECH IN THE LOCAL FORUM: THE RIGHT TO ASSEMBLE AND PETITION

The First Amendment guarantees the right of the people to assemble peaceably and to petition the government for redress of grievances. This guarantee is applicable to the states through the due process clause of the Fourteenth Amendment. Basic doctrines of First Amendment law discussed above are fully applicable to the rights of assembly and petition in the local forum. There is the demand for specificity and clarity when First Amendment rights are significantly burdened which is embodied in the prohibitions against vagueness and overbreadth. Prior restraints are especially burdened and government bears a heavy burden of justification when it uses such controls. Principles of equal protection merge into First Amendment law when government discriminates in regulating the exercise of First Amendment rights.

It is especially important for the student to emphasize the distinction between laws that are directed at the content (i.e., the idea or message) of expression and laws that are content-neutral but indirectly burden the exercise of First Amendment rights.

1. CONTROLLING SPEECH CONTENT
   a. The Danger of Disorder
      1) The Clear and Present Danger Test
      The courts often invoke the clear and present danger test in reviewing breach of the peace or disorderly conduct laws. Government must establish incitement to likely, imminent lawless conduct. *Brandenburg v. Ohio* (1969).

   Examples: (1) The state may not punish an individual for wearing a leather jacket blaring the words "Fuck the Draft" in a courthouse for breach of the peace. Absent a showing of an intent to incite illegal conduct (*i.e.*, not mere advocacy), an individual cannot be punished for the content of his speech. Nor did any of the categorical exclusions permitting regulation based on speech content apply. *Cohen v. California* (1971).

(2) An antiwar demonstrator could not be convicted for using words such as "we'll take the fucking street later." At worse, this amounted to nothing more than advocacy of illegal action at some future time. There was no showing that the defendant's words "were intended to produce, and likely to produce, *imminent* disorder." *Hess v. Indiana* (1973).

(3) A speech by NAACP leader Charles Evers warning of "discipline" against blacks violating an economic boycott of white merchants was protected speech. While constituting "strong language," Evers' speech did not authorize, ratify or directly threaten acts of violence. He did not engage in advocacy directed at inciting or producing imminent lawless action. No contemporaneous violence in fact ensued. Since Evers engaged only in protected expression, neither he nor the NAACP could be held liable for the lost earnings of white merchants in a state court action. *NAACP v. Claiborne Hardware Co.* (1982).

2) The Fighting Words Doctrine
    "Fighting Words" embrace words which have a direct tendency to cause acts of violence by the person to whom, individually, the remarks are addressed. Government has the power to punish the use of fighting words under carefully drawn statutes not susceptible of application to protected expression.

    a) Rationale
        The fighting words doctrine is based on the theory that fighting words are of such slight value as a step to truth as not to merit First Amendment protection. Such speech is not part of "freedom of speech" and is categorically excluded from First Amendment protection. While the doctrine originally was limited to face to face verbal encounters that are likely to produce a violent reaction from a reasonable person, it has increasingly been merged into the modern clear and present danger doctrine requiring incitement threatening imminent lawless action.

    b) Overbreadth and Vagueness
        The Court has provided little guidance on what words constitute fighting words. Instead it has tended to hold that the statute in question is not limited to fighting words, and therefore is overbroad or is so unclear as to be vague. Such laws are facially unconstitutional regardless of their application in the particular case.

Examples: (1) A Jehovah's Witness who called the City Marshal a "Goddamned racketeer" and a "damned fascist" could be validly prosecuted under a state statute which had received a narrowing construction from the state supreme court limited to punishing only those words which had a "direct tendency to cause acts of violence by the persons to whom individually the remark is addressed." *Chaplinsky v. New Hampshire* (1942).

(2) A state statute punishing the use of "opprobrious words or abusive language, tending to cause a breach of the peace" is unconstitutional. The law had not been construed by the state courts as limited to fighting words but had been read broadly to punish offensive language. *Gooding v. Wilson* (1972).

(3) An individual was prosecuted for saying to a police officer acting in the performance of his duties: "[Y]ou god damn m.f. police * * *." A narrowing construction by a state supreme court attempting to validate the statute under which the prosecution was brought making it unlawful "to curse or revile or to use obscene or opprobrious language" to a police officer fails where the state supreme court's construction is not limited to "fighting words" but extends to "words conveying or intending to convey disgrace." A statute so construed is constitutionally overbroad and facially invalid. *Lewis v. New Orleans* (1974).

(4) An ordinance forbidding "one or more persons to assemble * * * on any of the sidewalks * * * and there conduct themselves in a manner annoying to persons passing by * * * is a vague and overbroad intrusion on First Amendment rights. *Coates v. Cincinnati* (1971).

(5) A municipal ordinance making it unlawful intentionally to "oppose, molest, abuse or interrupt any policeman in the execution of his duties" is unconstitutionally overbroad under the First Amendment. Although city officials argued that the law dealt only with "core criminal conduct" and was content-neutral, the Court found that the ordinance also outlawed a substantial amount of

constitutionally protected speech. It was not narrowly tailored to reach only fighting words nor was it limited to situations presenting a clear and present danger of disorderly conduct. The law accorded police unconstitutional discretion in enforcement. The Court suggested that the fighting words exception is narrower where police officers are involved, since they may be reasonably expected to exercise restraint in the face of such verbal challenges. *Houston v Hill* (1987).

3) Hostile Audiences
If impending violence is due to the speaker's own provocations, then the speaker can be punished under narrowly drawn statutes (e.g., disorderly conduct, breach of the peace), limited to incitement to imminent, probable illegal action. Feiner v. New York *(1951).*
But if the source of the disruption is a crowd of listeners hostile to the speaker's message and the speaker is not seeking to incite them to disorderly conduct, the police usually must proceed against the crowd and protect the speaker. Gregory v. Chicago *(1969).*

The First Amendment protects speech even if it "induces a condition of unrest, creates dissatisfaction with conditions as they are, or even stirs people to anger." *Terminiello v. Chicago* (1949).

b. **Offensive and Abusive Language**
1) In *Chaplinsky v. New Hampshire* (1942), the Court indicated that insulting or abusive language constituted fighting words—words which by their very utterance inflict an injury (*i.e.*, verbal assault). This part of the original fighting words doctrine has been repudiated by the Court.

2) Government has no power to punish the use of words that are merely offensive, abusive, profane, or vulgar. Even abusive offensive dialogue can contribute to the marketplace of ideas. Government efforts to control such expression generally lack ascertainable standards. Further, often the emotive force of particular words is of equal or greater importance than their cognitive value. Finally, in suppressing offensive speech there is a substantial risk that ideas will also be suppressed.

Example: A defendant cannot be constitutionally convicted for wearing a jacket bearing the words "Fuck the Draft" in a county courthouse. Absent a particularized and compelling justification, the government cannot punish the use of offensive expletives. *Cohen v. California* (1971).

c. **Equal Protection as a First Amendment Doctrine**
Discrimination regarding who may use the public forum generally involves content-based distinctions. The Court subjects such content-based controls to strict scrutiny and demands substantial justification for discriminatory treatment which significantly burdens the fundamental rights of freedom of expression.

Examples: (1) A state statute barring all residential picketing except for labor disputes is unconstitutional. "When government regulation discriminates among speech-related activities in a public forum the Equal Protection Clause mandates that the legislation be finely tailored to serve substantial state interests, and the justifications offered for any distinctions it draws must be carefully scrutinized." The ban on nonlabor picketing was not narrowly tailored to promote privacy in the home. *Carey v. Brown* (1980).

(2) A university which has created a forum generally open for use by student groups violates the First Amendment freedom of speech and association when it discriminates in use of its facilities by denying access "for purposes of religious worship or religious teaching." In order to justify such discrimination in access to the public forum based on the religious content of the group's intended speech, the university must show "that its regulation is necessary to serve a compelling state interest and that it is narrowly drawn to achieve that end." The university policy is not justified by the desire to maintain separation of church and state mandated by the state and federal constitutions. *Widmar v. Vincent* (1981).

2. **REGULATING THE PUBLIC FORUM**
If government regulates speech in the "public forum," the law must be neutral as to the content of the regulated speech, it must serve a "significant governmental interest," and it must leave open ample alternative channels for communication of the information. Heffron v. International Society for Krishna Consciousness *(1981). If public property is determined to be a non-public forum, the government regulation may be based on speech content or the identity of the speaker but may not discriminate on the basis of viewpoint and must be reasonable.* Perry Educ. Assn. v. Perry Local Educators' Assn. *(1983).*

a. **The Nature of the Forum**
   1) Traditional Public Forum
      Government may not bar all communicative activity from the "quintessential" public forum, *e.g.*, streets and parks. Such places have historically been associated with expressive activity. *Hague v.*

CIO (1939). They are a natural and proper place for disseminating information. *Schneider v. New Jersey* (1939).

Examples: (1) Civil rights demonstrators who clapped, spoke, and sang but were otherwise peaceful may not be validly prosecuted for conducting a protest on traditionally public state capitol grounds. The state statute upon which the prosecution is based is so broad and all embracing as to jeopardize speech, press, assembly, and petition. *Edwards v. South Carolina* (1963).

(2) A law barring all picketing and leafletting on the sidewalks surrounding the Supreme Court is unconstitutional. Such a broad prohibition does not properly serve the public interests in protecting persons and property or maintaining proper order and decorum. *United States v. Grace* (1983).

(3) A provision of an ordinance prohibiting the display of signs within 500 feet of a foreign embassy if they tend to bring that government into public disrepute violates the First Amendment. The display clause, while not viewpoint-based, is a content-based regulation of core political speech—it focuses solely on the content of the speech and is sought to be justified as necessary to protect the dignity of embassy personnel by shielding them from critical speech. Even assuming this dignity interest is compelling, the regulation is not narrowly tailored since there are less restrictive alternatives available.

A regulation permitting police to disperse demonstrators within 500 feet of an embassy is constitutional. The congregation clause was narrowly interpreted by the lower court to permit dispersal of demonstrators only when police reasonably believe that a threat to the security or peace of the embassy is present. As interpreted, the law is not facially overbroad, but is a reasonable regulation of the place and manner of certain demonstrations. *Boos v. Barry* (1988).

2) Limited or Designated Public Forum
   a) In a number of cases, the public forum has been held to include other public property where expressive activity was not incompatible with the normal use to which the property is put.

Example: The First Amendment protects civil rights protesters engaged in a peaceful protest against segregation in a segregated public library from prosecution under a breach of peace statute. A reasonable, orderly, and limited exercise of First Amendment rights even in a public library is permissible. *Brown v. Louisiana* (1966).

b) Increasingly, the limited public forum is determined by government intent to open the property for expressive activity. When the government *designates* property as a public forum it is subject to the same limitations as apply to a traditional public forum except that government may withdraw the place from public forum designation.

Example: A state rule limiting the sale or distribution of goods and materials at a state fair to fixed locations, applied to prevent Krishnas from personal solicitation, is constitutional. State fairgrounds constitute a public forum. The fixed location rule is content-neutral and is narrowly-tailored to further the important state interest in traffic control on the crowded fairgrounds. Alternative forums such as speech at the fixed locations or personal contact off the fairgrounds, are available. *Heffron v. Int'l Society for Krishna Consciousness* (1981).

3) Nonpublic Forum

a) "Public property which is not by tradition or designation a forum for public communication" constitutes the nonpublic forum. Regulation of access to such property need only be viewpoint-neutral and reasonable. Reasonableness has been determined by a rationality test. The Court has yet to hold a regulation of the nonpublic forum unconstitutional.

(b) The sole fact that particular property is owned by the government does not make it part of the public forum. Certain publicly-owned places are inappropriate for any assembly or protest. Military bases, jails or prisons, rapid-transit cars, and mail boxes have been placed in this category.

Examples: (1) A number of students who were engaged in a demonstration at the county jail to protest the arrest on the day previous of other student civil rights demonstrators were validly convicted of trepass because not all public property is amenable to the exercise of First Amendment rights. While public property such as state capitol grounds may be open to the public, jails, built for security purposes, are not. *Adderley v. Florida* (1966).

(2) A federal statute which makes it unlawful for persons to use letter boxes, without payment of postage, to distribute notices, circulars or flyers is not an infringement of First Amendment rights. Since 1934, access to letter boxes has been unlawful except under the terms and conditions specified by Congress and the Postal Service and government has the power to preserve this property for the use to which it is lawfully dedicated. To insist upon more than viewpoint-neutral, reasonable regulation would be imposing an unreasonable burden on Congress' exercise of the authority to develop and operate a national postal system. *U.S. Postal Service v. Council of Greenburgh Civic Ass'ns.* (1981).

(3) A school district's grant of exclusive access to the interschool mail system and teacher mailboxes to the bargaining representative for the district's school teachers does not violate the First Amendment rights of a rival teacher group. School mail facilities are not by tradition or designation a public forum. They are not open to the general public or to other groups similar to a teacher's union. There was no evidence that the school district sought to discourage one viewpoint and advance another. Since use of the mail facilities allows the exclusive bargaining representative to perform effectively its obligations to all school district teachers, the differential access is reasonable. Substantial alternative channels of union-teacher communication remain open to the rival union. Equal protection cases requiring equal access apply only if there is a public forum. *Perry Educ. Assn. v. Perry Local Educators' Assn.* (1983).

(4) The federal government's exclusion of legal defense and political advocacy groups from participating in an annual charitable fund-raising drive conducted in the federal workplace does not violate the First Amendment. The Court concluded that the fund drive was neither a traditional public forum, nor a limited public forum for use by all

charitable organizations. The government could eliminate controversial groups from the fund drive to avoid disruption in the federal workplace and ensure the success of the campaign. On remand, the lower court could consider whether the exclusion was based on viewpoint discrimination. *Cornelius v. NAACP Legal Defense & Educ. Fund, Inc.* (1985).

(5) The application of a Postal Service regulation to prohibit solicitation on a post office sidewalk does not violate the First Amendment. The plurality reasoned that the postal sidewalk is not a traditional public forum since it does not have the characteristics of a general public sidewalk. It is not a public thoroughfare but leads only from the parking lot to the post office. Nor had the Postal Service dedicated the sidewalk to expressive activities. Permitting some First Amendment activity did not make the sidewalk a public fora. A plurality held that the regulation was to be reviewed under the reasonableness standards applicable to nonpublic fora.

The ban was reasonable because solicitation "is inherently disruptive of the Postal Service's business." Solicitation has the potential for evoking highly personal and subjective reactions; it impedes the normal flow of traffic. Given the difficulty of enforcing more limited regulations for the numerous post offices throughout the nation, a categorical ban is reasonable. The regulation does not discriminate on the basis of content or viewpoint.

Justice Kennedy concurred using a heightened review standard applicable to content-neutral time, place and manner regulation of protected speech. The regulation was narrowly tailored to serve significant government interests and left open alternative channels for communication. *United States v. Kokinda* (1990).

4) Privately-Owned Property
   a) Only when privately-owned property has taken on all of the attributes of publicly-owned property can it be labeled part of the public forum.

b) Generally, political protest on privately-owned property, such as shopping centers, is not privileged under the First Amendment. Trespass statutes may be constitutionally used to restrain even peaceful handbilling or demonstrations.

Examples: (1) Arrest of a Jehovah's Witness under a trespass law for distributing literature in a privately-owned company town violated freedom of speech. The property in this instance had acquired all of the attributes of a municipal area. *Marsh v. Alabama* (1946).

(2) A privately-owned shopping center may prohibit, consistent with the First Amendment, picketing on its property, even though the picketing is related to a labor dispute between the picketers and one of the lessees of the shopping center. The content of the picketing cannot render private property the functional equivalent of a municipality. Even a municipality could not discriminate in the regulation of expression on the basis of the content of that expression. If there is no First Amendment right to go on private property with respect to matters unrelated to the site of the protest, there is also no First Amendment right to go on private property with respect to a matter related to the site of the protest. *Hudgens v. NLRB* (1976).

b. **The Demand for Reasonable Regulation**
1) The *O'Brien* Standards
   The Court sometimes employs the *O'Brien* standards in reviewing regulations of the local forum. This is essentially the same standard applied in public forum cases.

Example: A law prohibiting the posting of signs on public property (utility poles) does not unconstitutionally abridge freedom of speech. Citing *O'Brien,* the Court concluded that the law is a reasonable regulation of the manner of communication closely tailored to serve the government's interest in improving the appearance of the city. The law is content-neutral and there are alternative channels of effective communication available. The mere fact that the government property could be used as a vehicle for communication does not mean the Constitution requires such uses to be permitted. Appellee failed to demonstrate the existence of a traditional right of access to utility poles for communication purposes nor had they been designated for such use. *Members of City Council of City of Los Angeles v. Taxpayers for Vincent* (1984).

2) **Determining Reasonableness**

When government regulates speech in the public forum, any time, place and manner control must be clear and precise. *The regulation must be justified without reference to the content of the speech.* Content-neutrality is not lost simply because a regulation incidentally burdens some speakers more than others. *Renton v. Playtime Theatres, Inc.* (1986). *The regulation must be narrowly drawn to further a substantial government interest but need not be the least-restrictive or least-intrusive means of achieving the interest. It is sufficient if the government interest would be achieved less effectively absent the regulation.* *Ward v. Rock Against Racism* (1989). As the public forum cases indicate, this is essentially a matter of interest balancing.

> *Example:* Two hundred protesters who conducted a protest one hundred feet from a high school, complaining that the principal had failed to redress the grievances of Black students were declared to have been validly convicted pursuant to an "anti-noise" ordinance directed to protecting schools. The ordinance was upheld because it was not a vague breach of the peace ordinance but a specific statute limited to protest during school hours. The same expressive conduct which may be constitutionally protected at other places or other times, may, when conducted next to a school while classes are in session, be validly prohibited. *Grayned v. Rockford* (1972).

a) **Speech Plus**

The fact that assembly and protest involves picketing, handbilling, or solicitation of funds does not deprive the conduct of First Amendment protection. *However, the Court frequently has suggested that when expression takes the form of "speech plus conduct", it is not entitled to the same degree of protection as "pure speech."*

> *Examples:* (1) A statute prohibiting willful obstruction of public passages, used to convict chanting, picketing, marching Black protesters on the sidewalks across the street from the jailhouse, was held vague and overbroad. But the Court rejected the proposition "that the First and Fourteenth Amendments afford the same kind of freedom to those who would communicate ideas by conduct such as patrolling,

marching, and picketing * * * as these
amendments afford to those who communicate ideas
by pure speech." *Cox v. Louisiana* (1965).

(2) *Compare:* The Court characterized clapping,
speeches, singing, and marching by a crowd of
demonstrators on statehouse grounds as "an exercise
of [First Amendment] rights in their most pristine
and classic form." *Edwards v. South Carolina* (1963).

b) **Sound Amplification and Interest Balancing**
Communication in the public forum can be subjected to content-
neutral regulation in the interest of privacy and tranquility.
Principles of freedom of speech used for the soap box orator do
not necessarily apply to forms of communication technology such
as sound trucks. While such broadcasting is protected under the
First Amendment, it may be subject to content-neutral, reasonable
regulation.

Examples: (1) A broad municipal ordinance prohibiting the use
of sound amplification devices without the permission
of the police chief and defining the permissible
subject of broadcast was held to be an
unconstitutional prior restraint. The law vested
excessive discretion in licensing administrators. *Saia
v. New York* (1948).

(2) An ordinance interpreted to prohibit the use of
only those sound trucks making "loud and raucous
noises" on city streets was held constitutional.
Kovacs v. Cooper (1949).

(3) A New York City ordinance designed to regulate
the volume of amplified music at a bandshell in
Central Park by requiring use of sound-amplification
equipment and a sound technician provided by the
City is constitutional. While the content-neutral law
employs flexible guidelines and vests considerable
discretion in administrators, "perfect clarity and
precise guidance have never been required even of
regulators that restrict expressive activity." New
York has substantial interests in protecting its
citizens from unwelcome noise even in the streets
and parks and in assuring its citizens of adequate
sound amplification at the bandshell. The regulation
is narrowly tailored since the government's

substantial interest in limiting sound volume is
served in a direct and effective way by requiring use
of the city's sound technician but giving the sponsor
autonomy regarding the sound mix. Since the city
regulation is limited only to the extent of the
amplification, the guidelines leave open ample
alternative channels of communication. *Ward v.
Rock Against Racism* (1989).

3) Protecting the Homeowner

Canvassing, handbilling and solicitation of homeowners is
constitutionally protected activity. *Martin v. Struthers* (1943) [ban on
residential handbilling held unconstitutional]. It is, however, subject
to clear, narrowly-drawn regulation designed to protect the privacy of
the homeowners or to avoid fraud.

Examples: (1) An ordinance prohibiting door-to-door solicitations
without the advance consent of the homeowner, used to
bar magazine sales, is a reasonable means of protecting
the privacy of the homeowner. *Breard v. City of
Alexandria* (1951).

(2) A federal statute permitting a homeowner to stop
mailings to his home that he considers offensive is
constitutional. "[A] mailer's right to communicate must
stop at the mailbox of an unreceptive addressee." *Rowan
v. United States Post Office Dept.* (1970).

(3) An ordinance requiring advance written notice for
purposes of identification by "any person desiring to
canvass, solicit, or call from house to house [for a
recognized charitable [or] political campaign or cause"
was held unconstitutionally vague. While solicitors may
be required to identify themselves, the ordinance vested
the undefined power in officials to determine what
messages residents could hear. *Hynes v. Mayor of
Oradell* (1976).

(4) A local ordinance prohibiting door-to-door solicitation
of contributions by charitable organizations that do not
use at least 75% of their receipts for charitable purposes
violates the First Amendment. It is facially overbroad
and unconstitutional regardless of whether or not a
narrowly drawn statute could be applied against the
challenging organization. While the village has a
substantial interest in preventing fraud and crime and

undue invasion of privacy, these interests could be sufficiently served by measures less destructive of First Amendment rights. *Village of Schaumburg v. Citizens for a Better Environment* (1980).

(5) A content-neutral city ordinance banning picketing "before or about" any residence, is constitutional. The law, as construed, prohibits only picketing focused on, and taking place in front of, a particular residence. The regulation of such focused picketing serves the significant governmental interest in protecting residential privacy and, as interpreted, leaves open ample alternative means of communicating a message. The ban is narrowly tailored since it eliminates no more than the exact evil it seeks to remedy; it forbids only targeted picketing directed at "captive" residents who are presumptively unwilling to receive the speech. *Frisby v. Schultz* (1988).

4) Licensing, Prior Restraint and the Duty to Obey
    Prior restraints on access to the public forum, embodied in permit systems, licensing requirements and court injunctions, are constitutional if they are clear, narrowly-drawn, time, place and manner regulations. In determining whether the regulation is reasonable, the courts balance the First Amendment interests against the government interests in preventing serious interference with the normal usage of the streets and in maintaining public peace and order.

    Example: Conviction of protestors under a state statute prohibiting street parades without a permit and imposing a licensing fee was held constitutional. "If a municipality has authority to control the use of its public streets for parades or processions, as it undoubtedly has, it cannot be denied authority to give consideration, without unfair discrimination to time, place and manner in relation to the other proper uses of the streets." *Cox v. New Hampshire* (1941).

    a) Facial Validity—Vagueness and Overbreadth
        Prior restraints on the use of the public forum are valid only if the regulation is drawn with precision and specificity. Vague and imprecise regulations, vesting excessive discretion in public officials, are invalid on their face, regardless of the manner in which they are administered.

        Examples: (1) Conviction of civil rights demonstrators who marched without a permit required by an ordinance directing issuance of such permits unless in the city commission's judgment "the public welfare, peace, safety, health, decency, good order, morals, or convenience require that it be refused" was overturned. As written, the ordinance was facially invalid since it vested "virtually unbridled and absolute power" in local officials. While the statute was given a narrowing interpretation by the lower court, the defendants could not have anticipated the saving construction. *Shuttlesworth v. Birmingham* (1969).

(2) A city ordinance giving the Mayor unfettered discretion to deny a permit for the placement of newsracks on public property as "not in the public interest" (he did have to give reasons) and unlimited authority to condition a permit on any terms he deems "necessary and reasonable" violates the First Amendment. The Constitution requires neutral licensing criteria to assure that official decisions are not based on the content or viewpoint of the speech being considered. *City of Lakewood v. Plain Dealer Publishing Co.* (1988).

b)   The Duty to Obey
   1) *Laws*—A licensing statute or ordinance which, if valid on its face but unconstitutionally administered, must be obeyed, until the action of the administrator is overturned. *Poulos v. New Hampshire* (1953) [denial of a license to conduct religious services in a park]. However, if the law is facially unconstitutional, it may be ignored and its invalidity established at the time of prosecution. The law is void *ab initio*. *Shuttlesworth v. Birmingham* (1969).

   2) *Injunctions*—But if the prior restraint is in the form of an injunction, it must be obeyed even if it is facially invalid. Only if the injunction is frivolous or if the court lacks jurisdiction may it be ignored. Otherwise you must obey and establish its invalidity on appellate review before marching.

      Example: An ex parte injunction issued pursuant to the ordinance later invalidated in *Shuttlesworth* could not be ignored. Conviction for contempt of court of marchers violating the injunction was upheld. The Court concluded that the protestors were not free "to ignore all the procedures of the law and carry their battle to the streets." *Walker v. Birmingham* (1967).

F. SYMBOLIC SPEECH

While action or conduct may be used as a vehicle for communicating ideas, it may also embody the idea itself—the medium can be the message. Such communicative conduct is referred to as symbolic speech. You should employ a two-part analysis in symbolic speech cases. First, ask if the conduct is communicative. Second, ask if the speech is protected by the First Amendment guarantees.

1. IS THE CONDUCT COMMUNICATIVE?
In determining whether conduct is speech, the Court examines the nature, factual context, and environment to determine if the actor has an intent to communicate a message and whether the audience viewing the conduct would understand the message. Spence v. Washington (1974).

2. IS THE SPEECH PROTECTED?
Government regulation of symbolic speech is permissible if (1) it furthers an important or substantial governmental interest; (2) if the governmental interest is unrelated to the suppression of free expression; and (3) if the incidental restriction on alleged First Amendment freedom is no greater than is essential to the furtherance of that interest. United States v. O'Brien *(1968).* If the regulation is based on the content of the symbolic speech, "the most exacting scrutiny" applies. *Texas v. Johnson* (1989).

Examples: (1) The governmental interest in the effective functioning of the Selective Service System is sufficiently legitimate and substantial to justify a law prohibiting the conduct of burning draft cards in spite of the incidental restraint on First Amendment expression. Assuring the continued availability of the certificates is an appropriately narrow means of protecting this government interest which is unrelated to the idea expressed; no alternative means would more precisely and narrowly serve the governmental interest. *United States v. O'Brien* (1968).

(2) The wearing of a black armband in school to protest the Vietnam War was "akin to pure speech" and hence protected by the First Amendment. In the absence of evidence that the symbolic conduct would "materially and substantially interfere with the requirements of appropriate discipline in the operation of the school," prohibition by school officials of the wearing of the armbands is impermissible. *Tinker v. Des Moines School Dist.* (1969).

(3) A flag misuse statute cannot be used to convict a person for displaying an American flag with a superimposed peace symbol on his own property. The nature of the activity, given the factual context and the environment, establishes this as a form of protected expression. Even assuming, arguendo, that the state has substantial interest in the physical integrity of the national flag as a symbol of our country, there was no impairment of this interest or any other governmental interest in this case. *Spence v. Washington* (1974).

(4) The federal government's passive enforcement policy for draft registration by which the government prosecutes only those who report themselves as having violated the law or who are reported by others does not violate the First Amendment. The national security interest is sufficiently important to justify regulating the nonspeech element of Wayte's conduct and the incidental limitations on his First Amendment freedoms. *Wayte v. United States* (1985).

(5) Application of a Park Service regulation to prohibit sleeping in Lafayette Park and the Mall in Washington, D.C., as part of a demonstration to protest homelessness, does not violate the First Amendment. Assuming that the demonstration is expressive conduct protected to some extent by the First Amendment, application of the regulation satisfies the *O'Brien* standards for content-neutral time, place and manner regulations. The regulation banning camping in these parks is narrowly focused to prevent wear and tear on the parks and preserve them in an attractive and intact condition. There were ample alternative channels for communication. *Clark v. Community for Creative Non-Violence* (1984).

(6) A Texas statute prohibiting desecration of a venerated object could not constitutionally be applied to convict a demonstrator for burning an American flag as part of a political protest at the Republican National Convention. The expressive and overtly political character of the flag burning as part of a protest when Ronald Reagan was renominated by the convention was intentional and apparent.

While the state sought to justify the application of the law by its interest in preventing breaches of the peace, no disturbance occurred or was threatened. The state may not presume provocative, offensive words will produce disorder and the expressive conduct involved did not constitute fighting words. The state's alternative interest in preserving the flag as a symbol of nationhood and national unity arises only from the content of the flag burner's message and is therefore content-based.

The state interest in the flag burning does not justify the means selected by the State—criminal punishment of a person for burning a flag as a means of political protest. Whether dealing with verbal speech or expressive nonverbal conduct, the State cannot proscribe speech because it is critical of the flag. *"If there is a bedrock principle underlying the First Amendment, it is that the Government may not prohibit the expression of an idea simply because society finds this idea itself offensive or disagreeable."* Texas v. Johnson (1989).

(7) The federal Flag Protection Act of 1989 which criminalizes the act of one who "knowingly mutilates, defaces, physically defiles, burns, maintains on the floor or ground, or tramples upon" a United States flag, except for conduct related to disposal of a "worn or soiled" flag is unconstitutional. Although there is no explicit content-based limit in the scope of the ban, the government interest in protecting the "physical integrity" of a privately owned flag is based on a perceived need to preserve the symbolic value of the flag. That value is implicated only when the person's treatment of the flag communicates a message that is inconsistent with the ideas which the flag symbolizes. The language of the Act also focused on disrespectful treatment of the flag and on acts likely to damage the flag's symbolic value. Since the Act is concerned with communicative impact, it is subject to the most exacting scrutiny. While the government may create and promote national symbols, it cannot proscribe expressive conduct because of its likely communicative impact, citing *Texas v. Johnson. United States v. Eichman* (1990).

G. COMMERCIAL SPEECH

1. DEFINITION
The Court has characterized as "classic commercial speech" expression that does "no more than propose a commercial transaction." *Virginia State Bd. of Pharmacy v. Virginia Citizens Consumer Council, Inc.* (1976). The Court has defined commercial speech as "expression related solely to the economic interests of the speaker and its audience." *Central Hudson Gas & Electric Corp. v. Public Service Com'n of New York* (1980). Nevertheless, there remains considerable uncertainty in determining what speech is commercial speech.

Example: Application of a federal law prohibiting the mailing of unsolicited advertisements for contraceptives to ban promotional and informational material which not only promotes a product but which discusses venereal disease and family planning was held unconstitutional. The Court initially determined that the material regulated did constitute commercial speech. Most of the mailings fell within the core notion of commercial speech in simply proposing a commercial transaction. The informational material did not become commercial speech simply by being included in an advertisement including references to products. Nor did the drug company's economic motivation turn the materials into commercial speech. But the combination of these considerations justified the lower court determination that the mailings constitute commercial speech. The Court then went on to hold that the application of the law to ban the mailings in question violated the *Central Hudson* test discussed below. *Bolger v. Youngs Drug Prods. Corp.* (1983).

2. APPLYING THE FIRST AMENDMENT

a. In early cases, the Court suggested that purely commercial speech was not First Amendment speech since it does not relate to self-government or promote individual self-dignity. See *Valentine v. Chrestensen* (1942). Further, there has been concern over the effect of extending First Amendment protection on government regulation of the economic marketplace.

b. It is now established that even commercial advertising (assuming the activity advertised is legal) enjoys some First Amendment protection. The protection, however, is not as substantial as the constitutional protection afforded political, social, or religious speech. It is argued that commercial speech has greater objectivity and hardiness permitting greater state regulation. For example, the prior restraint doctrine does not apply. The overbreadth doctrine applies only to the extent that the regulation applies to *noncommercial* speech; restriction of commercial speech will not be facially invalidated because of overbreadth. Further, even when government regulation is based on the content of the speech, the courts consider the commercial character of the speech as one factor, among others, in balancing the First Amendment interests against the governmental interests furthered by the regulation.

Example: A state statute declaring it unprofessional conduct for a licensed pharmacist to advertise the prices of prescription drugs was held invalid. Purely commercial speech is not removed from First Amendment protection. The fact that an advertiser's interest in a commercial advertisement is purely economic does not disqualify him from First Amendment protection. The consumer and society have a strong interest in the free flow of commercial information. *Virginia State*

Board of Pharmacy v. Virginia Citizens Consumer Council (1976).

3. UNPROTECTED COMMERCIAL SPEECH

Commercial speech providing information about activities which are illegal or contrary to public policy is not protected under the First Amendment. *Pittsburgh Press Co. v. Pittsburgh Com'n on Human Relations* (1973) [sex-designated help wanted ads, constituting illegal sex discrimination, not protected]. Similarly, false and misleading advertising is not protected. *Friedman v. Rogers* (1977) [state statute prohibiting use of trade names by those practicing optometry held constitutional]. Note that false defamatory publication, not involving commercial speech, does enjoy constitutional protection.

4. THE MODERN TEST

The Court now applies a four-part test to determine the constitutional protection provided commercial speech. First, the speech must not be misleading or related to unlawful activity—such speech is not protected by the First Amendment. Second, the asserted government interest must be substantial. Third, the government regulation must directly advance the governmental interest asserted. Fourth, the regulation must not be more extensive than is necessary to serve that interest. A prophylactic regulation designed to avert the potential for disruption is seldom sufficient to meet this test. The Court has held that a law can be "necessary" even if it is not the least restrictive means of achieving the substantial state interests, if it is narrowly-tailored. *Board of Trustees of State Univ. of New York v. Fox* (1989).

Examples: (1) A state prohibition on utility advertising to promote the use of electricity violates the First and Fourteenth Amendments. First, the commercial speech does not concern illegal activity and is not misleading, and, therefore, the First Amendment applies. Second, the government interests in fair rates and energy conservation are clear and substantial. Third, nevertheless, the prohibition of all advertising does not directly advance the government interest in fair rates since promotional advertising only has a speculative impact on rates. Fourth, while promotional advertising is directly related to the state's interest in energy conservation, a total prohibition is more extensive than is necessary to further the state's energy conservation interest. *Central Hudson Gas & Elec. Comm'n of New York v. Public Service Corp.* (1980).

(2) A city ordinance prohibiting outdoor advertising display signs, with the exception of on-site commercial billboards and twelve other specific categories of billboards, is an unconstitutional infringement of First Amendment rights. Only the third part of the test proved difficult. The city had reasonably decided that a

relationship exists between billboards and traffic safety and esthetics. Nevertheless, the Court accepted that a city may, for varying reasons, consider the interests of on-site advertisers to outweigh its own interests in safety and esthetics and, therefore, allow on-site billboards. The Court found the ordinance as it pertains to commercial speech, therefore, to be constitutional.

But providing a broad exemption for certain commercial messages while providing no similarly broad exemption for non-commercial messages, accords commercial speech a greater degree of protection than is accorded non-commercial speech. Because the ordinance excessively burdened protected non-commercial speech, it was unconstitutional on its face. The ordinance was not merely a reasonable time, place and manner restriction since it distinguished on the basis of content between permissible and impermissible signs. *Metromedia, Inc. v. City of San Diego* (1981).

(3) A state university has a substantial interest in regulating commercial speech in the form of Tupperware parties in college dorms, e.g., promoting an educational rather than a commercial atmosphere, promoting safety and security, preventing commercial exploitation of students and preserving residential tranquility. A regulation is narrowly tailored to advance these interests if the State proves that the law does not burden substantially more speech than is necessary to further the interest; there must be a "reasonable" fit. The case was remanded for a determination whether the regulation is constitutional as applied to commercial speech and to determine if the regulation is facially overbroad in reaching certain noncommercial speech. *Board of Trustees of State Univ. of New York v. Fox* (1989).

5. LAWYER ADVERTISING

Lawyer advertising concerning routine legal services is constitutionally protected. But not all regulation of lawyer advertising is unconstitutional under the modern commercial speech test.

Examples: (1) A flat state ban on advertising by lawyers violates the First Amendment at least in the case of advertising routine legal services describing the price and the nature of the services offered. The First Amendment interest in informed and reliable consumer decision-making necessitates invalidating a flat ban on advertising by lawyers. However, the Court left open whether competing state interests would authorize some regulation where advertising claims of quality are concerned or where the advertising is false and deceptive. Similarly, the problem of lawyer advertising in the unique context of the broadcast media was left unresolved. *Bates v. State Bar of Arizona* (1977).

(2) A state bar association constitutionally may discipline a lawyer for soliciting clients in person for pecuniary gain. In-person solicitation is not unprotected by the First Amendment. However, because it is essentially a business transaction of which speech is merely a part, the level of scrutiny is lower. The states have a strong interest in preventing the harm solicitation can cause. Disciplinary action in circumstances posing only potential danger is permissible as a prophylactic measure. *Ohralik v. Ohio State Bar Assoc.* (1978). *Compare In re Primus* (1978) [state concern over the potential for deception does not justify sanctions against an ACLU lawyer informing potential clients of the possibility of litigation].

(3) Missouri rules regulating lawyer advertising: (1) specify ten categories of information which may be included in a published advertisement in newspapers, periodicals, or the yellow pages and exclude all other information such as the jurisdiction in which the lawyer is licensed to practice; (2) delineate the precise manner in which the area or areas of practice may be described in ads; and (3) limit the mailing of professional announcement cards solely to "lawyers, clients, former clients, personal friends and relatives." Application of these rules to discipline an attorney in the absence of any showing that the lawyer's speech was misleading or that restrictions short of an absolute prohibition would be insufficient to prevent deception violates the First and Fourteenth Amendments. While commercial speech may be regulated, states must do so "with care and in a manner no more extensive than reasonably necessary to further substantial interests." *In re R.M.J.* (1982).

(4) A state supreme court reprimand of an attorney for newspaper advertising soliciting business from those injured by use of Dalkon Shields is unconstitutional. The ads were neither false nor deceptive and the government interest in the potential for deception is inadequate to justify a ban. Nor could the ban on the use of illustrations stand; the illustration involved was an accurate representation and the state's interest in preserving the dignity of the legal profession is not sufficient to justify a ban on all illustrations.

However, the decision to discipline the attorney for failure to disclose in his ads that clients might be liable for litigation costs if the lawsuit is unsuccessful does not violate the First

Amendment. Because extension of the First Amendment to commercial speech is justified by the value to the consumers of the information provided by the speech, the attorney's interest in not providing particular factual information is minimal. *Zauderer v. Office of Disciplinary Counsel of the Supreme Court of Ohio* (1985).

(5) A state may not prohibit lawyers from sending truthful, non-deceptive letters to potential clients known to face particular legal problems. There is much less risk of overreaching and undue influence from a mailed solicitation than from in-person solicitation. Nor does such mailed solicitation involve any special invasion of the recipient's privacy. A rule totally banning targeted, direct-mail solicitation by lawyers for pecuniary gain, without a particularized finding that the solicitation is false or misleading, violates the First Amendment. *Shapero v. Kentucky Bar Ass'n* (1988).

(6) The censure of an Illinois attorney by the Illinois Supreme Court for advertising himself as "Certified Civil Trial Specialist by the National Board of Trial Advocacy" on his letterhead is unconstitutional. The state cannot prohibit the advertising of facts that are true and verifiable simply because they are potentially deceptive. Only if the information is actually or inherently misleading does the state meet its heavy burden of justifying a categorical prohibition against disseminating accurate commercial information. The letterhead was neither actually nor inherently misleading and there is no dispute over the bona fides and relevance of NBTA certification. *Peel v. Attorney Registration and Disciplinary Comm'n of Illinois* (1990).

6. ADVERTISING HARMFUL ACTIVITY

The Supreme Court has indicated that truthful advertising on lawful but potentially harmful activity can be prohibited if the *Central Hudson* standards are met. In applying *Central Hudson*, the Court deferred to the legislative judgment on the appropriateness of the means—the legislature can ban advertising if this is a reasonable means. If government has the greater power to completely ban the activity, it has "the lesser power to ban advertising * * *" *Posadas de Puerto Rico Assoc. v. Tourism Co. of Puerto Rico* (1986).

Example: Although Puerto Rico has legalized casino gambling, it may ban advertising for casino gambling to the Puerto Rican public, while permitting restricted advertising outside of Puerto Rico. The government has a substantial "health, safety and welfare" interest in reducing the demand for casino gambling by the residents of

Puerto Rico (even though casino gambling by the residents is lawful). This interest is "directly advanced" by the ban since the legislature could reasonably conclude that ads would increase the demand. Puerto Rico's regulations are no more extensive than necessary since they apply only to ads aimed at residents, not tourists. It is for the legislature to decide whether to use a ban rather than a "counterspeech" policy of seeking to discourage gambling since the legislature could decide that residents, while aware of the risks of such gambling, would still be induced to engage in the harmful activity by the advertising. *Posadas de Puerto Rico Assoc. v. Tourism Co. of Puerto Rico* (1986).

H. FREEDOM OF THE PRESS

While it has been suggested that the press clause of the First Amendment be read independently of the speech clause to afford the media special constitutional protection, the Court has not accepted this reading. The press clause is read together with the speech clause as a single guarantee. Further, the Court has held that the press enjoys no First Amendment privileges or immunities beyond those afforded the ordinary citizen.

The protection afforded the press from restraints on publication is dealt with in a number of other places in the outline, e.g., prior restraint, obscenity. However, there are a number of issues of relevance to the media deserving special attention. Note, generally, that the constitutional protection afforded the press in the pre-publication, newsgathering stage is less extensive than the constitutional protection accorded against restraints on publication.

Examples: (1) A special state use tax imposed solely on the use of paper and ink in publishing violates freedom of the press regardless of the absence of any censorial motive. While the press was intentionally benefitted by a specific exemption from the general sales tax, the Court held that differential taxation of the press is permitted only if the state demonstrates "a counterbalancing interest of compelling importance that it cannot achieve without differential taxation." The state interest in raising revenues could be achieved by a generally applicable tax of businesses. Even though the state scheme imposed a lesser tax burden on the press than was applied to other businesses under the general tax laws, the Court concluded that the threat of different treatment of the press nevertheless has a censorial effect. Further, judicial assessment of the actual economic burdens of respective tax schemes was said to present too great a risk of error.

An exemption for the first $10,000 of ink and paper consumed, defended by the state as designed to create an equitable tax scheme, also was impermissible. The exemption presented a potential for abuse by singling out a few members of the press for special treatment while penalizing the remainder. The state failed to meet its heavy burden of justification. *Minneapolis Star & Tribune Co. v. Minnesota Com'r of Rev.* (1983).

(2) An Arkansas tax on general interest magazines which allows an exemption for newspapers and religious, professional, trade, and sports journals violates the freedom of the press. Selective taxation of a certain group of magazines poses a particular danger toward freedom of the press. Particularly disturbing is that such discrimination is content-based—magazines dealing with certain subjects are exempt from taxation. Applying strict scrutiny, the Court held that the tax was not necessary to the proffered state interests of raising revenue, encouraging low volume publications, or fostering communication on certain subjects. *Arkansas Writers' Project, Inc. v. Ragland* (1987).

1. NEWSGATHERING

The First Amendment does extend some protection to the newsgathering process. However, the press has not been accorded a privilege to gather information beyond that of the ordinary citizen. The court will balance the effect of a regulation on the free flow of information to the public with the state interest in maintaining the regulation. In determining the responsibilities of journalists to comply with the ordinary and neutral requirements of civil and criminal procedure, the standard appears to be that the press should not be either specially burdened or specially advantaged.

a. Newsman's Privilege

The First Amendment affords journalists no privilege, qualified or absolute, to refuse to give evidence to a grand jury at least so long as it is conducted as a good faith law enforcement effort and not as a harassment device. The uncertain burden on newsgathering by requiring disclosure is outweighed by the public interest in fair and effective law enforcement. *Branzburg v. Hayes* (1972). A number of lower courts have recognized a First Amendment-based journalists privilege in other contexts, e.g., civil cases.

b. Access to Public Information and Institutions
1) Prisons
a) Censorship of Mail
Censorship of prisoners' outgoing mail violates the First Amendment right of the recipient unless (1) it furthers substantial government interests in security, order or inmate rehabilitation; and (2) it is no greater than is necessary to further this substantial government interest. *Procunier v. Martinez* (1974). Internal correspondence may be limited if the

regulation reasonably relates to legitimate penological objectives. *Turner v. Safley* (1987). This more lenient standard of judicial review has also been applied to censorship of incoming material which is perceived as presenting more of a risk than outgoing materials. *Thornburgh v. Abbott* (1989).

b) Interviewing Prisoners

Where there is a reasonable basis for a government regulation on journalist interviews with prison inmates, and alternative avenues of communication are available, it is established that the state may restrict particular modes of communication between inmates and the public. *Pell v. Procunier* (1974). It is also clear that the press has no special right of access to the prisons beyond that of the public. It is unclear whether there is a First Amendment public right of access to the prisons. However, if public access is granted, government may not discriminate against the press. *Houchins v. KQED, Inc.* (1978).

2) Judicial Proceedings

a) Criminal Trials

Closure of criminal trials violates the First Amendment guarantee of access unless such closure is necessitated by a compelling government interest and the closure is narrowly drawn to serve that interest. The presumption of openness inheres the very nature of a criminal trial under our system.

Examples: (1) Closure of the fourth trial of a murder charge, ordered on defendant's motion, without objection by the prosecution, was held to violate freedom of expression. Citing the tradition and value of open criminal trials, a Court plurality held that absent an overriding interest, articulated in trial court findings, the trial of a criminal case must be open to the public. There were no such findings. *Richmond Newspapers, Inc. v. Virginia* (1980).

(2) A state statute requiring closure of trials of designated sex offenses during the testimony of minor witnesses is unconstitutional. The government interest in encouraging young victims of sex offenses to come forward and to protect them from psychological harm is compelling. However, automatic closure, rather than case-by-case determination, is not narrowly tailored but is, rather, excessively broad. *Globe Newspaper Co. v. Superior Court* (1982).

b)   Pretrial Proceedings

(1) The Court has held that the Sixth Amendment guarantee of an open trial is a personal right of the accused and does not create a right of public access to pretrial suppression hearings. However, a badly split Court avoided deciding the question whether the First Amendment guarantees a public right of access to suppression hearings. *Gannett Co. v. DePasquale* (1979).

(2) *Voir Dire*. The examination of prospective jurors in a criminal trial is presumptively open. This presumption can be overcome "only by an overriding interest based on findings that closure is essential to preserve higher values and is narrowly tailored to serve that interest." *Press-Enterprise Co. v. Superior Court* (1984) (*Press-Enterprise I*).

(3) *Preliminary Hearings*. A qualified First Amendment right of access to preliminary hearings which have traditionally been open to the public and which play "a particularly significant and positive role in the actual functioning of the process" exists. Given the importance of public access to such proceedings, they "cannot be closed unless specific, on the record findings are made demonstrating that 'closure is essential to preserve higher values and is narrowly tailored to serve that interest.' " *Press-Enterprise Co. v. Superior Court* (1986) (*Press-Enterprise II*).

c.   **Newsroom Searches and Seizures**
The First Amendment does not afford the press any special privilege from otherwise constitutional searches and seizures beyond that of the ordinary citizen. However, warrant requirements must be applied with particular searching exactitude when the search involves the newsroom. *Zurcher v. The Stanford Daily* (1978). *Compare New York v. P.J. Video, Inc.* (1986), holding, in an obscenity context, that an application for a warrant authorizing the seizure of materials presumptively protected by the First Amendment should be evaluated by the same standard of probable cause used to review warrant applications generally.

d.   **Cameras in the Courtroom**
Permitting radio, television, and still photographic coverage of criminal trials for public broadcast, even over the objections of the defendant, does not violate due process, absent a showing of prejudice to the defendant depriving him of a fair trial. *Chandler v. Florida* (1981).

e. Copyright

The First Amendment does not protect the publishing of as yet unpublished copyrighted expression of a public figure. The substantial import of the subject matter and the fact that the words themselves which the author has used may be newsworthy does not excuse a use of material which would not ordinarily be permitted nor does it justify the unauthorized copying of the author's expression prior to publication. Copyright law protects the First Amendment interest in free expression by distinguishing between copyrightable expression and uncopyrightable facts and ideas. To create a public figure exception to copyright would impede the copyright's functions of increasing knowledge. Moreover, First Amendment protection of freedom of thought and expression includes the right to refrain from speaking. *Harper & Row Publishers, Inc. v. Nation Enterprises* (1985).

2. PUBLIC ACCESS TO THE MEDIA

The public has a First Amendment right to receive suitable access to social, political, esthetic, moral, and other ideas and experiences. First Amendment protection extends not only to the interests of the speaker but also to those of the listener. This is necessary in order to preserve an uninhibited marketplace of ideas and to promote the role of the citizenry as citizen-critics of government action.

a. Public Access to the Electronic Media

1) Fairness Doctrine

The government may constitutionally require broadcasters to discuss public issues and to provide coverage to each side of an issue. This doctrine—the fairness doctrine—promotes First Amendment values in avoiding monopolization of the limited airwaves and in producing a more informed public. *Red Lion Broadcasting Co. v. FCC* (1969). The FCC has essentially abandoned the fairness doctrine.

2) A Right of Access

There is no First Amendment right of public access to the broadcast media. Government is not constitutionally required to assure that broadcasters provide access to ideas and issues. However, a limited, reasonable congressionally-mandated statutory right of access to broadcast line is constitutional.

Examples: (1) The First Amendment does not mandate that the FCC require broadcast licensees to accept paid editorials on controversial topics. Such a doctrine would not promote the public interest in access since it would intrude on journalistic independence by involving the government excessively into decisions on what to broadcast and would tend to permit the affluent to determine the issues to be discussed. *CBS v. Democratic Nat'l Comm.* (1973).

(2) Refusal to sell air time to a legally qualified candidate for federal elective office violates the Federal Election Campaign Act of 1971, which creates an affirmative, enforceable right of reasonable access to the use of broadcast stations for individual candidates seeking elective office. This holding does not create a general right of access to the media, but rather recognizes a limited statutory right to reasonable access that pertains only to legally qualified federal candidates. *CBS v. FCC* (1981).

b. Public Access to the Print Media
Newspapers cannot be compelled to publish that which they do not choose to print. Unlike the situation in the electronic media, in the case of the print media, government may not scrutinize the editorial function.

Example: A state statute granting a political candidate a right to equal space to reply to personal attacks by a newspaper violates the First Amendment. Government regulation of what materials should go into a newspaper with respect to size and content of the paper, and the treatment of public issues and public officials constitutes an impermissible exercise of editorial control and judgment. *Miami Herald Publishing Co. v. Tornillo* (1974).

c. Access to Cable
First Amendment considerations apply when government denies a cable television franchise and refuses access to public property for power lines. While the Court has indicated some form of balancing of interests is required, it has not yet defined the applicable standards.

Example: Summary dismissal of the complaint of an applicant for a cable franchise which is denied was inappropriate. Through original programming or by exercising editorial discretion over which stations or programs to include in its repertoire, a cable company seeks to communicate messages. Where speech and conduct are joined in a single action, the First Amendment values must be balanced with competing societal interests. When the government makes factual assertions to justify cable restrictions and these are disputed, a claim has been stated and the disputed issue must be more fully developed. *City of Los Angeles v. Preferred Communications, Inc.* (1986).

3. DEFAMATION

a. Public Officials and Public Figures

The First Amendment limits the ability of government to protect the reputation of citizens through defamation actions by erecting a qualified privilege to publish. A public official may recover damages for a defamatory falsehood relating to his official conduct only if he proves that the statement was made with "actual malice", i.e., with knowledge of its falsity or with reckless disregard of whether it was true or false. New York Times v. Sullivan *(1964).* The *New York Times* privilege has been extended to public figures. *Curtis Publishing Co. v. Butts* (1967). Both the public official and the public figure plaintiff also bear the burden of establishing that a defamatory publication involving matters of public concern is false. *Philadelphia Newspapers, Inc. v. Hepps* (1986).

1) Rationale

a) The First Amendment represents a profound national commitment to uninhibited, robust and wide-open debate on public issues free from government censorship or the need for self-censorship. Further, a qualified constitutional privilege for the citizen-critic of government is a necessary corollary of the privilege protecting public officials in performing their public duties.

b) But these interests do not require protection of calculated falsehood. Defamatory publications made with actual malice are not protected speech under the First Amendment.

2) Who Is a Public Official?

a) Public officials include all "those among the hierarchy of government employees who have, or appear to the public to have, substantial responsibility for or control over the conduct of governmental affairs." *Rosenblatt v. Baer* (1966) [nonelected supervisor of a publicly owned recreation area held to be a public official]. Lower courts have tended to extend the term to almost any government employee. Candidates for public office are also included.

b) The privilege extends to "anything which might touch an official's fitness for office." *Garrison v. Louisiana* (1964) [charge that certain judges were inefficient, lazy and hampering an investigation held privileged. Today, almost all publications concerning public officials probably fall within the privilege, including charges of criminal conduct, *Monitor Patriot Co. v. Roy* (1971) [claim that a candidate was former bootlegger] ; *Ocala Star-Banner Co. v. Damron* (1971) [claim that mayor had been charged with perjury].

3)   Who Is a Public Figure?
      a)   All-Purpose Public Figures
            A person "may achieve such pervasive fame or notoriety that he becomes a public figure for all purposes and in all contexts." *Gertz v. Robert Welch, Inc.* (1974).

      b)   Limited Purpose Public Figures
            A person may become a public figure for a particular range of issues if he is drawn into a public controversy or if he voluntarily injects himself into a public controversy in order to influence the outcome. *Gertz v. Robert Welch, Inc.* (1974). Increasingly the Court has required a *voluntary* involvement in a *public controversy* in order to qualify as a public figure.

            Examples: (1) Where a magazine article libeled a reputable attorney, the fact that the lawyer was active in community and professional affairs does not render him a public figure for all purposes. Absent clear evidence of general fame or notoriety in the community, and pervasive involvement in the affairs of society, an individual should not be deemed a public personality for all aspects of his life. This is particularly true where the libel plaintiff did not discuss the matter in controversy with the press, and did not thrust himself into the vortex of the public issue, nor engage the public attention in an attempt to influence the outcome of the case. *Gertz v. Robert Welch, Inc.* (1974).

            (2) When a magazine reported that a divorce had been granted on the basis of the wife's adultery but the divorce court had not made such a finding, and the wife brought a libel action against the magazine, the wife should not be deemed a public figure simply by virtue of her having been drawn into litigation. The wife, a prominent socialite, did not otherwise occupy a role of special prominence in the affairs of society and had not thrust herself to the forefront of particular public controversies in order to influence the issues involved. *Time, Inc. v. Firestone* (1976).

            (3) A researcher who received Senator Proxmire's "Golden Fleece" award criticizing federal support of his research is not a public figure in a defamation action against the Senator. The researcher had not voluntarily sought the public spotlight, his

professional writings reached a limited audience, and the only public controversy was that created by the Senator's award. *Hutchinson v. Proxmire* (1979).

(4) The fact that a person had refused to appear before a grand jury investigation of Soviet intelligence activities and was cited for contempt does not make him a public figure. He had not voluntarily sought public attention. Mere involvement in a matter attracting public attention does not make a person a public figure. *Wolston v. Readers' Digest Ass'n., Inc.* (1979).

4) Actual Malice

a) Do not confuse the "actual malice" required to overcome constitutional privilege with common law malice, i.e., ill will or spite. Actual malice requires knowledge of falsity or recklessness. Recklessness is not satisfied by proving that the publisher acted unreasonably. Only sufficient evidence demonstrating that the publisher "entertained serious doubts as to the truth of his publication" will suffice. *St. Amant v. Thompson* (1968).

b) Because actual malice requires proof of the subjective bad faith of the publisher, the plaintiff may ask questions during discovery probing the state of mind of the publisher and inquiring into the editorial process. *Herbert v. Lando* (1979).

c) The plaintiff must establish actual malice by "clear and convincing evidence." This evidentiary standard must be applied by a court ruling on a motion for summary judgment. *Anderson v. Liberty Lobby, Inc.* (1985).

d) An appellate court reviewing a jury finding of actual malice must review the entire record and exercise its own independent judgement to determine if actual malice has been proven by clear and convincing evidence. *Bose Corp. v. Consumer Union* (1984). The appellate court must itself examine the statements at issue and the circumstances to determine whether the speech is constitutionally protected. However, a jury's credibility determinations are reviewed under a "clearly erroneous" standard and are not subject to de novo review. *Harte–Hanks Commun., Inc. v. Connaughton* (1989).

b.   Private Figures

1)   Standards of Review

Even when the plaintiff is not a public official or public figure, the First Amendment imposes some limitations, at least where matters of public interest are involved. So long as a state does not impose liability without fault, it may define for itself the appropriate standard of liability for a publisher or broadcaster of defamatory falsehood injurious to a private individual. Gertz v. Robert Welch, Inc. (1974).

a)   A state may not employ liability without fault (i.e., strict liability) at least where a public issue is involved. A standard of negligence is the minimum required by the First Amendment. Most states have adopted negligence as the standard of liability.

b)   The private individual lacks the access to the channels of communication available to public officials and public figures and hence has less effective means to counteract false statements. Further, he has not voluntarily exposed himself to public view.

c)   This principle represents a balance of the First Amendment interest in avoiding media self-censorship and the state interest in protecting private reputation.

d)   *Dun & Bradstreet, infra,* raises serious question whether the constitutional ban against strict liability in private plaintiff defamation actions applies if the subject matter is solely a matter of private concern.

2)   Presumed and Punitive Damages

a)   If the subject matter of the defamation involves a matter of public interest, only actual damages, not presumed damages, are permitted. States may not permit recovery of punitive damages at least in the absence of a showing of actual malice. *Gertz v. Robert Welch, Inc.* (1974). However, actual damages includes not only out of pocket costs but also injury to reputation, humiliation, and mental suffering. *Time, Inc. v. Firestone* (1976).

b)   But in matters of purely private concern, the state may award presumed and punitive damages even absent a showing of actual malice.

Example: In a report circulated to five subscribers, Dun & Bradstreet, a credit reporting agency, falsely indicated that Greenmoss Builders, a construction contractor, had filed a voluntary petition for bankruptcy. A jury awarded $50,000 in compensatory or presumed damages and

$300,000 in punitive damages. The Supreme Court held 5–4 that such an award does not violate the First Amendment even if actual malice is not established. A plurality reasoned that the state interest in protecting reputation was sufficient to support such awards, even absent actual malice, "[i]n light of the reduced constitutional value of speech involving no matters of public concern." The First Amendment interest in speech involving matters solely of private concern "is less important than the one weighted in *Gertz*." In determining that the speech involved "no public issue," the plurality stressed the limited, specific audience to whom the defamation was addressed and the commercial character of the information communicated. Two concurring Justices would overrule *Gertz*. *Dun & Bradstreet, Inc. v. Greenmoss Builders, Inc.* (1985).

c. Proof of Falsity

The private figure plaintiff, like the public official and public figure plaintiff, bears the burden in the defamation action of proving that the statements at issue are false, at least where the statements involve matters of public concern. The common-law presumption that defamatory speech is false cannot stand when a plaintiff seeks damages against a media defendant for speech involving matters of public concern. *Philadelphia Newspapers, Inc. v. Hepps* (1986). *Dun & Bradstreet* raises a serious question whether this principle applies in private plaintiff defamation actions involving solely matters of private concern.

d. The Fact–Opinion Dichotomy

"Under the First Amendment there is no such thing as a false idea." *Gertz*. But this principle does not mean that there is a First Amendment privilege for matters of opinion. If a statement of opinion includes or implies false, defamatory statements of fact, a defamation action can be maintained. First Amendment concerns are adequately protected by the requirement that the plaintiff prove fault and falsity and the principle that a defamation action will not lie for publications that cannot reasonably be interpreted as stating actual facts about an individual. *Milkovich v. Lorain Journal Co.* (1990).

4. PRIVACY

a. Invasions of Privacy

Freedom of expression also limits the ability of government to award damages for invasions of privacy. But the scope of the constitutional protection available is uncertain.

b. False Light Privacy
A privacy action against the media cannot be maintained merely on grounds that the report was false if it was newsworthy. The Court has required that the plaintiff show that the publication was made with actual malice. Time, Inc. v. Hill (1967). Whether Gertz v. Robert Welch, Inc. (1974), alters this rule remains unclear.

Example: Life magazine contained a picture story on a play providing a misleading portrayal of the hostage ordeal of the Hill family, who had been held captive in their home by escaped convicts. The Hills brought suit under a privacy statute providing a cause of action even as to newsworthy events if the publication was fictionalized. The Court held that freedom of speech and the press require a showing of actual malice in order to recover for false publications. *Time, Inc. v. Hill* (1967).

c. Public Records
1) Truthful Reports Protected
    a) The press has a right to truthfully report facts disclosed in public court proceedings and in court records open to the public. However, the Court has declared that no *New York Times v. Sullivan* privilege will extend to shield a libel defendant if the alleged defamation relied on judicial records which were inaccurate. *Time, Inc. v. Firestone* (1976).

    Example: A cause of action for invasion of privacy pursuant to a state statute prohibiting publication of a rape victim's name may not be maintained where the information is a matter of public record. *Cox Broadcasting Corp. v. Cohn* (1975).

    b) The Court has, thus far, not held that truthful publication can never be punished consistent with the First Amendment. But "[i]f a newspaper lawfully obtains truthful information about a matter of public significance then state officials may not constitutionally punish publication of the information absent a need to further a state interest of the highest order." *Smith v. Daily Mail Pub. Co.* (1979).

    Example: An award of civil damages against a newspaper for negligently publishing the name of a rape victim obtained from a publicly released police report, in violation of a state statute forbidding such publication, was held unconstitutional. Imposition of damages was not a narrowly tailored means of furthering the state's interest in protecting privacy since government itself could take greater care in safeguarding private information. The law was deemed underinclusive since it punished disclosure by the media of the identity of the rape victims but not disclosure by other means. *Florida Star v. B.J.F.* (1989).

2) Closed Public Records
The Court has not yet decided the extent to which a state may deny public access to its records. However, a state law punishing a newspaper for publishing confidential material in connection with state judicial disciplinary commission proceedings is invalid. Discussion of judicial affairs lies near the "core of the First Amendment" and the state interest in protecting the reputation of judges and the judiciary was insufficient to constitute a clear and present danger to the administration of justice. *Landmark Communications, Inc. v. Virginia* (1978). A state cannot prohibit a grand jury witness from disclosing his own testimony after the grand jury term has ended. *Butterworth v. Smith* (1990).

d. Intrusion and Newsworthiness
The Supreme Court has not yet determined whether a privacy action can be maintained by a private individual where the publication is truthful. The common law privilege of "newsworthiness" protecting public disclosure of private facts may be constitutionally mandated.

e. Right of Publicity
Government protection of a person's "right of publicity", i.e., the publicity value of his name and activities, while permissible, is subject to constitutional limitations. However, an action for damages against a television station for broadcasting a performer's entire act does not violate the First Amendment. *Zacchini v. Scripps-Howard Broadcasting Co.* (1977).

5. INTENTIONAL INFLICTION OF EMOTIONAL DISTRESS
Public officials and public figures may not recover for the tort of intentional infliction of emotional distress without showing that the publication contains a false statement of fact which was made with actual malice.

Example: Hustler Magazine published a parody portraying the Reverend Jerry Falwell as a drunken hypocrite whose first time sexual encounter was with his mother in an outhouse. A judgment for Falwell for intentional infliction of emotional distress was unanimously reversed by the Supreme Court. Bad motive may not be made controlling for tort purposes in the area of public debate about public figures. "Outrageousness," a critical element of the tort, has an inherent subjectiveness about it which permits juries to impose liability based on a dislike for the expression. The publication could not reasonably have been interpreted as stating actual facts about Falwell. *Hustler Magazine v. Falwell* (1988).

I. OBSCENITY

1. NO FIRST AMENDMENT PROTECTION
Lewdness, offensiveness, and profanity are not excluded from First Amendment protection. Cohen v. California *(1971).* *["Fuck the Draft" emblazoned on a leather jacket is not obscene].* *However, obscenity is held not to be entitled to First Amendment protection since such expression lacks social importance.* Roth v. United States *(1957).*

a. Rationality Satisfied
The only substantive requirement, therefore, is that government obscenity regulations be rationally related to permissible state interests. The Court has stated that such regulations further the public interest "in the quality of life and the total community environment, the tone of commerce in the great city centers, and, possibly, the public safety itself ＊ ＊ ＊." *Paris Adult Theatre I v. Slaton* (1973).

b. A Matter of Definition
Since obscenity is not First Amendment speech or press, the essential focus is on the definition of "obscenity." Prior to 1973, no definition of obscenity was able to win support of a majority of justices.

2. THE MODERN DEFINITION
Each element of a three-part test must be satisfied in order to define material as obscene: "(a) whether the average person, applying contemporary community standards would find that the work, taken as a whole, appeals to the prurient interest, (b) whether the work depicts or describes, in a patently offensive way, sexual conduct specifically defined by the applicable state law, and (c) whether the work, taken as a whole, lacks serious literary, artistic, political, or scientific value." Miller v. California *(1973).*

a. Contemporary Community Standards
   1) No National Community Standard
      In applying the standards relating to pruriency and patent offensiveness, the courts need not apply any national community standard. The jury may be instructed to apply "contemporary community standards" without further specification.

   2) Federal Jury Standard
      In a federal proceeding, the prevailing community standard in the area from which the jurors are drawn may be used. *Hamling v. United States* (1974).

3) Identifying "Community" Members
In obscenity trials, children are not to be considered a part of the "community" for purposes of determining community standards. However, sensitive persons may be considered "community" members. *Pinkus v. United States* (1978).

4) Experts
Since the determination of pruriency and patent offensiveness are determined by community standards, no expert evidence is required to establish obscenity. *Paris Adult Theater I v. Slaton* (1973). Further, since community members can differ in their evaluation of materials, the fact that similar material to that in question is available in the community is not evidentiary. *Hamling v. United States* (1974).

5) Appellate Review
While *Miller* was meant to leave the determination of obscenity to local communities, this does not preclude independent judicial review *even* of the jury determination of obscenity. Constitutional standards must be satisfied.

>   *Example:* Conviction of a movie theater owner for showing the film "Carnal Knowledge" was reversed by the Supreme Court. While questions of pruriency and patent offensiveness are questions of fact for the jury, the Constitution does not permit condemnation of materials unless they "depict or describe patently offensive 'hard core' sexual conduct." The nude scenes in "Carnal Knowledge" did not satisfy this standard. *Jenkins v. Georgia* (1974).

b. Defining the Relevant Audience
1) The Average Person
Obscenity is to be judged in terms of the effect of the material on a person of average susceptibility. Neither the especially sensitive person nor the insensitive person is the measure, even though they are included in defining community standards.

2) Variable Obscenity: Minors and Deviants
Obscenity may be determined by considering the target audience to whom the work is addressed and their peculiar susceptibilities. Thus, a properly-drafted statute directed at distribution to minors would be constitutional. *Ginsberg v. New York* (1968). Similarly, jurors may be instructed to consider whether the material appeals to the prurient interest of members of sexually deviant groups, *e.g.,* sado-masochists. *Mishkin v. New York* (1966); *Pinkus v. United States* (1978).

c.   The Demand for Specificity

1)   Vagueness
The Court consistently has rejected the claim that all definitions of obscenity are necessarily unconstitutionally vague.

2)   Overbreadth
(a)   Sex and obscenity are not synonymous, although only *sexual* material may be obscene. Examples of obscene material include "patently offensive representations or descriptions of ultimate sexual acts, normal or perverted, actual or simulated" and "patently offensive representations or descriptions of masturbation, excretory functions, and lewd exhibitions of the genitals." *Miller v. California* (1973).

(b)   In *Miller,* the Court stated: "Conduct must be specifically defined by the applicable state law, as written or authoritatively construed, to make obscenity regulation constitutional." In fact, the courts often construe the obscenity laws to embody the obscenity standards and specific types of acts set forth in *Miller* and uphold the statutes. *Ward v. Illinois* (1977) [state statute read to incorporate the patently offensive standard of *Miller* and its examples of patently offensive acts].

(c)   The fact that an obscenity statute is overbroad in part does not mean that the entire statute is invalid.

Example: A statute defining "prurient" to include lust and not limited to shameful or morbid interest in sex is overbroad. However since the overbreadth is not incurable and need not taint all applications of the statute, it should be invalidated "only in so far as the word 'lust' is understood as reaching protected materials." *Brockett v. Spokane Arcades, Inc.* (1985).

3)   Pandering
In determining whether the three-fold definition of obscenity is satisfied, the circumstances of the presentation and dissemination of the material are material. *Splawn v. California* (1977).

Example: Where a publisher sought mailing privileges from the postmasters of Intercourse and Blue Ball, Pennsylvania, and where the leer of the sensualist permeated all the advertising for his publications, the purveyor's sole emphasis on the sexually provocative aspects of his publications can be decisive in the determination of obscenity. Inquiry can be validly directed to the context of such commercial exploitation in determining whether the material at issue can be treated as protected expression. *Ginzburg v. United States* (1966).

4) Racketeering Laws
There is no constitutional bar to the inclusion of substantive obscenity offenses under a state criminal RICO law. *Fort Wayne Books, Inc. v. Indiana* (1989).

d. Serious Value
Miller clearly rejects the requirement, fashioned in *Memoirs v. Massachusetts* (1966) that, to be labeled obscene, a work must be "utterly without redeeming social value." Today, the work, judged as a whole, must lack *serious* literary, artistic, political, or scientific value. Note that this element of the test is *not* judged by local community standards. The third prong is to be determined, not on a local community, but on an objective basis, i.e., whether a reasonable person would find serious literary, artistic, political, or scientific value in the material, taken as a whole, not whether such value would be found under contemporary community standards. *Pope and Morrison v. Illinois* (1987).

3. PRIVACY AND OBSCENITY
a. *The mere possession of obscene matter cannot constitutionally be made a crime. Privacy, a fundamental right, protects what an individual reads or watches in his own home.*

> *Example:* In the course of a search of a home for evidence of bookmaking activities, the police found obscene films and the accused was arrested and charged with possession of obscene matter. The Court declared that punishment of mere private possession of obscene material violates the right or privacy even though the public distribution of the very same material could be constitutionally punished. Public distribution, unlike private possession, may be punished because of the possibility such material may fall into the hands of children or may intrude upon the sensibilities or privacy of the general public. *Stanley v. Georgia* (1969).

b. But the right of privacy does not protect obscene displays in places of public accommodation even when effective safeguards are employed against exposure to juveniles and passersby. *Paris Adult Theater v. Slaton* (1973).

c. Nor does *Stanley* extend to child pornography. The state's compelling interests in protecting the physical and psychological well-being of minors and in destroying the market for the exploitative use of children distinguish the child pornography context from *Stanley*. *Osborne v. Ohio* (1990).

4. CIVIL CONTROL OF OBSCENITY AND INDECENCY
a. Prior Restraints
Control of obscenity may also take the form of civil statutes such as nuisance or zoning laws. Such controls usually constitute prior restraints involving licensing, injunction, and administrative censorship. However, the Court generally has taken a more favorable attitude to such prior restraints on the theory that they avoid many of the evils of obscenity control pursued through criminal laws. *Paris Adult Theater v. Slaton* (1973).

b. Content–Neutral Regulation
Frequently, zoning laws are treated as time, place and manner regulations rather than content controls. In cases where the regulation significantly effects protected activity, the law must be designed to achieve a substantial government interest and must leave open reasonable alternative channels of communication.

Example: (1) A zoning ordinance barring adult bookstores, theatres, etc., from being in a defined locational proximity is not an invalid prior restraint violative of the First Amendment or Fourteenth Amendment equal protection. While government must maintain neutrality regarding speech content, regulation of such establishments is unaffected by the content message in the films. Such a regulation is a place regulation, a reasonable means of implementing the city's interest in preserving the character of its neighborhoods. *Young v. American Mini Theatres, Inc.* (1976).

(2) A zoning ordinance which prohibits adult movie theatres from locating within 1000 feet of residential property, churches, parks, or schools does not violate the First Amendment. Such a regulation is a "content-neutral" time, place, and manner regulation aimed at the "secondary effects" of adult theaters. As such, it is acceptable under the First Amendment so long as it is designed to serve a substantial government interest and there are reasonable alternative avenues of communication. A city's interest in attempting to preserve the quality of urban life is an interest which must be accorded high respect. The law left open reasonable alternative channels of communication since 5% of the city's land could be used by adult theaters. The city need not engage in fact-finding regarding the harm in Renton but can

rely on findings and experience of other cities. *City of Renton v. Playtime Theatres, Inc.* (1986).

c. Vagueness and Overbreadth

1) "Indecent" publications and expressive activity which is not obscene remain constitutionally protected expression. Like criminal laws, civil regulations of obscene materials must be narrowly drawn to satisfy the three-fold test of obscenity. The sexual conduct proscribed must be specifically defined in the statute or be read in through authoritative judicial construction. Otherwise, when government seeks to shield the public from some kinds of speech or press on the ground of its special offensiveness by regulation, the First Amendment strictly limits its power.

Examples: (1) An ordinance that prohibits as a public nuisance drive-in theatres from showing films containing nudity ("bare buttocks * * * female bare breasts, or human bare pubic areas") when visible from a public street or public place sweeps too far beyond the permissible restraints on obscenity. Such an ordinance invalidly reaches films directed not only against sexually explicit nudity but reaches any nudity however innocent or educational. In such circumstances, the burden should be on the viewer to protect his sensibilities merely by averting his eyes. *Erznoznik v. Jacksonville* (1975).

(2) A zoning ordinance carrying penalties which excludes all commercial live entertainment, including nonobscene nude dancing, while permitting other commercial activity, violates the First and Fourteenth Amendment guarantee of freedom of expression. Nude dancing is not without its First Amendment protection from official regulation. But whatever protection nudity is afforded, this zoning ordinance was a substantial and overbroad intrusion on protected rights. It was not narrowly drawn to further a substantial governmental interest. State interests in traffic control and waste disposal, even if real, could be achieved by a more selective measure. It was not a reasonable time, place and manner control. *Schad v. Mount Ephraim* (1981).

(3) The New York Alcoholic Beverage Control Law which prohibits nude dancing in establishments licensed by the state to sell liquor for on-premises consumption, does not constitute a violation of the First Amendment. The State's power to ban the sale of alcoholic beverages

includes the lesser power to ban the sale of liquor on premises where topless dancing occurs. The elected representatives of New York have chosen to avoid the disturbances associated with mixing alcohol and nude dancing by means of a reasonable restriction upon establishments that sell liquor for on-premises consumption. Whatever artistic or communicative value may attach to topless dancing is overcome by the state's exercise of its broad powers and "the added presumption in favor of the state regulation" conferred by the Twenty-First Amendment. *New York State Liquor Authority v. Bellanca* (1981).

(4) A local ordinance prohibiting nude dancing in local establishments licensed to sell liquor on the premises, passed pursuant to a state delegation of its Twenty-First Amendment power to local electorates, is constitutional. The state's Twenty-First Amendment power and its police power interest in maintaining order outweighs any First Amendment interest in nude dancing. *City of Newport v. Iacobucci* (1986).

2) *If the regulation does not significantly burden expression or the effects of speech, the First Amendment protection does not apply and the law need only be rational.*

Example: The First Amendment does not bar enforcement of a statute authorizing closure of premises found to be used as a place for prostitution and lewdness simply because the premises are also used as an adult bookstore. The appellate court erred in applying *O'Brien* since the sexual activity being regulated in the present case involves no element of protected expression. The legislature properly sought to protect the environment of the community by directing the sanction at places knowingly used for unlawful activity involving no protected expression. The Court characterized the incidental burden on First Amendment activity as minimal; the owners remained free to sell their materials at another location. *Arcara v. Cloud Books, Inc.* (1986).

5.   BROADCASTING, DIAL–A–PORN AND INDECENT SPEECH
a.   Full First Amendment protection does not extend to broadcasting. The pervasiveness of broadcasting and concern over the presence of children in the audience, allows reasonable FCC regulation of indecent programming.

Example: George Carlin's 12–minute satiric monologue, "Filthy Words," was aired at two o'clock in the afternoon by a radio station owned by Pacifica. A man, who claimed that he had heard the broadcast while driving with his young son complained to the FCC. The Court upheld the FCC's power to regulate indecent programming under a nuisance rationale stressing the factual content involved. Broadcasting's "uniquely pervasive presence in the lives of all Americans" and its unique accessibility to children justify special treatment of government regulation of broadcasting. The deliberate repeated use of vulgar, offensive and shocking language, describing sexual and excretory functions in a patently offensive manner, broadcast at a time when children were undoubtedly in the audience, justified civil regulation. *FCC v. Pacifica Foundation* (1978).

b. But not all nonprint means of communication are necessarily subject to the diminished protection accorded broadcasting. Regulation of indecency on other forms of media may be subject to the more exacting standards of review normally used for content control.

Example: A total ban on sexually-oriented indecent, but nonobscene, telephone messages, is unconstitutional. Such speech can be regulated on the basis of its content only if the regulation is carefully tailored to achieve compelling government interest; government must use the least restrictive means available.

Pacifica was based on the unique aspects of broadcasting. Telephone communications require the recipient to take affirmative steps to receive the communication. There is no "captive audience" and dial-a-porn service "is not so invasive or surprising that it prevents an unwilling listener from avoiding exposure to it." There were feasible and effective ways to protect children other than a total ban. The Court upheld a statutory prohibition on obscene dial-a-porn telephone communication. *Sable Communications of California, Inc. v. FCC* (1989).

6. CHILD PORNOGRAPHY
Child pornography is a "category of material outside the protection of the First Amendment." Government can punish pornographic depictions of children even if the *Miller* standards are not satisfied.

Examples: (1) A New York criminal statute prohibiting persons from knowingly promoting sexual performances by children under the age of 16 by distributing such material is constitutional. The state has a compelling interest in protecting minors;

distribution of such visual material is intrinsically related to production involving sexual abuse of children; the economic benefits from distribution stimulate production of the materials; such productions have minimal constitutional value. The Court did limit its decision to live performances or visual reproduction of live performances, *i.e.*, production involving child actors. Since the New York law was not "substantially overbroad", it was not facially unconstitutional. The Court did not decide if "socially valuable" works are constitutionally protected. *New York v. Ferber* (1982).

(2) An Ohio statute which criminalized possession of any material depicting a nude minor, except under a number of limited circumstances and for proper purposes was found constitutional. The statute itself was not unconstitutionally overbroad, because the construction of the statute by the Ohio Supreme Court narrowly limited application of the law to lewd displays of nudity where such nudity involves a lewd exhibition or involves a graphic focus on genitals, and not merely nudity. The law was also read to include a requirement of scienter. Because the defendant had fair warning that his conduct was criminal, the statute, as interpreted, could be applied to him. However, since it was unclear that the jury had been properly instructed on the elements of the offense as due process requires, the conviction was reversed and the case remanded. *Osborne v. Ohio* (1990).

7. PROCEDURAL FAIRNESS
a. Administrative Regulation
1) Prior restraints are burdened procedurally as well as substantively. At least if the restraint involves administrative censorship, the following procedural requirements must be satisfied:
   (1) The censor has the burden of demonstrating that the material is unprotected.

   (2) There must be a prompt judicial proceeding in order to impose a valid final restraint on publication.

   (3) The censor must either issue a license for publication or go to court to justify the restraint. Freedman v. Maryland *(1965).*

2) *Other Licensing.* If the regulatory scheme does not involve the exercise of administrative discretion in passing on the content of any protected speech, there is dispute whether the *Freedman* standards are applicable.

Example: A Dallas ordinance embodying zoning, licensing and inspections of sexually oriented businesses was invalidated as an impermissible prior restraint which failed to provide the procedural protections required by *Freedman v. Maryland* (1965). The ordinance failed to place limits on the time within which the decision maker must issue the license and failed to provide for prompt judicial review. These faults made the law unconstitutional under *Freedman.* Three members of the Court would also have held, however, that since no censorship was involved in the licensing scheme, the city need not bear the burden of going to court and justifying the restraint as required by *Freedman.* Three justices would still apply all the *Freedman* standards to such licensing and three justices would not have applied any of the *Freedman* standards in the absence of content censorship. *FW/PBS, Inc. v. City of Dallas* (1990).

b.   Judicial Censorship
Procedural due process also limits the judicial determination of obscenity both at the hearing stage and in framing a remedy.

Example: A state nuisance statute authorizing a prior restraint of indefinite duration on the future exhibition of motion pictures that have not been judicially determined to be obscene was held unconstitutional. The restraint against future filming was based on a determination that obscene films had been shown in the past. The Court held that such an injunction must adhere to more narrowly drawn procedures than normally used in nuisance cases and that the burden of justifying such a prior restraint is greater than for justifying a criminal sanction for past activities. *Vance v. Universal Amusement Co., Inc.* (1980).

c.   Search and Seizure
   1) Large scale civil seizure of indecent materials for the purpose of their suppression or destruction must be preceded by an adversarial determination of obscenity. *Quantity of Books v. Kansas* (1964). This principle remains applicable if the seizure is taken pursuant to state civil racketeering (RICO) laws. *Fort Wayne Books v. Indiana* (1989).

   2) Search and seizure of a single copy of a work or film for use as evidence in a criminal proceeding pursuant to a warrant, describing the material to be seized, issued on a finding of probable obscenity, is permissible even if the warrant is issued *ex parte.* There is no

requirement in this context for a prior adversary determination of obscenity. *Heller v. New York* (1973).

J. SPECIAL CONTEXTS

In certain special contexts or "restricted environments", the ordinary speech-protective doctrines and rules are either not applied or applied in a markedly altered form. *In cases involving the military, government employees, prisons, and children in school, the special government interests involved result in a more deferential form of judicial review.*

1. POLITICAL ACTIVITY BY GOVERNMENT EMPLOYEES

a. *In determining what limitations may be placed on political action by government employees, the Court employs a balancing test. The interest of the employee as a citizen in participating in the political process is weighed against the interest of the government as employer in assuring the efficiency of its operations.*

> *Examples:* (1) Federal employees may be validly prohibited by the Hatch Act from undertaking an active and visible role in political management and political campaigning. The Court upheld the balance struck by Congress subordinating the interest of the employee as citizen to the interest of government in assuring efficiency and preserving public confidence by means of the prohibition. *United States Civil Service Commission v. National Association of Letter Carriers* (1973).
>
> (2) Although the state has interests as an employer in regulating the speech of its employees that differ significantly from those it possesses with respect to regulating the speech of the citizenry in general, a teacher may not, consistent with the First Amendment, be dismissed for making comments on matters of educational policy that are substantially correct. In such situations, a balancing test should be used to weigh the need for confidentiality as it relates to the function the state is performing against the interest of a teacher in commenting upon matters of public concern. *Pickering v. Board of Education* (1968).
>
> (3) A county law enforcement employee was overheard to say on hearing of an attempt on President Reagan's life, "If they go for him again, I hope they get him." She was fired because of her statement. The government's interest in discharging the employee under such circumstances did not outweigh her rights under the First Amendment. The

employee was fired because of the content of her speech. Since the employee served no confidential, policy-making or public contact role, the danger to governmental interests was minimal. Although a statement which constituted a threat to kill the President would not be protected by the First Amendment, this statement made in the context of a conversation which addressed the policies of the President's administration could not be so characterized. The employee's statement constituted protected speech on a matter of public concern. *Rankin v. McPherson* (1987).

b.   When the speech involves only matters of personal interest, rather than public concern, the courts exercise deference. "[W]hen a public employee speaks as an employee upon matters of personal interest, absent the most unusual circumstances, a federal court is not the appropriate forum in which to review the wisdom of a personnel decision taken by a public agency allegedly in reaction to the employee's behavior." *Connick v. Myers* (1983).

> *Example:*   Discharge of an assistant district attorney for protesting her transfer and for circulating a questionnaire to other assistant district attorneys requesting their views on transfer policies, office morale, confidence in supervisors, etc., does not violate the First Amendment. The government need not prove that the speech "substantially interfered" with official responsibility. The employer could reasonably believe the employee's behavior would disrupt the office, undermine his authority and destroy close working relationships. *Connick v. Myers* (1983).

c.   In order to establish a prima facie case, the government employee must prove that the protected activity was a substantial factor, *i.e.,* a cause, of the adverse government action against her.

> *Example:*   An untenured teacher who claims that his dismissal violates his First and Fourteenth Amendment rights has the burden of showing that his conduct was constitutionally protected and that this conduct was a substantial factor, a motivating factor, in the school board's decision not to rehire him. The burden is then on the school board to show by a preponderance of the evidence "that it would have reached the same decision as to respondent's reemployment even in the absence of the protected conduct." The Court concluded that "[t]he constitutional principle at stake is sufficiently vindicated if such an employee is placed in no worse a position than if he had not engaged in the conduct." *Mt. Healthy City School Dist. Bd. of Educ. v. Doyle* (1977).

2. THE ACADEMIC FORUM

Public education may properly seek to "inculcate fundamental values necessary to the maintenance of a democratic political system." *Ambach v. Norwick* (1979). Further, school officials have a special responsibility acting *in loco parentis* for the protection of students. On the other hand, public school officials may not impose political orthodoxy or exclude expression simply because of disagreement with the ideas expressed. Students retain First Amendment rights even in the schoolhouse, but "the special characteristics of the school environment" must be considered. *Tinker v. Des Moines School Dist.* (1969).

a. Library Censorship

The Court has held that the First Amendment does impose some limits on the power of a local school board to remove books from the school library. A plurality of the Court concluded that books could not be removed from public high school for the purpose of restricting access to ideas with which the board disagreed. The Justices generally agreed that books could be removed because they were pervasively vulgar or educationally inappropriate. *Board of Education v. Pico* (1982).

b. Student Speech

1) Student rights of free expression in the schoolhouse are not coextensive with the rights of adults in other settings. Schools can bar speech or expressive action that intrudes upon the work of the schools or the rights of other students.

> ***Examples:*** (1) The wearing of a black armband in school to protest the Vietnam War was "akin to pure speech" and hence protected by the First Amendment. In the absence of evidence that the symbolic conduct would "materially and substantially interfere with the requirements of appropriate discipline in the operation of the school," prohibition by school officials of the wearing of the armbands is impermissible. *Tinker v. Des Moines School Dist.* (1969).
>
> (2) A school district does not violate the Constitution by suspending a high school student for two days for delivering a speech at a student political assembly heavily laden with sexual innuendo which the Court characterized as vulgar and offensively lewd. Society has an overriding interest in teaching students "the boundaries of socially appropriate behavior." School officials could determine that such offensive speech would undermine the school's basic educational mission. The school disciplinary rule proscribing "obscene" language was held to have provided adequate warning to the

student of the potential for the sanctions. *Bethel School Dist. No. 403 v. Fraser* (1986).

2) *School facilities are public forums only if school officials have by policy or practice opened those facilities for general public use or for use by some segment of the public, e.g., student organizations. Schools can regulate "school sponsored" student speech that occurs in "curricular" activities so long as there is some reasonable basis, some legitimate pedagogical concern, for the regulation.*

> *Example:* Spectrum, a school newspaper written and edited by a school journalism class, carried two articles on teenage pregnancy and divorce which the school principal believed were "inappropriate, personal, sensitive and unsuitable." He deleted two full pages of the paper without any notice to the student editors. The censorship was held constitutional.
>
> There was insufficient evidence that school officials intended to make the school newspaper a public forum. It was a supervised learning experience for journalism students. Hence, the *Tinker* standard was not applicable—only reasonableness was required. Further, *Tinker* had not considered whether a school must affirmatively promote particular student speech. A school, acting in its capacity as sponsor of student speech, may disassociate itself from particular expression. In the school-sponsored expressive activity of publishing a newspaper the principal made a reasonable pedagogical decision that the articles in question were not suitable for publication. *Hazelwood School Dist. v. Kuhlmeier* (1988).

C. Academic Freedom

As the cases involving freedom of association and belief indicate, the First Amendment does extend protection to teachers from excessive governmental interference, including who may teach and what is taught. See, *e.g., Keyishian v. Board of Regents* (1967) [loyalty program held unconstitutional]; *Sweezy v. New Hampshire* (1957) [conviction of teacher for contempt for refusing to answer questions about the contents of a lecture held unconstitutional]. While the First Amendment embraces a concept of academic freedom, the First Amendment does not protect against every incidental burden on academic freedom.

> *Example:* The First Amendment right of academic freedom did not protect peer review materials involved in tenure decisions at universities from disclosure. Disclosure of peer review materials was deemed necessary by the Equal Employment Opportunity Commission to properly examine Title VII claims

of race and sex discrimination. The EEOC's subpoenas for the information would not direct the content of university discourse towards or away from particular subjects or points of view. There was no direct burden on who the University selects to teach. The indirect burden from disclosure on the University's choice of who will teach is too speculative and attenuated for the First Amendment to embrace the claim for confidentiality. *Univ. of Pennsylvania v. E.E.O.C.* (1990).

K. REVIEW QUESTIONS

1. T or F   Whether the burden on freedom of speech imposed by a government regulation is direct or indirect, the courts will require that the law be necessary to a compelling governmental interest.

2. T or F   Advocacy of illegal conduct is constitutionally protected speech.

3. T or F   Prior restraints on expression are prohibited by the First Amendment, i.e., they are *per se* impermissible.

4. T or F   A law that is vague and overbroad is unconstitutional even if it is applied narrowly in a way that conforms to First Amendment standards.

5. T or F   Even if political speech would normally be protected under applicable First Amendment law, a business corporate speaker would not be permitted to assert this constitutional protection.

6. T or F   The validity of a law that burdens freedom of association and belief is generally determined by a rationality test.

7. T or F   Government may not condition the receipt even of public benefits and privileges on the surrender of First Amendment rights.

8. T or F   The political activities of government employees, like citizens generally, are not subject to government restriction unless such activity is illegal.

9. T or F   Reasonable limitations on campaign expenditures by a candidate or a group are constitutional.

10. T or F   The freedom of association and belief implies a right not to associate and a freedom from compelled beliefs.

11. T or F   Government can punish fighting or offensive speech.

12. T or F When a speaker's message arouses a hostile crowd to take action against him or her, the police may arrest the speaker in order to preserve public peace and order.

13. T or F Speech in all publicly owned places is subject to regulation only if such a law serves a significant government interest and leaves open alternative channels of communication.

14. T or F While pure speech is constitutionally protected, when speech is joined with conduct, First Amendment standards no longer apply.

15. T or F Content-neutral licensing of First Amendment expression is constitutional if reasonable.

16. T or F Court injunctions usually must be obeyed even if they are facially invalid.

17. T or F In modern times, commercial speech receives the same constitutional protection afforded political speech.

18. T or F The press enjoys special privileges and immunities under the Press Clause of the First Amendment.

19. T or F There is a First Amendment right of access to the media.

20. T or F Government restraints on indecent, but not obscene, language in broadcasting are unconstitutional.

21. T or F Criminal proscription of the distribution of books and magazines which describe minor children in indecent, but not obscene, activity is constitutional.

22. T or F Private figure plaintiffs can never recover presumed or punitive damages absent proof of actual malice.

23. T or F There is a constitutional right of equality of access to public property when the expressive activity is not incompatible with the normal use to which the property is put.

24. Which of the following is a *per se* restraint on freedom of association and belief that is unconstitutional regardless of the government interests:

    a. Prohibition on membership in an association advocating illegal conduct.

    b. Forced disclosure of the membership lists of such an association.

    c.   Loyalty oaths.

    d.   All of the above (a, b, c) are *per se* invalid.

    e.   None of the above (a, b, c) are *per se* invalid.

25. Which of the following standards is *not* used in assessing the constitutionality of time, place and manner controls of speech in the public forum?

    a.   The law must be clear and precise.

    b.   The law must be content neutral.

    c.   The law must be narrowly drawn to reflect a significant government interest.

    d.   The availability of alternative forums will be considered.

    e.   All of the above standards are used in determining the validity of time, place and manner controls.

26. Which of the following most accurately describes the legal status of "symbolic speech"?

    a.   It is conduct which does not involve First Amendment law.

    b.   If the nature, factual content, and environment indicate that the conduct is intended and understood as communication, any restraint violates the First Amendment.

    c.   Conduct which qualifies as "symbolic speech" is judged by First Amendment standards.

    d.   Conduct labeled "symbolic speech" receives the same constitutional protection as obscenity.

27. Which of the following is most accurate under the present public law of defamation?

    a.   Defamation of public officials is fully protected under the First Amendment.

    b.   The law of defamation of public figures and private persons is left to the states.

    c. In defining the defamation standards relating to private figures, states may choose actual malice, negligence, or strict liability.

    d. Defamation actions by public officials and public figures are permitted only if actual malice is shown.

    e. Punitive and presumed damages can be recovered.

28. Which of the following is *not* part of the present test of obscenity?

    a. The material must appeal to the prurient interests of the average person applying contemporary community standards.

    b. The work must be patently offensive.

    c. The work must lack redeeming social value.

    d. Pruriency and patent offensiveness need not be judged by a national community standard.

29. Which of the following procedures are constitutionally required for valid civil censorship of obscene materials?

    a. The publisher has the burden of demonstrating that the material is protected.

    b. Administrative censorship must not be used.

    c. Only a judicial determination of obscenity will suffice to permanently restrain publication.

    d. The publisher must appeal the censor's determination to a court to eliminate the restraint.

30. Prepare an essay in response to this question:

An ordinance has recently been enacted by the City Council of Lincoln City, West Lincoln, prohibiting the posting of real estate "For Sale" and "Sold" signs. During the 1970s, the non-white population of Lincoln City rose from 60 to over 5000, or from .005% of the population to 18.2%. The City Council enacted the new ordinance because, in the words of a city councilman, "a major cause in the decline in the white population was 'panic selling' exploited by unscrupulous real estate brokers and salesmen who have been encouraging whites to sell their houses at low prices in order that they might sell them at much higher prices to incoming black residents." A real estate company, Beautiful Homes, Inc., has filed suit in the appropriate federal district court asking for a declaratory judgment that the ordinance is unconstitutional and requesting injunctive relief to prevent its enforcement. At the trial, expert real estate witnesses testified that only 2% of the homes that had been sold in Lincoln City during the past decade were chiefly sold because of the panic selling techniques of a few real estate agents. Is the ordinance constitutional? Why or why not?

31. The state of Eureka has enacted a law requiring all groups advocating racial hatred to register with the state Attorney General and to disclose the organization's membership lists. Pursuant to the law, the state has ordered the Ku Klux Klan to register and file a disclosure statement. Discuss the First Amendment claims that might be raised by the KKK in challenging the Eureka law.

IX

FREEDOM OF RELIGION

Analysis

A. The Meaning of the "Establishment" Clause
B. The Meaning of the "Free Exercise" Clause
C. The Meaning of Religion
D. Review Questions

The First Amendment guarantees both the "free exercise" of religion and freedom from "law respecting an establishment of religion." Both guarantees have been incorporated into the Due Process Clause and are therefore applicable to the states. However, these guarantees are often in conflict. For example, providing fire and police services constitute government support for religious institutions. But denial of such services, critical to their survival, might be said to impair the free exercise of religion. Remember, both guarantees may be involved in a freedom of religion case and the tensions will have to be reconciled. While the basic command is government neutrality courts have wavered as to how strict the neutrality must be and how much government accommodation of religion is permissible.

A. THE MEANING OF THE "ESTABLISHMENT" CLAUSE

In most cases, the courts presently employ a three-fold test to determine if the command of neutrality imposed by the Establishment Clause is violated. Each of the three requirements must be satisfied: (1) the government action must have a secular legislative purpose; (2) the primary effect of the government action must be one that neither advances nor inhibits religion; (3) the government action must not foster an excessive government entanglement with religion. The Court has increasingly asked whether a law constitutes an *endorsement* of religion or a particular religious belief.

The Establishment Clause is not merely a prohibition of a government sponsored religion or simply a command of equal treatment among religions. Government cannot "pass laws which aid one religion, or prefer one religion over another." Everson v. Board of Educ. *(1947).*

Example: A state statute vesting in the governing bodies of churches and schools the power effectively to veto applications for liquor licenses within a five hundred foot radius of the church or school violates the Establishment Clause. While the state can regulate the environment around schools, churches, hospitals, etc., when the state delegates its zoning power to a private religious entity, the deference due to legislative zoning (including the deference accorded under the 21st Amendment) is inappropriate. While the law has a valid secular purpose (in protecting the centers from the hurly-burly associated with liquor outlets), it has a primary effect of advancing religion. Since the law is standardless, it "does not by its terms require that churches' power be used in a religiously neutral way." Further, the law provides "significant symbolic benefit to religion" by creating a joint exercise of legislative authority. Finally, the third test is violated since the law "enmeshes churches in the exercise of substantial governmental powers." *Larkin v. Grendel's Den, Inc.* (1982).

1. RELIGION IN THE SCHOOLS
  a. Released Time
     While released time for religious education is permissible, it violates the
     First Amendment to conduct the classes within the schools. *Zorach v.
     Clauson* (1952). An on-premises religious program involves the expenditure
     of public resources for promoting religious goals, places public support
     behind the programs, and involves a close working relationship between
     public and religious authorities. Therefore, it has a primary effect which
     is sectarian, which violates the Establishment Clause. *McCollum v. Board
     of Education* (1948).

  b. Prayers, Bible Reading, Moments of Silence and Devotional Exercises
     1) While an objective study of the Bible or religion may be included as
         part of a secular program of study, government may not require
         religious exercises in the schools. *Required prayers, even when non-
         denominational, or other religious exercises have the purpose and primary
         effect of aiding religion.* Engel v. Vitale *(1962)* [required recitation of
         prayer, composed by Board of Regents, held unconstitutional].

     2) *Excusal or exemption to avoid coercion of students having religious
         objections to the exercises is irrelevant.* When the state aids or
         encourages religion in violation of the Establishment Clause,
         accommodation for free exercise claims is not determinative.

         Example: The First Amendment forbids state required recitation of a
                     prayer and daily Bible reading even though the state
                     provides for excusal of the nonconforming child upon the
                     written request of a parent and even though the prayer is
                     not state composed. Even if it argued that the purpose of
                     the mandatory Bible reading is non-religious in character
                     and designed to serve secular values, such as promotion of
                     moral values and the teaching of literature, the religious
                     character of the exercise is manifest from, among other
                     things, the provision for nonattendance at the exercises by
                     non-conforming children. In such circumstances, the
                     primary effect of the enactment is the impermissible
                     advancement of religion. *School District of Abington
                     Township v. Schempp* (1963).

     3) A moment of silent prayer is a religious exercise designed to promote
         prayer and endorse religion and therefore violates the Establishment
         Clause. Whether a moment of silence with no reference to prayer or
         religion would survive Establishment Clause review remains undecided.

         Example: A state statute which authorizes a period of silence for
                     "meditation or voluntary prayer," which is proven to be

motivated by a legislative purpose to endorse religion and by no secular purpose, violates the Establishment Clause. Enacted to convey a message of state endorsement and promotion of prayer, the statute is not consistent with the established principle that the government must pursue a course of neutrality toward religion. *Wallace v. Jaffree* (1985).

c.   Teaching Religious Values
1)   Curriculum Control
While the state has broad leeway in prescribing the school curriculum, it may not use the power to advance particular religious tenets or beliefs.

Examples: (1) A state statute prohibiting the teaching of evolution in public schools is unconstitutional. A particular segment of a body of knowledge cannot be proscribed "for the sole reason that it is deemed to conflict with a particular religious doctrine." The anti-evolution or "monkey law" was clearly enacted for a religious purpose. *Epperson v. Arkansas* (1968).

(2) A state statute which forbids the teaching of the theory of evolution in public schools unless accompanied by instruction in the theory of "creation science" is facially invalid as violative of the Establishment Clause because it lacks a clear secular purpose. While the Court is "normally deferential to a State's articulation of a secular purpose," the statement of a secular purpose must be "sincere and not a sham." The state "creationism" law sought to discredit evolution by counterbalancing the teaching of evolution "at every turn with the teaching of creation science." The state statute impermissibly attempted to endorse religion by advancing "the religious viewpoint that a supernatural being created humankind." *Edwards v. Aguillard* (1987).

2)   Covert Religious Purpose
Even when the state seeks to justify a law by claiming that it serves secular objectives of teaching fundamental values and traditions, the law will not be upheld if the Court determines that the program or practice is primarily religious in character or has the purpose of advancing religion.

Example: A state statute requiring the posting of the Ten Commandments in public schools furthers only sectarian purposes and hence violates the Establishment Clause of the First Amendment. The fact that the public school displays carry a statement on the importance of the Ten Commandments in our laws and our legal system and that the display was paid for with private funds is insufficient to negate the religious purpose. *Stone v. Graham* (1980).

d. Equal Protection

1) As the released time cases indicate, not all government accommodation of religious programs in public forums violates the Establishment Clause. *Discrimination against groups in the use of the public forum based on the religious content of their message can be justified only by showing a compelling government interest.*

   Example: A university which has created a forum generally open for use by student groups violates the First Amendment freedom of speech and association when it discriminates in use of its facilities by denying access "for purposes of religious worship or religious teaching." The university policy is not justified by the desire to maintain separation of church and state, mandated by the state and federal Constitutions.

   While compliance with the federal non-establishment principle is a compelling interest, an equal access policy is not incompatible with the non-establishment requirement. An open forum policy would serve a secular purpose of promoting exchange of student ideas and would not foster excessive entanglement of government with religion since enforcement of the exclusion policy risks greater entanglement (i.e., determining which groups are to be excluded and monitoring meetings to assure compliance). Nor does equal access have a primary effect of advancing religion since the policy does not confer any imprimatur of state approval on the religion and the benefit is available to a broad spectrum of groups, secular and sectarian. *Widmar v. Vincent* (1981).

2) Laws designed to promote equal access to school facilities by prohibiting discrimination against religious speech do not violate the Establishment Clause.

   Example: The 1984 federal Equal Access Act, extending *Widmar* to public secondary schools, does not violate the Establishment Clause. Since Westwood High School allows one or more "noncurriculum related groups" to meet on school premises, it creates a "limited open forum" under the Act, and is therefore prevented from discriminating based on speech content. Denial of a request to form a religious group and meet on school premises during noninstructional time is a denial of "equal access" which violates the Act.

The logic of *Widmar* applies with equal force to the Equal Access Act. A plurality applied the *Lemon* test. Congress' avowed purpose of preventing discrimination against religious and other types of speech is "undeniably secular." The Act grants equal access to both secular and religious speech; its purpose is not to endorse or disapprove of religion. Nor does the Act have the primary effect of advancing religion. Secondary school students are sufficiently mature to appreciate that a school does not endorse student speech merely because it is permitted on a nondiscriminatory basis. Participation of school officials is expressly limited under the Act, minimizing the possibility of official endorsement or coercion. The wide spectrum of clubs at the school also limits any possible message of official endorsement or preference. The limited oversight role of school officials does not impermissibly entangle government in religious activities. *Board of Educ. of the Westside Community Schools v. Mergens* (1990).

2. FINANCIAL ASSISTANCE TO RELIGIOUS SCHOOLS
a. Public Benefits: Busing and Books
The fact that government action provides some aid to religion does not necessarily mean it is an impermissible establishment of religion. *If the state only acts for the secular purpose of serving the public welfare and well-being, the fact that religion is incidentally benefited does not condemn the program.*

Examples: (1) A state law authorizing reimbursement to parents for the expense of bus transportation for their children on buses operated by the public transportation system does not violate the Establishment Clause of the First Amendment. The law was designed to provide safe transportation to school age children, not to aid private schools. State power is no more to be used as to handicap religions than it is to favor them. *Everson v. Board of Education* (1947).

(2) A state law permitting the loan of state-approved secular textbooks to children in secondary schools does not violate the

Establishment Clause. The purpose of the law is to advance the education of the young. Parents and children, rather than the religious school, receive the primary financial benefits of the law. *Board of Educ. of Central School Dist. No. 1 v. Allen* (1968).

b. Financial Aid to Schools

The Court is sharply divided on the application of the Establishment Clause to various forms of aid to religious schools. While the three-part test is applied, each case is decided on an ad hoc basis reflecting shifting coalitions of the Justices. While aid is usually found to be in furtherance of a permissible secular purpose, it is frequently held to have a primary sectarian effect or involve excessive government entanglement with religion.

Among the factors you should consider in evaluating aid programs are: (1) whether the aid is to elementary and secondary education or to higher education, (2) the type of assistance provided (especially whether the aid is directed to citizens generally or is given directly to the religious institution, whether the aid is available generally or is limited to benefiting religious institutions, and whether it involves a continuing church-state relationship or affords an opportunity for inculcating religious values), (3) the location of the assistance, i.e., on public or private school grounds.

1) Elementary-Secondary v. Higher Education

Aid to elementary and secondary education is more likely to be held unconstitutional since the pupils are more impressionable and subject to ideological persuasion. Political divisiveness is more common at this level of education. Higher education has its own internal discipline and stresses academic freedom.

Examples: (1) State salary supplements for the teachers of secular subjects in nonpublic elementary schools involves excessive government entanglement with religion since parochial schools have substantial religious activity, the teacher is amenable to religious discipline, such aid involves a continuing government relationship with the schools, the children are of impressionable age and there is danger of political divisiveness. *Lemon v. Kurtzman* (1971).

(2) Federal construction grants for buildings and facilities to be used strictly for secular activities at private colleges are constitutional, although only a 20-year limit on the use to which such facilities could be put violates the First Amendment. Such construction aid is dispensed on

a one-time basis, is religiously neutral involving limited government surveillance, and does not involve institutions permeated with religious education involved in educating impressionable young people. *Tilton v. Richardson* (1971).

(3) State annual noncategorical grants to private colleges, including sectarian institutions requiring theology courses, is not unconstitutional. First, the purpose is secular, i.e., supporting higher education generally. Second, the state aid did not go to institutions so "pervasively sectarian" that secular and sectarian activities could not be separated—the aid was directed exclusively to the secular activities. No entangling relationship was created given the character of the institutions aided, review of the class content was not required in the approval process, and there was minimal danger of political divisiveness. *Roemer v. Board of Public Works of Maryland* (1976).

2) **Tax Relief and Tuition Benefits**
When the aid is given to citizens rather than provided directly to the religious institutions it is more likely to be upheld. But if the aid is limited only to citizens involved with religious institutions rather than to citizens generally, it may still be held unconstitutional.

Examples: (1) A state law providing direct unrestricted reimbursement grants to parents with children in non-public elementary and secondary schools was held to have the direct and immediate effect of aiding religion. Similarly, state tax relief to the parents was held unconstitutional. Finally, grants for the maintenance and repair of facilities and equipment was struck down. There was no assurance that any of these grants would be used to support solely the secular activities of the schools. *Comm. for Public Educ. & Religious Liberty v. Nyquist* (1973).

(2) A state law permitting taxpayers to deduct certain educational expenses is constitutional. Assuring a well-educated citizenry is the secular purpose of the law and the legislature could conclude that assuring the financial health of private schools serves that end to the benefit of taxpayers generally. Nor does the aid have a primary effect of advancing the sectarian aims of the private schools. Education is only one of the many deductions allowed, encouraging desirable expenditures. "Most importantly, the deduction is available for educational

expenses incurred by *all* parents, including those whose children attend public schools and those whose children attend non-sectarian private schools or sectarian private schools." This neutrality of the program distinguishes *Nyquist*. Further, "by channeling whatever assistance it may provide to parochial schools through individual parents, [the state] has reduced the Establishment Clause objectives. ∗ ∗ ∗ " The Court rejected the usefulness of statistical evidence indicating that the law primarily benefits religious institutions. *Mueller v. Allen* (1983).

(3) State vocational rehabilitation aid to a blind student which is used by him for education at a Christian college is not precluded by the Establishment Clause. The second prong of the *Lemon* test is not violated. First, the state aid goes directly to the student and flows to the religious institution only as a result of the independent and private choice of the recipient, (i.e., it is not a "direct subsidy" to the religious school). Further, it is not likely that any significant part of the aid expended under the program would support religious education. Finally, the aid is in no way skewed towards religion and creates no financial incentive for students to attend sectarian institutions. Nor is there any state endorsement of religion. *Witters v. Washington Dept. of Services for the Blind* (1986).

3) Testing, Recordkeeping, and Other Services
The validity of state support for such services in elementary and secondary schools is likely to turn on the opportunity the particular program affords for indoctrination, *e.g.*, do state officials or private school administrators prepare the test. Also, if the program takes place on public school grounds and under the supervision of public school officials, it is more likely to be upheld.

Examples: (1) The Court upheld a statute authorizing the state to furnish pupils in non-public schools with standardized tests and scoring services. Similarly, the Court upheld the furnishing by public employees of speech, hearing, and psychological diagnostic services, stressing the non-ideological character of the aid. However, the Court did rule unconstitutional those portions of the statute providing for the loan of instructional materials and equipment to non-public school parents or their children and providing for field trip services to non-public schools since such services could be used to disseminate religious teachings. *Wolman v. Walter,* 433 U.S. 229 (1977).

(2) State cash reimbursement of nonpublic schools for state required testing and reporting services does not violate the Establishment Clause. The state retained total control over the content of the tests and the grading and recordkeeping could not be used as a part of religious teaching. The non-ideological services are discrete and readily identifiable and the pervasive religious atmosphere of the schools is not determinative. *Committee for Public Educ. & Rel. Lib. v. Regan* (1980).

(3) A released time education program in which remedial and enrichment courses are offered to non-public students at public expense in classrooms located in and leased from the private schools violates the Establishment Clause. A community education program taught by public employees in classrooms leased from the sectarian schools is unconstitutional. "First, the teachers participating in the programs may become involved in intentionally or inadvertently inculcating particular religious tenets or beliefs. Second, the program may provide a crucial symbolic link between government and religion, thereby enlisting—at least in the eyes of impressionable youngsters—the powers of government to the support of the religious denomination operating the school. Third, the programs may have the effect of directly promoting religion by impermissibly providing a subsidy to the primary religious mission of the institutions affected." *School Dist. of Grand Rapids v. Ball* (1985).

(4) A program involving use of federal funds to pay the salaries of public school teachers to provide remedial instruction and guidance services to educationally deprived children from low income families violates the Establishment Clause. The pervasive sectarian character of the environment and the need for ongoing inspection to assure that teachers will not deliver any religious message involves "a permanent and pervasive state presence in the sectarian schools" violative of the bar against excessive government entanglement with religion (*i.e., Lemon's* third prong). *Aguilar v. Felton* (1985).

3. OTHER ESTABLISHMENT CONTEXTS

a. Blue Laws

1) The Court has thus far upheld Sunday closing laws against challenges based on the Establishment and Free Exercise Clauses.

2) Whatever the historical purpose of the Blue Laws, the Court considered that their present purpose and effect is secular. They are designed to promote a common day of rest. *McGowan v. Maryland* (1961).

3) However, if it were established that a particular law was enacted for the purpose of advancing religion, it would be unconstitutional, even if it also had the secular effect of providing a day of rest. See *Epperson v. Arkansas* (1968). Further, a law affording an employee with an absolute unqualified right not to work on the Sabbath of his choice was held to have the primary effect of advancing a religious practice in violation of the Establishment Clause. *Estate of Thornton v. Caldor, Inc.* (1985).

4) Note that, unlike the religious exemptions granted in many free exercise cases, the law in *Estate of Thornton* did not exempt the employee from any government imposed obligation in order to further free exercise concerns. The Court has stated: "[I]t is a permissible legislative purpose to alleviate significant governmental interference with the ability of religious organizations to define and carry out their religious missions." *Corporation of Presiding Bishop of the Church of Jesus Christ of Latter-Day Saints v. Amos* (1987) [religious exemption from Title VII prohibition against discrimination in employment is a permissible accommodation consistent with the Establishment Clause]. Granting a religious exemption from generally applicable laws does not necessarily violate the Establishment Clause. Indeed, the Court has suggested, (1) that such legislation is valid; and (2) that it is more appropriate that such exemptions be created by the legislatures than by the courts.

b. Tax Exemptions

Property tax exemptions for places of religious worship as part of a general scheme relieving nonprofit organizations from tax obligations, are constitutional in spite of the indirect support provided religion. A history of exemption has demonstrated that such benefits do not involve sponsorship (*i.e.*, money is not given to support religion). Tax exemptions, in fact, result in less government administrative entanglement with religion than would tax assessments, liens, foreclosures, etc. This is "benevolent neutrality." *Walz v. Tax Comm'n* (1970). However, a state may not grant exemptions from sales and use taxes exclusively to religious periodicals. Such exemptions violate the Establishment Clause in that they constitute a state endorsement of religious beliefs. Such a subsidy to religion does not have the secular purpose and primary effect mandated by the Establishment Clause. *Texas Monthly, Inc. v. Bullock* (1989).

c. Legislative Prayer

While prayer in the schools has been invalidated by the Court, legislature opening prayer led by a state-paid chaplain has been upheld. Instead of employing the *Lemon* three-part test, the Court relied on history in holding that those who drafted the First Amendment had not perceived legislative prayer as a threat to the Establishment Clause. The First Congress voted to pay a chaplain to open sessions with a prayer. *Marsh v. Chambers* (1983).

d. Religious Displays

The Court has employed history and tradition in upholding governmental recognition of holidays. However, government may not recognize a religious holiday in a way that has the effect of endorsing religious beliefs.

Examples: (1) Inclusion of a nativity scene as part of a municipal Christmas display does not violate the Establishment Clause. The Court emphasized "the government's acknowledgement of our religious heritage and governmental sponsorship of graphic manifestation of that heritage." While minimizing the value of the *Lemon* test, the Court characterized the display as having the secular purpose of celebrating the holiday. Any benefit to religion from use of the nativity scene to depict the origins of the holiday was "indirect, remote and incidental." There was no entanglement since minimal funds were involved and there were no contacts between church and city authorities. *Lynch v. Donnelly* (1984).

(2) The placement of a Christmas creche on the Grand Staircase, the main part of the Allegheny County Courthouse, given the setting, violates the Establishment Clause. The creche stood alone with no other secular symbols of the holiday season. In this context, the display endorsed a patently Christian message glorifying God for the birth of Jesus Christ.

On the other hand, the placement of an 18–foot Chanukah menorah in front of a government building, next to a Christmas tree and a sign saluting liberty, does not violate the Establishment Clause. In this context, the menorah is part of an overall holiday setting; a secular celebration of the cultural event of Christmas coupled with an acknowledgment of Chanukah as "a contemporaneous alternative tradition." It is not "sufficiently likely" that citizens will interpret the display as an endorsement or disapproval of religious choices. *Allegheny County v. ACLU* (1989).

e. Denominational Preferences

The Court has suggested that when a law aids or advances only selected religions, rather than religions generally, i.e., it grants denominational preferences, the law is suspect and a strict scrutiny standard applies. Government must demonstrate that the law is closely tailored to furthering a compelling public interest. The Lemon *three part test must be satisfied.*

Examples: (1) A Minnesota law imposing registration and reporting requirements only on religious organizations that solicit more than 50 percent of their funds from nonmembers violates the Establishment Clause. The clear command of the clause is that one religious denomination cannot be officially preferred over another. Such a law must be closely fitted to furthering a compelling interest. While the State has a compelling interest in protecting its citizens from abusive practices in solicitations, the law is not closely fitted to further that interest. The record does not support the assumption that membership control over solicitation will occur when the 50 percent figure is reached, that this will protect the public and that the need for public disclosure rises in proportion with the percentage of non-member contributions.

While the *Lemon v. Kurtzman* Establishment Clause test is intended to apply to laws affording a uniform benefit to all religions rather than a discriminatory law, the "excessive entanglement" test of *Kurtzman* is implicated since the law creates a risk of politicizing religion. *Larson v. Valente* (1982).

(2) The refusal of the IRS to recognize payments made by members of the Church of Scientology to that church for training and auditing sessions as charitable contributions does not violate the Establishment Clause. The applicable section of the IRS code was neutral in design and purpose, even though it might impose a disparate burden on certain groups that rely on sales for fundraising. There is no unconstitutional denominational preference since the rule applies to all religious entities. There is no significant danger of an excessive entanglement between church and state through enforcement of the rule since it involves

routine regulatory action rather than any inquiry into religious doctrine. *Hernandez v. CIR* (1989).

(3) Imposition of a state sales and use tax on religious materials sold by a religious organization does not violate the Establishment Clause. Applying the *Lemon* test, the Court first concluded that the tax was "neutral and nondiscriminatory on questions of religious beliefs." Nor was there a danger of excessive entanglement. Even assuming that there were significant administrative burdens imposed by the tax, this would not violate the Establishment Clause. Since the materials are subject to the tax regardless of content or motive, government would not be required to inquire into the religious basis for selling the materials. *Jimmy Swaggart Ministries v. Board of Equalization* (1990).

f. Internal Church Disputes

Courts are not to decide purely internal church disputes. However, courts may decide legal questions, which can be settled by the application of "neutral principles of law", i.e., questions which will not require an inquiry into religious doctrine. Jones v. Wolf *(1979)* [state court could decide which group would control church property following a separation within the church].

B. THE MEANING OF THE "FREE EXERCISE" CLAUSE

If government undertakes to burden persons because of their religious beliefs, there is a violation of the Free Exercise Clause. Most laws, however, only incidentally burden or coerce religious beliefs while pursuing a secular public welfare objective. Coercion of religious belief is the essence of a free exercise claim.

Free exercise cases generally involve a claimed exemption from an otherwise generally applicable law. In reconciling the secular public welfare interests of government with the free exercise interests of the individual, the courts engage in balancing. For example, it is doubtful whether the members of a religious group which did not believe in paying taxes to the state would be permitted to withhold their taxes.

Since the 1960's, the courts have employed a two step test. Initially, the court examines the severity of the burden on the individual's religion. If the burden is significant, government must demonstrate that the law is narrowly tailored to achieve a compelling state interest. The availability of less burdensome alternatives is considered. Doctrines employed in freedom of expression cases, *e.g.,* the prior restraint doctrine, prohibition against vagueness and overbreadth, are often applied in free exercise cases. In many cases, this strict scrutiny standard has resulted in an exemption from religion-neutral laws that have the effect of significantly burdening a religion.

However, in Employment Div., Dept. of Human Resources of Oregon v. Smith *(1990), and* Lyng v. Northwest Indian Cemetery Protective Ass'n *(1988), discussed below, the Court held that this strict scrutiny standard did not apply to a generally applicable and otherwise constitutional law, even though application of the law incidentally imposed a significant burden on a religion.* These holdings may portend a general doctrinal revision rejecting strict scrutiny review of laws having only an incidental effect of significantly burdening religious freedom. If this trend solidifies, a key question will become whether the challenged government action directly, rather than incidentally, burdens free exercise. Incidental burdens on religion would be insufficient to generate strict scrutiny review.

1.   BELIEF–CONDUCT

While religious belief and opinion is absolutely protected, the practice of religious activities must be accommodated to valid government interests. The respective interests of the government in regulating conduct injurious to the public well-being is balanced against the burden on the individual's exercise of his religion if the conduct is prohibited.

Examples: (1) Application of a federal law prohibiting polygamy to a Mormon who claims that polygamy is a fundamental tenet of his faith does not violate the Free Exercise Clause. The law is a permissible regulation of conduct which is subversive of good order and violative of social duties. *Reynolds v. United States* (1878).

(2) A state law compelling a flag salute by public school children in violation of their religious beliefs offends the guarantee of free exercise of religion. The state cannot prescribe what is orthodox in politics, nationalism, and matters of opinion. Religious freedom is susceptible of restriction only to prevent grave and immediate dangers to interests which the state may lawfully protect. *West Virginia Bd. of Educ. v. Barnette* (1943).

(3) A state law prohibiting clergymen from being delegates to the state constitutional convention violates the free exercise guarantee. Treating the law as directed at conduct rather than beliefs, the Court still found no state interest of sufficient magnitude to justify the significant burden on religion. *McDaniel v. Paty* (1978).

2.   CENTRALITY AND SINCERITY

In resolving free exercise claims, the courts are prohibited from assessing the truth or falsity of the claimant's religious beliefs. United States v. Ballard *(1944)* [lower court erred in allowing jury to consider truth or falsity of religious claims of a member of the "I Am" movement who was being prosecuted for using the mail for false pretense]. *However, the courts can inquire into whether the religious belief is sincerely held. The courts have also probed the centrality of a belief or practice to a religion in assessing the significance of the burden on free exercise.* Wisconsin v. Yoder *(1972).* However, in Employment Div., Dept. of Human Resources of Oregon v. Smith *(1990),* discussed below, the Court states: "It is no more appropriate for judges to determine the 'centrality' of religious belief before applying a 'compelling interest' test in the free exercise field, than it would be for them to determine the 'importance' of an idea before applying the 'compelling' interest test in the free speech field." This may be the prelude of eliminating the centrality inquiry in free exercise cases.

3. GENERAL INDIRECT BURDENS

The fact that a religion-neutral, generally applicable law imposes a burden on a religious group does not, without more, require an exemption under the Free Exercise Clause. Absent a significant burden on the claimant's free exercise of her religious beliefs, i.e., a uniquely religious impact, strict scrutiny is not appropriate.

> *Examples:* (1) Application of the Fair Labor Standards Act (FLSA) to workers (identified as "employees" under the Act because they are not truly "volunteers" but receive "wages" in the form of benefits) engaged in the commercial activities of a religious foundation (identified as a business "enterprise" under the Act) does not violate the Free Exercise or Establishment Clauses. The Free Exercise Clause requires an exemption from a governmental program only if the law actually burdens the claimant's freedom to exercise religious rights. Application of the FLSA does not force the workers to accept wages nor does it prevent their returning the wages to the Foundation. Nor does the recordkeeping required by the FLSA foster an excessive government entanglement with religion violative of the Establishment Clause. The Act is limited to commercial activities and the inquiries made relate only to routine factual information and are not equal to significantly intrusive "government surveillance" into religious affairs. *Tony & Susan Alamo Foundation v. Secretary of Labor* (1985).
>
> (2) California's imposition of sales and use tax liability on religious materials does not violate the Free Exercise Clause. The incrementally larger tax burden experienced by the religious group does not significantly burden their free exercise of their religious beliefs. Claimant's religious beliefs do not forbid payment of the tax. California's generally applicable tax is not a flat license fee imposed as a precondition for evangelical activity; it is not a prior restraint to engaging in religious activity.

Compare Murdock v. Pennsylvania (1943) [convictions of Jehovah's Witnesses for soliciting without a license requiring payment of a license fee held unconstitutional]. The Free Exercise Clause does not require the state to grant an exemption from its generally applicable tax absent proof of a more significant burden on religious freedom. *Jimmy Swaggart Ministries v. Board of Equalization* (1990).

4. BLUE LAWS

The Court has rejected a challenge to Sunday closing laws based on the Free Exercise Clause by characterizing the laws as imposing only an indirect economic burden on the Sabbatarian. Balanced against the state interest in having a uniform day of rest, the free exercise claim failed.

Example: An orthodox Jewish merchant who celebrates the Sabbath on Saturday and closes his shop that day but who keeps his shop open on Sunday may be validly prosecuted under a state Sunday closing law. When the state regulates conduct by enacting a general law within its power, the purpose and effect of which is to advance the state's secular goals, the statute is valid despite its indirect burden (i.e., an economic hardship) on religious observance unless the state may accomplish its purpose by means which do not impose such a burden. *Braunfeld v. Brown* (1961).

5. CONDITIONING PUBLIC WELFARE BENEFITS

a. *The government cannot condition the receipt of governmental benefits on the surrender of constitutional rights, including the free exercise of one's religion. Conditioning the receipt of public benefits, such as unemployment compensation, on the willingness to violate one's religious principles, imposes a significant burden on free exercise. Only a compelling government interest, which cannot be realized by means less burdensome on constitutional values, justifies such coercion.*

Examples: (1) A Seventh Day Adventist was disqualified for benefits under a state unemployment compensation law because she would not work on Saturday, the Sabbath day of her faith, thus falling afoul of a provision in the state law disqualifying those who refuse to accept "suitable work when offered * * *." The state may not force an individual to choose between following the precepts of her religion and forfeiting governmental benefits. The application of the provision violated free exercise because it involved a significant burden and no compelling state interest was advanced to justify such a burden. *Sherbert v. Verner* (1963).

(2) A state denial of unemployment benefits to a claimant who terminates his job because his religious beliefs forbade participation in production of armaments violates the free exercise guarantee. As long as the person terminates his work because of an honest conviction that such work was forbidden by his religion, he can make a free exercise claim. The state interest in avoiding wide-spread unemployment and avoiding detailed probing by employers of a job applicant's religious beliefs were not sufficiently compelling to justify the substantial burden placed on the employee's religious liberty. The benefit to the employee of receiving benefits does not constitute an establishment of religion but reflects nothing more than the governmental obligation of neutrality in the face of religious differences. *Thomas v. Indiana Employment Security Div.* (1981).

(3) A state denial of unemployment benefits because of the "misconduct" of a Seventh Day Adventist who, because of religious objections, refused to work her assigned hours, violates the Free Exercise Clause. Even though her religious objections developed after she commenced employment, *Sherbert* and *Thomas* controlled. *Hobbie v. Unemployment Appeals Comm'n* (1987).

(4) The federal statutory requirement that a state agency "shall utilize" social security numbers in administering federal assistance programs does not violate the Free Exercise Clause even where the claim is made that state compliance with the requirement would burden the litigant's religious beliefs. The Free Exercise Clause does not afford an individual a right to dictate the conduct of the government's internal procedures on religious grounds. The law, requiring use of Social Security numbers already in the government's possession, imposes no significant burden on the claimant's ability to exercise his religion.

A further requirement was that the number be provided by the individual as a condition for welfare eligibility. Three justices stressed that eligibility for welfare benefits rather than government compulsion of conduct was involved and would not apply strict scrutiny. Since the requirement is facially neutral in religious terms applying to all applicants for the benefits involved, and clearly promotes a legitimate and important governmental interest, they would uphold the requirement. Preventing fraud in these programs is an important goal, and the social security number requirement is a reasonable means of promoting that goal. Four justices would have used strict scrutiny on the basis of *Thomas* and *Sherbert*. Two justices did not reach the issue. *Bowen v. Roy* (1986).

(5) State denial of unemployment benefits to a worker who refused a job because of his belief that as a Christian he could not work on Sunday as the job required, violates the free exercise guarantee. A person cannot be made to choose between fidelity to religious belief and employment absent compelling justification. *Frazee v. Illinois Dept. of Emp. Sec.* (1989).

b. *Exception: Employment Div., Dept. of Human Resources of Oregon v. Smith* (1990), discussed below, indicates that benefits can be denied if the denial is only the incidental effect of applying a generally applicable and otherwise valid criminal law. *In such a case, strict scrutiny is not applicable.* Since prohibition of the religious practice is constitutional, imposition of the lesser burden of denying unemployment benefits to persons engaging in the proscribed conduct is constitutional. *Employment Div., Dept. of Human Resources of Oregon v. Smith* (1988) (*Smith* I).

6. COMPELLED EXPRESSION

a. *When government requires an individual to engage in practices contrary to central tenets of his or her religion, it imposes a direct burden on the free exercise of religion. Only a compelling or overriding government interest justifies such a significant burden on free exercise.*

Examples: (1) State prosecutions of members of the Amish church who refuse to send their children to public school after the eighth grade thus violating a state law compelling public school attendance to age 16 violates the free exercise guarantee. Utilizing a balancing test, the Court ruled the prosecutions invalid on the ground that the Amish had sustained the heavy and difficult burden of showing that their alternative mode of continuing informal vocational education served to meet exactly those interests advanced by the state in support of its requirement of compulsory high school attendance. In such circumstances, the legitimate claims to free exercise of religion overbalance the interests of the state. *Wisconsin v. Yoder* (1972).

(2) Imposition of social security taxes on a member of the Amish faith who objected on religious grounds to receipt of public insurance benefits and to payment of taxes to support public insurance funds does not violate the free exercise

guarantee. While payment of such taxes does violate Amish religious beliefs, the government limitation on religious liberty is justified by its showing that "it is essential to accomplish an overriding governmental interest." Government has a vital interest in maintaining a mandatory and continuous participation in and contribution to the social security system since widespread individual voluntary coverage would undermine the system. *United States v. Lee* (1982).

b. But the courts exercise extreme deference to government authority in reviewing free exercise claims by military personnel.

Example: The First Amendment does not preclude an Air Force regulation, prohibiting members of the Air Force from wearing headgear while indoors, from being applied to an Orthodox Jew's wearing of a yarmulke even though the effect is to restrict the wearing of the headgear required by his religious beliefs. Review of military regulations challenged on First Amendment grounds is far more deferential than constitutional review of similar laws or regulations designed for civilian society. When evaluating whether military needs justify a particular restriction on religiously motivated conduct, courts must give great deference to the professional judgment of military authorities concerning the relative importance of a particular military interest. The regulation reasonably and evenhandedly served the military's perceived need for uniformity in visible apparel. *Goldman v. Weinberger* (1986).

7. NONCOERCIVE LAWS

If the government regulation has the incidental effect of making it significantly more difficult to practice a religion, but does not compel or coerce action contrary to a religious belief, strict scrutiny does not apply. Note that the government is not required by the Free Exercise Clause to accommodate its own internal processes and operations to the religious needs and desires of particular claimants, even if the government action imposes a significant burden on religious belief. See also *Bowen v. Roy* (1986) (supra), where the Court characterized the burdensome effect of such government action as insignificant.

Example: The Free Exercise Clause does not bar the federal government from permitting timber harvesting and road construction in a national forest traditionally used for religious purposes by three Indian tribes. Such an incidental effect on religion does not constitute a "prohibition" of free exercise. Even if the government action "would virtually destroy" the religious practice, government could not operate if it were required to satisfy every citizen's religious needs and desires. *Lyng v. Northwest Indian Cemetery Protective Ass'n* (1988).

8.   PROSCRIBED RELIGIOUS PRACTICES
The free exercise guarantee is not violated by a generally applicable and otherwise constitutional criminal law which has the incidental effect of prohibiting a religious practice. Such religion-neutral laws are presumptively valid; strict scrutiny does not apply. This principle applies even if the proscribed practice is central to a religion.

> *Example:*   Denial of unemployment compensation to workers who were fired from their jobs with a private drug rehabilitation organization for work-related misconduct resulting from the use of the drug peyote during sacramental worship of the Native American Church did not deny free exercise of religion. The use of peyote violates state criminal drug laws which make no exception for religiously inspired uses. Such a prohibition is permissible under the Free Exercise Clause.
>
> Free exercise does not relieve an individual of the obligation to comply with valid, neutral laws of general applicability. Strict scrutiny is inapplicable to challenges to "an across-the-board criminal prohibition on a particular form of conduct." The *Sherbert* strict scrutiny test has never been used to invalidate government action outside the context of unemployment compensation, a context where individualized assessment of the reasons for the government action is appropriate. To apply strict scrutiny would establish "a private right to ignore generally applicable laws" which would be a "constitutional anomaly." Strict scrutiny is not required even if the practice is "central" to religion, since determining the "centrality" of a practice is inappropriate for judges. A rule of presumptive invalidity "would open the prospect of constitutionally required religious exemptions from civic obligations of almost every conceivable kind." Such religious accommodation should be left to the legislature. *Employment Div., Dept. of Human Resources of Oregon v. Smith* (1990).

C.   THE MEANING OF RELIGION

The Court has not directly addressed itself to the question of what qualifies as a religion or a religious belief under the Establishment and the Free Exercise Clauses. Indeed, it is not even clear that it is appropriate for a court to probe the meaning of "religion." But the Court has stated: "Although a determination of what is a 'religious' belief or practice entitled to constitutional protection may present a most delicate question, the very concept of ordered liberty precludes allowing every person to make his own standards on matters of conduct in which society as a whole has important interests." *Wisconsin v. Yoder* (1972).

The Court has clearly rejected any limitation of "religion" to theistic religions. *Torcaso v. Watkins* (1961). While there must be a sincerely held "religious belief" to qualify for free exercise protection, it is not required that the claimant be a member of organized religion or a particular sect. *Frazee v. Illinois Dept. of Emp. Sec.* (1989) [denial of religious exemption to a claimant for unemployment compensation who belonged to no sect, but sincerely believed that as a Christian he could not work on Sunday as the job required, violates free exercise].

1. CONSCIENTIOUS OBJECTION

a. In cases involving the conscientious objector provisions of the draft laws, the Court has indicated that the test of whether a belief is religious "is whether a given belief that is sincere and meaningful occupies a place in the life of its possessor parallel to that filled by the orthodox belief in God * * *."

b. A plurality of the Court has gone even further, extending conscientious objector status even to those whose objections primarily reflect public policy considerations. *Welsh v. United States* (1970). However, the Court has refused an exemption to those opposed to a particular "unjust" war and has upheld the exclusion of such persons as based on neutral and secular reasons. *Gillette v. United States* (1971).

D. REVIEW QUESTIONS

1. T or F Released time for religious instruction, on or off school grounds, violates the Establishment Clause.

2. T or F Requiring non-denominational prayers violates the First Amendment even if objecting students are excused.

3. T or F Use of state funds for busing or the loan of state approved textbooks for students attending religious-affiliated schools does not violate the Establishment Clause.

4. T or F State tax relief for parents with children in non-public elementary and secondary schools violates the Establishment Clause.

5. T or F A tax break for educational expenses, available to all citizens, is constitutional even if statistically sectarian schools receive the primary economic benefit.

6. T or F   A shared time program for children attending sectarian schools is constitutional so long as public school teachers are used to teach only secular subjects.

7. T or F   A law providing favorable treatment for traditional religions with a large, established membership is probably constitutional.

8. T or F   A state law granting a religious exemption from a generally applicable law has the purpose of aiding religion and therefore violates the Establishment Clause.

9. T or F   Courts may not decide legal questions involving ownership of religious property.

10. T or F   While religious belief is absolutely protected, religious practices are subject to public regulation.

11. T or F   If a government regulation of conduct significantly burdens a sincerely held religious belief, it necessarily violates the Free Exercise Clause.

12. T or F   An exemption from generally-applicable laws for persons having a sincere religious objection to conforming is always required by the Free Exercise Clause.

13. T or F   Courts cannot constitutionally inquire into the meaning of "religion" or "religious belief".

14. T or F   If a law significantly burdens a religious belief, strict scrutiny is always required by the Free Exercise Clause.

15. Which of the following programs would be most likely to violate the Establishment Clause?

    a.   Tax exemption for churches and other property owned by religions.

    b.   A requirement that the Ten Commandments be posted in public school classrooms.

    c.   Sunday Closing Laws.

    d.   State building grants to colleges.

    e.   State reimbursement of nonpublic elementary schools for state required testing and reporting.

16. Which of the following is the *least accurate* statement of the law relating to the Establishment of Religion Clause?

    a.   The government action must have a secular legislative purpose to be valid.

    b.   The Establishment Clause is directed principally against laws discriminating among religions.

    c.   If the primary effect of a law is to advance or inhibit religion, the Establishment Clause is violated.

    d.   Laws fostering an excessive entanglement with religion, or promoting political devisiveness, violate the non-establishment guarantee.

17. A member of the Seventh Day Adventist Church was discharged by her employer because she would not work on Saturday, the sabbath day of her faith. She was unable to obtain other employment because of her refusal to work on Saturdays. She, therefore, filed a claim for unemployment compensation benefits under the State Unemployment Compensation Act. The State Commission handling such matters said that she was disqualified for benefits because she failed, without good cause, to accept suitable work when offered by the State Employment Office. The state courts affirmed the State Commission's ruling. The Seventh Day Adventist has now challenged the state decision to disqualify her from benefits on the grounds that it is unconstitutional. Is it?

X

STATE ACTION

Analysis

The mechanism that makes most constitutional guarantees operative is state action. In the Civil Rights Cases of 1883, the Court delimited the significance of state action under the Fourteenth Amendment: "Individual invasion of individual rights is not the subject matter of the Amendment." In other words, private discrimination against other individuals with respect to jobs, housing, and services are not a constitutional (as distinguished from a statutory) matter reached by the Fourteenth Amendment. This is equally true of most rights and liberties protected by the Constitution—it is government wrongdoing that provides the subject matter for constitutional judicial review. In applying the state action requirement, the Court has described it as preservative of personal liberty, federalism and separation of powers.

In the fairly recent past, efforts were made, with some success, to have the Court view private action as quasi-public and therefore subject to constitutional standards. Thus, where a private activity fulfills a public function or where the state involvement and the private involvement were intertwined, the Court has been willing to categorize an entire activity as the equivalent of state action.

In the 1970's, the movement to judicially expand the state action concept to reach more private conduct came to a halt. The Court has significantly increased the level of government involvement in private conduct that is needed to establish state action and has required litigants to demonstrate a close nexus between government and the particular private action being challenged. In other words, the Court is limiting the occasions when private conduct will be subject to constitutional limitations.

A. THE STATE ACTION REQUIREMENT

1. THIRTEENTH AMENDMENT
The Thirteenth Amendment provides that "neither slavery nor involuntary servitude * * * shall exist within the United States * * *." It is not limited to state or public action denying the guarantee but applies directly against private action as well.

2. FOURTEENTH AMENDMENT
The Fourteenth Amendment, § 1, provides that "no *State* shall make or enforce any law which shall abridge the privileges or immunities of citizens of the United States; nor shall any *State* deprive any person of life, liberty, or property, without due process of law; nor [may the State] deny to any person within its jurisdiction the equal protection of the laws." [Emphasis added.] It has been held that state action is required if the courts are to find these guarantees violated. *Civil Rights Cases* (1883).

3. **FIFTEENTH AMENDMENT**
   Similarly, the Fifteenth Amendment, § 1 requires governmental action in order
   to prove a violation. It provides that "the right of citizens of the United
   States to vote shall not be denied or abridged *by the United States or by any
   State* on account of race, color, or previous condition of servitude." [Emphasis
   added.]

4. **THE PRESENT STANDARD—STATE RESPONSIBILITY**
   *The mere fact that the government is somehow involved in challenged private
   action is not sufficient to establish "state action." It is only when the government
   is so significantly involved in the action that it can be said that the government is
   "engaged in the challenged conduct or is responsible for it" that the requisite
   threshold is satisfied. There must be a close nexus between government and the
   particular private conduct being challenged.*

B. OFFICIAL MISCONDUCT AND JOINT ACTION

1. **ACTION CONTRARY TO LAW**
   *Challenges to laws and to official action pursuant to a law clearly involve state
   action. But even if an official acts contrary to law, the state action requirement is
   satisfied. The government has put the official in a position of authority where he
   can misuse his power.*

   Example: Three state law enforcement officials beat and killed a young Black
   man. Suit was brought against the officers under a federal civil
   rights statute alleging that the officers, acting under color of law,
   had violated the victim's due process rights to life, trial, and
   punishment according to law. The acts of the officers were
   considered by the Court to be under "color of law" because that
   term embraces acts of officers who undertake to perform official
   duty whether they act properly or improperly. *Screws v. United
   States* (1945).

2. **PUBLIC ADMINISTRATION**
   *Official supervision, control or management of a facility, even when the
   government is only indirectly entwined in the management, constitutes state action.*

   Example: A testator left a park as a gift to a city on condition that it be
   used only by whites. The park was maintained by the city as a
   public facility and was also granted a tax exemption. The
   appointment of "private" trustees did not take the park out of the
   public sector and did not dissipate the momentum the park
   acquired as a public facility. If the city remains entwined in the
   management or control of the park, it is subject to Fourteenth
   Amendment standards. In such circumstances, even if the formal

title to the park is in private hands, the public character of the park requires that it be subject to the commands of the Fourteenth Amendment. *Evans v. Newton* (1966).

3. JOINT ACTION
If a private individual engages in joint activity with government officials, state action is established.

Example: Eighteen defendants, three of them state law officers, were responsible for the deaths of three civil rights workers. The lower court upheld counts charging a violation of a federal civil rights statute against the three law officers but dismissed as to the fifteen private individuals on the ground that they had not acted under color of law. The Supreme Court reversed holding that one acts under color of law if he is a willful participant in a joint activity with the state or its agents. *United States v. Price* (1966).

C. PUBLIC FUNCTIONS

Some activities are so public in character that the government will not be allowed to disclaim responsibility. Government inaction in the face of private actions in such areas will be deemed to establish state action. Only if a function is traditionally and exclusively a function of government will it constitute state action.

1. WHITE PRIMARIES
Primary elections are "an important function relating to the exercise of sovereignty by the people." Even when the primary is administered by normally private persons or groups, the action remains that of the government. *Terry v. Adams* (1953). [Primary held by a private group prior to regular Democratic primary which was tantamount to election, held to constitute state action.]

2. COMPANY TOWNS
If a privately-owned place becomes the functional equivalent of a public forum, such as a municipality, it may become part of the public forum.

Examples: (1) When a company-owned town refused to permit a Jehovah Witness to distribute religious pamphlets on the town's main street, the Court declared that such a company-owned town, where no alternative forum was present, should be deemed sufficiently public as to prevent a restraint on First Amendment rights. The touchstone of this decision was that the streets of the company town, albeit privately owned, served a public or governmental function sufficient to cause them to be viewed as quasi-public for purposes of application of the state action concept. *Marsh v. Alabama* (1946).

(2) The Court has suggested that operation of a park could constitute a public function. "The service rendered even by a private park of this character is municipal in nature," citing *Marsh. Evans v. Newton* (1966). But, this approach has not prevailed. *Evans v. Abney* (1970).

3. TRADITIONALLY AND EXCLUSIVELY SOVEREIGN

At the present time, the Court requires that the private entity must be exercising powers traditionally and exclusively reserved to government, i.e., powers "traditionally associated with sovereignty, such as eminent domain * * *," in order to find state action using the public function theory. *Jackson v. Metropolitan Edison Co.* (1974) [privately-owned utility is not engaged in state action].

Examples: (1) A warehouseman's enforcement of a lien by the sale of the stored goods, as authorized by New York's Uniform Commercial Code, was held not to constitute state action. In authorizing self-help as a means of resolving private disputes, the statute does not delegate a function "traditionally and exclusively reserved to the state", because there remains a wide range of debtor's remedies available and the state has not delegated to the creditor "an exclusive perogative of the sovereign." The statute is merely a legislative determination that courts should not prevent self-help in this situation. State acquiescence in private action does not constitute state action. *Flagg Bros. Inc. v. Brooks* (1978).

(2) Operation of a nominally private school for maladjusted high school students, located on private grounds and managed by a private Board of Directors, is not state action, for purposes of a lawsuit alleging denial of free speech and due process rights of an employee. Until recently, the state had not undertaken responsibility for students who could not be served by traditional public schools. Nor is education of maladjusted students the *exclusive* province of the state merely because it extensively funds the private education. *Rendell-Baker v. Kohn* (1982).

(3) Operation of a nursing home which houses Medicare patients, challenging their transfer or discharge without notice or hearing, does not constitute state action. The fact that the state has legally assumed financial responsibility for the nursing care of such patients does make the activity state action. The decisions made in the day-to-day administration of a nursing home are not the kind of decisions "traditionally and exclusively made by the

sovereign for and on behalf of the public." *Blum v. Yaretsky* (1982).

D. SIGNIFICANT STATE INVOLVEMENT

1. **SYMBIOTIC RELATIONSHIPS**

   a. *The Court will sometimes inquire into the facts and circumstances to determine whether the aggregate of all the contacts between the government and the private actor constitute such a significant involvement as to make the government responsible for the private action. Critical in such a weighing is the existence of a "symbiotic relationship" between the government and the private actor.*

   > ***Example:*** A privately-owned restaurant, located within a municipal parking authority, which refused to serve a Black man food or drink solely because of his race was held bound by the proscriptions of the Fourteenth Amendment. The land and building were publicly owned, acquired, constructed, and maintained. Guests of the restaurant were thereby afforded a convenient place to park their autos, and the restaurant's convenience for diners may well have provided more business for the Parking Authority. In short, the state had so far insinuated itself into a position of interdependence with the restaurant that the state had to be recognized as a joint participant in the challenged activity. Therefore, the restaurant could not be viewed as so "purely private" as to fall outside the scope of the Fourteenth Amendment. *Burton v. Wilmington Parking Authority* (1961).

   b. The fact that the government and private party are in a close working relationship or even in a contractual relationship does not necessarily establish a symbiotic relationship or joint action. There must be a sufficiently close relationship between the government and the private party that the acts of the latter may fairly be treated as the acts of the State itself.

   > ***Example:*** Disciplinary actions taken by the University of Nevada Las Vegas (UNLV) against its basketball coach, Jerry Tarkanian, under threat of sanction for violation of NCAA rules, does not mean that the NCAA engaged in state action. This case is the "mirror image" of the usual state action case since it was the State that performed the final act complained of in response to the influence of the private party. Since UNLV actively resisted the imposition of sanctions, the parties were more in an adversarial posture than partners. The NCAA was

not an agent of the State but acted in response to its other members to enforce its rules. UNLV was free to leave the NCAA and establish its own standards. No power was delegated by the State to the NCAA to discipline a State employee; the rules were enforceable only by sanctions against the University itself. The NCAA imposition of sanctions was not taken pursuant to Nevada law and the organization remained a private entity acting at odds with the State. *National Collegiate Athletic Ass'n v. Tarkanian* (1988).

2. GOVERNMENT REGULATION AND LICENSING

Even extensive government regulation of a private activity or the provision of public benefits on a neutral basis is not, without more, sufficient to constitute state action. Further, the fact that the state licenses the actor does not make the state a partner to the actions of the licensee.

Example: A Black who was refused service by a national fraternal organization, contended that because the state liquor board had issued the organization a private club liquor license, the refusal of service to him was state action for purposes of the Equal Protection Clause. The Court rejected this contention, reasoning that discrimination by an otherwise private entity does not violate the Equal Protection Clause merely because the private entity receives some state benefit or is subject to extensive state regulation. The Court emphasized that unlike *Burton v. Wilmington Parking Authority* (1961), there was nothing in the record to suggest the presence of a symbiotic relationship between the private entity and the state. *Moose Lodge No. 107 v. Irvis* (1972).

3. GOVERNMENT FINANCIAL SUPPORT

The fact that government provides financial support for a private actor does not necessarily make the conduct of the private action into state action. Numerous privately-owned businesses and institutions rely on government contracts. Further, government grants and subsidies flow to numerous persons and institutions. Only if the assistance somehow makes the government a partner to the challenged conduct by encouraging, authorizing, or approving it (see below) is it likely to constitute state action.

Examples: (1) The fact that a state directly reimburses 90 percent of the medical expenses of the patients in privately-owned nursing facilities and subsidizes the operating and capital costs of the home, does not make the state constitutionally responsible for the home's decisions. *Blum v. Yaretsky* (1982).

(2) The fact that a privately-owned and operated school depends on public funds for 90 to 99 percent of its operating budget does not make the acts of the administrators the acts of the state. *Rendell-Baker v. Kohn* (1982).

(3) State purchase of textbooks, like state tuition grants, directed to students attending public and private schools, regardless of whether the participating school practiced racial discrimination violates the Fourteenth Amendment. Such support is a form of financial assistance money to the benefit of the private school itself. *Norwood v. Harrison* (1973).

(4) A city under a desegregation order violates equal protection when it permits exclusive use of its recreational facilities, even on a temporary basis, by segregated private schools since it makes attendance at such schools more attractive. The Court remanded the question of whether non-exclusive use would constitute state action to the lower court. *Gilmore v. Montgomery* (1974).

E. ENCOURAGEMENT, AUTHORIZATION AND APPROVAL

1. NEUTRAL LAW ENFORCEMENT
Generally, the neutral enforcement of its laws by state officials will not, without more, constitute state action. In the absence of any encouragement, authorization, or approval of the challenged act, the State is not responsible for the conduct.

Example: A public park could not constitutionally be operated on a racially discriminatory basis as directed by the testator who had asked that his property be held in trust by the city as a park "for whites only". The state court's refusal to apply the *cy pres* doctrine to the will in order to keep the park open to all races and its decision permitting the trust property to revert to the heirs of the testator did not violate the Fourteenth Amendment. The Court emphasized that there was not the slightest indication that the state judges were motivated by any discriminatory intent in construing the will. Similarly, there was no indication that the testator had been persuaded to draw his will as he did by the fact that state statutes permitted racial restrictions at the time of the writing of the will. *Evans v. Abney* (1970).

2. INVOLUNTARY DISCRIMINATION
However, even a neutral enforcement of state law by a state official cannot be used to force racial discrimination on unwilling parties.

Example: A willing seller may not be barred from transacting a sale of real estate with a willing buyer because of state judicial enforcement of restrictive covenants, designed to exclude persons from the ownership of real property on the basis of race. Such judicial action bears the clear and unmistakable imprimatur of the state. Judicial action is no less state action under the Fourteenth Amendment because taken under a state's common law policy or because the particular private discrimination, enforced by the state, has its original impetus in a private agreement. This conclusion is fortified by the public policy against housing discrimination and in favor of free alienation of property. *Shelley v. Kraemer* (1948).

3. SIGNIFICANT ENCOURAGEMENT
When the challenged private actions are overtly or covertly encouraged by public officials or government measures, state action is present.

Examples: (1) Convictions against civil rights demonstrators participating in a "sit-in" protesting segregation in a privately-owned restaurant were reversed by the Court because the facts disclosed that the separation of the races which was being protested had been precipitated by the oral command of the police superintendent and the mayor. *Lombard v. Louisiana* (1963).

(2) A new provision of a state constitution was submitted to the electorate by referendum which was designed to prevent the enactment by the state of legislation designed to secure fair housing, i.e., to prevent racial discrimination in the rental and sale of real estate. The Court held that the embodiment of a right of discrimination on racial grounds in the state's charter would encourage private racial discrimination to a degree which would offend the Fourteenth Amendment. *Reitman v. Mulkey* (1967).

4. AUTHORIZATION AND APPROVAL
a. *The fact that the government acquiesces in the wrongful acts of a private party does not make the government responsible for the conduct. Only if the government authorizes or compels the particular conduct being challenged, thus making itself responsible for the action, is there a sufficient nexus to satisfy the state action requirement.*

Examples: (1) The termination of a customer's electric service by a privately-owned utility company for non-payment, in the absence of notice, hearing and an opportunity to pay any amounts found due, is not attributable to the state. This is so even though the state public utilities commission approved a tariff which authorized termination of service in such circumstances. State action was still not present because the state public utility commission had not directly approved or authorized the termination provision. The fact that public utility regulation by the state is extremely comprehensive does not in itself establish state action. *Jackson v. Metropolitan Edison Co.* (1974).

(2) A warehouseman's enforcement of a lien by the sale of stored goods, as authorized by the state Commercial Code, did not constitute state action. Action by a private party, without any action by public officials, did not make the person a public actor. In the absence of "something more", there was no state action. *Flagg Brothers, Inc. v. Brooks* (1978).

(3) Dismissal of employees by a privately-owned school because of their speech activity does not constitute state action. Even though the school was heavily regulated, there was no showing that the personnel decisions were "compelled or even influenced" by the state regulation. *Rendell-Baker v. Kohn* (1982).

(4) A private nursing home's decision to discharge or transfer a Medicaid patient is not state action sufficient to support a § 1983 claim. The fact that the state required the facility's staff to evaluate a patient's condition on a particular form, to make "all possible efforts" to place the patient in a facility providing the "appropriate level of care", and the fact that the state could impose penalties on nursing homes, was not deemed to be regulation that would "dictate the decision to discharge or transfer in a particular case." Here, the ultimate decision turned on medical judgments made by private parties according to professional standards not established by the State. *Blum v. Yaretsky* (1982).

b.   *In order to find state authorization and approval of private conduct, two conditions must be satisfied. "First, the deprivation [of the right] must be caused by the exercise of some right or privilege created by the state or by a rule of conduct imposed by the state or by a person for whom the state is responsible. Second, the party charged with the deprivation must be a person who may fairly be said to be a state actor."*

Example: Invocation of state prejudgment attachment proceedings by a private party, whereby the county sheriff executes a writ of attachment issued by the clerk of the state court, constitutes state action. The constitutional challenge was to the state law creating the attachment proceeding thus satisfying the first test. The private party's joint participation with state officials in the seizure of the disputed property was sufficient to make the private party a "state action" under the second test. *Lugar v. Edmonson Oil Co., Inc.* (1982).

F. REVIEW QUESTIONS

1. T or F The Thirteenth Amendment applies to private conduct.

2. T or F Any government involvement with private discrimination will establish the requisite state action under the Fourteenth Amendment.

3. T or F When a public official acts contrary to state law, this is not state action under the Fourteenth or Fifteenth Amendments.

4. T or F If the government financially contributes a substantial portion of the funds of a private concern, the action of that concern constitutes state action.

5. T or F If an activity is traditionally and exclusively a function of the sovereign, government will not be allowed to disclaim responsibility for it.

6. T or F Neutral law enforcement which forces unwilling private parties to racially discriminate constitutes state action violative of the Equal Protection guarantee.

7. T or F Even state authorization and approval of the challenged private action does not constitute state action if the government is not in a joint venture with the private actor.

8. Which of the following is the *least likely* basis for a funding of state action?

   a.   State management of a facility.

   b.   Joint action by public officials and private persons.

   c.   Government regulation and licensing.

   d.   Public encouragement of the challenged act.

   e.   The existence of a symbiotic relationship between government and the private actor.

9. Which of the following is most likely to constitute state action?

   a. Warehouseman's enforcement of a lien by selling the stored goods, as authorized by the State Commercial Code.

   b. Termination of a customer's electric service by a privately-owned utility service subject to extensive state regulation.

   c. Dismissal of employees by a privately-owned school receiving 90% of its funds from the government.

   d. Invocation of a state prejudgment attachment law by a private party, whereby the sheriff executes a writ of attachment issued by the clerk of the state court.

10. Western Broadcasting Company, which operates a radio station in Lincoln City, West Lincoln, had a policy of requiring political candidates to submit the script of their campaign messages prior to broadcast to the station news director in order to insure the material was in good taste. On several occasions, one of the candidates for mayor of Lincoln City, Joe Luzer, was ordered by the station news director, Carr E. Full, to excise from his campaign messages material the news director considered to be in bad taste. Station news director Full never found it necessary to review the scripts of Abel Goode, the winning candidate for mayor. Luzer has filed suit for damages in the federal district court on the grounds that the censorship of his campaign messages by the station violated his First Amendment rights. The defendant station has moved to dismiss. What is the principal constitutional law ground for the motion to dismiss? Explain.

XI

CONGRESSIONAL LEGISLATION IN AID OF CIVIL RIGHTS AND LIBERTIES

Analysis

A. IN GENERAL: FEDERAL LEGISLATIVE JURISDICTION

1. COMMERCE CLAUSE

As indicated in Ch. II of the Outline, Congress has plenary power to regulate interstate commerce even for social welfare purposes. It has used this constitutional power in the 1964 Civil Rights Act to provide remedies for private and state discrimination in places of public accommodation. *Heart of Atlanta Motel v. United States* (1964); *Katzenbach v. McClung* (1964).

2. SPENDING POWER

As indicated in Ch. II of this Outline, Congress has power to condition federal grants in the exercise of its spending powers. Congress used this constitutional power in Title VI of the 1964 Civil Rights Act providing for the termination of federal funds to grantees who discriminate.

3. FEDERAL RIGHTS

Congress also has power to reach state or private action which interferes with the exercise of "federal rights" arising from the relationship of the citizen to the national government.

Examples: (1) In an action based on a federal civil rights statute brought by Blacks for damages against white persons who mistook them for civil rights workers, stopped them on the highway and beat them, the Court found (1) that the statute could constitutionally be applied to protect the right of interstate movement; (2) that the right did not necessarily rest on the Fourteenth Amendment; and (3) that right was assertable against private as well as governmental interference. *Griffin v. Breckenridge* (1971).

(2) A provision of the 1970 Federal Voting Rights Act eliminating the use of state residency requirements in presidential and vice-presidential elections is constitutional since the imposition of durational residency requirements unreasonably burdens the privilege of taking up residence in another state. The constitutional authorization for the legislation in this regard was based on the power of Congress to protect the privileges of federal citizenship without reference to § 5 of the Fourteenth Amendment despite the availability of that source of legislative power. *Oregon v. Mitchell* (1970).

4. AUTHORITY TO ENFORCE AMENDMENTS

The Thirteenth, Fourteenth, Fifteenth, Nineteenth [women's rights to vote], Twenty-third [vote for the District of Columbia in presidential elections], Twenty-fourth [abolishes poll tax], and Twenty-sixth [18 year old vote] Amendments all have provisions giving Congress power to enforce the amendment by appropriate legislation.

B. ENFORCING THE THIRTEENTH AMENDMENT

1. PRIVATE ACTION COVERED

The guarantee of the Thirteenth Amendment, § 1, against the imposition of slavery or involuntary servitude runs against private as well as governmental action.

2. BADGES OF SLAVERY

Section 2 of the Thirteenth Amendment gives Congress authority "to enforce this article by appropriate legislation." Congress has power under this provision to enact direct and primary legislation which is necessary and proper for abolishing all badges and incidents of slavery in the United States. As long as the legislation is a rational means of achieving that end, Congress has power to act under the Thirteenth Amendment, subject only to rights and liberties guaranteed by the Constitution.

> *Examples:* (1) White sellers who refused to sell a home to Blacks were sued pursuant to 42 U.S.C. § 1982 which provides: "All citizens of the United States shall have the same right, in every State and Territory, as is enjoyed by white citizens thereof to inherit, purchase, lease, sell, hold, and convey real and personal property." The Court held that § 1982 bars *all* racial discrimination, private as well as public, in the sale or rental of property, and that the statute thus construed is a valid exercise of the power of Congress to enforce the Thirteenth Amendment. Under the Thirteenth Amendment, Congress has the power to legislate against the badges and incidents of slavery such as those imposed by racial barriers to the acquisition of real and personal property. *Jones v. Mayer* (1968).
>
> (2) A federal statute interpreted to prohibit discrimination against Blacks by private commercially operated nonsectarian schools constitutes a valid exercise of federal legislative power under § 2 of the Thirteenth Amendment. Such an interpretation does not offend freedom of association. Although parents have a First Amendment right to send their children to schools teaching segregation, the First Amendment does not protect the practice of excluding racial minorities from such institutions. Parents still have a due process right to send their children to private schools. *Runyon v. McCrary* (1976).

C. ENFORCING THE FOURTEENTH AMENDMENT

Section 5 of the Fourteenth Amendment provides that "Congress shall have power to enforce, by appropriate legislation, the provisions of this article." This provision gives

Congress the power to enforce the privileges and immunities, due process and equal protection guarantees of the Fourteenth Amendment, § 1. As long as Congress could rationally conclude that legislation is appropriate to securing the guarantees of the Fourteenth Amendment, the legislation is constitutional.

1. DEFINING REMEDIES

Congress can enact legislation which is reasonably designed to secure Fourteenth Amendment rights, as defined by the Court through judicial review.

Example: Section 4(e) of the federal Voting Rights Act of 1965 provides that no person who had successfully completed the sixth grade in school in Puerto Rico in which the language of instructions was other than English shall be denied the right to vote because of inability to read or write English. The federal statute served to prohibit the enforcement of New York laws making literacy in English a condition to voting. One basis for the Court's decision upholding the law was that Congress could have reasonably concluded that elimination of literacy requirements was a means of promoting nondiscriminatory treatment by government in providing and administering public services. Eliminating voting discrimination was an appropriate remedy for eliminating other modes of discrimination against Puerto Ricans. *Katzenbach v. Morgan* (1966).

2. DEFINING SUBSTANTIVE RIGHTS

Katzenbach may also indicate that Congress can define the substantive scope of the Fourteenth Amendment rights, at least when it acts to expand the degree of constitutional protection afforded. Congress can act even though the Court has previously read the substantive guarantee more narrowly. It has been suggested that this interpretation would allow Congress to define its own powers and overrule the allocation of powers in defining the Constitution recognized in *Marbury v. Madison*. Alternatively, *Katzenbach* may mean only that Congress, in exercising its remedial power under § 5, may examine the facts and determine that a state lacks sufficient justification of the voting discrimination produced by a literacy test.

Example: Congress could reasonably determine that literacy requirements violate the equal protection guarantee, even though the Court had held to the contrary. The Court rejected the contention that a judicial determination that the enforcement of the state literacy requirement violated the Fourteenth Amendment was necessary before Congress could validly enact the provision. Section 5 of the Fourteenth Amendment grants to Congress the same broad powers expressed in the Necessary and Proper Clause. *Katzenbach v. Morgan* (1966).

a. Exception—The Rachet Theory (No Dilution)
In using its Fourteenth Amendment, § 5, powers, Congress cannot dilute the scope of the Fourteenth Amendment guarantees as previously defined by the Court. Section 5 is limited to power "to enforce" the guarantees by "appropriate" legislation. This is sometimes referred to as the "rachet theory", since the enabling clause is said to work in only one direction— Congress can increase, but cannot dilute, constitutional guarantees.

b. Exception—Constitutional Limits on Congressional Power
Congress cannot violate other provisions of the Constitution in the exercise of its Fourteenth Amendment, § 5, powers.

Example: The provision of the federal Voting Rights Act of 1970 lowering the voting age to 18 in state elections is invalid. Art. I, § 2, makes clear that the states are to determine the qualifications of their own voters for state officers. Congress has power, however, to set aside state voter qualifications when those qualifications reflect racial discrimination. In the latter circumstance, the explicit ban on racial discrimination reflected in the Civil War Amendments to the Constitution necessarily qualifies the division of powers between the state and national governments. *Oregon v. Mitchell* (1970).

3. PRIVATE ACTION
Since the Fourteenth Amendment, § 1, requires state action when judicially enforced, there has been some question whether Congress, using its Fourteenth Amendment, § 5, powers could legislate against private action.

a. Historic Barrier
In the *Civil Rights Cases* (1883), the Court held that Congress had power only to provide remedies for state action violating the Fourteenth Amendment, § 1. Section 5 did not give Congress power to enact the equivalent of a municipal code for private rights.

b. Basis for Expansion
However, six Justices in concurring opinions in *United States v. Guest* (1966), would have held that where the right secured by the Fourteenth Amendment runs against private interference (in that case, the right to use state-owned facilities free from racial discrimination), Congress may use its § 5 powers to legislate remedies against such interference, governmental or private.

c. Thirteenth Amendment and Commerce and Spending Powers
The Court's broad reading of Congress' power under the Thirteenth Amendment and its commerce and spending powers has made it unnecessary to determine the potential scope of *Guest.*

D. ENFORCING THE FIFTEENTH AMENDMENT

1. CONSTITUTIONAL TEXT

The Fifteenth Amendment, § 1, provides that "the right of citizens of the United States to vote shall not be denied or abridged by the United States or by any State on account of race, color, or previous condition of servitude."

2. ENFORCEMENT CLAUSE

Section 2 of the Fifteenth Amendment gives Congress the power to enforce this article by appropriate legislation. Any legislation which Congress could rationally conclude is appropriate to effectuate the constitutional prohibition against racial discrimination in voting is a constitutional exercise of Congress' power under the Fifteenth Amendment, § 2.

Examples: (1) The federal Voting Rights Act of 1965 prohibiting voter registration requirements denying the right to vote on the basis of race was upheld. Congress had legislative jurisdiction to enact the statute under § 2 of the Fifteenth Amendment. As against the reserved powers of the states, Congress may use any rational means to effectuate the constitutional prohibition of racial discrimination in voting. The Court declared that the powers of Congress, under § 2 of the Fifteenth Amendment, is complete in itself, may be exercised to its utmost extent, and acknowledges no limitations, other than are prescribed in the Constitution. *South Carolina v. Katzenbach* (1966).

(2) The provisions of the federal Voters Right Act prohibiting literacy tests were upheld as a proper exercise of congressional legislative jurisdiction under § 2 of the Fifteenth Amendment in view of the long history of discriminatory use of literacy tests to disenfranchise voters on account of their race. *Oregon v. Mitchell* (1970).

(3) Even if only purposeful racial discrimination in voting violates the Fifteenth Amendment, Congress under § 2 of that Amendment may outlaw voting practices that are discriminatory in effect. While such practices do not violate § 1 of the Amendment, prohibitions against practices having a discriminatory racial effect on voting are "appropriate" and "reasonable" means of enforcing the voting guarantees of the Fifteenth Amendment. The extension of the Voting Rights Act of 1965 for an additional seven years was held to be a reasonable means of promoting the purposes of the Fifteenth Amendment. *City of Rome v. United States* (1980).

(4) A multimember electoral scheme which resulted in black voters having less opportunity to elect representatives of their choice was challenged as violative of Sec. 2 of the Voting Rights Act. In 1982, Congress had amended Sec. 2 to provide that the Act is violated if the "totality of the circumstances" established that a voting standard or practice "results in a denial or abridgement of the right" to vote on a racial basis. According to the Court, the Amendment was to make clear that "a violation could be proven by showing discriminatory effect alone and to establish as the relevant legal standard the results test. . . ." A district court finding that Sec. 2, as interpreted, was violated was not clearly erroneous. *City of Rome* had established that Congress has power to legislate against discriminatory effects under the Fifteenth Amendment, even if Sec. 1 of the Fifteenth Amendment requires a showing of racially discriminatory purpose. *Thornburg v. Gingles* (1986).

E. REVIEW QUESTIONS

1. T or F   Congress can legislate against private action under its commerce and spending powers.

2. T or F   Congress can legislate against private action imposing "badges of slavery".

3. T or F   Congress can provide remedies to enforce the guarantees of the Fourteenth and Fifteenth Amendments as long as the laws are reasonable.

4. T or F   In the exercise of its plenary enforcement powers under the Fourteenth and Fifteenth Amendments, Congress can increase or diminish the rights as defined by the courts.

5. T or F   It is established that Congress cannot use its enforcement powers under the Fourteenth and Fifteenth Amendments against private action.

6. T or F   In enforcing the Fifteenth Amendment, Congress can legislate against state action that has the *effect* of racially discriminating in the exercise of the franchise.

7. Which of the following Congressional enactments is the *least likely* to be upheld pursuant to Congress's enforcement powers under the Thirteenth, Fourteenth, and Fifteenth Amendments?

a.   A law prohibiting the use of literacy tests.

b.   A law lowering the voting age to age 18 in federal elections.

c.   A law prohibiting gender discrimination in private schools.

d.   A law prohibiting private racial discrimination in the sale or rental of housing.

8. A federal statute, 42 U.S.C. § 1981, has been read to prohibit private schools from excluding qualified children solely because they are black. A private commercially operated non-sectarian school contends that this statute so interpreted constitutes an invalid exercise of federal legislative power under Section 2 of the Thirteenth Amendment. Does it?

PART ONE: THE ALLOCATION OF GOVERNMENTAL POWER: NATIONAL AND STATE

CHAPTER 1: JUDICIAL REVIEW

1. *False.* Although it is possible to argue on the basis of the grant of judicial power in Art. III and constitutional supremacy in Art. VI that there is a textual basis for judicial review, most authorities agree that Justice Marshall in *Marbury v. Madison* (1803) created the doctrine. It is, at best, an implied power.

2. *False.* The doctrine of judicial review applies to the actions of all government officials, state or federal, as was held by the Supreme Court in *Cooper v. Aaron* (1958) and *United States v. Nixon* (1974).

3. *True.* Art. VI of the Constitution has been read to give state courts concurrent jurisdiction in federal constitutional matters.

4. *False.* The Supreme Court of the United States has constitutional power to review cases coming from the state as well as the federal courts because Art. III makes the touchstone for review the case and not the

tribunal. This helps to further the policy of assuring uniformity of constitutional interpretation.

5. *False.* The policy of judicial self-restraint counsels that the courts not anticipate constitutional questions. Instead, the courts should decide the constitutional question only when there is no alternative basis for deciding the case.

6. *True.* While it might be held today that separation of powers principles would be violated by such a massive assault on the federal courts, a critical reading of Art. III which refers to lower federal courts which Congress "may create", supports this conclusion.

7. *True.* While the Eleventh Amendment bans suits against a sovereign state in federal courts (absent the state's consent), *Ex parte Young* (1908) has created an enduring exception permitting suit against a state official who acts unconstitutionally.

8. *True.* The Art. III requirement of "case and controversy" requires that a litigant demonstrate a factual injury caused by the government action being challenged. The injury must be "fairly traceable" to the action and must be "redressible" if the court grants the requested relief.

9. *False.* At least in the absence of congressional legislation authorizing suit, a citizen lacks standing. There is controversy about whether the bar to citizen standing is born of concern whether injury in fact exists or is a rule of judicial self-restraint (i.e., a prudential limitation). The Court generally treats it as an Art. III bar.

10. *False.* The *jus tertii*-third-party standing rule is not a requirement of Art. III. It proceeds from the belief that the best plaintiff, if possible, is the one most directly involved in the controversy. But the facts of the particular case may move a federal court to waive the rule.

11. *True.* Under *Younger v. Harris* (1971), a federal court should exercise its discretion and abstain, absent a showing of bad faith harassment, when a state criminal prosecution is pending. If no good faith prosecution is pending, a federal court may issue injunctive and declaratory relief against vague and overbroad intrusion on First Amendment rights.

12. *True.* The courts decide many cases involving political matters, *e.g., United States v. Nixon* (1974). The political question doctrine is based on separation of powers concerns or the constitutional commitment of the issue to another branch of government. In either instance, the case is not appropriate for judicial resolution.

13. c. Art. III federal courts cannot give advisory opinions because of the Art. III requirement of a case and controversy. All of the other limitations on judicial review indicated are prudential rules born of judicial self-restraint, *e.g.,* avoidance of judicial review until necessary, the desire to secure the best plaintiff.

14. b. While state officials can be sued when they act illegally (hence, c is a wrong answer), suit is barred if the award would be a retroactive charge on the state treasury. A is wrong since a state may waive its sovereign immunity. D is wrong since ancillary monetary relief, such as attorney's fees, is permitted in spite of the Eleventh Amendment. Similarly, e is wrong since prospective relief, such as a desegregation order involving busing (which involves added costs), has been approved by the Court.

15. b. A builder seeking to build housing in the area who is prevented from doing so by the zoning ordinance has injury in fact caused by the challenged enactment. A is wrong since any injury suffered by Metro taxpayers would be speculative and the causation would be questionable. C is not the best answer since simply being a member of a racial minority has not been held sufficient to establish standing—the Black would have to prove he or she was prevented from living in Suburbia because of the ordinance. D is not the best answer. While an association may have standing to represent its members, it must demonstrate that the members have Art. III standing. There are no facts indicated that establish this prerequisite.

16. The awarded back pay does not offend the Eleventh Amendment. In *Edelman v. Jordan* (1974), the Supreme Court held that even in a suit directed against a public official, if relief involves a charge on the general revenue of the state, it cannot be distinguished from an award of damages against the state. Therefore, the Eleventh Amendment would bar such an award. However, the award in this case is different. In this case, unlike *Edelman*, Congress has specifically provided for suits against the state pursuant to the authority it possesses under § 5 of the Fourteenth Amendment. The Eleventh Amendment bar to a back pay award against the state without its consent is thus limited by the Fourteenth Amendment duty imposed on states and the accompanying power of Congress to provide remedies for violation of the state's duties pursuant to § 5. In short, the threshold fact of congressional authorization distinguishes this case from *Edelman*. Or, to put it another way, the Eleventh Amendment is *pro tanto* qualified by § 5 of the Fourteenth Amendment in these circumstances. *Fitzpatrick v. Bitzer* (1976).

17. Since Doctor Kildare would benefit financially from the grant of the injunction against the Sterilization Law, he has standing under Art. III to challenge its constitutionality. He alleges financial injury resulting from the operation of the Purity law that would be abated by the grant of the injunction. This satisfies the standing requirement derived from the Art. III case and controversy mandate. While the Third Party Standing Doctrine would normally prevent a doctor from raising the rights of a person not before the Court, this is a rule of judicial self-restraint. In the present case, the doctor can claim the rights of his female patients given the closeness of the doctor-patient relationship, the difficulty of the woman's raising her own privacy claims and the intimate involvement of the doctor in the woman's sterilization decision. See *Singleton v. Wulff* (1976).

CHAPTER II: NATIONAL LEGISLATIVE POWERS

1. *False.* This is a government of enumerated powers. Congress has no inherent domestic legislative powers. There must be a constitutional grant of power, express or implied, in order for Congress to legislate.

2. *True.* While Justice Marshall in *McCulloch* indicated that a granted power cannot be used as a pretext for legislating in regard to matters outside congressional power, this pretext principle has not endured. The courts will not probe the motive or purpose behind otherwise valid exercises of congressional powers. Congress, therefore, can achieve social welfare objectives by using broad powers, such as the commerce power.

3. *True.* Congress can regulate local activity if it can rationally conclude that such activity has a substantial adverse effect on interstate commerce. Since federal law overrides contrary state law under the Art. VI Supremacy Clause, the displacement of state police powers is not an impediment to regulation. Insofar as federal regulation of *private* activity is concerned, the Tenth Amendment is a truism.

4. *True.* While the taxing power is a fiscal power rather than a regulatory power, the courts today do not probe the congressional motive or purpose. If the law is facially a revenue-producing tax measure, it will not be held to be invalid under the penalty doctrine.

5. *False.* Congress has power to tax and to spend for the general welfare. But these are fiscal, not regulatory powers.

6. *True.* Congress may define the conditions under which federal monies are spent. While states may thereby be induced to submit to federal regulation in order to obtain needed funds, they remain free to refuse the monies and the accompanying conditions. In modern times, the Tenth Amendment has not proven an impediment to such indirect federal regulation.

7. ***False.*** While this statement would have been true under *National League of Cities*, it is false under *Garcia*. The *Garcia* Court rejected judicial efforts to identify provinces of state autonomy. It is the national political process that now protects federalism. The judicial role is limited to assuring that this political process is working.

8. ***True.*** In *McCulloch v. Maryland*, the Necessary and Proper Clause was broadly interpreted to cover all reasonable means for achieving the delegated powers. Under Art. VI Supremacy Clause doctrine, Congress can preempt state law.

9. **c.** Congress can tax and spend money derived therefrom for the general welfare. Congress can impose taxes even if the law has an incidental regulatory effect. The courts will not probe Congress's purpose. Further, A is wrong since a law will not be invalidated as a penalty if it is facially revenue-producing. B is wrong since Congress can only spend, not regulate, for the general welfare. D is wrong since Congress can impose reasonable conditions as a prerequisite to receiving federal monies. The State is free to reject the grant.

10. No, the town does not have a constitutional defense. Whatever the consequences to itself, the *Garcia* case makes it clear that the judiciary cannot interpose itself between what would otherwise be the appropriate exercise of federal legislation, such as the FLSA, validly authorized by the federal commerce clause and the states. Although these facts may stretch the point, local or state sovereignty cannot be a limitation on federal commerce power jurisdiction. Sometimes it is said that an exception to federal regulation of state activities might be congressional regulation of the location of the State House itself. It might be argued that this regulation comes close to that but it is unlikely that the courts would find that these facts come close enough. The Tenth Amendment today serves only as a minimal limitation on the congressional commerce power. Even if the Supreme Court were inclined to resurrect some portion of *National League of Cities*, it is questionable that the provision of life guard service at municipal beaches would be considered such an essential element of state or local sovereignty as to override the federal interests embodied in the Fair Labor Standards Act, especially in light of the fact that the interests served by that legislation have been considered appropriate for commerce clause regulation.

CHAPTER III: STATE POWER IN AMERICAN FEDERALISM

1. ***False.*** The commerce power is, at least partially, a shared power. While Congress has plenary power over interstate commerce, this is not necessarily inconsistent with state regulation of the same subject.

2. *False.*   The Dormant Commerce Clause, as interpreted by the courts, has "negative implications" which limit the states ability to regulate when interstate commerce is burdened.

3. *False.*   The central purpose of the Commerce Clause, i.e., to assure a national Common Market, is violated by protectionist laws. Such barriers are "virtually per se" impermissible.

4. *True.*   State laws which discriminate in the means used or in their impact are, at least in theory, capable of justification. The state must show overriding benefits and the absence of nondiscriminatory alternatives.

5. *False.*   Even if the state law is nondiscriminatory, it will be held unconstitutional if it imposes an undue burden on interstate commerce. Determination of whether a burden is excessive is determined by ad hoc balancing. There is increasing sentiment on the Court for limiting the Dormant Commerce Clause to discriminatory state laws. The Court, however, has not thus far abandoned undue burdens analysis involving a balancing of the national and state interests.

6. *True.*   Given the historic local control of highway management, state highway laws enjoy a heavier presumption of validity. But states cannot excessively burden interstate commerce even when regulating highways.

7. *True.*   When a state is not regulating commerce, but instead is participating in the marketplace, the negative implications of the Dormant Commerce Clause will not prohibit a state from favoring its own citizens.

8. *True.*   While Art. IV, § 2, prohibits unreasonable discrimination against out-of-state citizens, the Court has held that the Clause is implicated only if fundamental interests, which bear on the vitality of the Nation as an entity, are burdened.

9. *True.*   When the state runs a business in the market place, it acts as a market participant, not as a regulator. In such a capacity, it is not subject to the Dormant Commerce Clause.

10. *False.*   Interstate commerce can be made to pay its way but the burden imposed by the taxing state must reasonably reflect the benefits the taxpayer receives in doing business in the state.

11. *False.*   It is the economic incidence of the tax, not its name, that determines its validity. The modern test requires that: (1) the activity taxed

must be sufficiently connected to the taxing state (due process); (2) the tax must be fairly related to the benefits provided the taxpayer; (3) the tax must not discriminate against interstate commerce; (4) the tax must be fairly apportioned in light of the local contacts and the benefits received by the taxpayer.

12. **d.**   The Court in *Commonwealth Edison v. Montana* upheld the state tax under the *Complete Auto Transit* test which is indicated in answer d. State taxes regularly burden out-of-state consumers (answer a) and out-of-state businesses (answer c) but are nevertheless upheld. Answer b is wrong since the tax applies regardless of the destination of the coal.

13. *False.*   State legislation is preempted only if it conflicts with federal law, Congress has expressly precluded state regulation on the area, or an analysis of the congressional action indicates an intent to occupy exclusively the field.

14. *False.*   Congress has plenary regulatory power over interstate commerce and may legitimate state laws which would otherwise violate the Dormant Commerce Clause.

15. **e.**   When the courts determine if federal law is intended to preempt state law, the courts will consider each of the factors as well as legislative history and the historic federal and state roles in regulating the subject. Preemption turns on the particular facts of each case.

16.   The law is constitutional. It creates no barriers whatsoever against interstate independent dealers. It does not prevent the flow of interstate goods, nor does it place added costs upon them. Furthermore, the statute does not distinguish between in-state and out-of-state companies in the retail market. While some out-of-state integrated petroleum companies will not enjoy the same privileged status in the West Lincoln market that they have in the past, the statute does not give a competitive advantage to in-state independent dealers against out-of-state dealers. The presence of discriminatory impact here—the fact that the burden of a state regulation falls on interstate companies—does not by itself establish a claim of discrimination against interstate commerce. The negative implications which flow from the Commerce Clause are not offended by this kind of state regulation. *Exxon Corp. v. Governor of Maryland* (1978).

CHAPTER IV: THE EXECUTIVE POWER

1. *False.*   At least in the absence of an extreme emergency, the President has no inherent law-making power. However, his power to see that the laws are faithfully executed does appear to create some power to act subject to congressional authority.

2. *True.*   While not expressly provided for in the Constitution, the Court in *United States v. Nixon* recognized such a constitutionally based privilege for confidential matters based on the separation of powers principle and the powers set forth in Art. II.

3. *False.*   The President's power of removal over officials exercising quasi-judicial or quasi-legislative functions is subject to congressional control. While Congress' power to restrict the President's removal of purely executive officials is more circumscribed, limited restrictions which do not impede the President's ability to perform his constitutional duty are constitutional.

4. *True.*   While the President has acquired a dominant role in foreign affairs, both Congress and the Executive have constitutional powers in foreign affairs.

5. *True.*   While there is no express constitutional authority for executive agreements, their legality is now established. As federal law, they prevail over state law in cases of conflict.

6. *True.*   Art. I, § 8, vests the power to *declare* war in Congress. However, as Commander-in-Chief (Art. II, § 2), the President has power to make war and some ill-defined power to commit the nation to hostilities. The war power, therefore, is a shared power.

7. *False.*   The President's unique role in our constitutional scheme has been held to afford him absolute immunity against civil suits even when he acts in the "outside perimeter of his official responsibility."

8. c.   When the President invokes privilege, it is presumptively valid and the burden is on the party seeking disclosure to make a strong showing of the need for rejecting the privilege. "A" may be true in foreign affairs and national security matters since this has not yet been decided, but it has been rejected in domestic matters. Since a presumption of validity attaches to the claim of privilege, b is not the best answer. *United States v. Nixon* establishes that the courts are the final arbiters of a claim of privilege. Therefore, d is not correct.

9. c.   Members of Congress and their aides enjoy constitutional immunity for "legislative acts." They are subject to prosecution but the prosecutors cannot rely on legislative acts in securing a conviction.

10.   Yes, the legislation was unconstitutional. Article 2, § 2, cl. 2, established the power to appoint officers of the United States and provides that the Congress may vest the appointment of inferior officers in either the President alone, in the courts of law, or in the heads of departments. Congress violated Article 2

by providing that a majority of the voting members of the Federal Election Commission should be appointed by the President pro tem of the Senate and the Speaker of the House. Neither of these legislative officials come within the terms "courts of law" or "heads of departments" as required by the appointments clause. *Buckley v. Valeo* (1976).

PART TWO: INDIVIDUAL RIGHTS AND LIBERTIES

CHAPTER V: CONSTITUTIONAL LIMITATIONS ON GOVERNMENTAL POWER

1. *False.* The sole function of the Privileges and Immunities Clause of the Fourteenth Amendment is to protect rights secured to individuals in their capacity as federal citizens. The Clause has not been interpreted, as has the Due Process Clause, to incorporate Bill of Rights guarantees.

2. No, he is wrong. The Supreme Court has definitively held that the Privileges and Immunities Clause of the Fourteenth Amendment was not designed to protect individual economic liberties against state legislation. The sole function, it has been held, of the Privileges and Immunities Clause of the Fourteenth Amendment is to protect the right secured to individuals in their relationship to the federal government, i.e., in their capacity as federal citizens. *Slaughterhouse Cases* (1873).

CHAPTER VI: DUE PROCESS OF LAW

1. *True.* Only if a law severely impairs contract relationships on which the parties have relied to the point that the law is unreasonable will it unconstitutionally impair the Obligation of Contracts Clause (Art. I, § 10 for state laws) or the Fifth Amendment Due Process Clause (federal laws).

2. *False.* A state may contract away its fiscal powers but it may thereafter impair such contract if it is necessary to do so to serve important state interests.

3. *False.* While "taking" is not limited to condemnation of land, the mere fact that property values are diminished will not require just compensation under the Fifth Amendment (federal laws) or Fourteenth Amendment Due Process Clause (state law). If a regulation is a reasonable use of governmental power, *e.g.*, the state police power, it is probably not a taking even if property values decline.

4. *True.* Social and economic regulatory and tax legislation which does not seriously interfere with fundamental constitutional rights is reviewed under the traditional rational basis test. The law is presumed constitutional and the burden is on the challenging party to establish that it is arbitrary and irrational. This burden is essentially insurmountable.

5. *False.* The Court adheres to a selective incorporation approach, applying only those guarantees determined to be essential to "the concept of ordered liberty" or "fundamental to the American scheme of justice" to the state. Thus far, the Seventh Amendment right to trial by jury in civil cases, the right to grant jury indictment, freedom from excessive bail and the requirements of a 12-person jury and of a unanimous verdict for conviction, have not been incorporated.

6. *True.* Once a Bill of Rights provision is held applicable to the states under the Fourteenth Amendment, it has the same substantive meaning as it has for the national government. But note that the Court has, at times, read the Bill of Rights guarantees narrowly, thus leaving the states free to pursue their own policies.

7. *True.* When a fundamental right is significantly burdened, the Court employs a stricter standard of review. Frequently the government bears the burden of demonstrating that the law is necessary to further a compelling government interest. A law must be narrowly tailored to achieve the overriding government objective.

8. *True.* The right of privacy is not significantly burdened if government fails to make the right of privacy effective by funding abortions for those dependent on government-supplied medical care. There is no right to abortion funding. Nor is equal protection violated.

9. *False.* While the right to travel interstate is a fundamental right, the Court has never clearly identified the source of the right. It has been variously ascribed to the Commerce Clause, to the Privileges and Immunities Clauses of the Fourteenth Amendment or Art. IV, § 2, or to be an inherent federal right arising from the character of our National Union.

10. *False.* Procedural due process must be accorded only if the government deprives a person of significant life, liberty, or property interests which are presently enjoyed. Once this threshold is met, then, the Courts balance the following interests: (1) the severity of the harm if procedures are not given; (2) the risk of error if the procedures are not afforded; and (3) the administrative difficulty and cost of providing the added procedures.

11. *True.* The Court has held that imposition of a stigma by government officials does not, without more, qualify as a liberty interest. But when the official action affects a legal interest or status created by law, or, perhaps, when a tangible interest is lost, liberty interests are implicated.

12. *False.* Denial of an opportunity to challenge critical facts which are presumed true, which result in the loss of fundamental liberty or property interests, generally do violate due process. However, when no significant liberty or property interest is impaired by the presumption, e.g., non-contractual claims to public benefits, the presumption is constitutional if it is rationally based.

13. *False.* The right-privilege distinction has been abandoned. Whether the person's interest is characterized as a constitutional right or is only a life, liberty or property interest, due process must be accorded.

14. a. The courts generally do not probe to discover the true legislative purpose in reviewing laws under the rationality standard. If there is a permissible government objective that is sufficient. That a law may incidentally serve other objectives that would be impermissible, will not render a law unconstitutional.

15. b. The Court in *Bowers v. Hardwick* (1986) rejected the claim that there is a fundamental right to engage in homosexual relations in private. The Court specifically did not decide the constitutional claims raised by a, c and d.

16. b. Such a law was upheld in *Ashcroft*. Laws giving parents an absolute veto over the abortion decision of a minor (a) have regularly been held unconstitutional although some limited substitute consent laws providing for parental or judicial consent have been upheld. A law limiting abortions to hospitals was held unconstitutional in *City of Akron*, although requiring use of a licensed medical facility was upheld in *Simopoulus*. Spousal consent was rejected in *Danforth*.

17. b. A mere subjective expectancy of continued employment is not enough to qualify as a property interest. Similarly, if the government specifically conditions the character of the entitlement afforded, making it only a limited employment interest, it will not suffice as a property interest. However, if government creates an entitlement, either expressly or impliedly, it will constitute a property interest. A, c, and d have all been held sufficient to require due process to be afforded.

18. Yes, it is. The Supreme Court no longer follows the line of decisions which used to exalt substantive due process by striking down state legislation which

a majority of the Court deemed unwise. State legislatures are not to be put in a straitjacket when they attempt to deal with economic situations which they regard as offensive to the public welfare. The courts may not use the Due Process Clause of the Fourteenth Amendment to sit as a super-legislature to weigh the wisdom of legislation. The West Lincoln statute may be wise or unwise but relief, if it is needed, should be addressed to the legislature of West Lincoln and not to the courts. Since the law is rationally related to promoting the public health and safety, it is constitutional. *North Dakota State Board of Pharmacy v. Snyder's Drugstores* (1973).

CHAPTER VII: EQUAL PROTECTION

1. *True.*   Like due process law, equal protection generally affords a wide measure of discretion to government in fashioning classifications. The burden is on the challenger to prove that the classification is not rationally related to any permissible government interest. If any state of facts reasonably can be conceived that would sustain a law, the existence of that state of facts at the time of enactment will be presumed.

2. *False.*   Before strict scrutiny is used, the challenger must prove that the discrimination was purposeful, either overtly or covertly. Discriminatory impact may be evidentiary of this impermissible purpose but it is seldom sufficient alone to prove discriminatory purpose.

3. *False.*   If a decision is motivated even in part by racial hostility, government must prove that it *would* have reached the same decision regardless of the discriminatory purpose.

4. *True.*   A *de jure* segregated school district is under an affirmative duty to desegregate. Action that has the effect of impeding fulfillment of that duty is prohibited.

5. *False.*   Equal protection does permit the use of voluntary racial classifications if government makes a proper showing. But this requires more than proof of a rational basis. Whenever race is used as the basis for awarding public benefits or imposing burdens, strict judicial scrutiny is used.

6. *False.*   State classifications based on alienage are judged by strict scrutiny, unless the political community exception applies. When states set qualifications for voting or for appointment of officials to important government positions, only a rational basis for the classification is required.

7. *False.*   It is only *purposeful* gender classifications which must meet the higher standard of review. Since gender is not a suspect classification, but shares some common characteristics with race, an intermediate standard is used—but only when the discrimination is intentional.

8. *True.*   Benign gender classifications are generally upheld when narrowly drawn. But the Court will probe the legislative purpose in order to determine if the classification is truly benign.

9. *False.*   Illegitimacy, while sharing some characteristics with race as a classifying trait, is not suspect. Like gender, it generally receives intermediate scrutiny, i.e., the classification must be substantially related to an important government interest.

10. *True.*   Strict scrutiny may be used because of the nature of the personal interest which is burdened. If government significantly burdens the exercise of a constitutional right, rational basis review would be inappropriate. Generally, the Court will employ strict scrutiny—the classification must be necessary to a compelling government interest.

11. *False.*   Only a significant burden on the right of interstate travel will trigger strict scrutiny review. The Court has required a showing of deterrence or a penalty on the right. On occasion the Court has invalidated laws burdening interstate travel purporting to use a rational basis test.

12. *True.*   There is no express right to vote in the Constitution, nor has such a right been implied. But equality of access to the franchise is a fundamental right protected by the Equal Protection Clause itself. The franchise is an interest of such vital importance that classifications significantly burdening the exercise of the franchise in both general and special purpose elections have been judged under a strict scrutiny standard of review, i.e., the classification must be necessary to a compelling interest.

13. *False.*   Residency requirements are generally held not to violate equal protection. It is durational residency requirements that are judged by the more stringent standard of review. Nevertheless, even durational residency requirements may be upheld when of short duration and narrowly tailored to prevent electoral fraud.

14. *False.*   It is only when a local government uses popular elections relating to the performance of governmental functions and employs single member districting that one person-one vote applies.

Barron & Dienes—Const'l Law, 3d BLS—13

15. *False.* In order to violate equal protection, a political gerrymander must be intentionally discriminatory *and* must have the effect of discriminating against an identifiable political group. A plurality in *Davis v. Bandemer* (1986) would require a showing that the electoral system is arranged in a manner that will consistently degrade a voter's or a group of voters' influence on the political process as a whole.

16. *True.* While education is not a constitutional right, when this fundamental interest is denied to a discrete underclass of children, e.g., illegal aliens, while it is available to other children, more than rationality is required. Only a law furthering a "substantial" state goal will satisfy equal protection.

17. e. When the strict scrutiny standard is used, the ordinary presumption of validity no longer applies. The government bears the extremely difficult burden of proving that the classification is necessary to a compelling government interest and that no less burdensome alternative is available.

18. d. Wealth classifications, without more, are judged under the traditional rationality standard. Race and national origin classifications (a & b) are subject to strict scrutiny. Gender and illegitimacy classifications (c & e) are judged by an intermediate form of review, i.e., the classification must be substantially related to an important government interest.

19. c. While decent housing is an important social interest, it has not been held to be a fundamental right. Classifications significantly burdening access to housing, like access to welfare benefits, are subject only to traditional rational basis review.

20. No, the West Lincoln Welfare program does not violate the Equal Protection Clause. In the area of social and economic legislation, a state does not violate the Equal Protection Clause merely because the classifications made by its laws are imperfect. As long as the classification has a reasonable basis, it is constitutionally permissible even though the classification may in practice result in some inequality. A basis for this legislation can be found in the legitimate state interest in encouraging employment and avoiding discrimination between welfare families and the families of the working poor. The Equal Protection Clause does not require a state to choose between attacking every aspect of a problem or not attacking the problem at all. The state's action need only be reasonably based and free from invidious discrimination, a test which the statute meets. The courts may not second-guess state officials in their task of the allocation of limited public welfare funds among competing categories of potential recipients. *Dandridge v. Williams* (1970).

21. A law is generally constitutional under the Equal Protection Clause if the classification is rationally related to a permissible government interest. In the present case, however, the recipient would claim that the burden of the law impacts more severely on Blacks and that such a racial classification must be shown to be necessary to a compelling government interest. However, a disproportionate racial impact is insufficient to trigger this strict scrutiny standard. Only if it is shown that the law was born of a purpose to racially discriminate will the Court depart from rationality review. The recipient would also claim that the law's classification significantly burdens the fundamental right of privacy. If this allegation is established, the state would be required to prove that the classification is necessary to a compelling governmental objective. It is doubtful that the state interest in curtailing welfare costs or discouraging illegitimacy would support the law. If the rationality standard is used, the law would probably be held constitutional under the Equal Protection Clause.

CHAPTER VIII: FREEDOM OF EXPRESSION

1. *False.* When government regulates freedom of speech directly because of the content of the speech, the courts demand substantial justification, *e.g.,* clear and present danger test, strict scrutiny. But when the law only indirectly burdens free expression, *e.g.,* content-neutral time, place or manner regulation, a lesser degree of judicial scrutiny is used, *e.g.,* interest balancing to determine the reasonableness of the law.

2. *True.* Advocacy of illegal conduct, without more, is protected. It is only when the advocacy takes the form of incitement which will probably produce imminent lawless action, that the expression may be controlled because of the content of the speech.

3. *False.* Prior restraints are highly suspect, both substantively and procedurally, and there is a heavy presumption against their constitutionality. The government bears a heavy burden of justification when it seeks to use such a restraint.

4. *True.* A law that fails to inform persons of ordinary intelligence what actions are proscribed and thereby burdens First Amendment speech is facially unconstitutional. Similarly, if a law indiscriminately reaches both protected and unprotected activity it is facially invalid. Substantial overbreadth is required. Such facial unconstitutionality cannot be redeemed by a narrow application of the law.

5. *False.* The Court has not stated definitely whether a corporation is a person capable of possessing First Amendment rights. However, if expression is constitutionally protected, it does not lose its protected status simply because the source of the speech is a corporation.

6. *False.* Freedom of association and belief are implicit in the First Amendment guarantees. The extent of the burden imposed by a law on the individual rights to associate and hold particular political, economic, or social beliefs is weighed against the interests of the government in maintaining the regulation. The courts often employ more stringent forms of review, including strict scrutiny.

7. *True.* This is the Unconstitutional Conditions Doctrine. Such a forced surrender of constitutional rights is itself unconstitutional.

8. *False.* The government employee's political activities are subject to greater restraint than those of the ordinary citizen. The Court employs a balancing test, weighing the interests of the employee as a citizen against the interests of the government as employer. If private speech is involved, only rationality is required.

9. *False.* Restrictions on expenditure excessively reduce the quality and quantity of communications about political matters, and, therefore, violate the First Amendment. Reasonable regulation of campaign contributions or spending on ballot questions are constitutional.

10. *True.* Government may not define what is orthodox in politics or other matters of opinion. An individual possesses a First Amendment right to be free of government-compelled association and belief. Only a compelling government interest will justify such a restraint.

11. *False.* Government can punish fighting words under carefully drawn laws which are not susceptible of application to protected expression, i.e., not vague or overbroad. However, government has no power to punish the use of words that are merely offensive, abusive, vulgar, or profane.

12. *False.* If impending violence is due to a speaker's incitement of a crowd to imminent and probable illegal conduct, then the speaker can be punished under properly drawn laws. But if the source of the disruption is a hostile audience and the speaker is not seeking to incite illegal conduct, the police must generally proceed against the crowd and protect the speaker. "Heckler's veto" is inconsistent with the First Amendment.

13. *False.* The more demanding standard of review is limited to speech in places which are parts of the "public forum". Speech in publicly-owned places which are not parts of the "public forum", *e.g.,* military bases, jails or prisons, rapid transit cars, mailboxes, can be regulated by laws that are viewpoint-neutral and reasonable.

14. *False.* The Court has at times suggested that when expression takes the form of "speech plus conduct", it is not entitled to the same degree of First Amendment protection accorded "pure speech". Nevertheless, conduct which provides the means for communication, *e.g.,* handbilling, picketing, or solicitation of funds, is protected under the First Amendment.

15. *True.* Prior restraints on access to the public forum are constitutional if they are clear, narrowly drawn (i.e., not vague or overbroad) time, place and manner controls. When the regulation is content-neutral, reasonableness is determined by balancing the severity of the burden on First Amendment expression against the government interests in preventing excessive interference with the normal usage of the streets and in maintaining public peace and order.

16. *True.* While statutes which are facially invalid may be disobeyed and tested at the time of prosecution, court injunctions must generally be obeyed even if they are patently invalid. Only if the order is frivolous or if the issuing court lacks jurisdiction may it be ignored.

17. *False.* While commercial speech is protected under the First Amendment, its hardiness and the ability of the speaker to determine its accuracy causes it to be subject to a lesser standard of First Amendment protection. A four-part standard is used for commercial speech: (1) the speech must not be false or misleading since such speech is unprotected under the First Amendment; (2) the government interest in regulating must be substantial; (3) the regulation must directly advance the substantial government interest; and (4) the regulation must be no broader than is necessary to achieve that interest.

18. *False.* The Press Clause and the Speech Clause are read as a single guarantee. The press enjoys no special privileges or immunities under the First Amendment beyond those afforded the ordinary citizen.

19. *False.* The First Amendment does not impose any duty on the government to intrude on journalistic discretion by forcing either the electronic or print media to make access available. Further, the First Amendment prohibits laws that require the print media to publish particular material. However, the First Amendment is not violated by a limited, reasonable, congressionally-mandated statutory right of access to broadcast time.

20. *False.* While indecent or offensive speech and print publication is constitutionally protected, the unique context of broadcasting (*e.g.,* the limitations on its availability, its pervasiveness, the need to protect

children) have been held to permit broader government control, including regulation of indecent programming.

21. *False.*   The exclusion of the distribution of materials involving child pornography was limited to live productions and reproductions of live productions. If no live actors are involved, distribution does not promote production involving child abuse.

22. *False.*   While *Gertz* does suggest such a broad principle, *Dun & Bradstreet* limits the constitutional bar on presumed and punitive damages to matters of public concern. If the defamation in a private figure plaintiff case involves only a matter of purely private concern, the state may award such damages.

23. *False.*   Characterization of public property as part of the limited public forum increasingly turns on government intent to designate it as open to expressive activity. While the compatibility of the speech with the normal functions of a place is evidentiary of government intent, it is not determinative. Outside of the traditional public forum, government can close public property to particular speech or speakers so long as it acts in a viewpoint-neutral, reasonable manner.

24. c.   Laws burdening the rights of association and belief are constitutional if reasonable which is determined by a balancing test. Restraints on group membership (answer a) are valid if limited to active membership which requires knowledge of the organization's illegal objectives (scienter) and specific intent to further those illegal objectives. Forced disclosure of a group's membership lists may be constitutional if the government's interests in a narrowly tailored law are sufficiently compelling. Even loyalty oaths probing an individual's associations may be constitutional if vagueness and overbreadth are avoided.

25. e.   While government regulation of speech outside of the public forum need only be content-neutral and reasonable, a more demanding standard of review is used for time, place and manner control of speech in the public forum. In defining this more stringent standard, the Court uses all of the elements indicated in a, b, c, and d.

26. c.   When conduct embodies the idea itself, such symbolic speech is judged under the First Amendment (Answers a and d are wrong). Conduct qualifies as symbolic speech if all the circumstances indicate that the speaker intends to communicate and the audience understands the speech. But even symbolic speech is subject to regulation if the law meets First Amendment requirements (b is wrong).

27. **d.** Public officials and public figures may recover in defamation only if they prove that the publication was made with knowledge of its falsity or reckless disregard of its truth or falsity, i.e., actual malice (a is wrong and d is correct). While states may define the applicable standards for private figures, public figures enjoy the same measure of First Amendment privilege as public officials (b is wrong). In defining the applicable standard for private figures, states may not impose strict liability (c is wrong). Note that *Dun & Bradstreet, Inc.,* may portend a change in this principle if the defamatory material involves solely a matter of private concern. Absent proof of actual malice, presumed and punitive damages cannot be recovered if the defamation involves a matter of public concern (e is not completely accurate). Even in private figure defamation cases, presumed and punitive damages can be recovered only if actual malice is shown, unless private speech is involved (e is not accurate).

28. **c.** The modern obscenity definition set forth in *Miller* requires only that the work, taken as a whole, lacks serious literary, artistic, political, or scientific value. The requirements of prurient interest (answer a) and patent offensiveness (answer b) are subject to "contemporary community standards" which need not be a national community (answer d). Thus, a, b, and d are all accurate statements of the modern obscenity definition.

29. **c.** Temporary administrative censorship, under narrowly drawn procedures, does not violate the First Amendment (b is wrong). But, the censor has the burden of demonstrating that the material is unprotected (a is wrong) and it is the censor who must remove the restraint or go to court to justify it (d is wrong). Only a prompt judicial determination that the material is obscene justifies a permanent suppression of the materials.

30. The ordinance violates the Constitution. A regulation of truthful commercial speech is constitutional only if the government has a substantial interest, the regulation directly advances that interest and the regulation is no more extensive than is necessary. *Central Hudson Gas & Elec. Corp. v. Public Service Commission of New York* (1980).

Government has a substantial interest in promoting a stable, racially integrated community and stemming "white flight." But this end cannot be achieved by keeping its citizens from obtaining information. [But see *Posadas de Puerto Rico Assoc. v. Tourism Co.* (1986), upholding a ban on advertising casino gambling to Puerto Rican residents].

The fact that the ordinance here restricts only one method of communication has some significance to First Amendment analysis. A law which regulates the time, place, or manner of expression has a different status than a law prohibiting a category of expression altogether. Nevertheless, the ordinance is still unconstitutional since reasonable alternative means of communication do not exist here. Leaflets, sound trucks, demonstrations—all of them alternative forms of expression—would be no substitute in this context for "For Sale" signs.

Furthermore, this ordinance is not a time, place, or manner regulation since the basis for the ordinance must be ascribed to the town's interest in regulating the content of the communication rather than on the interest in regulating the form of expression, i.e., the place. Thus, the town has not prohibited all signs but only "For Sale" signs indicating that content rather than the form of expression is the purpose behind the ordinance. See *Linmark Associates, Inc. v. Township of Willingboro* (1977).

31. The Klan would allege that the law violates the rights of association and belief of Klan members. While no right of association and belief is expressly guaranteed by the First Amendment, the right, including a right of privacy in associational memberships, has been implied from the express rights and has been applied to the states as a guarantee of the Fourteenth Amendment Due Process Liberty Clause. Whether the Eureka law violates this right would be determined by a balancing test. The burden on the protected rights would be weighed against the state interest in maintaining public order and discouraging racial conflict and dissention. The Klan would argue that the Court should employ strict scrutiny since the registration and disclosure law significantly burdens protected First Amendment activity. In the past, however, the Court has tended to employ strict scrutiny for "legitimate" groups engaged in First Amendment activity, using ad hoc balancing for groups such as the Communist Party and the KKK. In any case, it would be argued that the law is vague and overbroad intrusion on the rights of association and belief. It would be argued that persons of common intelligence could not determine which groups are covered by the "advocating racial hatred" provision. Since advocacy, even of illegal conduct, is constitutionally protected, it would be argued that the law is unconstitutionally overbroad.

CHAPTER IX: FREEDOM OF RELIGION

1. *False.*   Released time, off school grounds, is a permissible accommodation of religion. On-campus released time programs have a primary effect which is sectarian by placing public support behind religious programs.

2. *True.*   The First Amendment forbids required recitation of prayers or Bible reading. Even if the prayer is non-denominational and students are excused, the Establishment Clause is violated. A moment of silent *prayer,* for the purpose of endorsing religion, has also been held unconstitutional.

3. *True.*   If a state acts for the secular purpose of serving the public welfare, the fact that the program incidentally benefits religion does not

condemn the program. Such non-ideological aid as busing and books does not have a *primary* effect of fostering religion and does not involve excessive government entanglement with religion.

4. *True.* Such assistance has been held to have the direct and immediate effect of aiding religion. The Court has not yet dealt with a case of tax relief for all parents with school-age children.

5. *True.* Aid for meeting tuition expenses, available only to parents having children in sectarian schools, is unconstitutional. *Comm. for Public Educ. v. Nyquist* (1973). But, an aid program available to citizens generally was upheld in *Mueller.*

6. *False.* The shared time program held unconstitutional in *Grand Rapids School Dist. of the City of Grand Rapids v. Ball* (1985), used public school teachers to teach secular subjects. The critical factor was that the instruction took place in the pervasively sectarian atmosphere of the private school.

7. *False.* When a law aids or advances only selected religions, rather than religions generally, i.e., it grants denominational preferences, the law is suspect and must meet the rigorous strict scrutiny standard. Only if the law is necessary to a compelling government interest is it constitutional.

8. *False.* Accommodation of religion by granting exemptions from significant burdens on a religious belief or practice which would result from application of general laws is a legitimate public purpose. The Court has indicated that it is more appropriate for the legislature than the courts to fashion such exemptions. Any such preference must be nondenominational, *i.e.,* it must not prefer particular religions over others.

9. *False.* Courts may not decide purely internal church disputes. However, they may apply neutral principles of law, not requiring an inquiry into religious doctrines, to settle questions of ownership of religious property.

10. *True.* Religious belief and opinion is not subject to government control. However, conduct, even when it is an expression of religious beliefs, must be accommodated to overriding government interests.

11. *False.* The Court applies a two-part test in free exercise cases. If a burden on religion is determined to be significant, the government must demonstrate a compelling or overriding interest for the law. There

must be no less burdensome alternative available. But even a significant burden on religion can be justified.

12. *False.* Government cannot condition the receipt of public benefits on the surrender of Free Exercise rights. Further, a direct burden on a religious adherent by requiring conduct contrary to one's faith demands substantial justification. But even though neutral laws of general applicability may impose a significant burden on a religious adherent, the government may require uniform application if this is essential to achieve an overriding government interest, if the law does not coerce the surrender of religious beliefs or if the law is a general criminal prohibition which only incidentally burdens religion.

13. *False.* While the Court has not yet directly addressed the meaning of "religion" in the First Amendment, the Court has recognized that ordered liberty precludes allowing every person to provide their own constitutional standard of religion. The closest the Court has come to addressing this issue is the parallel beliefs doctrine which asks whether a particular belief occupies a place in the life of its possessor parallel to that filled by the orthodox belief in God.

14. *False.* Even if a generally applicable law incidentally imposes a significant burden on religion, strict scrutiny is not required if the law does not coerce surrender of religious freedom. Further, strict scrutiny is not applied to a generally applicable criminal law that has only the incidental effect of significantly burdening a particular religion or religious pratice.

15. b. Such a law has been held unconstitutional even where private funds were used. While the state argued that the law served secular purposes, the Court held that it was religious in purpose and primary effect. Tax exemptions, Sunday Closing Laws, government funds for college buildings and non-ideological aid for state-required activities all have been upheld as secular in purpose and primary effect and as not involving excessive government entanglement with religion.

16. b. The Establishment Clause is not merely a command of equal treatment among religions, but instead, is a command of government neutrality as to religion generally. Answers a, c, and d embody the three-part test used in Establishment Clause cases. If a law is secular in purpose or primary effect or fosters excessive government entanglement with religion, the Clause is violated.

17. Yes. The disqualification for benefits by the state imposes a significant burden on the free exercise of the Seventh Day Adventist religion. Even though the disqualification may be, in a sense, indirect, if a welfare benefits law

significantly impedes the observance of one or all religions or discriminates invidiously between religions, that law is unconstitutional absent compelling justification. The Seventh Day Adventist is forced to choose between following the precepts of her faith and forfeiting benefits or not following the precepts of her faith and receiving benefits. The government imposition of such a choice significantly burdens free exercise.

There is no compelling state interest which can be asserted on behalf of the state which justifies so substantial an infringement of the Seventh Day Adventist's First Amendment rights. The only state interest that can be suggested is the possibility that the filing of fraudulent claims by unscrupulous claimants who pretend religious objections to Saturday work might drain the state unemployment compensation fund, but there is no proof of such malingering under these facts. Furthermore, this decision does not amount to fostering the "establishment" of the Seventh Day Adventist religion in the state. Extending unemployment benefits to Sabbatarians in common with Sunday worshippers is merely maintenance of the government's obligation of neutrality in the face of religious differences. Finally, a decision to extend benefits to the Seventh Day Adventist did not involve religious and secular institutions which it is the object of the establishment of laws to prevent. *Sherbet v. Verner* (1963).

CHAPTER X: STATE ACTION

1. *True.* Unlike the Fourteenth and Fifteenth Amendments, the Thirteenth Amendment is not limited to state action but applies directly against private action. Slavery or involuntary servitude is prohibited, regardless of its source.

2. *False.* The modern Court is increasingly narrowing the concept of state action. It is only significant involvement in the particular conduct being challenged, making the government responsible for the challenged activity, that will satisfy the state action requirement.

3. *False.* While illegal action by a public official may not be the actions of the state for Eleventh Amendment purposes, it is state action under the Fourteenth and Fifteenth Amendments. The official has been clothed with state authority, thus putting him in a position where he or she can misuse public power.

4. *False.* The fact that the government financially supports a private actor does not necessarily make the state a partner to the activities of that actor. Only if the government funds are shown to constitute encouragement, authorization, or approval of the activity being challenged is a finding of state action likely.

5. *True.*   Some activities, such as elections or maintaining public order on municipal streets are so public in character that even state failure to control private actions, constitute state actions. However, the Court today requires that the activity be *traditionally and exclusively* a function of sovereign government in order to apply the Public Function Doctrine.

6. *True.*   Generally, neutral enforcement of valid state laws does not constitute state action violative of the Fourteenth Amendment. However, the Court has held that the neutral judicial enforcement of a racially restrictive covenant against a willing white seller does constitute impermissible state action. *Shelley v. Kraemer* (1948).

7. *False.*   While government acquiescence in the wrongful action does not make the state responsible for the conduct if the state authorizes or compels the particular conduct being challenged, it is a responsible party. Joint action is a means of establishing state action but it is not the only test of state action.

8. **c.**   Neutral enforcement of government regulations will not constitute state action. Even pervasive regulation and licensing of a private actor engaged in discrimination does not make the state responsible for the discrimination. However, if government actually manages or supervises the challenged activity (answer a) or public officials become vicariously responsible by acting in concert with the discriminating party (answer b) or the government encourages, authorizes, or approves the challenged action (answer d), there is state action. Similarly, if government and the private actor are so interdependent that a symbiotic relationship exists, state action is present.

9. **d.**   The action was taken pursuant to a state law authorizing the private action and the private party's joint participation with the public officials fairly makes him a state actor. *Lugar v. Edmonson Oil Co., Inc.* (1982). "A" was held not to constitute state action in the absence of some public enforcement—it was held to be only a policy of noninvolvement. *Flagg Bros., Inc. v. Brooks* (1978). "B" was held not to constitute state action in absence of a showing of government authorization or approval of the policy under which service was terminated. Pervasive government regulation of private action is inadequate. *Jackson v. Metropolitan Edison Co.* (1974). Financial support of a private actor (answer c), without a closer government involvement in the challenged act, does not constitute state action. *Rendell-Baker v. Kohn* (1982).

10.   The state action principle is the principal constitutional law ground for the motion to dismiss. The mere fact that broadcasting is a licensed industry is not sufficient to establish "state action". First Amendment obligations run only to the government and not to private broadcasters. The mere fact that the broadcasting industry is extensively regulated by government does not serve to transform the actions of this private industry into state action. Furthermore, the fact that government licenses the actor does not make the state a partner to the action. *Moose Lodge No. 107 v. Irvin* (1972).

CHAPTER XI: CONGRESSIONAL LEGISLATION IN AID OF CIVIL RIGHTS AND LIBERTIES

1. *True.* Congress may use its plenary commerce and spending powers against private action detrimental to civil rights and liberties. Similarly, Congress can legislate against private or state action which interferes with the exercise of "federal rights" protected by the Constitution.

2. *True.* Section 2 of the Thirteenth Amendment gives Congress authority to enforce the prohibition against slavery and involuntary servitude. Legislation designed to eradicate the badges of slavery is a reasonable means of enforcing the Thirteenth Amendment guarantee which reaches even private action.

3. *True.* Section 5 of the Fourteenth Amendment and § 2 of the Fifteenth Amendment grant power to Congress to enforce the substantive guarantees in those amendments. Congress can enact reasonable laws to protect against conduct which the courts hold violates these amendments.

4. *False.* *Katzenbach v. Morgan* may indicate that Congress has power to define the substantive content of the guarantees of the Fourteenth and Fifteenth Amendments, although some persons see this as a usurpation of the judicial function. Others read the opinion as limited to broad remedial power. However, even *Katzenbach* indicated that Congress cannot dilute rights judicially recognized (rachet theory). This would not constitute "appropriate" legislation to "enforce" the amendments. Further, Congress cannot violate other constitutional limitations in exercising its enforcement powers.

5. *False.* In the *Civil Rights Cases* (1883), the Court did hold that Congress in exercising its enforcement powers could provide remedies only against "state action". However, more recently there has been judicial support for the proposition that Congress can legislate against private conduct which interferes with Fourteenth Amendment rights. *United States v. Guest* (1966) (concurring opinions).

6. *True.* Even if a showing of discriminatory state purpose is required to establish a Fourteenth or Fifteenth Amendment violation, Congress, in the exercise of its enforcement powers, can legislate against

discriminatory impact.   As long as the law is a reasonable means of implementing the constitutional guarantee in the Amendment, it is constitutional.

7. c.   While it is possible that this law might be upheld, it is the *least likely* to be held valid. The Thirteenth Amendment, which provides possible support for the law, is generally held to be limited to racial (not gender) discrimination. The Fourteenth Amendment, which would reach gender discrimination, at least thus far, usually requires state action. "A" was upheld in *Oregon v. Mitchell* (1970) as a reasonable means of enforcing the Fifteenth Amendment. "B" was also upheld in *Oregon v. Mitchell,* although a provision lowering the voting age in state elections was held unconstitutional. "D" was upheld in *Jones v. Mayer* (1968), under Congress' Thirteenth Amendment, § 2, powers, as a reasonable means of eradicating "badges of slavery".

8. No, it does not. Congress has power to legislate under Section 2 of the Thirteenth Amendment to enact direct and primary legislation which is necessary and proper for abolition of badges and incidents of slavery, subject only to the rights and liberties guaranteed by the Constitution. The interpretation of 42 U.S.C., § 1981 prohibiting discrimination against Blacks by private schools does not offend freedom of association. Although parents have a First Amendment right to send their children to schools which teach segregation as a value, the First Amendment does not protect the practice of excluding racial minorities from such institutions. *Runyan v. McCrary* (1976). The statutory interpretation of § 1981 as reaching private conduct was reaffirmed in *Patterson v. McLean Credit Union* (1989).

APPENDIX B

PRACTICE EXAMINATION

There are six unevenly weighted exam questions. The exam will last four hours. An additional 20 minutes will be given for you to read the questions. You should not use more than two blue books writing on only one side of the page. Do not write abnormally small and do not write in the margins. Avoid a rambling general discourse on law and/or policy. Keep your discussion relevant to the fact pattern and issues raised by the question. You may use your textbook, materials provided by the instructor, a copy of the Constitution, your notes, and whatever materials you have personally produced or produced with a study group, i.e., no commercial outlines, canned briefs, other books, or xeroxed articles or cases may be used.

Read each question carefully and organize your answer. Do not make unnecessary assumptions. If you feel that any assumptions are necessary to enable you to develop an issue, state these assumptions in your answer and indicate why they are necessary. If you believe additional information is necessary to properly resolve an issue, state the nature of the required information and why it is needed. Even if you decide that a particular theory decides the issue, you are required to discuss alternative theories. Formulate your answers, whenever possible, to reflect the competing policy considerations or values that are involved. A mere statement of issues without analysis or of rules with no analysis of their rationale is to be avoided. Once you discuss a subject do not repeat the discussion—merely cross-reference to your original discussion.

Question I
(1¼ Hours)

The community of Purewhite is a high income residential community. Less than 1% of the community is non-white. While there are three luxury apartment units in the town, it is primarily composed of single family dwellings built on large lots. The average price of these homes is approximately $500,000 and land values have risen rapidly. Schools in the community are among the finest in the country and the municipal services provided are correspondingly excellent.

Purewhite is across the river from the city of Urbana. A typical urban area, Urbana has become increasingly populated by non-whites as whites have fled to Purewhite and other adjoining white communities. Metropolitan Urbana is over 60% non-white. The declining tax base of Urbana has aggravated the municipality's problems. Little new housing is being built and older housing is falling into a severe state of disrepair. Urbana has made a number of efforts to secure assistance from surrounding white communities, including Purewhite, in meeting its problems but has been consistently rebuffed. While various land-use controls of Purewhite have been struck down by the courts as racially discriminatory, Purewhite remains heavily segregated. Purewhite has never applied for federal funds available to assist in developing lower-income racially integrated housing.

In 1990, Bild–A–Lot, Inc., a privately-owned, open housing developer, announced plans to build a large-scale, racially-integrated, low-income, multi-unit apartment housing project in Purewhite on land on which it holds an option. Architects were hired and plans were drafted for the project. A furor of adverse reaction broke out in Purewhite. Under public pressure, the Purewhite Community Council took the unusual step of scheduling a public meeting on the subject of the future development of Purewhite. At the meeting, there were statements made about "undesirable elements" entering the community and even blatantly racist appeals. But there were also statements reflecting economic and aesthetic concerns.

Shortly thereafter, the Purewhite Council enacted an "Anti–Apartment Ordinance," zoning the entire town to exclude any further apartment dwellings. Provision was made for individual exceptions or variances granted by the zoning board and for the apartment units already built. The ordinance recited the high costs to the community of multi-unit developments created by the need to provide schools, fire and police protection, sewage and sanitation, adequate access roads, etc. Bild–A–Lot applied to the zoning board for an exception or variance. A hearing was held but the application was denied, citing the problems indicated in the Anti–Apartment Ordinance.

A. A black resident of Urbana who desires housing in Purewhite, a small number of white residents of Purewhite who desire to enjoy the social and economic benefits of living in an integrated community, and Bilt–A–Lot Inc., want to bring suit to challenge the Anti–Apartment Ordinance as violative of the Equal Protection Clause of the Fourteenth Amendment. However, the plaintiffs are concerned over standing problems if the suit is brought in federal district court. Discuss the nature of the standing problems. In your answer, assume there is no applicable federal fair housing law.

B. Assuming that standing problems are overcome, discuss the merits of a federal court challenge to the Purewhite ordinance based on the Equal Protection Clause. Do not discuss equal protection law involving fundamental rights and interests.

Question II
(30 Minutes)

For the past twenty years, Central High School, a state operated public school, has conducted an annual baccalaureate ceremony for graduating seniors. The baccalaureate ceremony, held separately from the regular commencement ceremony where degrees are awarded, is held in the school gym. Costs for programs, decorations, etc. are met by voluntary private contributions. Attendance is voluntary, although over 90% of all graduating students do attend.

The baccalaureate has always been conducted by Dr. Paul Pastor, an ordained Protestant minister, who is an active and respected member of the community. He is not paid for his participation. While the contents of the ceremony are generally left to Dr. Pastor, the baccalaureate always contains an invocation and closing benediction, asking for God's protection and guidance of the graduates. Dr. Pastor has always sought to make the invocation and benediction non-denominational and very general, reflecting our Judeo–Christian heritage. The ceremony itself typically involves a speech by Dr. Pastor on traditional social values of service, dedication, patriotism, morality and decent living.

When a few graduates and their parents complained to the school, the principal stated that he and the governing board had concluded that the program was important to the educational process and furthers the school's objective of developing decent persons and citizens. He noted that no one is required to attend. Further, he asserted, "to deny the majority of parents and students an opportunity for such a ceremony of gratitude and dedication would violate their constitutional rights."

Suit has been filed by parents and graduates seeking to enjoin the baccalaureate ceremony as unconstitutional under the Establishment Clause. Discuss the merits of the establishment claim and the merits of the principal's defense of the program.

Question III
(30 Minutes)

The trucking freight business in the state of Utopia has hit hard times. Almost all local Utopia trucking firms do business primarily within the state using conventional single unit trucks. However, many interstate trucking companies using large double and triple unit trucks are seriously cutting into local truckers' business. Because of the large capacity of the double and triple unit trucks, interstate companies are able to carry a number of loads at one time. They are generally able to deliver freight between points within a state (as part of a larger shipment) at cheaper rates than can be charged by domestic companies using single unit trucks. Trucking companies in Utopia have been lobbying the state legislature for relief.

Utopia's Department of Transportation has been concerned with the road safety hazards posed by large doubles and triples. Studies indicate that they are involved in a disproportionate number of road accidents. When accidents do occur, they tend to be more severe and produce far greater road congestion than other highway accidents. The studies show that the large trucks, when temporarily parked on road shoulders, often hang out into the roadway producing increased highway danger. All this information, derived from the Department's studies, has been forwarded to appropriate committees of the Utopian state legislature.

In 1990, the Utopian legislature enacted the "Highway Safety Act" (HSA), which provides: "All companies doing business with the state of Utopia are required to use only single unit trucks, (i.e., no double or triple unit trucks may be used) for all their business involving hauling." The HSA applies to companies doing business with the state which use their own trucks for hauling as well as those companies doing business with the state which hire trucking freight companies to haul their products.

Suit has been brought challenging the HSA as violative of the Commerce Clause. Discuss the issues that will be raised in the litigation. Limit your discussion solely to Commerce Clause issues.

Question IV
(30 Minutes)

Studies indicate that a highly disproportionate number of drunk driving accidents involve drivers under 21. Drivers under 21 are responsible for 20% of all traffic related accidents although they comprise only 8% of all licensed drivers. It is estimated that alcohol related accidents involving drivers under 21 cost the nation $2 billion a year in lost wages, productivity, medical and legal costs and purchasing power. In states where the drinking age has been raised to 21, alcohol-related fatalities in the 16–20 years old age group have dropped an average of 28%. The Chairman of the National Transportation Safety Board has stated that if the drinking age is raised to 21 across the nation, over 1,250 lives can be saved per year.

Congress is presently considering two bills designed to combat drunken driving. The first, "Drunk Driving Regulation Act" (DDRA), would make drunken driving "in or affecting interstate commerce," a federal criminal offense. Stringent criminal penalties, enforced by federal authorities, would be prescribed. The second, the "Drunken Driving Spending Act" (DDSA) would require states to adopt stringent criminal sanctions for drunken driving as a condition for receiving federal highway funds. Cut-off of federal funds would follow a determination by U.S. Department of Transportation that the state laws fail to meet federal standards.

Critics of the proposed legislation claim that Congress lacks constitutional power to enact either law and that either measure would violate the powers reserved to the states under the Tenth Amendment. Discuss the merits of these claims.

Question V
(15 Minutes)

Malcom Y, accompanied by 50 followers, marched to a local neighborhood park on Martin Luther King's birthday. At the park, Malcom made a fiery speech, stressing that King had made one serious mistake—he had ruled out violence. Malcom stated:

> Violence is all that whites understand. You've got to burn, destroy and kill to make it. And you have to start now. Knock the whites down and don't let them up.

Pointing to some white construction workers standing near by, he said, "Look at those Fucking Sons of Bitches. Those are the ones who have the jobs you need." As he continued, his followers became increasingly agitated and so did the whites in the area. One of the construction workers said, "We should shut that Son of a Bitch up." At this point, police moved in, arrested Malcom Y and dispersed the crowd.

Malcom Y was convicted of violating the Penal Code, § 111 which provides:

> Sec. 111 *Disorderly Conduct.* It shall be unlawful and constitute disorderly conduct for any person to intentionally use language that is highly abusive, offensive or indecent or to use language that threatens to produce immediate violence and disorder.

Malcom has appealed his conviction. Discuss the constitutional issues that might be raised on the appeal.

Question VI
(One Hour)

St. Marks Church is located in the central business district of the town of Hustler. Erotica Bookstore wishes to move into a location only 500 feet from St. Marks. In doing so, Erotica would violate a Hustler township ordinance (Adult Business Activity Ordinance, ABAO) providing that "adult entertainment business" may not locate within 1000 feet of any lot upon which there is located a school, a public park, another adult entertainment business, or a church. The ordinance does not apply to preexisting uses; it was applicable only to future locational decisions. An adult business activity includes adult bookstores, defined as:

> An establishment having as a principal activity the sale of material which emphasizes portrayals of human genitals and pubic regions or act of human masturbation, sexual intercourse or sodomy.

No other definitions are provided.

The Adult Business Activity Ordinance (ABAO) was enacted in 1990 after a number of protests at Hustler town Hall by religious organizations and civic groups. Many of the protestors expressed moral outrage at the influx of "indecency and filth" into the town and expressed concern "for the well-being of children." These sentiments as well as expressions of concern over the effect of the intrusion of adult business activity in the town on the civility of communal life, the threat of urban deterioration, and effect on the township's image were repeated in the debate of the Hustler town council leading to the enactment of ABAO. There were no specific findings by the council or any government agencies on the effects of the location of adult establishments, although some council members noted the increasing use of such zoning ordinances in other communities and the Supreme Court decisions that have upheld similar ordinances. It was noted in the debate that the area of land in Hustler township where adult businesses could locate under the ordinance is approximately 3% of the total urban area; most of the land where adult businesses could locate would be outside of the central business area.

Erotica Bookstore filed suit in federal district court seeking a declaration that the Hustler ABAO is unconstitutional and an injunction against the ordinance's enforcement. Discuss the issues raised by the suit.

ANSWERS
Question I

A.   Standing raises the question whether the litigant is entitled to have the court decide the case on the merits. This involves both constitutional limitations on federal court jurisdiction and prudential rules governing the proper exercise of the judicial review powers.

Art. III of the Constitution requires that litigation be presented in an adversary form and context capable of judicial resolution and that its resolution not violate separation of powers principles, *i.e.*, that there be a "case or controversy." Art. III standing requires that the plaintiff demonstrate a "personal stake" in the outcome of the controversy. In order to establish this personal stake, the plaintiff must establish actual or threatened "injury in fact," which is "fairly traceable" to the government action being challenged, and which is "redressable" through judicial relief.

Even assuming *arguendo* that the Purewhite Anti–Apartment Ordinance is purposefully racially discriminatory, the black resident of Urbana would not, simply by reason of his race, satisfy Art. III standing requirements. Stigmatic injury is sufficient only if the litigant is personally denied equal treatment by the discriminatory treatment. The minority litigant must prove that his inability to find suitable housing in Purewhite is fairly traceable to the restrictive ordinance and that absent the ordinance there is a substantial probability that he could live in the community. *Warth v. Seldin* (1975). However, if the black plaintiff could establish that he is seeking apartment housing such as that planned in the Bild–A–Lot project (or similar project) which is actually being stopped because of the challenged law, and that he would qualify for such housing, the indirect injury can satisfy Art. III. *Village of Arlington Heights v. Metropolitan Housing Dev. Corp.* (1977).

The white residents of Purewhite claim injury in fact to their interest in the social and economic benefits from living in an integrated community. Such an intangible injury can satisfy Art. III standing requirements. However, a generalized grievance common to citizens generally is not sufficiently personal to the plaintiff to satisfy Art. III requirements; ideological injury common to all citizens is insufficient. In *Gladstone Realtors v. Village of Bellwood* (1979), the white plaintiffs claimed under federal fair housing laws recognizing their intangible interest. The denial of their statutory interest then provided the requisite injury in fact. Further they were residents of a 12–13 block racially integrated neighborhood being transformed by the challenged practices. While injury to this interest was held sufficient to satisfy Art. III standing requirements, it is not certain that the more attenuated interests of Purewhite residents in the racial integration of the community generally would suffice.

The developer Bild–A–Lot would have the clearest claim to Art. III standing. Bild–A–Lot has been denied a variance under the challenged ordinance and seeks to remove the obstacle, thus satisfying causation requirement that the injury is fairly traceable and redressable.

If the Art. III standing requirements are satisfied, both the white resident plaintiffs and Bild–A–Lot would still have to overcome prudential obstacles, insofar as they rely on the equal protection claim of racial discrimination suffered by racial minorities. Generally, litigants are not allowed to raise the legal claims of third parties not before the court, *i.e.,* the third party standing rule. Courts will decide a constitutional question only when necessary and usually only when litigated by the "best plaintiff" who can fully represent the legal interests at stake.

But the *jus tertii* rule is a prudential doctrine, a non-jurisdictional rule of judicial self-restraint, which can be overcome when there are overriding considerations. The close relationship of the racial discrimination claim to the interests of the white resident plaintiffs and the developer might suffice. On the other hand, there is no apparent reason why the disappointed members of the racial low-income minority cannot litigate their own legal claim. If the black resident of Urbana is found to have standing, the third party standing rule would pose no obstacle to litigating the equal protection claim.

B. The plaintiffs challenge the Purewhite ordinance as violative of the Fourteenth Amendment Equal Protection Clause. In most equal protection cases, the plaintiff has the burden of proving that the classification is not "rationally related to furthering a legitimate government interest." He must prove that the law is arbitrary and irrational. The courts will assume that the legislature found any state of facts that would sustain the law. In short, the courts traditionally defer to the legislature or agency when reviewing socio-economic legislation under the Equal Protection Clause and the law is generally sustained. Given the economic and aesthetic interest recited in the Anti–Apartment ordinance, a general ban on future building with provision for variances when appropriate would probably be upheld.

While the Supreme Court in some recent socio-economic cases has invoked a more demanding mode of equal protection review, the facially neutral, generally applicable, *i.e.,* non-discriminatory, character of the Purewhite apartment ban makes the present case an unlikely candidate for more intensive judicial review.

The plaintiffs will endeavor to have the court invoke a more demanding review than that used in traditional socio-economic cases. However, the fact that the ordinance discriminates against the poor, will not, without more, produce a stricter classifying trait.

The plaintiff's best argument will be that the Purewhite ordinance is a racially discriminatory law. When the state intentionally discriminates on the basis of race, it has the burden of establishing that the classification is necessary to a compelling interest. There must be no less burdensome alternative available. However, to trigger this strict scrutiny standard of review, the plaintiffs must prove that the Anti–Apartment law, while facially neutral, was covertly enacted for the purpose of racial classification.

The requirement of purpose cannot be satisfied by proving that the government knew or could have foreseen the discriminatory consequences of the law. The government must act "because of" and not merely "in spite of" its impact on the racial minority. But the purpose to racially classify need not be the sole or even the dominant purpose for using the electoral system; race must be shown to have been a motivating factor in the decision.

In determining whether there is discriminatory purpose, the courts are to consider the totality of the relevant facts, including circumstantial and direct evidence of intent.

In proving the intentional use of race in enacting the Purewhite ordinance, plaintiffs will use the foreseeability and statistical evidence indicating a disproportionate burden on racial minorities and the perpetuation of racial segregation resulting from the exclusion of apartment dwellings such as the Bild–A–Lot project (*e.g.*, while metropolitan Urbana is 60% non-White, Purewhite is only 1% non-white). The plaintiffs can also employ other contextual evidence such as the community reaction to the Bild–A–Lot project, the departure from normal procedures in calling public meeting, and racist remarks made at the meeting. This can be added to evidence indicating past racial housing discrimination in Purewhite, the socio-economic conditions on the metropolitan area, Purewhite's refusal to aid Urbana and its failure to participate in federal fair housing programs (although it has no legal obligation to participate).

If the plaintiffs succeed in establishing a prima facie case of purposeful race discrimination, the burden would shift to the government. Purewhite could seek to rebut the prima facie case by arguing that the racial segregation is a product of wealth disparities (*e.g.*, cost of housing) and not race, that the public meeting was meant to provide a forum for differing views on the future development of the community faced with a major new housing development, that the testimony at the meeting was mixed and that there were pressing public welfare (i.e., aesthetic and economic) concerns reflected in the ordinance.

The community can also argue that even if the enactment of the Anti–Apartment ordinance was partially motivated by racial consideration, the law would have been enacted in any case given the economic and aesthetic concerns of the community. Finally, the community could argue that the apartment ban is necessary to compelling public interest in avoiding the adverse social consequences of high density dwellings. However it is unlikely that community could meet the strict scrutiny standard of review which is generally "strict in theory, fatal in fact."

Question II

The parents and children challenging the law would contend that the baccalaureate program constitutes an establishment of religion prohibited by the First Amendment, made applicable to the state by the Fourteenth Amendment Due Process Clause. The Establishment Clause requires that government be neutral between religions and between religion and non-religion. On the other hand, the

Constitution does not mandate total separation of government and religion; it permits accommodation of religion by government.

In most Establishment Clause cases, the Court applies a three part test: (1) the state action must have a secular purpose; (2) the primary effect of the state action must neither advance nor inhibit religion; and, (3) the state action must not create an excessive government entanglement with religion. *Lemon v. Kurtzman* (1971). If any of these principles are violated, the state action is unconstitutional under the Establishment Clause.

State support of a baccalaureate ceremony must serve a secular purpose. If the *only* purpose of the program is to endorse, advocate or promote religion, it violates the Establishment Clause. For example, in *Wallace v. Jaffree* (1985), a moment of silent prayer statute enacted solely for religious purposes was unconstitutional. The inclusion of prayers in the baccalaureate—prayer is inherently a religious exercise—would be cited by the challengers as indicating that the program is religious. In fact, the values discussed at the baccalaureate ceremony could be argued to be religious. Further, the use of a second ceremony, in addition to the commencement ceremony, would indicate a religious purpose; the secular objectives of the state could be accomplished at the commencement ceremony. Arguably, when valid secular objectives can readily be accomplished by less religious means, the less religious means must be used.

The defendants would argue that the baccalaureate was intended to serve the secular purpose of promoting traditional patriotic and other social values in graduates. If there is a secular purpose, they would assert, the fact that there are also religious objectives will not make state action unconstitutional. Even use of a prayer by the state does not necessarily mean that the state action is designed to solely promote or endorse religion. See *Marsh v. Chambers* (1983), where the opening of legislative sessions with a prayer was held constitutional. It should be noted, however, that *Marsh* did not apply the *Lemon* three-part test and was based on the unique history of legislative prayer.

Even if the state action is held to serve a secular purpose, it must not have a primary effect of advancing religion. Those challenging the holding of the baccalaureate will note that public schools facilities and funds are used to support a program fashioned and conducted by an ordained minister. Such state support actually and symbolically endorses religion; it places state power behind the religious message of the baccalaureate ceremony. The fact that the ceremony took place in the gym rather than the classroom is not determinative. Nor is the fact that the program is voluntary determinative in Establishment Clause analysis; coercion applies primarily to free exercise issues.

The school district will contend that any aid to religion is only "indirect, remote and incidental"; the baccalaureate program is primarily a secular public ceremonial event, simply acknowledging the role of religion in our society and in the lives of the graduate. It is an accommodation of religion similar to public recognition of Christmas upheld in *Lynch v. Donnelly* (1984).

While student prayer in the classroom might be coercive, the baccalaureate is conducted in the gym and participation is voluntary. Making available the school gym (which is totally separate from the classroom) for the program does not communicate a message of government endorsement of religion. Most of the costs of the baccalaureate are paid by private contributions. Dr. Pastor is selected for the ceremony, not because of his ministry but because of his reputation in the community. He is not paid for his participation.

The challengers could also allege that the program involves excessive government administrative entanglement with religion given the use of public facilities and funds. Further the objections raised by parents and students indicate that potential for political divisiveness in the community (a form of entanglement). However, there is no evidence of ongoing involvement of state authorities with religious authorities in fashioning or conducting the ceremony. The monetary value of the state support is *de minimus*. There is no evidence of any substantial community divisiveness over the baccalaureate service. In any case, political divisiveness alone cannot invalidate an otherwise permissible program.

The challengers might also argue that the selection of a Protestant minister to conduct the ceremony involves a denominal preference, constituting a form of discrimination prohibited by the Establishment Clause. Such a law would be suspect, and subject to strict scrutiny—it must be "closely fitted" to a compelling governmental interest. While promoting traditional values would be a significant interest in the present case, the use of a separate religiously-oriented ceremony would not be a narrowly tailored means.

However, the school can argue that the selection of Dr. Pastor does not favor a particular religion; there is no indication that he is selected in order to prefer a certain religion.

Defendants argue that the baccalaureate ceremony is only an accommodation of religion; it facilitates the free exercise of religion by the majority of students. Government may seek to relieve citizens of burdens on their religious freedom without violating the Establishment Clause. But in the present case, the government is not simply lifting a burden it has imposed on the free exercise of religion as in the cited cases, but arguably is endorsing the religious event.

Elimination of the program, plaintiffs would argue, involves no significant burden on the free exercise rights of majority parents and students. They remain free to pray and even conduct a private graduation ceremony, free of state involvement. If the free exercise rights of the majority does not permit the state to use prayer in the classroom (*Wallace v. Jaffree* (1985)), it is unlikely that it would support a state supported baccalaureate service.

Question III

Utopia's "Highway Safety Act" (HSA) can be challenged as violative of the negative implications of the Dormant Commerce Clause. Although the commerce power is a concurrent power, a state cannot adopt policies which discriminate against interstate commerce or which unduly burden the free flow of interstate commerce.

If the Court finds that the purpose of HSA is to favor local trucking firms against competition from out-of-state truckers, then it is virtually *per se* impermissible. Such a discriminatory purpose would violate the intent of the Commerce Clause to establish a National Common Market. Moreover, out-of-state citizens lack recourse to the state's political process for redress of such discrimination. Since the burden of the law would not fall on local residents, there is no internal political check. While HSA is facially neutral in that it applies to all truckers, it could be argued that there is evidence of discriminatory purpose in that Utopia's trucking business has hit hard times, almost all local firms use single unit trucks, and local truckers have been lobbying for relief. The Court, however, has been increasingly reluctant to probe behind an asserted state interest to find a covert discriminatory purpose.

The Court could also find that HSA, while intended to serve the state's interest in highway safety, is discriminatory in impact. Arguably, HSA is discriminatory in that the restriction on trucking impacts more heavily on out-of-state truckers who use doubles and triples and eliminates a competitive advantage they previously held over local trucking firms which use singles. If the Court accepts this argument, the state would have to prove that HSA is narrowly-tailored to achieve a substantial state interest and that no less discriminatory alternative legislation is available.

In defense of HSA, Utopia could argue that the law is not discriminatory since it applies to all trucking companies using doubles and triples, whether in-state or out-of-state. Further, out-of-state trucking firms are not restricted from doing business in Utopia as long as they use singles. The fact that the structure of the trucking industry is such that most local firms use single unit trucks, while out-of-state trucking firms use double and triples, does not make the law discriminatory.

If the Court finds that HSA is not discriminatory, the law might still violate the Dormant Commerce Clause if it unduly burdens the free flow of interstate commerce. The burden on interstate commerce must be balanced against Utopia's interest in highway safety. Utopia can argue that the highway safety interests of the state have traditionally been given great weight by the Court. In fact, if the safety interests are not illusory, the Court has indicated that it would not second-guess the legislative judgment by balancing the competing interests. Further, under the HSA, out-of-state firms remain free to do business in the state using doubles and triples, only companies doing business *with* the state are affected. The out-of-state firms, on the other hand, will stress the loss of business and the resulting pressure to convert to singles for business in Utopia which would impair their competitive advantage. They may also challenge the state's safety evidence and note the alternatives available to the state to promote highway safety.

The analysis above proceeds on the assumption that the state is *regulating* the marketplace. However, the state might assert that it is acting as a market participant rather than a market regulator. When a state participates in the marketplace, the normal negative implications of the Dormant Commerce Clause do not apply. The Commerce Clause is directed solely at state regulation and not at state action taken to provide benefits to its citizens. Further, when the state enters the market, fairness dictates that it be treated similarly to private participants who are not subject to the Dormant Commerce Clause. Utopia would argue that it is directly acting in the marketplace by choosing those companies with whom it will deal and defining the conditions of the contract.

The interstate truckers, on the other hand, would argue that the effects of the HSA are not limited only to firms entering contracts with the state but others as well. Businesses dealing with the state must limit their trucking contracts to firms using singles. Further, this requirement appears to apply to all of the hauling business of the company, even if Utopia is not a party. When a state imposes conditions that effect parties who are not in privity to the contract and with which it has no business relationship, *i.e.*, a "ripple" effect, it acts as a regulator rather than as a participant. If Utopia is held to be a market regulator rather than a market participant, the negative implications of the Dormant Commerce Clause, discussed above, would apply.

Question IV

The claim that Congress lacks constitutional power to enact (DDRA) should be rejected. No federal statute based on the commerce power has been held unconstitutional for want of a source of congressional legislative power since the New Deal. The Commerce Clause provides a plenary source of constitutional power to regulate driving in interstate commerce, including the power to limit or exclude such commerce. This regulatory power to define the substantive conditions under which interstate commerce shall occur is complete in itself, subject only to the limitations of the Constitution.

Congress also has implied power to enact all regulations necessary and proper to effectuate the Commerce Clause. Pursuant to this implied grant, Congress may regulate local interstate activity if Congress could rationally conclude that such activity has a substantial effect on interstate activity, even if the effect is only indirect. This includes the power to impose criminal sanctions even absent proof that the particular defendant is engaged in activity affecting interstate activity— "[w]here the *class of activities* is regulated and that *class* is within the reach of federal power, the courts have no power 'to excise, as trivial, individual instances' of the class." *Perez v. United States* (1971). The only constitutional requirement is that the means selected be reasonable. Congress is the judge in the first instance of what means are to be employed in the exercise of its granted powers; the courts ask only whether that congressional judgment is rational.

Under these deferential standards, the proposed DDRA would be constitutional. The Act is expressly drawn in terms of drunk driving "in or affecting interstate commerce." In light of the statistical evidence concerning the relationship of drunken driving and automobile accidents, Congress could rationally conclude that stringent federal criminal sanctions applied to the whole class of drunk drivers is an appropriate means of regulating the movement of interstate commerce. The fact that the law furthers police power objectives or that its primary effect is local is immaterial if the regulated activity substantially affects interstate commerce. The courts will not inquire into the purpose and motive of Congress.

The constitutional objections to the "Drunken Driving Spending Act" (DDSA) should also be rejected. Congress may spend for the general welfare. *U.S. Const. Art. I, § 8.* The Spending Clause is an independent source of fiscal power, authorizing Congress to spend for matters of national concern. It is not limited to spending as a means to effectuate other granted powers. While the Clause is not a grant of regulatory power, Congress may impose reasonable conditions on grants as a condition for state participation. The reach of this spending power is at least as broad as the regulatory powers of Congress.

As indicated above, there is ample basis for congressional regulation of drunk driving. It is a matter of national concern subject to the congressional spending power. The condition imposed by DDSA is reasonably related to the subject of the grant, *i.e.*, highway safety.

While the Court has held that the Tenth Amendment imposes some limitation on the commerce power when Congress regulates "the states as states" [*National League of Cities v. Usery* (1976), overruled in *Garcia v. San Antonio Metropolitan Transit Auth.* (1985)] that principle has no application to DDRA which regulates only private activity. Insofar as the proposed laws would displace state police power to regulate private activity, *i.e.*, highway safety, the Tenth Amendment is not a limitation. In the context of regulation of private activity, the Tenth Amendment is only a truism—that Congress may not regulate if it lacks power. But Congress can act when it has power to regulate the private conduct even if the federal law displaces state power in a traditional area of local concern. As indicated above, Congress' commerce power extends to private driving activity and the Tenth Amendment, therefore, provides no barrier to this exercise of the commerce power.

It could be argued that the Tenth Amendment limits Congress' ability to use its spending power to require that the state use its sovereign legislative powers against drunken driving. Indeed, in overruling *National League of Cities,* the Court in *Garcia* indicated that there may be some remaining "affirmative limits" that the "constitutional structure might impose on federal action affecting the states under the Commerce Clause." But whatever these undefined limits on the commerce power might be, it is doubtful that the Tenth Amendment imposes similar limits on Congress' power to impose conditions under its spending powers. First, the Court in *Garcia* stressed that the primary protection of state sovereignty lies not in judicial enforcement of the Tenth Amendment, but in the political processes. Further, when a state voluntarily participates in a federal spending program, it accepts reasonable conditions attached to the grant. The state may preserve its sovereign choice by refusing to participate in the federal program.

Question V

Malcom Y will challenge his conviction as a violation of his First Amendment right of freedom of speech made applicable to the states as part of Fourteenth Amendment liberty. Malcom would argue that his remarks, while abusive and offensive are constitutionally protected. The state will argue that Malcom's speech constitutes "fighting words," *i.e.,* words which have a direct tendency to cause acts of violence by the person to whom, individually, the remarks are addressed. Fighting words are so devoid of social worth as not to enjoy any First Amendment protection. If Malcom's abusive remarks to the construction workers are held to constitute fighting words, the Disorderly Conduct statute could be constitutionally applied to punish Malcom because of the content of his speech. The conviction, therefore, would be affirmed.

Alternatively, the state could contend that Malcom's speech presented a clear and present danger of violence which government could prevent by suppressing his speech. The government would have to establish that Malcom's speech was intended to incite or produce imminent unlawful action and that such imminent lawless action was likely to result. The mere abstract advocacy of unlawful conduct would be insufficient to justify Malcom's conviction. Malcom's language must be held to have constituted advocacy of action, *i.e.,* incitement. Further, there must have existed a real probable and imminent threat that violence would result from the indictment if the conviction is to be upheld.

If the danger of violence arose only because of a hostile audience reaction to Malcom's otherwise protected speech, the conviction should be reversed. Speech that is offensive, vehement and caustic is constitutionally protected even if it produces an angry hostile crowd reaction. Normally the Police must protect the speaker from the hostile crowd; there is no "heckler's veto."

Assuming that the Court held that Malcom's speech was not constitutionally protected, Malcom could still seek to overturn his conviction by arguing that the Disorderly Conduct Statute is facially unconstitutional since it is vague and overbroad. Even though Malcom could be convicted under a properly drawn law, under the First Amendment overbreadth doctrine, he has standing to challenge the facial constitutionality of the statute. This is an exception to the third party standing rule that a litigant normally cannot raise the legal claims of parties not before the Court who might be chilled from asserting their own rights.

Malcom's challenge to the facial validity of § 111 might well succeed. First the statute does not satisfy the special demand for precision and clarity when First Amendment rights are at stake. Since it does not clearly define the types of proscribed speech, persons of ordinary intelligence would be forced to guess at its meaning and could differ as to its application. This, in turn, chills free speech and leads to indiscriminate and improper law enforcement. Second, the statute arguably is overbroad; i.e., it proscribes both protected and unprotected speech. Abusive, offensive and indecent speech, which the statute proscribes, is protected by the First Amendment unless perhaps the speech is imposed upon a "captive" audience. The statute is not limited to fighting words or speech which is intended to and is likely to incite imminent unlawful acts. It seems unlikely that the Court would provide a savings construction which would limit the statute to unprotected speech and the law would probably be held facially unconstitutional.

Question VI

Erotica will argue that the Hustler ordinance violates freedom of speech protected by the First and Fourteenth Amendments. While obscene publications are not part of the "freedom of speech" protected by the Constitution, the First Amendment does protect sexually offensive and indecent adult materials and businesses that deal in such materials. This constitutional protection applies to both criminal and civil regulation, *e.g.,* the zoning law involved in the present case. While a plurality of the Court has asserted that indecent and offensive speech enjoys a lesser degree of constitutional protection than other fully-protected speech, *e.g.,* political speech, this has not been accepted by a majority of the Court.

However, the Court has upheld two adult zoning ordinances similar to that employed by Hustler township on the basis that they were reasonable, content-neutral time, place and manner regulations. *City of Renton v. Playtime Theatres* (1986) and *Young v. American Mini Theatres, Inc.* (1976).

The initial issue is whether the Hustler ordinance is content-based or content-neutral. If the law was enacted for the purpose of restraining the content of the speech it would presumptively violate the First Amendment. Such a content-based law is valid only when the speech is categorically excluded from "the freedom of speech," (*e.g.,* obscenity), or if the law is narrowly-tailored to serve compelling government interests.

While the Hustler ordinance does distinguish between bookstores whose principal activity is the sale of designated adult materials and other materials—facially a discrimination reflecting the content of the materials sold—this does not necessarily mean that the law is content-based. If the law is enacted for a predominant, primary purpose which is not based on the content of the regulated speech, it may still be deemed content-neutral. The fact that *one* of the motivating factors for a law is speech content will not necessarily trigger strict scrutiny review.

In this case, Hustler township will argue that the law was enacted because of the expressed concerns over the tone and civility of communal life, the image of the community and urban deterioration. Erotica will argue that the context in which the law was enacted (*i.e.,* the protests and lobbying focused on concerns of offensiveness and indecency), the legislative debate reflecting these concerns and the lack of governmental findings on urban blight prove that the primary concern of the Hustler town council was combatting sexually offensive, indecent expression. Given the Court's reluctance to probe behind a facially valid purpose, it seems unlikely that the Court would accept the argument that the law is content-based.

If the ordinance is held to be a content-neutral time, place and manner regulation, the Court will apply the *United States v. O'Brien* test, asking whether the law furthers an important or substantial governmental interest unrelated to the restriction of free expression and if the incidental restriction on alleged First Amendment freedoms is no greater than is essential to the furtherance of that interest. This does not require the state to adopt the least burdensome alternative. If the law directly and effectively furthers its legitimate objective, it is constitutional. Further, courts have traditionally extended presumptive validity to a city's use of its zoning powers.

However, Erotica will argue that Hustler has failed to prove that the claimed state interests are really threatened by adult business activities in the town. In *American Mini Theatres,* Detroit had made extensive factual findings on the effect of adult businesses on urban life. In *City of Renton,* the city had relied heavily on studies produced by other cities. While the *City of Renton* Court did not require the city to produce its own studies, it did note the city's reliance on some particularized studies. Erotica will argue that the court should invalidate adult zoning based solely on unsupported declarations and not based on factual findings.

Hustler township can argue that precedent does not require conclusions and explicit findings of fact in the legislative record. The city can rely on the findings of other cities and the Supreme Court decisions accepting the legislative recognition of the documented relation of adult business activities and urban deterioration. They will contend that as long as there is expressed justification for the city ordinance, the city need not make explicit findings.

Erotica will also argue that the ordinance does not leave "reasonable alternative avenues of communication." The effect of the ordinance is to ban adult businesses from most of the central business areas. Only 3% of total city area is available to such establishments whereas 5% of the land area was available in Renton. The Hustler ordinance suppresses or greatly restricts access to lawful speech.

Hustler township will argue that the zoning ordinance, effects only future locational decisions. It permits location of adult businesses in approximately 3% of the land area, including portions of the central business area. The community has not used its zoning power to exclude adult businesses; adult businesses remain free to operate in Hustler. Hustler has not denied adult bookstores a reasonable opportunity to operate.

Erotica may also argue that the Hustler ordinance is unconstitutionally vague. The ordinance applies to business establishments having as a "principle activity" the sale of the designated materials. But the ordinance nowhere defines "principal activity." In the First Amendment area, laws must be narrow and specific. Persons of common intelligence must be able to ascertain its meaning. Precision and clarity in drafting are essential to assure that protected speech will not be chilled and that the law will be properly enforced.

Hustler township will argue that, to the extent that any ambiguity exists in the ordinance, it can be given a narrowing construction by the state courts. Further there is nothing in the record indicating that Erotica is not clearly subject to the ordinance; any lack of warning does not harm this plaintiff.

APPENDIX C

TEXT
CORRELATION CHART

Constitutional Law: Black Letter Series	Barrett & Cohen Constitutional Law: Cases and Materials (8th ed. 1989)	Barron, Dienes, McCormack & Redish Constitutional Law: Principles and Policy Cases and Materials (3d ed. 1987)	Brest & Levinson Processes of Constitutional Decisionmaking: Cases and Materials (2d ed. 1983)	Freund, Sutherland, Howe & Brown Constitutional Law: Cases and other Problems (4th ed. 1977)	Gunther Cases & Materials on Constitutional Law (11th ed. 1986)
PART ONE: THE ALLOCATION OF GOVERNMENTAL POWER: NATIONAL AND STATE					
I. JUDICIAL REVIEW					
A. Establishing Judicial Review	26–40; 48–53	1–39	86–108; 889–901	3–35	1–40
B. Source of Judicial Power: Article III	40–47	1269–1278; 1287–1342	988–1015; 1381–1390	36–48; 136–146	40–69
C. Constitutional and Policy Limitations on Judicial Review	54–78; 92–95	1278–1287	903–922; 1017–1028	48–87	1532–1590; 1633
D. Specific Doctrines Limiting Judicial Review	79–91; 96–161	39–59; 1342–1354	1028–1074	87–135	1541–1589
II. NATIONAL LEGISLATIVE POWERS					
A. The Scope of the National Legislative Power	164–185	61–74	9–59	147–162; 603–621	70–98
B. Commerce Power	185–193; 203–217; 222–242	74–145	61–86; 237–258; 313–332; 335–336	163–174; 207–237; 242–253; 273–286; 293–309	99–169
C. The Taxing Power	245–248	145–150	258–259; 332–335	237–242	192–202
D. The Spending Power	217–222; 248–251	150–163	260–263	253–273	202–222
E. Intergovernmental Immunities	405–448		263–265; 336–352	286–293; 621–647	169–191; 331–335
III. STATE POWER IN AMERICAN FEDERALISM					
A. State Power to Regulate Commerce	193–202; 270–271; 274–393	165–173; 231–241	127–153; 352–393	174–184; 200–205; 339–478	317–331
B. State Power to Tax Commerce	271–273; 505–507; 1194–1195	228–231		185–200; 479–602	331–333
IV. THE EXECUTIVE POWER					
A. The Domestic Arena	449–450; 466–493	243–278		649–679	336–362
B. The Foreign Arena	252–262; 457–466	278–299		690–726	220–229; 362–377
C. Impeachment and Immunity	493–501	299–315	922–928	673–690	377–402

Constitutional Law: Black Letter Series	Barrett & Cohen Constitutional Law: Cases and Materials (8th ed. 1989)	Barron, Dienes, McCormack & Redish Constitutional Law: Principles and Policy Cases and Materials (3d ed. 1987)	Brest & Levinson Processes of Constitutional Decisionmaking: Cases and Materials (2d ed. 1983)	Freund, Sutherland, Howe & Brown Constitutional Law: Cases and other Problems (4th ed. 1977)	Gunther Cases & Materials on Constitutional Law (11th ed. 1986)
PART TWO: INDIVIDUAL RIGHTS AND LIBERTIES: CONSTITUTIONAL LIMITATIONS ON GOVERNMENTAL POWER					
V. PRIVILEGES AND IMMUNITIES OF NATIONAL CITIZENSHIP	511–523	315–332	195–210	753–788	405–419
VI. DUE PROCESS OF LAW					
A. Traditional Substantive Due Process	503–511; 525–526; 551–621	385–405	108–120; 153–193; 211–237; 287–313	1077–1111; 441–500	419–420
B. The Process of Incorporation	526–550	332–341		993–1075	422–440
C. Substantive Due Process Revisited; The Right of Privacy and Other Fundamental Rights	969–1067	405–469	657–717	1112–1130	501–566
D. Procedural Fairness	524–525; 1069–1101	348–383	719–746	939–943	566–585
VII. EQUAL PROTECTION					
A. General Standards	690–697	471–472		869–876	586–593
B. Traditional Equal Protection	697–716	472–488	549–569	876–881	593–621
C. New Equal Protection					
1. Classifying Traits	716–917; 612–689	489–677	265–286; 401–547; 569–622	881–902; 907–939	621–787
2. Fundamental Rights and Interests	917–1067	677–770	622–655; 746–817	907–939; 948–974; 981–987	787–853
VIII. FREEDOM OF EXPRESSION					
A. The Basic Doctrine of Freedom of Expression	1197–1266	771–823; 918–942	1091–1098; 1137–1144	1130–1175	972–1044; 1157–1160
B. Freedom of Association	1450–1467; 1480–1533	824–863	1074–1088; 1102–1111; 1330–1366	1230–1247; 1260–1283; 1315–1344	1349–1360
C. Freedom from Compelled Expression	1447–1449; 1467–1480		1098–1109		
D. Speech in the Local Forum: The Right to Assemble and Petition	1307–1311; 1319–1323; 1347–1435	863–898	1178–1194; 1224–1288	1175–1205	1044–1049; 1196–1291
E. Symbolic Speech	1436–1447	898–910	1366–1377	1205–1210	1169–1196
F. Commercial Speech	1324–1346	942–969	1149–1163	1252–1257	1128–1146
G. Freedom of the Press	1534–1590	1041–1071	1137–1144; 1289–1330	1247–1260; 1305–1315	1291–1300; 1431–1462

Constitutional Law: Black Letter Series	Barrett & Cohen Constitutional Law: Cases and Materials (8th ed. 1989)	Barron, Dienes, McCormack & Redish Constitutional Law: Principles and Policy Cases and Materials (3d ed. 1987)	Brest & Levinson Processes of Constitutional Decisionmaking: Cases and Materials (2d ed. 1983)	Freund, Sutherland, Howe & Brown Constitutional Law: Cases and other Problems (4th ed. 1977)	Gunther Cases & Materials on Constitutional Law (11th ed. 1986)
H. Defamation and Privacy	1266–1290	969–999	1144–1195; 1163–1178	1210–1230	1049–1064
I. Obscenity	1290–1307; 1311–1318	999–1040	1194–1224	1283–1304	1064–1128
IX. FREEDOM OF RELIGION					
A. The Meaning of the Establishment Clause	1591–1661	1073–1131		1350–1385	1463–1509
B. The Meaning of the Free Exercise Clause	1661–1684	1132–1155		1344–1349	1509–1520
C. The Meaning of Religion	1676–1684	1182–1155			1520–1531
X. STATE ACTION					
A. The State Action Requirement	1109–1110	1157–1164	279–286; 480–485; 819–821	788–841	860–865
B. Official Misconduct and Joint Action				841–850	913–918
C. Public Functions	1110–1118	1166–1171; 1195–1215	845–869	797–808	865–877
D. Significant State Involvement	1128–1151	1171–1176; 1187–1194	821–837	823–837	884–903
E. Encouragement Authorization and Approval	1118–1128	1176–1187; 1195–1215	837–845	808–814; 837–841	877–883
XI. CONGRESSIONAL LEGISLATION IN AID OF CIVIL RIGHTS AND LIBERTIES					
A. In General: Federal Legislative Jurisdiction	1102–1109	1217–1228	883–885; 928–988	841–869	903–905; 918–924
B. Enforcing the Thirteenth Amendment	1155–1163	1259–1268	870–883; 885–886	814–822	924–929
C. Enforcing the Fourteenth Amendment	1164–1169	1228–1242; 1248–1259	942–988	851–857; 902–906; 980	905–918; 929–953
D. Enforcing the Fifteenth Amendment	1169–1195	1242–1248	930–942	974–980	953–968

Constitutional Law: Black Letter Series	Kauper & Beytagh Constitutional Law: Cases and Materials (5th ed. 1980)	Lockhart, Kamisar, Choper & Shiffin Constitutional Law: Cases—Comments—Questions (6th ed. 1986)	Rotunda Modern Constitutional Law: Cases and Notes (3d ed. 1989)	Stone, Seidman, Sunstein, & Tushnet Constitutional Law (1986)	Redlich, Schwartz & Attanasio Constitutional Law (1989)
PART ONE: THE ALLOCATION OF GOVERNMENTAL POWER: NATIONAL AND STATE					
I. JUDICIAL REVIEW					
A. Establishing Judicial Review	5–23	1–35	1–26	1–47	1–27
B. Source of Judicial Power: Article III	101–137	55–75	26–33	69–76; 111–115	27–34
C. Constitutional and Policy Limitations on Judicial Review	24–32	1521–1527; 1581–1585	34–40	76–78	34–42
D. Specific Doctrines Limiting Judicial Review	32–101	35–55; 1527–1580; 1585–1601	41–57; 1026–1073	78–111	42–71
II. NATIONAL LEGISLATIVE POWERS					
A. The Scope of the National Legislative Power	139–152	76–86; 157–158	58–69	115–127	71–79
B. Commerce Power	152–227	86–141	142–174; 189–200	127–196	79–123
C. The Taxing Power	227–237	141–146	174–179	216–219	123–132
D. The Spending Power	237–257	146–154	179–189	219–233	132–146
E. Intergovernmental Immunities	489–535	159–187	200–212	196–212	159–201
III. STATE POWER IN AMERICAN FEDERALISM					
A. State Power to Regulate Commerce	345–390; 456–480	243–315	70–134	249–287; 290–334	203–243
B. State Power to Tax Commerce	390–456	316–376	134–141	287–290	
IV. THE EXECUTIVE POWER					
A. The Domestic Arena	312–329	188–214	219–227; 279–288; 296–297; 304–341	339–395	248–282
B. The Foreign Arena	277–312	214–219	213–219; 227–267	418–433	282–304
C. Impeachment and Immunity	329–343	219–242	267–304	395–413	304–322
PART TWO: INDIVIDUAL RIGHTS AND LIBERTIES: CONSTITUTIONAL LIMITATIONS ON GOVERNMENTAL POWER					
V. PRIVILEGES AND IMMUNITIES OF NATIONAL CITIZENSHIP	547–568; 602–638; 861–870	384–389	342–347	334–336	192–196

Constitutional Law: Black Letter Series	Kauper & Beytagh Constitutional Law: Cases and Materials (5th ed. 1980)	Lockhart, Kamisar, Choper & Shiffin Constitutional Law: Cases—Comments—Questions (6th ed. 1986)	Rotunda Modern Constitutional Law: Cases and Notes (3d ed. 1989)	Stone, Seidman, Sunstein, & Tushnet Constitutional Law (1986)	Redlich, Schwartz & Attanasio Constitutional Law (1989)
VI. DUE PROCESS OF LAW					
A. Traditional Substantive Due Process	695–751; 794–859	377–430	304–359; 390–423	724–751	409–459
B. The Process of Incorporation	568–602	1131–1149; 431–458	359–362	707–724	316–409
C. Substantive Due Process Revisited; Privacy and Other Fundamental Rights	1561–1598	458–591	593–690	751–791; 802–900	459–548
D. Procedural Fairness	751–793; 1096–1103	591–627	362–390	791–802; 900–924	548–566
VII. EQUAL PROTECTION					
A. General Standards	875–891	1130–1131			
B. Traditional Equal Protection	891–897	1131–1149	477–482	495–528	
C. New Equal Protection					
1. Classifying Traits	897–986; 1039–1096	1149–1316	483–593	435–495; 528–652; 685–689	566–675; 675–734; 844–882
2. Fundamental Rights and Interests	930–949; 986–1047; 1085–1096	1316–1409	593–690	652–685	906–976

Constitutional Law: Black Letter Series	Kauper & Beytagh Constitutional Law: Cases and Materials (5th ed. 1980)	Lockhart, Kamisar, Choper & Shiffin Constitutional Law: Cases—Comments—Questions (6th ed. 1986)	Rotunda Modern Constitutional Law: Cases and Notes (3d ed. 1989)	Stone, Seidman, Sunstein, & Tushnet Constitutional Law (1986)	Redlich, Schwartz & Attanasio Constitutional Law (1989)
VIII. FREEDOM OF EXPRESSION					
A. The Basic Doctrine of Freedom of Expression	1151–1191	629–665; 670–675; 803–829; 1007–1026	725–752	925–991; 1036–1058	976–1015; 1079–1094
B. Freedom of Association	1410–1461	968–1026	876–900; 908–922	1306–1322	1015–1077
C. Freedom from Compelled Expression	1410–1461	962–968		1300–1306	
D. Speech in the Local Forum: The Right to Assemble and Petition	1192–1235; 1247–1280	741–756; 866–884	752–790	997–1017; 1146–1201	1193–1201; 1222–1286
E. Symbolic Speech	1235–1247	846–866	900–908	1201–1218	1317–1336
F. Commercial Speech	1280–1294	776–803	826–845	1091–1114	1365–1398
G. Freedom of the Press	1295–1333	829–846; 922–961	790–862	1017–1036; 1322–1360	1079–1148
H. Defamation and Privacy	1333–1359	675–703	845–875	1058–1091	1148–1191
I. Obscenity	1359–1410	709–740; 754–765	922–956	1114–1146	1398–1434
IX. FREEDOM OF RELIGION					
A. The Meaning of the Establishment Clause	1463–1532	1027–1095	957–1005	1373–1410	1434–1567
B. The Meaning of the Free Exercise Clause	1532–1560	1095–1118	1005–1021	1410–1423	1567–1594
C. The Meaning of Religion	1544–1560	1118–1129	1021–1025	1423–1426	1584
X. STATE ACTION					
A. The State Action Requirement	638–651	1410–1414	424–430	1467–1476	323–327
B. Official Misconduct and Joint Action	651–655	1416–1419			327–331
C. Public Functions	655–659	1414–1470	430–442	1521–1534	327–331
D. Significant State Involvement	659–675; 681–694	1419–1427; 1446–1460	442–461	1499–1513	331–334
E. Encouragement Authorization and Approval	675–681; 691–694	1428–1446	461–476	1513–1521	327–331

Constitutional Law: Black Letter Series	Kauper & Beytagh Constitutional Law: Cases and Materials (5th ed. 1980)	Lockhart, Kamisar, Choper & Shiffin Constitutional Law: Cases—Comments—Questions (6th ed. 1986)	Rotunda Modern Constitutional Law: Cases and Notes (3d ed. 1989)	Stone, Seidman, Sunstein, & Tushnet Constitutional Law (1986)	Redlich, Schwartz & Attanasio Constitutional Law (1989)
XI. CONGRESSIONAL LEGISLATION IN AID OF CIVIL RIGHTS AND LIBERTIES					
A. In General: Federal Legislative Jurisdiction	1105–1108; 1146–1149	1472–1478		233–245; 247	336–337
B. Enforcing the Thirteenth Amendment	1138–1146	1514–1520	702–713	245–246	359–376
C. Enforcing the Fourteenth Amendment	1118–1138	1490–1514	691–702	246	337–359
D. Enforcing the Fifteenth Amendment	1108–1118	1478–1490	713–724		359–376

GLOSSARY

A

Abortion The constitutional right of privacy extends to the decision of a woman to terminate a pregnancy. Only narrowly drawn government regulation designed to promote the state's compelling interest in maternal health or the potential life of the fetus (from the point of viability) are constitutional. While the minor female has a right to privacy, extending to abortion, the state has a greater interest in regulating the abortion of minors. Parental notification and consent laws are constitutional if narrowly drawn and if they include a judicial bypass provision. *Hodgson v. Minnesota* (1990).

Abortion Funding Government has no affirmative constitutional duty to provide funds for abortions for those who could not otherwise, because of financial reasons, obtain them. This is so even though government may choose to provide financial assistance to those who need it to encourage childbirth.

Abstention Federal courts use the discretionary "abstention" doctrine to avoid the unnecessary adjudication of a constitutional issue, especially where such issue rests on an unsettled interpretation of state law. Thus, a federal court may give a state court the chance to interpret a challenged state statute or to complete a pending state trial, even if the federal court has jurisdiction. Also, a federal court will not enjoin a pending state criminal proceeding (and some civil proceedings) nor grant declaratory relief, absent bad faith harassment.

Adequate State Grounds The Supreme Court will not review state court judgments that clearly and expressly rest on "adequate and independent state grounds," even if the state court erroneously decided an alternate federal ground.

Advisory Opinions   Art. III, § 2, of the Constitution confines federal court jurisdiction to "cases and controversies." The Court has interpreted this as a bar to any Art. III court rendering an "advisory opinion." *Muskrat v. United States* (1911).

Affirmative Action   Race-based affirmative action by a state or locality is constitutional only if the law satisfies strict scrutiny, *i.e.,* necessary to a compelling government interest. The plan must be narrowly drawn and race-neutral means must be considered. *City of Richmond v. J.A. Crosson Co.* (1989). Because of the judicial deference accorded Congress, a congressionally sanctioned affirmative action program need only serve important government interests and be substantially related to the achievement of those objectives. *Metro Broadcasting, Inc. v. F.C.C* (1990).

Affectation Doctrine   Congress can regulate local activities which it could reasonably conclude have a substantial effect on interstate commerce. Such regulation is necessary and proper to effectuating Congress' power to regulate "Commerce among the states."

Alienage Classifications (Standard of Review)   When a state classifies on the basis of alienage, strict scrutiny normally applies. The reason for this is said to be that such classifications involve a discrete and insular minority requiring special judicial protection. However, where a state regulates on the basis of an alienage classification in matters concerning qualifications for voting or for appointment of officials to important government positions which involve the definition of self-government (*i.e.,* political function exception) the traditional equal protection-rational basis test applies.

Appellate Jurisdiction   Art. III vests the appellate jurisdiction in the Supreme Court, subject to congressional exceptions. The failure of Congress to grant jurisdiction is treated as an implied exception. While the power of Congress to withdraw appellate jurisdiction may be plenary, it may be subject to limitations arising from separation of powers principles and constitutional rights and liberties.

Appointment Power   Art. II, § 2, cl. 2, vests the power to appoint principal federal officials, subject to the Senate's advice and consent, in the President. Congress may vest the power to appoint inferior officers in the President, courts of law, or heads of departments. Congress may not vest appointment powers in itself. *Buckley v. Valeo* (1976). Whether an officer is a principal or inferior officer depends on a functional analysis of the official's subordination or independence, the scope of her jurisdiction, and the extent of the functions performed. *Morrison v. Olson* (1988).

Association and Belief   While the First Amendment does not expressly mention a right of association and belief, it has been interpreted to protect a right of expressive association to achieve First Amendment objectives and a freedom of belief. Burdens on these implied rights are usually reviewed by a balancing test, often strict scrutiny.

Authorization and Approval (State Action)   The fact that the state acquiesces in the wrongful acts of a private party does not make the state responsible for the conduct. The termination of a customer's electric service by a privately-owned public utility company for non-payment, in the absence of notice, hearing, and an opportunity to pay any amounts found due, is not attributable to the state. Only if the state authorizes or compels the particular conduct being challenged, thus making itself responsible for the action, is there state action. *Jackson v. Metropolitan Edison Co.* (1974).

B

Badges of Slavery (Thirteenth Amendment Enforcement of)   Congress has power under § 2 of the Thirteenth Amendment to enact direct and primary legislation which is necessary and proper for abolishing all badges and incidents of slavery in the United States.

Thus, it has been held that 42 U.S.C. § 1982 which has been construed to bar *all* racial discrimination, private as well as public, in the sale or rental of property, is a valid exercise of the power of Congress to enforce the Thirteenth Amendment. *Jones v. Mayer* (1968).

Balance of Interests Test (Interstate Commerce) Even non-discriminatory state regulation of interstate commerce may violate the Commerce Clause if it excessively burdens interstate commerce (Negative Implications or Dormant Commerce Clause Doctrine). In ruling on whether a state statute setting forth the number of permissible passenger and freight cars in a train was unconstitutional as violative of the Commerce Clause, the Court stated "reconciliation of the conflicting claims of state and national power (concerning interstate commerce) is to be attained only by some appraisal and accommodation of the competing demands of the state and national interests involved. *Southern Pacific Co. v. Arizona* (1945). The courts weigh the burden on the free flow of interstate commerce against the state interests furthered by the regulation.

Balancing Test (First Amendment) When government regulation only indirectly burdens First Amendment rights, the courts apply a balancing test. Thus, in reviewing a contempt of Congress conviction for refusal to answer during a government inquiry into alleged Communist infiltration of the field of education, the Court stated: "Where First Amendment rights are asserted to bar government interrogation, resolution of the issue always involves a balancing by the courts of the competing private and public interests at stake in the particular circumstances shown." *Barenblatt v. U.S.* (1959). Balancing takes a variety of forms including simple ad hoc balancing of interests to more stringent forms of review requiring a more narrow tailoring of means to overriding government objectives.

Belief-Conduct Distinction, Freedom of Religion While religious belief and opinion is absolutely protected, the practice of religious activities must be accommodated to valid government interests. Thus, a federal law prohibiting polygamy was enforceable against a nineteenth century Mormon who claimed that polygamy was a practice fundamental to his faith. The federal law did not violate the Free Exercise Clause but was a permissible regulation of conduct which was subversive of good order and violative of social duties. *Reynolds v. United States* (1878).

Blue Laws (Freedom of Religion) Thus far, challenges to Sunday closing laws based on the Free Exercise Clause have been rejected. The Supreme Court has balanced the state interest in a common day of rest against the free exercise claims of Sabbatarians and concluded that Blue Laws impose only an indirect economic burden on the Sabbatarian. *Braunfeld v. Brown* (1961).

C

Campaign Finance (Contributions v. Expenditures) The rights of association and expression are burdened by attempts to limit contributions and expenditures for political campaigns. However, reasonable limits on contributions by individuals and groups are permissible since the government has a substantial interest in preventing corruption or the appearance of corruption resulting from large contributions. Expenditure restrictions, though are unconstitutional because they excessively reduce the quality and quantity of communication. *Buckley v. Valeo* (1976). However, restrictions on expenditures by corporations are constitutional if they are narrowly drawn to serve the state's compelling interest in preventing the distorting and corrosive effect of corporate wealth on the political process. *Austin v. Michigan Chamber of Commerce* (1990).

Case and Controversy The Art. III limitation of federal judicial power to various enumerated "cases" and "controversies" requires that a case be in an adversary form and content which is capable of judicial resolution and that its resolution not violate separation of powers principles.

Child Pornography Sexually indecent live productions involving minors or visual reproductions of such performances are not protected by the First Amendment. The state may criminally punish those who knowingly promote such activity by distributing child pornographic material.

Clear and Present Danger "The most stringent protection of free speech would not protect a man in falsely shouting fire in a theatre and causing a panic. * * * The question in every case is whether the words used are used in such circumstances and are of such a nature as to create a clear and present danger that they will bring about the substantive evils that Congress has a right to prevent." *Schenck v. U.S.* (1919). "[F]ree speech and free press do not permit a state to forbid or proscribe advocacy of the use of force or of law violation except where such advocacy is directed to inciting or producing imminent lawless action and is likely to incite or produce such actions." *Brandenburg v. Ohio* (1969).

Commerce Power Congress has the power to regulate "commerce among the states" which has come to mean interstate commerce. However, the Commerce Power includes, in addition, the power to regulate local activities, not part of interstate commerce, which substantially affect interstate commerce. In reviewing laws enacted pursuant to the Commerce Power, courts will not probe the congressional purpose or the local effects of the law in determining whether Congress has power to act. Thus, Congress may achieve social welfare objectives through the use of the Commerce Power.

Commercial Speech Precisely what speech will be labeled commercial speech remains uncertain. The Court has noted that "Expression related solely to the economic interests of the speaker and its audience," constitutes commercial speech. *Central Hudson*

Gas & Electric Corp. v. Public Service Corp. (1980).

Commercial speech, such as commercial advertising, does enjoy First Amendment protection but not as extensive as that enjoyed by political, social, or religious speech. *Virginia State Board of Pharmacy v. Virginia Citizens Consumer Council* (1976). *Central Hudson* sets forth a four-part test for determining the constitutionality of commercial speech regulations: (1) The speech must not be false or misleading or related to unlawful activity; (2) the asserted government interest must be substantial; (3) the regulation must directly advance the government interest; (4) the regulation must be no more extensive than necessary.

Compact Clause Article I, § 10, cl. 3, requires that Congress consent to any agreement or compact by a state with another state or with a foreign country. This consent requirement has been limited by judicial interpretation to apply to agreements which increase the powers of the states in such a way as to potentially interfere with federal supremacy.

Company Towns (State Action) If a privately-owned town operates as the functional equivalent of a municipality, it may be deemed a public forum. Thus, where the streets of a company owned town are denied to Jehovah's Witnesses for purposes of distributing religious pamphlets, and no alternative forum is present, they will be deemed quasi-public for purposes of the state action concept. The action of the company town denying access to its streets to the Jehovah's Witnesses will be deemed sufficiently public to render the town's action a violation of the constitutional rights of the Jehovah's Witnesses. *Marsh v. Alabama* (1946).

Compelled Speech Since the First Amendment protects the right to speak and the right of freedom of association and belief, it has been held that there also must be a correlative right to be free from compelled association and compelled speech. *Wooley v. Maynard* (1977).

Conclusive Presumption A conclusive presumption is created when a law irrebuttably presumes that certain facts exist which result in categorizing individuals into a class. The class is subjected to burdens not visited on others, even though in fact the presumption may be incorrect as applied to a particular individual whom the presumption places in the class. The denial of the opportunity to challenge the presumption in regard to fundamental liberty or property interests has generally been held to violate due process. *Cleveland Board of Education v. LaFleur* (1974).

Congressional Immunity Art. I, § 6, the Speech and Debate Clause, provides absolute immunity for "legislative acts," *i.e.*, matters which are an integral part of the communicative and deliberative process. Congressional aides can share in this constitutional immunity.

Contemporary Community Standards, Obscenity, Definition of In applying the standards relating to pruriency and patent offensiveness as aspects of the definition of what is obscene, *i.e.*, unprotected expression under the First Amendment, the courts need not seek to apply a "national community standard" but may instruct the jury without further specification.

Content Control Government regulation based on the content or subject matter of speech. Content-based control is considered a form of regulation which requires substantial justification under the First Amendment. When a regulation is based on the content of the speech, *i.e.*, a harm associated with the message, government must establish that the regulation is necessary to compelling government interest. *Cohen v. California* (1971).

Cooley Doctrine In determining whether a state regulation is valid under the dormant Commerce Clause, the Cooley Doctrine focuses on the subject of the regulation. When the subject is national, requiring uniformity of regulation, the states may not regulate. Today, the doctrine is generally used as part of the balancing of national and local interests to determine if the state regulation is an undue burden on interstate commerce.

Corporate Speech Although corporations have been held to be "persons" under the due process clause of the Fourteenth Amendment, it has not yet been determined whether a business corporation, not engaged in the communications business, may claim First Amendment protection. Nevertheless, expression which is protected under the First Amendment does not lose its protected status simply because the source of the speech is a corporation. *First National Bank v. Bellotti* (1978).

Cumulative Effects Doctrine Even though the impact of a particular transaction on interstate commerce may be trivial in itself, it still may be sufficient to be covered under federal regulation pursuant to the Commerce Clause, when it is considered that the impact of the transaction, taken together with many others similarly situated, is far from trivial. Hence, taken overall, the transaction can be seen to substantially affect interstate commerce. *Wickard v. Filburn* (1942).

D

Defamation (Private Persons) "[S]o long as they do not impose liability without fault, the states may define for themselves the appropriate standard of liability for a publisher or broadcaster of defamatory falsehood injurious to a private individual." *Gertz v. Robert Welch, Inc.* (1974). In *Time, Inc. v. Firestone* (1976), the Court held that the mere existence of public interest is not sufficient to make someone a "public figure" so as to require the plaintiff to show "actual malice" under the *New York Times v. Sullivan* doctrine. If the defamation involves a matter of purely private concern, the private figure plaintiff can recover presumed and punitive damages, even absent actual malice. *Dun & Bradstreet, Inc. v. Greenmoss Builders, Inc.* (1985).

Defamation (Public Officials and Public Figures) "The constitutional guarantees (of freedom of speech and press) require, we think, a federal rule that prohibits a public official from recovering damages for a defamatory falsehood relating to his official conduct unless he proves that the statement was made with 'actual malice'—that is, with knowledge that it was false or not." Actual malice also includes reckless disregard of truth or falsity. *New York Times Co. v. Sullivan* (1964). The actual malice requirement also applies to public figures. Whether he is a public official, public figure or private person, the plaintiff also has the burden of proving falsity, at least for defamation involving matters of public concern.

De Jure and De Facto Segregation De Jure segregation is racial separation created by purposeful, government action. De Jure segregation in the public school is inherently unequal and violative of equal protection. *Brown v. Board of Educ.* (1954). This principle has been extended to public facilities such as beaches and parks. A de jure segregated school system is under an affirmative duty to desegregate.

De Facto segregation is not intentionally created by government action. It is the product of factors such as housing patterns and migration. The Court has held that De Facto segregation does not violate equal protection.

Delegation of Legislative Powers Congress can delegate legislative powers to the Executive or to independent agencies if it formulates reasonable standards to guide the exercise of the delegated powers. The courts today defer to the congressional judgment of reasonableness.

Deprivation (Procedural Due Process) When an individual is injured by a negligent rather than a deliberate act, no "deprivation" requiring procedural due process protection

arises. The lack of due care by government officials does not constitute the type of abusive treatment that the Due Process Clause was designed to protect against. *Davidson v. Cannon* (1986); *Daniels v. Williams* (1986).

Diluting the Franchise Government regulations limiting the effectiveness of the vote of particular classes may significantly burden equality of access to the franchise in violation of the Equal Protection Clause. The franchise is diluted by unreasonable state limits on access to the ballot of minority parties and independents or by legislative reapportionment which denies the equal protection right to vote on a one person-one vote basis. [*Reynolds v. Sims* (1967)] or by a political gerrymander [*Davis v. Bandemer* (1986)].

Direct v. Indirect Burden (Free Exercise) A direct burden on the free exercise of religion results when government requires an individual to engage in practices contrary to central tenets of his or her religion. Only a compelling government interest justifies such a significant burden on free exercise. The free exercise of religion is severely burdened where a state prosecutes Amish church members for refusing to send their children to school as required by law. *Wisconsin v. Yoder* (1972).

An indirect burden on the free exercise of religion results when government places an incidental burden on religious observance. The Court has held that when a state regulates conduct by enacting Blue Laws, the purpose of which is to advance the secular goal of a uniform day of rest, the statute is valid despite its indirect burden on religious observance unless the state may accomplish its purpose by less restrictive means. *Braunfeld v. Brown* (1961). The Court has usually reviewed indirect burdens under the same strict scrutiny standards used for direct burdens. *Sherbert v. Verner* (1963); *Frazee v. Illinois Dep't. of Emp. Sec.* (1989). However, there are increasing indications that a law that is generally applicable and religion-neutral, which imposes only incidental burdens on a particular religion, will not be reviewed by strict scrutiny. *Employment Div., Dept. of Human Resources of Oregon v. Smith* (1990).

Discrimination (Interstate Commerce) State laws which discriminate against out-of-state interests in favor of local interests are likely to be held violative of the negative implications of the Dormant Commerce Clause. Only a law which is narrowly tailored, *i.e.*, nondiscriminatory alternatives are available, to achieve important state interests will survive judicial scrutiny. Discriminatory laws violate the historic purpose of the Commerce Clause and its Common Market philosophy. Out-of-state interests lack political power to protect themselves in the legislature of the regulating state.

Division of Powers Federalism reflects the values of diversity while preserving unity. Governmental powers in the United States are allocated between the national government and the states. Governmental powers not delegated to the national government are, under the Tenth Amendment, reserved to the States, or to the people. Today, the Tenth Amendment is not a meaningful limit on the national power to regulate private action and provides only a limited check on Congress' power to regulate the states.

Dormant Commerce Clause Even if Congress has not legislated, the Dormant Commerce Clause limits the ability of states to regulate interstate commerce. States may not discriminate against interstate commerce unless the law is narrowly tailored to legitimate state interests and nondiscriminatory alternatives are not available. Even a nondiscriminatory law may violate the Dormant Commerce Clause if it unreasonably burdens interstate commerce. Whether the burden is excessive is determined by balancing the competing interests. (See *Balance of Interests Test, Interstate Commerce*).

Due Process (Procedural) The guarantee of procedural fairness which flows from both the Fifth and Fourteenth Amendment Due Process Clauses. For the guarantees of procedural due process to apply, it must first be shown that a deprivation of a significant life, liberty, or property interest has occurred. This is necessary to bring the Due Process Clause into play. Minimal procedural due process requires notice and hearing. Procedures which due process requires beyond that minimum must be determined by a balancing analysis based on the specific factual context. *Goldberg v. Kelly* (1970).

Due Process (Economic Substantive) The idea that certain notions of substantive social policy, such as freedom of contract or the right to enjoy property without any interference by government regulation, should be read into the Due Process Clause of the Fourteenth Amendment, particularly the words "liberty" and "property" in that clause. Thus, freedom of contract was declared to be part of the liberty of the individual protected by the Due Process Clause of the Fourteenth Amendment. Today, social and economic regulation which does not interfere with specific fundamental rights is not accorded close scrutiny by the courts. State and federal regulation in the economic area is, therefore, routinely upheld as long as there is any rational basis for the legislation in question. (See *Fundamental Rights*).

Durational Residency Requirements While residency requirements for voting do not violate equal protection, durational residency requirements do significantly burden the exercise of the franchise and impair the fundamental personal right to travel. A one year state residency requirement as a precondition for voting has been held to be an unconstitutional denial of equal protection. *Dunn v. Blumstein* (1972).

E

Editorial Autonomy (First Amendment) The exercise of editorial judgment in the print media, unlike the situation in the electronic media, may not be scrutinized by government. Editorial autonomy in the print media is protected by the First Amendment. *Miami Herald Publishing Co. v. Tornillo* (1974).

Eleventh Amendment The Amendment, as interpreted, provides that the judicial power does not extend to suits against a state or its agencies by citizens of another state or a foreign country or by its own citizens. However, the Amendment does not bar suit in federal court against local governments, where the state has waived immunity, where a state official is sued in his or her individual capacity or where Congress has authorized suit pursuant to its powers under the Fourteenth Amendment, § 5, or the Commerce Clause.

Equal Protection (Administrative or Enforcement Discrimination) Although a law is nondiscriminatory on its face, if it is applied and administered by public authority unfairly so as to illegally discriminate between persons in similar circumstances, equal protection is nonetheless still violated. *Yick Wo. v. Hopkins* (1886).

Equal Protection (Discriminatory Purpose and Effect) While discriminatory effect may be evidence of discriminatory purpose, it does not in itself trigger review beyond the rational basis test. In order to authorize the judicial departure from the traditional equal protection standard of review, a governmental purpose to discriminate must be shown.

Equal Protection (Federal) There is no specific textual guarantee of equal protection vis-a-vis the federal government in the Constitution. However, the federal government has been held to be bound by "equal protection" through an interpretation of the Due Process Clause of the Fifth Amendment. *Bolling v. Sharpe* (1954).

Equal Protection (Traditional) Classifications which do not intentionally discriminate on the basis of a suspect or quasi-suspect trait or significantly burden fundamental rights, are reviewed under traditional equal protec-

tion standards. Usually the classification will be upheld if it is rationally related to a legitimate government interest. The burden is on the challenging party. Over-and under-inclusion is not fatal. Recently, the Court has occasionally employed a more searching review demanding a greater showing of justification for the classification.

Establishment Clause, Test for Violation of The Establishment Clause has been interpreted to mean that the government may not aid one religion, may not prefer one religion over another, and may not aid religion in general. For government action to survive a constitutional attack under the Establishment Clause, three criteria must be met: (1) The government action must have a secular legislative purpose; (2) the primary effect of the government action must be one that neither advances nor inhibits religion; and (3) the government action must not foster an excessive government entanglement with religion. *Lemon v. Kurtzman* (1971).

Executive Agreements Executive Agreements are agreements entered into by the Executive with foreign powers. They do not require Senate concurrence. Executive Agreements prevail over contrary state law. Even though there is no express constitutional authority for such agreements, their constitutional validity has been long established. *United States v. Belmont* (1937).

Executive Immunity The President of the United States enjoys absolute immunity from civil damages for actions while in office within the "outside perimeters" of his official responsibilities. Lower executive officials enjoy only a qualified immunity. They are liable for violations of clearly established rights knowable to a reasonable person.

Executive Impoundment The President impounds funds when he withholds or delays the expenditure of congressionally appropriated funds. Whether this is a constitutional exercise of the executive power to execute the laws (*e.g.* budget limits) or in an intrusion on the legislative power to make the laws, has not been finally decided.

Executive Privilege The Court has recognized executive privilege regarding confidential domestic matters. A claim of privilege is presumptively valid, imposing a heavy burden of justification on the party seeking disclosure. Courts are the final arbiter of this domestic privilege which takes its life from the separation of powers doctrine. Executive privilege is designed to protect the expectations of a President in the confidentiality of his conversations and correspondence. The President and those who work with him in the executive branch must be able freely to explore policy alternatives. The Court reasoned that this would be impossible unless the privacy of executive deliberations were at least presumptively protected. *United States v. Nixon* (1974).

Executive Removal Power Quasi-legislative and quasi-judicial officers can be removed only for cause and only by the processes indicated in the legislation creating the office. The President has greater freedom to remove purely executive officials. But congressional restrictions on such removal may be constitutional if they do not impede the President's constitutional duties *Morrison v. Olson* (1988). Congress violates separation of powers by vesting executive functions in officials subject to its power of removal. *Bowsher v. Synar* (1986).

Ex Post Facto Law This is a specific limitation on federal and state government which is found in Art. I, § 9, cl. 3, and Art. I, § 10, cl. 1, which prohibits the enactment of retroactive criminal legislation which significantly disadvantages the offender. It should be remembered that the *ex post facto* law prohibition does not apply to civil legislation.

F

False Light Privacy Where a privacy action is brought against the media because a report has been published that is false, the privacy plaintiff will be required to show, if the report was newsworthy, that the publication was made with actual malice. *Time, Inc. v. Hill* (1967).

Fighting Words "There are certain well-defined and narrowly limited classes of speech, the prevention and punishment of which have never been thought to raise any (First Amendment) problem. These include 'fighting' words—those which by their very utterance inflict injury or tend to incite an immediate breach of the peace." *Chaplinsky v. New Hampshire* (1942). Words which have a direct tendency to cause acts of violence by the person to whom, individually, the remarks are addressed may be punished by government under carefully drawn statutes not susceptible of application to protected expression. Such verbal assaults are not part of "the freedom of speech."

Fourteenth Amendment, § 5, Enforcement Powers In *Katzenbach v. Morgan* (1966), the Court held that the language of § 5 of the Fourteenth Amendment ("The Congress shall have power to enforce, by appropriate legislation, the provisions of this article") gives to Congress "the same broad powers expressed in the Necessary and Proper Clause, Art. I, § 8, cl. 18." Laws reasonably designed to protect Fourteenth Amendment guarantees are constitutional. This includes not only remedial power but perhaps some power to define the substantive right itself.

Free Exercise, Test for Violation of If government undertakes to burden persons because of their religious beliefs, there is a violation of the Free Exercise Clause. Coercion of religious belief is the heart of the free exercise claim. Today, courts examine the severity of the alleged governmental burden on the individual religious beliefs. If the burden is significant, government usually will be required to demonstrate a compelling or overriding public interest. Here, as elsewhere in First Amendment law, the availability of less burdensome alternatives to realize the governmental interest will be considered. However, if the law is a generally applicable, religion-neutral criminal law, which only incidentally burdens religious freedom, strict scrutiny may not be used even if the burden is significant. *Employment Div., Dept. of Human Resources of Oregon v. Smith* (1990).

Fundamental Rights Challenged legislation that significantly burdens a "fundamental right" (examples include First Amendment rights, (privacy, and the right to travel interstate)) will be reviewed under a stricter standard of review. A law will be held violative of the Due Process Clause if it is not closely tailored to promote a compelling or overriding interest of government. A similar principle applies under Equal Protection law.

G

Gender Classifications (Standard of Review) The Court applies an intermediate standard of review for gender classifications. This standard of review is not as severe as the strict scrutiny standard of review, which is used in racial discrimination cases. However, it is more difficult for the state to meet than the traditional equal protection-rational basis standard of review. Under the intermediate standard of review, purposeful gender classifications "must serve important governmental objectives and must be substantially related to achievement of those objectives". *Craig v. Boren* (1976).

Group Litigation (First Amendment) Litigation engaged in by groups to further organizational goals is viewed as expressive and associational conduct entitled to First Amendment protection. Government may regulate group litigation and legal services only for substantial reasons and with specificity. *In re Primus* (1978).

I

Illegitimacy Classifications (Standard of Review) The Court appears to use an intermediate standard of review for illegitimacy classifications. For classifications directed against illegitimates to be upheld, the state must usually show that the classification is substantially related to an important government interest. Although illegitimacy classifications have many of the characteristics of suspectness, *i.e.*, it is a status beyond the control of the child, there is a history of pervasive discrimination, and illegitimates are a politically insular minority, the Court has as yet declined to treat illegitimacy classifications as suspect classifications warranting the application of the strict scrutiny standard of review.

Intergovernmental Immunities (In General) Under the Supremacy Clause (Art. VI), the states may not tax or regulate the national government or its instrumentalities. "[T]he power to tax involves the power to destroy * * *" *McCulloch v. Maryland* (1819). Nor may the state discriminate against the federal government and those dealing with the federal government. Nondiscriminatory federal taxes on the states, which are reasonable in light of the benefits conferred on the state, are constitutional.

Intergovernmental Immunities (Federal Regulation of States) In *National League of Cities v. Usery* (1976) the doctrine of state sovereignty, reflected in the Tenth Amendment, was interpreted to hold that federal regulations should not displace state choices involving the integral operations of state governments thereby interfering with their traditional governmental functions. *National League* was overruled in *Garcia v. San Antonio Metropolitan Transit Auth.* (1985). The test for identifying traditional functions was said to be unworkable. It was deemed inappropriate for unelected federal judges to determine what functions are traditional or integral to state sovereignty. Federalist values are best protected by the political process.

Interpretivism/Non–Interpretivism These two approaches reflect different views on how Courts should make constitutional decisions. Interpretivism emphasizes reliance on the Constitution itself as the basic norm for decision. Non–Interpretivism looks both at the Constitution and outside the document itself for values to guide the determination of constitutional questions.

J

Joint Action (State Action) If a private individual is engaged in joint activity with state officials, state action is established. A private individual acts under color of law if he is a willful participant in a joint activity with the state or its agents. *United States v. Price* (1966).

Journalist Privilege The idea that journalists should have a privilege, either qualified or absolute, to refuse to give evidence is based on the theory that such disclosures would dry up their news sources and thus work to the detriment of First Amendment interests. The First Amendment does not afford journalists the privilege, qualified or absolute, to refuse to give evidence to a grand jury, at least where the grand jury is undertaking a good-faith law enforcement effort. *Branzburg v. Hayes* (1972). However, lower courts have increasingly recognized a qualified privilege, especially in civil cases where the journalist is not a litigant.

Judicial Review "[T]he particular phraseology of the Constitution of the United States confirms and strengthens the principle, supposed to be essential to all written constitutions, that a law repugnant to the Constitution is void." *Marbury v. Madison* (1803). The power of constitutional review by the courts is also extended to executive and judicial acts, national and state. "The judicial power shall extend to all Cases, in Law and Equity, arising under this Constitution, the Laws of the United States, and Treaties made, or which shall be made, under their Authority; * * *" U.S. Constitution, Art. III, Sec. 2.

Justiciability The Court has used justiciability to refer both to case and controversy jurisdictional limitations on judicial power

and prudential limitations on judicial power. It is used to refer to considerations of judicial self-restraint relating to the proper role of the federal courts in our constitutional system, *i.e.,* the ability of the federal courts to define duties and rights and fashion remedies.

L

Legislative Investigations (First Amendment Limitations) When an investigation intrudes on First Amendment rights of speech and association, government must show a substantial relation between the information sought and a subject of overriding and compelling government interest. *Gibson v. Florida Legislative Investigation Comm.* (1963).

Legislative Veto Congress delegates authority to the Executive but retains power to review and veto the exercise of such authority. In *Immigration & Naturalization Service v. Chadha* (1983), the Court held a one-house veto of executive orders involving deportation violative of the Bicameralism and Presentment Clauses since legislative action was involved.

Legitimization Since Congress has plenary power over interstate commerce, it can legitimize state action which would be unconstitutional under the Dormant Commerce Clause. Where Congress allows a state to regulate an area of interstate commerce, "any action taken by a State within the scope of the congressional authorization is rendered invulnerable to Commerce Clause challenge." *Western & Southern Life Ins. Co. v. State Bd. of Equalization* (1981). Thus, Congress can legitimize a discriminatory state tax on out-of-state companies in interstate commerce. *Prudential Ins. Co. v. Benjamin* (1946).

Liberty Interest (Procedural Due Process) The broad concept of liberty is not limited to conditions of confinement such as imprisonment. Liberty also includes fundamental constitutional rights such as the freedom of choice to marry and raise a family. Liberty interests also include values which have special importance in American society. Reputation may be a liberty interest but the Court has held that injury to reputation alone, without any more tangible interest, does not constitute liberty. *Paul v. Davis* (1976). The Due Process Clause mandates that no person's liberty interest may be deprived without fair processes.

Limitations on Congressional Power Under § 5 of the Fourteenth Amendment Congress cannot violate other provisions of the Constitution in the exercise of its Fourteenth Amendment, § 5, powers. Thus, the provision of the Federal Voting Rights Act of 1970 lowering the voting age to 18 in state elections is invalid. Art. I, § 2, makes clear that the states are to determine the qualifications of their own voters for state officers. *Oregon v. Mitchell* (1970).

M

Marketplace of Ideas Theory The principle that it is the responsibility of government not to limit or restrain dialogue in the marketplace of ideas. The theory, Darwinian in essence, is that if government does not intrude, free play will be given to the struggle of ideas and those with the greatest social value will triumph. "[T]he best test of truth is the power of the thought to get itself accepted in the competition of the market." *Abrams v. United States* (1919).

Market Participant (Interstate Commerce) When the state acts as a participant in the marketplace rather than as a regulator of the market, the Dormant Commerce Clause Doctrine does not apply. Like any private actor, the Dormant Commerce Clause imposes no limitation. The state may choose those with whom it will deal. The more that state action affects parties who are not in any contractual relation with the state, *i.e.*, the "ripple effect" of state contractual activity, the more likely it is that the state will be treated as a regulator.

Militia Clauses Article I, § 8, clauses 15 and 16, grant Congress the power to call forth the Militia "to execute the Laws of the union, suppress insurrections, and repeal invasions," and "[t]o provide for organizing, arming, and disciplining the Militia." The second Militia Clause reserves the power to appoint officers and to train the Militia to the states. However, this does not prevent Congress from providing that the consent of the state Governor is not required for assignment to duty outside the United States if the state National Guard is called to active service. The Militia Clauses increase rather than limit the congressional war powers. *Perpich v. Department of Defense* (1990).

Mootness Judicial review will be denied under the "mootness" doctrine if a judicial determination is no longer necessary to compel the result originally sought. Exceptions to this doctrine include: (1) cases which are capable of repetition, yet evading review; (2) the continued existence of collateral consequences; (3) voluntary cessation of illegal actions where there is a reasonable likelihood they will reoccur.

N

Necessary and Proper Clause Art. I, § 8, states: "The Congress shall have Power * * * To make all Laws which shall be necessary and proper for carrying into Execution the foregoing (enumerated) powers, and all other Powers vested by this Constitution in the Government of the United States." In its historic discussion of implied powers in *McCulloch v. Maryland* (1819), the Court gave the Clause a broad interpretation: "Let the end be legitimate, let it be within the scope of the constitution, and all means which are appropriate, which are plainly adapted to that end, which are not prohibited, but consistent with the letter and spirit of the constitution, are constitutional." If the law is reasonably designed to effectuate an express constitutional power, it is constitutional in the absence of some other constitutional violation.

Newsgathering (Access to Judicial Proceedings) The First Amendment extends some protection to the newsgathering process. Criminal trials may not be closed unless such closure is mandated by a compelling government interest and the closure is narrowly drawn to serve that interest. Absent an overriding interest articulated in trial court findings, the trial of a criminal case must be open to the public. *Richmond Newspapers, Inc. v. Virginia* (1980).

Nonpublic Forum Public property not designated or traditionally considered a public forum for communication constitutes the nonpublic forum. Government regulation of the nonpublic forum need only be viewpoint-neutral and reasonable to be constitutional. Regulation may be based on subject matter and speaker identity as long as the government doesn't take sides. *Perry Education Assn. v. Perry Local Educators' Assn. (1983).* (See *Public Forum*).

O

Obscenity "Obscenity is not within the area of constitutionally protected speech or press." *Roth v. U.S.* (1957). In *Miller v. California* (1973), the Court set forth the modern test: "(a) whether 'the average person, applying contemporary community standards' would find that the work, taken as a whole, appeals to the prurient interest. * * * (b) whether the work depicts or describes, in a patently offensive way, sexual conduct specifically defined by the applicable state law, and (c) whether the work, taken as a whole, lacks serious literary, artistic, political, or scientific value."

Obscenity in Broadcasting The law of obscenity is not applied in broadcasting. Indeed, material that would not be considered "obscene" if published in the print media may be deemed "indecent" and prohibited on broadcasting. The unique nature of broadcasting, particularly its pervasiveness and the difficulty of excluding children from the broadcast audience, may require legal controls in the field of broadcasting which would not be tolerated elsewhere. *FCC v. Pacifica Foundation, Inc.* (1978).

Origination Clause Art. I, § 7, states: "All Bills for raising Revenue shall originate in the House of Representatives." But a bill which only incidentally raises revenue for achieving the bill's primary purpose is not a "Bil[l] for raising revenue." *United States v. Munoz–Flores* (1990).

Overbreadth A law may be void on its face if it is substantially overbroad in that the law indiscriminately reaches both constitutionally protected and unprotected activity. A statute regulating activity protected under the First Amendment must be precisely drawn so that protected expression is not chilled or suppressed. *Coates v. Cincinnati* (1971).

P

Pardon Power Under Art. II, § 2, the President has the power to grant pardons for offenses against the United States except for impeachment. The power of the President to pardon is plenary, but it is subject, possibly, to constitutional prohibitions.

Penalty (Equal Protection) When a classification significantly burdens the exercise of a fundamental right, the classification ordinarily must withstand strict scrutiny. If the law does not deter, penalize or otherwise significantly burden the exercise of the protected right, the classification must only satisfy the traditional rational basis test. For example, a one year state residency requirement for divorce did not violate the Equal Protection Clause since the state had an important interest in divorce and because of the insignificant burden of the alleged deprivation, *i.e.*, the petitioner was merely delayed. *Sosna v. Iowa* (1975).

Penalty Doctrine (Federal Taxing Power) A tax law which has the facial characteristics of regulation and punishment may be judged as a penalty rather than a tax. As such, it must be justified as an exercise of Congress' regulatory power rather than its fiscal powers. Today the courts will not probe the congressional purpose. If the law is facially revenue-producing, it is likely to be treated as a tax rather than a penalty.

Penumbral Rights The view that specific guarantees in the Bill of Rights have penumbras formed by emanations from constitutional guarantees. This approach was used as a basis for creating a right of privacy. This penumbral right of privacy was found by the Court to flow from emanations in the First, Third, Fourth, Fifth, and Ninth Amendments. *Griswold v. Connecticut* (1965).

Pervasively Sectarian Atmosphere Institutions in which secular and sectarian activities can't be separated reflect a pervasively sectarian atmosphere. A community education program taught by public employees *in classrooms leased from sectarian schools* violates the Establishment Clause since the program may subsidize religious training, create a symbolic line between religion and government, and inadvertently inculcate religious beliefs. *School Dist. of Grand Rapids v. Ball* (1985). The use of federal funding to pay the salaries of public school teachers tutoring educationally deprived children *in sectarian schools* violates the Establishment Clause since the need to ensure that the teachers are not delivering religious messages would require government supervision and religious entanglement with the state. *Aguilar v. Felton* (1985).

Political Function (See *Alienage Classifications*).

Political Gerrymanders The deliberate and arbitrary drawing of political district lines for partisan advantage is political gerrymandering. An equal protection challenge to such districting is justiciable. The challenger must prove both intent to discriminate against an identifiable group and an actual discriminatory effect on this group.

Political Question Under the "political question" doctrine, federal courts will not decide certain cases. While holding that reapportionment was not a political question, *Baker v. Carr* (1962) set forth several formulations of what a political question is, including classic, functional and political considerations such as: (1) "a textually demonstrable constitutional commitment of the issue to a coordinate political department"; (2) "the impossibility of deciding (the question) without an initial policy determination of a kind clearly for nonjudicial discretion"; and (3) "the impossibility of a court's undertaking independent resolution without expressing lack of the respect due coordinate branches of government." The political question doctrine reflects the concerns of justiciability and separation of powers. It focuses on the capabilities of the federal courts and their proper role *vis a vis* the Congress and the Executive.

Preemption Under the Supremacy Clause, a federal law or regulation preempts any conflicting state law or regulation. Further, a state law is preempted if it frustrates the full purposes and objectives of Congress. Finally, Congress may occupy a field of regulation. In determining congressional intent, courts look at factors which include: (1) the pervasiveness of the federal regulatory scheme; (2) whether national uniformity necessitates federal occupation of the field; (3) the danger of conflict between the state law and the administration of the federal program.

Prematurity and Abstractness Even if a case is sufficiently ripe to satisfy the Art. III requirement of a case and controversy, the Court may still decline to decide the case on the merits because the issue is premature or the record is too abstract. Such considerations, born of judicial self-restraint, are often included under the term "justiciability."

Prior Restraint Prior restraints are especially burdened under the First Amendment. Government bears a heavy burden of justification when it undertakes to regulate speech or press prior to publication. *Nebraska Press Association v. Stuart* (1976).

Prior Restraint (Civil Obscenity Procedures) "[A] noncriminal process which requires the prior submission of a film to a censor avoids constitutional infirmity only if it takes place under procedural safeguards designed to obviate the dangers of a censorship system. * * * [T]he exhibitor must be assured, by statute or authoritative judicial construction, that the censor will, within a specified brief period, either issue a license or go to court to restrain showing the film." The court must promptly determine whether the material may be suppressed. The censor bears the burden of proof. *Freedman v. Maryland* (1965).

Privacy (Obscenity) "Whatever may be the justifications for other statutes regulating obscenity, we do not think they reach into the privacy of one's own home. If the First Amendment means anything, it means that a State has no business telling a man, sitting alone in his own house, what books he may read or what films he may watch." *Stanley v. Georgia* (1969).

Privacy (Sexual) In reviewing a state criminal statute which proscribed assisting in or counseling in the use of contraceptive devices, the Court recognized a constitutional "right of privacy" by reasoning that "specific guarantees in the Bill of Rights have penumbras." *Griswold v. Connecticut* (1965). This privacy right has since been extended to protect a woman's right to choose whether to terminate a pregnancy. *Roe v. Wade* (1973). But it does not include homosexual relations even in private. *Bowers v. Hardwick* (1986).

Private Action (Thirteenth Amendment) The Thirteenth Amendment's prohibition against slavery or involuntary servitude encompasses private as well as governmental action.

Privileges and Immunities (Article IV) Absent substantial justification, the state is required to treat alike all citizens, resident and non-resident, with respect to those privileges and immunities which are fundamental to the nation as a single entity. Nonresidents must be shown to be a particular source of a problem and the law must bear a substantial relation to eradication of the problem.

Privileges and Immunities Clause (Fourteenth Amendment) This clause does not incorporate any of the Bill of Rights nor does it protect all civil rights of individual citizens against state action. Instead, it only protects those rights peculiar to federal citizenship. *Slaughterhouse Cases* (1873).

Property Interest (Procedural Due Process) A property interest requires a legal entitlement created by the state. Property is not limited to interests in realty or personalty, but the interest must be recognized by the state, *e.g.*, wages, welfare benefits, a driver's license. If the state seeks to deprive a person of a property interest, procedural due process must be accorded.

Protecting Personal Mobility (Interstate Commerce) The negative implications which flow from the Dormant Commerce Clause may serve as a basis to invalidate state restrictions on the free movement of persons into the state. *Edwards v. California* (1941).

Public Benefit (Establishment Clause) Government action in the form of busing and books which provides some incidental aid to religion constitutes public benefits. If the state acts only for the secular purpose of serving the public welfare and well-being, the fact that religion is incidentally benefitted does not constitute an impermissible establishment of religion. *Everson v. Board of Educ.* (1947).

Public Figure (definition of) Public figures, for purposes of the application of the *New York Times v. Sullivan—Gertz v. Welch* doctrines, have been defined into two categories as follows:

All-purpose public figures—a person who has achieved such pervasive fame or notoriety that he is deemed to be a public figure for all purposes and in all contexts. By universal acclamation, Johnny Carson falls in this category.

Limited-purpose public figures—people who would not otherwise be public figures but who have become so for a particular range of issues because they have voluntarily injected themselves into a public controversy in order to influence its outcome. *Gertz v. Robert Welch, Inc.* (1974).

Public Forum Places like streets and parks, which have historically been associated with expressive activity constitute the "quintessential" public forum. *Hague v. CIO* (1939). The First Amendment bars government from restricting all communicative activity in natural and proper places for disseminating information. *Schneider v. New Jersey* (1939). The public forum has been expanded to include such property as the government may designate as a public forum (the limited or designated public forum). Government may regulate the time, place and manner of speech in the public forum if the regulation is content-neutral, is narrowly tailored to serve a significant government interest and leaves open alternative channels of communication. *Perry Education Assn. v. Perry Local Advocators Assn.* (1983). (See *Nonpublic Forum*).

Public Function (State Action) Some activities are so public in character that the government will not be allowed to disclaim responsibility even though the activity is entirely private in terms of ownership. To qualify as a public function, the activity must be traditionally and exclusively associated with sovereignty.

Public Records, First Amendment Protection For The press has a right to publish an accurate report of facts obtained from public court proceedings or from public court records. However, the actual malice test of *New York Times v. Sullivan* will not shield a defendant if the defamation was based on judicial records, even though public, if they were inaccurate. *Time, Inc. v. Firestone* (1976).

R

Rachet Theory (Fourteenth Amendment, Congressional Enforcement of § 5) In using its enforcement powers under § 5, Congress can increase, but cannot dilute, the scope of Fourteenth Amendment guarantees as previously defined by the Court.

Released Time (Freedom of Religion) While released time for religious education is permissible, it violates the First Amendment to conduct the classes within the schools. Released time for religious instructions within the public schools provides religion so invaluable an aid that it constitutes a violation of the Establishment Clause. *McCollum v. Board of Education* (1948).

Religion, Meaning of The Court has not, thus far, provided any consistent definition of the meaning of "religion" in the First Amendment. The concept is not limited to theistic beliefs and practices. It protects sincere and meaningful beliefs which occupy a place in the life of the person claiming it parallel to that filled by more traditional notions of religious belief and practice.

Right of Publicity Legal protection for a person's "right of publicity", the publicity value of his name and activities, may *vis-a-vis* a media defendant be subject to some First Amendment limitations. But an action for damages against a television station for broadcasting a performer's act does not violate the First Amendment. *Zacchini v. Scripps-Howard Broadcasting Co.* (1977).

Right to Assemble and Petition The First Amendment guarantees the right of the people to assemble peaceably and to petition the government for redress on grievances. This guarantee is applicable to the states through the Due Process Clause of the Fourteenth Amendment.

Right to Refuse Treatment The Court has recognized a significant liberty interest in avoiding the unwanted administration of medical treatment. This liberty interest includes the refusal of life supporting treatment. But, through a balancing test, the Court held that a state may require that the individual's intent to terminate such treatment be established by clear and convincing evidence. *Cruzan v. Director, Mo. Dept. of Health* (1990).

Ripeness Art. III "case and controversy" requires that there be an immediate injury or a threat of imminent injury for a case to be timely.

S

Selective Incorporation The theory that some, but not all, of the provisions of the Bill of Rights are incorporated by the Due Process Clause of the Fourteenth Amendment and are thus made applicable to the states.

Separate but Equal Doctrine In *Brown v. Board of Education* (Brown I) (1954), the Court stated that "segregation of children in public schools solely on the basis of race, even though the physical facilities and other 'tangible' factors may be equal, deprive(s) the children of the minority group of equal educational opportunities" in violation of the equal protection guarantee of the Fourteenth Amendment.

Separation of Powers Principles governing the allocation of powers among the three coordinate branches of the national government. When powers come into conflict, the courts consider whether one Branch is invading the constitutional prerogatives of another Branch or is usurping powers which are properly shared. Formalists tend to focus on the text of the Constitution and stress the formal separation of governmental functions. Functionalists stress the principle of checks and bal-

ances and the interaction of institutions sharing government powers.

Speech Plus The Court has suggested, at various times, that when speech is joined with conduct ("speech plus"), it is not entitled to the same degree of First Amendment protection as pure speech. Reasonable laws directed at the conduct element may be held constitutional even though speech is indirectly burdened.

Spending Power Congress has power to spend, but not directly regulate, for the general welfare. General welfare objectives are not limited to the specifics of Art. I, § 8, but include all matters of national concern. Congress can attach reasonable conditions to its grants of money.

Standing Art. III standing has two requirements, both of which must be met if standing is to be present in litigation before an Art. III court. First, the litigant must show injury in fact; second, he must show that he will personally benefit from the required judicial relief and that but for the action of the defendant, the injury in fact of which he complains would not occur (*i.e.,* causation). This includes both a requirement that the injury is "fairly traceable" to the government act being challenged and that the injury is "redressible" if the court grants relief.

Standing (Taxpayers) "We (courts) have no power per se to review and annul acts of Congress on the ground that they are unconstitutional. * * * The party who invokes the (judicial review) power must be able to show not only the statute is invalid but that he has sustained or is immediately in danger of sustaining some direct injury as the result of its enforcement, and not merely that he suffers in some indefinite way in common with people generally." *Frothingham v. Mellon* (1923). This "impenetrable barrier" to taxpayer suits was lowered in a challenge by taxpayers to aid to religious schools under a federal statute. In *Flast v. Cohen* (1968), the Court stated "A taxpayer may or may not have the requisite personal stake in the outcome, depending upon the circumstances of the particular case. * * * First, the taxpayer must establish a logical link between (taxpayer) status and the type of legislative enactment attacked. * * * Secondly, the taxpayer must establish a nexus between the status and the precise nature of the constitutional infringement alleged." A federal taxpayer must be challenging on the basis of a specific limitation on Congress' Taxing and Spending Power. Only the Establishment Clause has been held to be a specific limitation on the Taxing and Spending Power.

Standing (Third Party Rights) While a party generally does not have "standing" to assert the rights of a third party, a court may make an exception after weighing: (1) the importance of the relationship between the complainant and the third party; (2) the third party's ability to vindicate its own rights; (3) the risk that third party rights will be diluted if standing to the complainant is not allowed.

Standing ("Zone of Interests") For claims based on a federal statute, the plaintiff must allege not only that the challenged action has caused "injury in fact, economic or otherwise" to the complainant (i.e., Art. III standing) but also that the specific interests sought to be protected are within the "zone of interests" protected by the applicable statute. *Association of Data Processing Service Organization v. Camp* (1970).

State Action Most constitutional guarantees are not violated by private action. Only significant government involvement, making the government responsible for the challenged acts, will constitute state action. The Court requires a close nexus between the government and the private actions being challenged.

State Taxation of Interstate Commerce States may tax interstate commerce if the tax reasonably reflects the benefits derived from the taxing state, the tax is not discriminatory, the taxpayer has minimal local contacts with

the taxing state and the tax is fairly apportioned to avoid multiple burdens. *Complete Auto Transit, Inc. v. Brady* (1977).

Stream of Commerce In Commerce Clause analysis, local activities which are part of the current or stream of interstate commerce are considered part of the interstate movement. Congress can regulate such local incidents directly under its commerce power.

Suspect Classifications The Court will employ the "strict scrutiny" standard under the Equal Protection Clause in determining the legitimacy of classifications that are based upon a trait which itself seems to contravene established constitutional principles so that any purposeful use of the classification may be deemed "suspect." Examples include race, national origin and alienage (with exceptions). Classifications for which the Court has not adopted the strict scrutiny standard include illegitimacy, gender, wealth, and age. State alienage classifications are suspect unless the "political function" exception applies.

Supremacy Clause Article VI provides that, "[t]his Constitution, and the Laws of the United States which shall be made in Pursuance thereof * * * shall be the Supreme Law of the Land * * *." State laws which conflict with federal law, impede federal objectives or which are preempted, yield to the federal law.

Symbiotic Relationship When the action of government and private actors is so intertwined as to constitute a "symbiotic relationship", their combined activities will be viewed by the courts as constituting state involvement sufficient to invoke the "state action" doctrine and thereby subject the private actor, in such circumstances, to constitutional obligation. *Burton v. Wilmington Parking Authority* (1961).

Symbolic Speech The Court has rejected both the view that there is no First Amendment protection if expression involves conduct and the idea that a "limitless variety of conduct can be labeled 'speech' whenever the person engaging in the conduct intends thereby to express an idea." Conduct is deemed symbolic speech when all the factual circumstances indicate that the actor intends to communicate and the audience can understand the communication. It is then necessary to determine if the law regulating the symbolic speech is constitutional under the First Amendment. "When 'speech' and 'non-speech' elements are combined in the same course of conduct, a sufficiently important government interest in regulating the non-speech element can justify incidental limitations on First Amendment freedoms." *United States v. O'Brien* (1968).

T

Takings Clause When government "takes" property for public use, the Fifth and Fourteenth Amendment require that just compensation be given. In determining whether a law constitutes a taking requiring just compensation or a regulation which does not, the courts consider the law's economic impact, investment expectations, and the extent to which the property is occupied.

Tax Exemptions Tax exemptions for places of religious worship are constitutional even though, indirectly, they provide support for religion. Tax exemption for religious institutions constitutes a historically-acceptable "benevolent neutrality" on the part of government because they involve, in fact, less government entanglement with religion than would tax assessments, liens, and foreclosures. *Walz v. Tax Commission* (1970).

Taxing Power Congress has the fiscal power to raise monies through taxes. But a regulatory "penalty" may not be imposed under the guise of raising revenue. If a law is revenue producing on its face, it is likely to be treated as a tax, not a penalty.

Total Incorporation The idea that the Due Process Clause incorporates each of the Bill of Rights and makes them applicable against the states. The Court has never accepted the total incorporation theory. *Adamson v. California* (1947).

Travel (Interstate Migration) The right to interstate travel or interstate migration is protected under the Constitution. However, it does not have a specific constitutional locus. At various times, it has been said to be protected by the Commerce Clause, the Privileges and Immunities Clause of the Fourteenth Amendment, and the Interstate Privileges and Immunities Clause of Art. IV, § 2. At other times, it is referred to as a national right implicit in the federal Union established by the Constitution.

Tuition Aid (Establishment Clause) Tuition aid given to citizens generally is more likely to be upheld than aid given only to citizens involved with religious institutions. A state law allowing taxpayers to deduct tuition expenses is not violative of the Establishment Clause where its purpose is to promote a well-educated citizenry and where the deduction is available on a neutral basis to parents of all students. *Mueller v. Allen* (1983).

U

Unconstitutional Conditions, Doctrine of Government may not unconstitutionally condition the receipt of government benefits on the surrender of constitutional rights such as First Amendment rights. Thus, a refusal by a state board of bar examiners to admit an applicant to its bar solely because of past association is invalid. *Schware v. Board of Bar Examiners of State of N.M.* (1961).

V

Vesture Clause Art. II, § 1, vests the Executive Power in the President. It may be a separate source of power, a reference to other Art. II powers, or a reference to the Framer's choice of a single Executive.

Viewpoint Control Government regulation which endorses a particular belief or opinion over competing positions is viewpoint-based. It is considered a form of censorship which is heavily burdened under the First Amendment. The courts will sustain such regulation "only if the government can show that the regulation is a precisely drawn means of serving a compelling state interest." *Consolidated Edison Co. of New York v. Public Service Comm'n. of New York* (1980).

Void but Not Non-Frivolous Order, Doctrine of The treatment of court orders or injunctions which are void *ab initio* differs from the treatment of legislation which is void *ab initio*. The latter need not be obeyed; the former must be. The rationale for this distinction is that the "rule of law" requires a duty to obey judicial procedures. *Walker v. Birmingham* (1967).

Void for Vagueness Doctrine A statute is void for vagueness if it is not drawn with sufficient clarity and definiteness to inform persons of the course of conduct they must follow to avoid the ban of the statute. The First Amendment requires special clarity so that protected expression will not be chilled or suppressed. Statutes which are void for vagueness are fundamentally unfair thus violating the due process guarantee as well.

Voting Practices, Racially Discriminatory in Effect (Congressional Power to Legislate Against Pursuant to § 2 of the Fifteenth Amendment) Under § 2, any legislation which Congress could rationally conclude is appropriate to effectuate the constitutional prohibition against racial discrimination in voting is constitutional. Even though only purposeful racial discrimination in voting violates the Fifteenth Amendment, Congress, under § 2 of that Amendment, may outlaw voting practices that are discriminatory in effect. While such practices do not violate § 1 of the Amendment, prohibitions against practices having a discriminatory racial effect on voting are "appropriate" and "reasonable" means of enforcing the voting guarantees of the Fifteenth Amendment. *City of Rome v. United States* (1980); *Thornburg v. Gingles* (1986).

W

Wealth Classifications In the absence of some fundamental right or interest, a classification which operates to disadvantage the poor is not suspect. The Court employs a rational basis standard of review.

Welfare Legislation (Standard of Equal Protection Review) While welfare assistance involves basic human needs, welfare legislation will be measured by the rational basis test unless a suspect classification is involved. *Dandridge v. Williams* (1970).

APPENDIX E

TABLE OF CASES